Mapping Texts

Advance praise for Mapping Texts

"Stoltz and Taylor have managed to create a work that confidently takes even a beginner to a position of sophistication and technical virtuosity, leading to not only a practical mastery of cutting edge techniques, nor just that plus a clear understanding of the mathematical bases, but also gives the reader an intuitive feel for the larger social contexts that produce the text data analyzed, and all this without dropping a single equation in the reader's lap! A true gem."—John Levi Martin, Florence Borchert Bartling Professor of Sociology at The University of Chicago and author of *Thinking Through Methods*

"Language is pragmatic, language is habitual, language is relational. I have been waiting for a book like this. One that seamlessly integrates philosophy and theory with tools and reproducible examples and does so in a deeply sociological way. If you read this book, if you teach with this book, you and your students will have everything needed to successfully do computational text analysis in the social sciences. An extraordinary contribution."—Laura K. Nelson, Assistant Professor of Sociology at The University of British Columbia

"Packed with interesting examples, *Mapping Texts* reveals the exciting possibilities of computational text analysis for social science. It's one of those rare books that offers useful advice about both what to do and how to do it. I think many readers will love Stoltz and Taylor's decision to use no equations and illustrate key ideas with code in R. *Mapping Texts* will be helpful to anyone hoping to learn more about this dynamic and important area of research."—Matthew J. Salganik, Professor of Sociology at Princeton University and author of *Bit by Bit: Social Research in the Digital Age*

"This book is an excellent entry-point to modern ideas and tools for the quantitative analysis of textual data. Well-organized, approachable, and pragmatic, the book does a terrific job of showing why researchers find the ideas so interesting while also teaching the reader how to use the tools for themselves."—Kieran Healy, Professor of Sociology at Duke University and author of *Data Visualization: A Practical Introduction*

"*Mapping Texts* provides a timely and accessible foray into the evolving domain of computational text analysis, enriched with fascinating examples and cutting-edge techniques. The book is perfectly tailored for newcomers to text-based methods. Guiding readers through computational techniques without the complications of equations, the authors equip you with everything, including all the essential R code, to dive directly into text analysis. Moreover, the authors' approach is grounded in a philosophy of language and text that harmonizes the positivist and interpretive traditions, making the book an excellent fit for an especially wide range of social science and humanities scholars and students."—Anjali M. Bhatt, Assistant Professor of Business Administration at Harvard Business School

"Stoltz and Taylor's book is easily one of the clearest and most comprehensive introductions to computational text analysis written to date. With impressive dexterity, they take readers through the principles and workflows that are necessary for studying texts with computational techniques, never forgetting that words are complex and multifaceted cultural objects. In its style, organization, and pedagogical approach, this book is nothing short of an exceptional achievement."—Juan Pablo Pardo-Guerra, Associate Professor of Sociology the University of California, San Diego, and co-editor of *The Oxford Handbook of the Sociology of Machine Learning*

"This book could not be more welcome. Authored by two of the leading sociological researchers in the field of text analysis, it offers a comprehensive guide to state-of-the-art text analysis methods. But beyond just an introduction to methods, it provides a thoughtful and theoretically informed engagement about how we should think about, and interpret, the wealth of textual data that is now available. This is essential reading for anyone with an interest in computational social science."—Carly Knight, Assistant Professor of Sociology at New York University

Dustin S. Stoltz and Marshall A. Taylor

Mapping Texts

COMPUTATIONAL TEXT ANALYSIS
FOR THE SOCIAL SCIENCES

OXFORD

UNIVERSITY PRESS

OXFORD

UNIVERSITY PRESS

Oxford University Press is a department of the University of Oxford.
It furthers the University's objective of excellence in research, scholarship,
and education by publishing worldwide. Oxford is a registered trade mark of
Oxford University Press in the UK and in certain other countries.

Published in the United States of America by Oxford University Press
198 Madison Avenue, New York, NY 10016, United States of America.

Library of Congress Cataloging-in-Publication Data

Names: Stoltz, Dustin S., author. | Taylor, Marshall A., 1989– author.
Title: Mapping texts : computational text analysis for the social sciences
/ Dustin S. Stoltz, Marshall A. Taylor.
Description: New York, NY : Oxford University Press, [2023] | Series:
Computational social science series | Includes bibliographical
references and index.
Identifiers: LCCN 2023033955 (print) | LCCN 2023033956 (ebook) | ISBN
9780197756881 (paperback) | ISBN 9780197756874 (hardback) | ISBN
9780197756904 (epub)
Subjects: LCSH: Social sciences—Methodology. | Text data mining. |
Qualitative research.
Classification: LCC H61 .S874 2023 (print) | LCC H61 (ebook) | DDC
300.72/1—dc23/eng/20230920
LC record available at https://lccn.loc.gov/2023033955
LC ebook record available at https://lccn.loc.gov/2023033956

Integrated Books International, United States of America

To Our Students

Contents

Preface

METAPHORS orient us. Many guides to text analysis use the *mining* metaphor. When mining, we search for a valuable vein to extract from valueless gangue. Information retrieval scholars pioneered computer-assisted text analysis by confronting the problem of (as you might guess) retrieving the most relevant documents from ever-growing databases. Parts of the documents were less helpful for completing this task. This was especially true when computational resources were minimal. Mining was an apt metaphor.

Mapping, by contrast, is not about extraction. It is about *reduction* to aid interpretation. When mapping texts, we simplify their information, but always for particular uses. Many useful cartographies are based on the same territory: road maps, contour maps, political maps, to name a few. Wrangling, pruning, stopping, and transforming text all involve a decision informed by a particular goal. To put it plainly: *there is not a sole kernel of truth to be extracted, but rather a range of empirical patterns.* There is an unfinished quality to text analysis—perhaps all science. Repeating, then, is a cornerstone of this book. While *scale* can undoubtedly be useful, *iteration* is the unsung hero of computational methods.

Merging computational techniques with social scientific text analysis blurs qualitative and quantitative methods. While computational methods involve quantification, there is **interpretation** before, during, and after any quantification. Text analysis is about establishing whether patterns are present in a collection of texts and how they vary. Determining what these patterns mean and which are important, however, is a qualitative process. So, we look toward the centuries of scholarly analysis of texts to guide our computational workflows.

WHAT YOU WILL LEARN

This book complements conceptual discussions of text analysis with step-by-step guides for putting ideas into practice, focusing on social scientific questions and data[1] (with some digital humanities and corpus linguistics sprinkled in for good measure). We outline the text analysis workflow, from building corpora to visualizing outputs, paired with the theoretical impetus behind each step.

Through reproducible examples spanning data as diverse as fake news articles, presidential campaign speeches, and Reddit AITA[2] posts, we'll

[1] Our examples do lean toward sociology, though, because we are, after all, sociologists.

[2] Don't know the acronym? Read on! Or Google it.

learn how to select and acquire text, wrangle and structure, annotate and tag, and apply inductive and deductive approaches for discovering meaningful patterns from text. The examples use R , a widely used and open-source programming language for data analysis. Our conceptual discussions, however, are applicable across programming languages. Our intent is not to teach how to use specific tools (although we do), but rather to think about the motivations underlying the major techniques of contemporary computational text analysis.

We organized this as follows. In Part I (**Bounding Texts**), we introduce our general approach to language and text as an object of study and consider how selection influences the patterns we may find in corpora. In Part II (**Prerequisites**), we introduce basic computing ideas with R .[3] We then briefly review basic mathematical concepts. Together, these chapters provide a primer, refresher, and cheat sheet we refer back to throughout the book—pay attention to **margin notes**!

In Part III (**Foundations**), we discuss how different kinds of texts are acquired and converted into a machine-readable form and then outline the initial steps involved in converting texts into numbers using fundamental data structures. In Part IV (**Below the Document**), we discuss "wrangling" text by removing and replacing characters and words, followed by a chapter on corpus annotation, tagging, and parsing. We move to the document and corpus level in Part V (**The Document and Beyond**). We organize these chapters into **inductive** and **deductive** approaches.[4] In the first, researchers allow patterns to emerge from the data; in the second, researchers seek out preconceived patterns. Although, the specific techniques discussed can often be used inductively or deductively. In practice, researchers will combine these into an abductive workflow, oscillating between these modes. Finally, we group techniques into **core** and more **extended**, with the latter building upon concepts and methods provided in the former.

WHAT WE LEFT OUT

This book touches on computational social science, critical data science, and research design, but is not a comprehensive introduction to any of those topics. For research design we recommend *Evidence* (Becker 2017), *Thinking Through Methods* (Martin 2017), *Abductive Analysis* (Tavory and Timmermans 2014) and *Thinking Clearly With Data* (de Mesquita and Fowler 2021). For critical data science, we recommend *Decoding the Social World* (González-Bailón 2017) and *Data Feminism* (D'ignazio and

[3] Those already familiar with R can mostly skip this chapter save for installing the required packages. We also recommend heading to the **Appendix** for the table of all packages used, and the table of all functions associated with their respective packages.

[4] Inductive: What are the themes in a set of news articles? Deductive: Which news articles talk about Akira Kurosawa?

Klein 2020). For computational social science, we recommend *Bit by Bit* (Salganik 2019), *Doing Computational Social Science* (McLevey 2021), *Data Analysis for Social Science* (Llaudet and Imai 2022), and *Statistical Rethinking* (McElreath 2020).

Finally, no equations! Regarding the mathematical details of a given measure, we show it with reproducible examples instead of formal equations. This does mean we sometimes must sacrifice precision for clarity. Anyone with at least high school math (and our **Math Basics** chapter) should be able to complete the analyses in this book. That being said, for a deeper understanding of the content in the **Extended** chapters, we suggest Strang (2020) and Roberts et al. (2022).

Suggested Course Readings for Instructors

Below are some selections from this book for various courses not specific to computational text analysis.[5] These suggested readings could pair well with other materials for a week on text data, for example. Chapters 3 and 4 are listed in almost every set, but these might be removed for upper-level courses.

- *Introduction to Social Data Science*: Chapters 3 and 4 for an overview of computing and math basics, the sections on "Supervision and Validation" and "Classic Training with Supervision" for an introduction to supervised learning, the section on "Document Clustering" in Chapter 10 (**Core Inductive**) for an introduction to unsupervised learning, and Chapter 13 (**Project Workflow and Iteration**) for data management.
- *Supervised Learning*: Chapters 3 and 4 for an overview of computing and math basics, and Chapters 9 and 12 on **Core Deductive** and **Extended Deductive** methods, respectively.
- *Unsupervised Learning*: Chapters 3 and 4 for an overview of computing and math basics, and Chapters 10 and 11 on **Core Inductive** and **Extended Inductive** methods, respectively.
- *Network Science*: Chapters 3 and 4 for an overview of computing and math basics, the section on "Document Similarity" in Chapter 10 (**Core Inductive**) and the section on "Inference with Text Networks" in Chapter 12 (**Extended Deductive**).
- *Sociology of Language*: Chapter 1 (**Text in Context**) and Chapter 2 (**Corpus Building**).

[5] We, of course, recommend that you use the *whole* book for that class! Although, **Extended** chapters could be omitted for lower-level courses and the **Computing Basics** and **Math Basics** could be omitted for upper-level courses.

Acknowledgments

This book emerged out of teaching: being taught, teaching others, and teaching ourselves. It would be appropriate to start with our very first teachers, but we'd be here all day, so we'll start by thanking our most recent: Omar Lizardo, Erin Metz McDonnell, Terry McDonnell, and Ann Mische. Many of the chapters in this book started as short guides and lecture notes for our text analysis classes, so we also owe much to our students at Notre Dame, New Mexico State, and Lehigh.

We are lucky to be part of a growing community of computationally inclined scholars in sociology. Among them, Chris Bail, Matt Salganik, Laura Nelson, Bart Bonikowski, J. P. Pardo-Guerra, Kieran Healy, and Clayton Childress have offered both inspiration and encouragement along the way. This community, in turn, would not be what it is without the pioneering work of Kathleen Carley, John Mohr, and Paul DiMaggio.

Of course, this book would be impossible without the editorial work of James Cook. Along the way, Katherine Wiley combed through an earlier draft, interrogating each line of prose for clarity and purpose. This book would not be the same without her careful eye and thoughtful feedback. Bruce Archer, in turn, went over each line of code for errors and inefficiencies. Mike Wood was a constant sounding board from start to finish on matters big and small. We also received valuable feedback from anonymous reviewers. We hope that they will read the final book and appreciate how they improved it. We thank John Levi Martin, Alessandra Lembo, Oscar Stuhler, and members of the Culture Action Network for comments on content that became **Corpus Building** and **Project Workflow and Iteration**. Jeremiah Bohr and Petko Bogdanov generously shared text data we use in **Basic Deductive** and **Tagging Words**, and we are indebted to every scholar who posts their data and code for all to study. We also appreciate our colleagues at New Mexico State and Lehigh, who have been steadfast supporters of our work.

This book would have been a futile feat without the infrastructure built by legions of volunteer programmers. Our deepest gratitude to the R community and text analysis package developers. We'd also be remiss if we forgot the patient commenters on Stack Overflow. Much of the code presented in this book was probably influenced or derived from Stack Overflow community posts! Any errors are, of course, our own (or downstream dependencies . . .)

Lastly and especially, from Dustin to Kc and Galileo, and from Marshall to Natalie, Freddie, and Wednesday: something cool.

Part I

Bounding Texts

1
Text in Context

'Don't be such an ass!', 'You silly ass!', 'What an ass he is!' ... the word ass is in familiar and habitual company, commonly collocated with you silly-, he is a silly-, don't be such an-. **You shall know a word by the company it keeps!**
—J. R. Firth

LANGUAGE is generous. It is a window into the mind, an echo of shared meaning, and a tool people use to remake the social world. Language, typically, enters social scientific examination in the form of text; either transcribed by the examiners or written by the examinees. Text allows us to map meanings across time, space, and people.

Pre–1950s Science Fiction

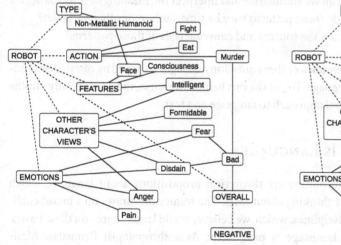

1970–80s Science Fiction

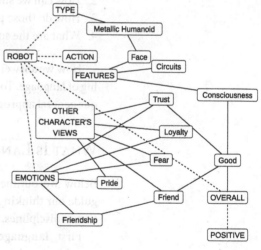

Figure 1.1: Shared perceptions of 'robot' unique to pre-1950s and 1970s–80s (adapted from Carley 1994:301–4).

Through text we can examine, for instance, how science fiction authors define "robot" (see Figure 1.1). By mapping conceptual associations found in 27 texts published between 1818 and 1988, we would find robots originally caused pain and fear but later are associated with trust and loyalty

Mapping Texts: Computational Text Analysis for the Social Sciences. Dustin S. Stoltz and Marshall A. Taylor, Oxford University Press. © Oxford University Press 2024. DOI: 10.1093/oso/9780197756874.003.0001

(Carley 1994:301–4). Or, we may consider how changes in women's educational attainment in the last century in the United States track shifts in gendered stereotypes in American print media. We would find, among other things, that as "studying" becomes feminized, "intelligence" gains masculine connotations (Boutyline et al. 2023). We can also survey 800,000 books, newspapers, and articles spanning 350 years to identify key themes surrounding Black women's experiences. The patterns in word use emblematic of these themes can then be used to rescue previously unidentified African American writings (Brown et al. 2016, 2019)

Language is also slippery. It cannot be censused. It grows and decays vigorously. Every day, new words are spoken, written, gestured, and forgotten. We continuously improvise around a relatively stable core of linguistic habits, fueling an illusion of clear boundaries between *languages*. Just as cartographers must grapple with ever-changing rivers and roads, the text analyst must grapple with the implications of language's dynamic and unbounded essence. Text mapping engages this open-ended nature of language by exploring four interrelated questions:

1. How can we identify patterns in a selection of texts?
2. How can we summarize and interpret the meaning of those patterns?
3. How do those patterns vary by time, author, or other variables?
4. What are the sources and consequences of those patterns?

How we answer these questions, though, is shaped by our understanding of language. To put the cart behind the horse, then, let's briefly outline our general approach to language and text.

WHAT IS LANGUAGE?

Below we outline six theoretical propositions about language which guide our thinking about texts. The framework draws on a broad coalition of disciplines, which, we believe, would largely agree on these basics.

First, **language is pragmatic**. As anthropologist Bronisław Malinowski argued, humans use language to do things: "to direct, to control and to correlate human activities" (1937:172). We also acquire language through use (Tomasello 2009; Croft and Cruse 2004). However frustrating for researchers, any sample of language will be missing information. In particular, what is often not present are the authors. Patterns in language emerge within social action. Words are a product and facilitator of what is going on "around" them. The meanings they evoke are not static but change with context—and, indeed, meaning does not stop at the boundary of what can be said.[1]

Second, **language is not meaning**. Influenced by Malinowski (Rose 1980; Gellner 1998:149), the philosopher Ludwig Wittgenstein ([1953] 2009:80, 109) suggested that in a "large class of cases...the meaning of a word is its use in the language."[2] We modify this slightly: a word's meaning is its use *by* the language *community* (Bloomfield 1933:29, 37). Words are not their meanings nor do individuals decide their meanings in isolation; rather, their meanings are determined and modified by how people use them to do things with other people.[3] True, language is intimately connected to many meaning-making processes (Fauconnier 1997). Yet, without people to interpret words—spoken, gestured, written, or otherwise—there is no meaning. This entails a cautionary stance toward distinctions between *signs*, *sounds*, or *syntax*, on the one hand, and *semantics*, on the other (Goldberg 1995).

Third, **language is habitual**. This means "language is embodied" and "human bodies are linguistic" (Di Paolo et al. 2018:5; Johnson [1987] 2015). What we say, and how we say it, are the accrual of all our prior experiences, stored in our bodies as habits (Bloomfield 1933:30–34; Bourdieu 1991; Croft and Cruse 2004). We are shaped by our language (Ong 2013; Dennett 2017) and what language can be is constrained by us—by our physiology and biography. As everybody has similarities and differences, so too does every language-user become a locus of stability and change within a language community. The regularities of language are, in part, human conventions grounded in the flesh-and-blood, dirt-and-stone.

Fourth, **language is relational**. The linguist John Firth—again influenced by Malinowski (Firth 1935:68–9; Young 2011)—argued we "know a word" by the "company it keeps." But what is a word's company? Researchers can specify a word's meaning when they know the words occurring with it (see also Harris 1954). When we say relational, though, we suggest a more general proposition (Mohr 1998; Mohr et al. 2020:94–127; Robins 2013). People infer a word's meaning from its relation to other words, but also to the people, objects, organizations, and other texts that form the contexts of their use.

Fifth, **language is unfinished**. The notion of crisp lines around *a* language is, in the final analysis, a red herring (Davidson 2005:89–108).[4] Contrary to the desires of various classist, racist, and nationalist projects (Fishman 2011; Bourdieu 1991; Rosa and Flores 2017), there is no pure specimen of *a language*. There is no right and wrong way to

[1] "One great part of every human existence is passed in a state which cannot be rendered sensible by the use of wideawake language, cutanddry grammar, and goahead plot."—James Joyce

[2] "Social science is still burdened with the superstition that words contain their meanings" (Malinowski [1947] 2015:86).

[3] Except, of course, for Humpty Dumpty: "When *I* use a word...it means just what I choose it to mean—neither more nor less" (Carroll 1925:246).

[4] Generally, two people are said to speak *different* languages if there is low **intelligibility** between those people. Even this is a fuzzy criterion. Intelligibility is graded and may not even be symmetrical. For example, "speakers of Portuguese can understand Spanish but this applies less well the other way around" (Dixon 1997:7–8).

speak, write, and gesture. There is no sufficient set of rules that speakers *must* follow (Fillmore 1979; Bauer 1998). The divisions between styles, accents, dialects, and languages are always drifting.

Sixth, **language is a field**. Language is organized and patterned, and so scholars commonly describe language as a "system." But, "system" connotes an autonomous set of arranged parts where change is internal: altering one part alters all parts.[5] While it is true that language is patterned, has regularities, and may even have internal sources of change, language is "too unwieldy to be understood directly as a whole" (Di Paolo et al. 2018:106). Understanding language as a *field*—an organized yet open-ended structure—better captures both the regularities and dynamics inherent in speaking and writing.

The preceding propositions have implications for how we think about the *boundaries* of language. No sample of language, no matter how large, is ever a self-contained whole. No language change is wholly instigated by internal mechanisms. Meaning is not constituted *solely* by relations between words or other linguistic units. There is no necessarily correct instance of language use. No crisp set of linguistic rules sufficiently explains all patterns in language data. All this complexity makes carrying out a text analysis more difficult. Still, by thinking through each step and documenting our decisions clearly, we can contribute to the scholarly understanding of language and its role in social life.

WHAT IS TEXT?

Writing is a subset of language. Like speaking or gesturing, it is an attempt to associate a perceptible *form* with meanings such that, through it, a writer's intentions are communicated to a reader, even when the writer is absent.[6] Here, we attempt to "bound" our object of investigation further by outlining five propositions about written text.

First, **texts are a set of characters**. That text can be *segmented* is a precondition of computer-assisted text analysis (c.f. Aronoff 1992)[7]— numerals, alphabets, abjads, logographics, alphasyllabaries, syllabaries, punctuation, diacritics, and even spaces or other word dividers. These characters are not abstractions but perceptible through sight and touch. A writer arranges this set so a reader could, more or less, recover meaning—provided that the writer generally follows conventions familiar to the reader. That text comprises a *relatively finite set of re-arrangeable characters* is a minimal assumption in contemporary text analysis.

Second, **texts re-present**. "The ethnographer," Geertz (1973:19) tells us, "inscribes" social activity and "turns it from a passing event ... into an

[5] The linguist Ferdinand de Saussure, for example, asserted that language is a "self-contained whole" and "everything that changes the system in any way is internal" (Saussure 1986:23).

[6] For this book, we are not dealing with meaningful content which may accompany text, for example, diagrams or pictures (Prior 2003; Bauer and Gaskell 2000).

[7] Characters are often associated with speech sounds, with varying degrees of refinement (Daniels and Bright 1996; Okrent 2021). The "International Phonetic Alphabet" aims for maximum fidelity to articulation. Specialized systems for capturing prosody also exist (Jefferson and Others 2004). While sound shapes language (e.g., Hinton et al. 2006), we'll presume characters do not necessarily represent sound.

account, which exists in its inscriptions and can be reconsulted."[8] Interview researchers, similarly, transcribe their analytic conversations with participants. Speeches, music lyrics, dictated instructions, or recorded meetings may also be transformed from sound into writing. Writing is an attempt to capture an event, and text is the means through which such occurrences are captured. Text does *re*-present other modes of communication, mediums of perception and expression, or even thoughts.

Third, **texts are language**. Speaking likely preceded writing. This prompted the linguist Leonard Bloomfield to assert: "Writing is not language, but merely a way of recording language" (Bloomfield 1933:21; see also Saussure 1986:23). Those inspired by the linguist Noam Chomsky go further by presuming both speaking and writing are simply reflections of language in the mind (c.f. Aronoff 1992). True, writing does record speech and thought, but it does not only record. The written word also has its own norms, intents, and constraints—which shape other modes of communication, our minds, and our very theories of language (Ong 2013; Olson 1996; Coulmas 2003).

Fourth, **texts are durable and decay**. Text is an attempt to fix the fleeting; it is durable. Yet, no text is indestructible; it decays.[9] We can only analyze what is *preserved*, and "all other things equal, selectivity increases with the age of documents" (Martin 2017). We are only privy to a small portion of these ancient texts and thus the range of meanings within these communities. This remains true in the digital age, with "bitrot" an ever-present concern and texts easily deleted with a few keystrokes or perhaps irreversibly encrypted. More troubling for the social scientist, text is not lost and preserved at random (e.g., King et al. 2013). This means we must theorize the political and organizational projects that shape access to texts to accurately interpret those texts (Brown et al. 2016).

Fifth, **texts are objects**. Texts are objects because they are durable and decay, but also because they are produced and maintained (Prior 2003). Whenever we encounter a text, an interconnected network of people, groups, organizations and other texts are all implicated. For example, the novel is produced and distributed by an author, but also literary agents, publishers, editors, book stores, book clubs, critics, etc. (Childress 2017).

Taken together, with our working theory of language, the above five propositions have important implications for the first step in any text analysis: **selection**. We can never study the entire population of any language, as text or otherwise. We'll always—intentionally or not—study a subset of all the texts that could be studied. Being principled about selection is essential for rigorous and reproducible text analysis.

[8] *Verba volant, scripta manent*

"Everything not saved will be lost."—Nintendo 'Quit Screen' Message.

[9] Consider, for example, the origins of writing such as the Jiahu bone inscriptions, the tattoos on the mummified Ötzi, the Vinča symbols on pottery, or the cuneiform clay tablets of ancient Uruk.

2
Corpus Building

Words don't mean anything. People mean things with words, and you need to know what they are trying to do to know what their words mean.

— J. L. Martin

CARTOGRAPHY involves establishing the boundaries around the domain or terrain to be mapped. What is determined to be inside and outside of the mapping space determines not only what is to be represented but also **what it means**. For example, detailed topographical maps of the Bob Marshall Wilderness Preserve in Montana are indispensable to the hiker and useless to the motorist driving around it. This is also the case for the text analyst. Before any analysis can take place, we must *bound text*. That is, we must determine which texts we will include and which we will exclude, and importantly, how it is a given text is available for us to select at all.

For at least four hundred years, humans have used text as data in systematic analyses (Krippendorff 2018:3–5). This began with theological studies, followed closely by analyses of newspapers. Several studies of the press emerged in the early 20th century, with the most optimistic suggesting that such data "would constitute a series of observations of the 'social weather' comparable in accuracy to the statistics of the United States Weather Bureau" (Tenney [1912] 2008:19).

In these early analyses, newspapers were treated like surveys of *representative* samples of people, as if tapping into national attitudes. J. G. Speed's (1893) "Do newspapers now give the news?"—likely the first quantitative analysis of newspaper content[1]—suggests why we may want to be cautious about such an assumption.

[1] Sociologists Willey and Weinfeld (1934) conducted quantitative studies of newspapers using Hollerith cards, offering perhaps the first *computational* analyses of newspapers (cf. Sumpter 2001).

In 1883, Joseph Pulitzer bought the *New York World* and used sensationalism to sell more papers—a technique adopted by other newspapers in New York. Speed believed that these changing journalistic norms were also changing newspaper content. To answer this question, he examined "representative New York newspapers of twelve years ago [1881] and compare[d] them with the same papers of this year [1893]" (1893:706). Indeed, the quantity of "gossip" had replaced "literary" and "editorial" (see Figure 2.1), leading him to conclude:

Mapping Texts: Computational Text Analysis for the Social Sciences. Dustin S. Stoltz and Marshall A. Taylor, Oxford University Press. © Oxford University Press 2024. DOI: 10.1093/oso/9780197756874.003.0002

There is a conventional phrase—"a newspaper is the history of the world for a day"—that is more or less believed in. Nothing could be falser than this. Our newspapers do not record the really serious happenings, but only the sensations, the catastrophes of history. (1893:710)

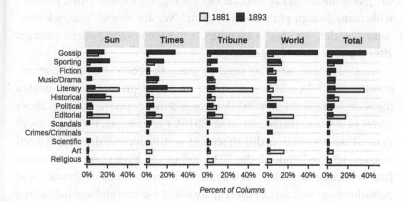

Figure 2.1: Columns of Subjects in New York Newspapers, 1881 and 1893 (adapted from Speed 1893:707).

We must understand how and why a **corpus**[2] is bounded as it is; otherwise, we may confuse patterns in how our corpus is produced for patterns within our texts.

Take, for example, a study of "cognitive distortions" using the 2020 Google Books N-gram Corpus. Beginning as early as 2002 with "Project Ocean," Google joined several other projects—such as Project Gutenberg, HathiTrust, and JSTOR—in the large-scale digitization of books. The search giant started scanning books to eventually allow search within *full texts*. By the late 2010s, Google's team estimated that 129 million editions had been published since the "Printing Revolution" fomented by movable type printing press; they had scanned 15 million. In 2009, Google released this treasure trove, not as full text, but as lists of n-grams for each year.[3] In 2020, Google released an updated n-gram corpus.

The next year, a team published evidence of a supposed "surge in cognitive distortions"—"thinking patterns ... associated with internalizing disorders" (Bollen et al. 2021:1)—across four countries using this updated corpus. With a dictionary[4] to associate phrases with a given "cognitive distortion"—for example, "not that great" indicating the distortion "disqualifying the positive"—they counted the frequency with which distortions occurred per year. Limiting their study to 1855 to 2019, they concluded (Bollen et al. 2021:5):

[2] Corpus (singular) or corpora (plural) is any collection of texts. These can be quite large or quite small and used for many purposes.

[3] An n-gram is a phrase up to n words long. Google's corpus included all phrases of one to five words per year. A corpus as an n-gram list is one technique to overcome copyright issues.

[4] See **Core Deductive**.

[O]ur results indicate historically high levels of the expression of a large set of lexical markers of cognitive distortions in three languages.... [T]his points to the possibility that large populations are increasingly stressed by pervasive cultural, economic, and social changes.

Why were other researchers skeptical? The Google Books N-gram Corpus is the dataset behind the Google Ngram Viewer. Using that tool with many benign phrases—"I'm calm," "we are loved," "puppy kisses," "time traveler," or "dog"—we notice a fairly common pattern emerges after the year 2000. They all *surge*.

To understand why, we need to grasp the context of this corpus's construction.[5] In addition to larger questions prompted by Google's focus on *books* (Schwartz 2011), there is a more specific concern about *genres* or *domains* (Pechenick et al. 2015). For example, if there is more fiction than non-fiction, this affects any conclusions we draw from word frequencies. And, indeed, the 2020 corpus did have significantly more fiction because of shifting relationships between Google, libraries, and publishers—as well as the rapid expansion of e-books and self-publishing during that period. The study of "cognitive distortions" was possibly measuring a surge in the proportion of fiction in the corpus after the year 2000 (Schmidt et al. 2021).

Following Leech (2014:xix), "[W]e have to be cautious in drawing general inferences from the results of a corpus analysis, and alert to the influence of hidden variables implicit in the way we collected and sampled the data." For example, in critiquing a study (Bearman and Stovel 2000) of the "narrative networks" of Nazis based on "life stories," Biernacki (2012:29–30) argued that the study used abridged stories. The abridger, moreover, "was prone to deleting the musings on personal life decisions or self-reflection on family relations ... the very stuff [reported] as strangely missing [in the original study]." By relying on abridged stories, the study's conclusions were, at best, incomplete.

Computational advances do not allay these concerns; indeed, they potentially compound them. Researchers may be inclined toward "analysing only what is easy to find, and counting what is easiest to count" (Ball 1994:295). Just like the study of individuals or groups in a population, we must take care that we select "a site that isn't predisposed to mislead [us] into overly confident inference" (Martin 2017:38).[6] This is more of a concern for text analysis, since the ability to collect a large amount of data is getting easier. Size does not guarantee a fair sample; rather, it may increase one's confidence while reducing one's ability to manually validate conclusions.

[5] Unfortunately, as of this writing, another glaring problem with the 2020 corpus is a lack of documentation about the corpus construction process.

[6] This overlaps with **coverage error** in survey research: the misalignment of a sampling frame and the target population.

Texts Are Not People

The growing interest in the analysis of newspapers and radio broadcasts in the early 20th century consolidated around the work of Lazarsfeld, Katz, Merton, Cantril, and Stanton.[7] Very often in this work—but certainly not always—newspapers were treated as surveys of *representative* samples from a well-defined population of people. Quantitative content analysis often follows suit and argues that there is probability and nonprobability sampling of texts, where the former is always preferred (e.g., Weber 1990; Neuendorf 2017:83–88; Riffe et al. 2019:95–112). We should be cautious with this framing because *texts are not people*. We mean this in three senses.

First, even if we could collect all a population's texts, there is no reason a random sample is representative of the people in that population. Not everyone produces texts, and among those who do, they do not produce it in similar volumes.[8] When it comes to ready-made text, there is likely a long-tail distribution whereby a minority produces far more than the rest of the population.[9]

Second, the absence or presence of a text does not mirror human demographic processes. When selecting texts via the Internet, for example, Riffe and colleagues caution that traditional sampling frames – and therefore probability samples—are (probably) not applicable. They note, "the Internet is like a city without a telephone book or map to guide people. New houses are being built all the time, and old houses are being deserted with no listing of the changes. Sampling requires creative solutions" (Riffe et al. 2019:118). We want to stress: this applies to most texts. We encounter selection bias that is largely outside of our control. Furthermore, these selection pressures are bound up with what authors and audiences are trying to do with their words. For example, if we collected every electronically available *New York Times* article, we could get most, *but not all*, articles. Those missing are unlikely to be missing at random.[10] Articles may be misplaced, deleted, and destroyed for all sorts of organizational, custodial, ideological, and technological reasons.

Finally, what constitutes a "unit" in text analysis—computational or otherwise—is a notoriously tricky question. Traditionally, a "unit" is a single survey respondent or interviewee. What is so tricky about defining a unit in text analysis? In short, we may *select units* that are not our *units of analysis*—and we may not even settle on a unit of analysis before we begin selecting. A single document in our analysis need not be a document as commonly understood—for example a single bound book,

[7] Beginning with the Radio Research project in the late 1930s, this eventually became the study of *communications*.

[8] Furthermore, we must consider the contexts of production where bans on writing or discriminatory publishing practices may erase certain voices (e.g., Brown et al. 2016)

[9] For example, a study by Pew Research found that of all tweets produced by adult US users between June 2 and September 12 of 2021, the top 25% of users (by tweet volume) produced about 97% of all tweets (McClain et al. 2021).

[10] Archaeology is a disciplinary kith: a "discipline with the theory and practice for the recovery of unobservable hominid behavior patterns from indirect traces in bad samples" (Clarke 1973:17).

a single tweet, or a single speech. These *can* be our units of analysis, but so are chapters within that book, the pooled collection of tweets by a single Twitter user, or the paragraphs in the speech.[11] We may, say, select the opinion section of three national newspapers. These articles may be our units of analysis, but perhaps paragraphs or sentences are better suited for our research question. For another example, Nelson (2021a) digitized more than 200 articles published by women's liberation movement organizations, but her corpus consisted of more than 1,100 scanned pages from these articles. The problem is, how do we chunk what is, roughly, a "continuous stream of information" (Neuendorf 2017:73)? While the boundaries around some documents might be easily identified, this is not always the case.

BALANCE, RANGE, AND REPRESENTATIVENESS

Early quantitative linguists were quick to generate **frequency lists** (Bontrager 1991). Without corpora, only intuition could provide evidence for how common a word or phrase was in a given language community. An early concern was whether these frequencies could be generalized to *a language* from a corpus, rather than the peculiarities of a given genre. To address this concern, Kučera and Francis at Brown University composed 500 samples of American English, totaling 1 million words (Table 2.1). This **Brown Corpus** was structured to *balance* contributions across a range of fifteen genres in an attempt to be representative of work published in 1961.

Table 2.1: Large-Scale, Balanced Corpora

Corpus	Language	Tokens
Brown	American English	1 million
Lancaster-Oslo/Bergen	British English	1 million
British National	British English	100 million
American National	American English	22 million
BYU Corpus of American English	American English	560 million
Oxford English Corpus	English	2.1 billion
Bank of English	English	4.5 billion

Drawing on corpus linguistics and qualitative content analysis, **balance, range**, and **representativeness** are broad guidelines for creating a

[11] This is known as the problem of *unitization* (Neuendorf 2017:71)—what we call *chunking*. Chunking has a statistical allure: it can increase a corpus size on the cheap. But, chunking should be guided by the meaningfulness of the unit and determined after selection.

In the 1970s, the Lancaster-Oslo/Bergen (LOB) Corpus was based on the same selection strategy as the Brown Corpus. Linguists constructed the British National Corpus (BNC) and the American National Corpus (ANC) following similar selection strategies.

fair selection of texts. By "balance," we mean different sources of variation are equally proportioned across our corpus. By "range," we mean more than one dimension of variation is accounted for when selecting texts. By "representativeness," we mean the extent our selection of texts includes all sources of variability relevant to our case (Biber 1993:243).

The following **sources of variation** may be a principle for *delimiting* a corpus or a principle for *balancing* a corpus. For example, we can select only recent fiction, but balance with a range of genres. Each source of variation "reweight[s] the probabilities" of observing a given linguistic pattern (Martin 1997:85).

These sources of variation may be more internal to a text's content or more external to this content. We use this observation to organize our sources of variation. **Text metadata** is information associated with a text, but perhaps only indirectly derived from the text's contents, including: authors and audiences, publication location and date, and domain and media. **Text data** is information derived from the text's contents, including: languages and dialects, genres and topics, registers and styles. We discuss each below.

Text Metadata

Authors and Audiences

Documents must be written.[12] This is the first act of selection; an act that is typically outside researchers' control. To understand authors' motivations for writing anything, we could dive into the content. But, we must still understand why they wrote at all. What compelled and enabled them to produce a piece of text? What types of authors may be underrepresented (Brown et al. 2016)? And, later, we can consider why *these* words in *this* order and quantity?

Related, we must consider to whom the author is writing as well as those who will eventually read it—that is, the audiences of the text. Broadly, the text we use for analysis can either be *custom-made* or *ready-made* (Salganik 2019). Custom-made text data is made explicitly to answer a scientific question. Here, researchers are audience members who craft its production. This includes interviews, observational fieldnotes, and open-ended survey questions. The reasons such text is produced are largely aligned with motivations for participation in any other kind of social-scientific study.

Ready-made text, by contrast, is produced to communicate with friends, advertise products, persuade political rivals, entertain audiences,

[12] Authors are the people responsible for producing a given text. Ascertaining authorship is sometimes straightforward—*The Parable of the Sower*—and other times reasonably contested—*The Odyssey*. Furthermore, texts may be written by more than one person or group and are often altered on the journey from initial writing to our analyses.

[13] Some argue this mitigates desirability bias. This is true regarding the researchers' desires, but not the audiences'.

[14] This is called diachronic analysis. If a corpus is continually updated, this is called a **monitor corpus**.

generate revenue, etc. Ready-made texts tend to evoke a different set of selection biases: what is available is, typically, *all that is available*. In other words, "the data are already in" (Martin 2017:194).[13] We must theorize audiences—and the authors' assumptions about their audiences—when making our selection. Authors are producing texts *for someone* and this shapes the meanings in those texts.

Time and Location

A recurring question for text analysis is: How do textual variables change over time?[14] As in the study of "cognitive distortions" discussed earlier, we must be mindful of how text's internal *and external* properties may change. Commenting on an initial study of cultural change using the Google Books corpus, Schwartz (2011) remarks: "If the fossil record shows more dinosaur footprints in one period than another, it does not necessarily mean that there were more dinosaurs—it may be that there was more mud."

Focusing on a specific time, as many corpora implicitly do, does not solve this issue. Some phrases may be especially common or uncommon in a given year, but this may or may not be unique to that year. Such problems plague the use of "generations" in studies of social change. How one sets the cutoffs may change the findings.

These concerns are paralleled when considering the locations from which texts are produced. Moving from the roughly one billion Anglophones worldwide—those who inhabit India, New Zealand, South Africa, Barbados, Canada, the United Kingdom, etc.—to the English spoken in only Australia systematically increases homogeneity. Taking the whole Anglophone world, we may find some phrases are over-represented precisely because specific locations produce (or maintain) the bulk of the texts.

Domains and Media

Each piece of text is produced within a broad social domain and through a given form of media. Using domain and media as principles of variation means being oriented toward the social activity involved in the production and maintenance of the text, as well as the affordances offered by different avenues of communication.

Is the speech originally spoken, but then transcribed? Was the written text in a book or a newspaper? An email or a text message? Was the document intended for public consumption or personal uses

(Martin 2017:190–4)? Are there certain conventions that structure the texts, such as routine introductions and closings (Weber 1990:43)?

We must also consider why a given document is preserved. The Enron Corpus, for example, includes roughly 600,000 emails sent and received by 158 employees the year the company collapsed following a scandal. The Federal Energy Regulatory Commission hired Aspen Systems to create it. Leslie Kaelbling, a computer scientist, purchased the corpus, a team cleaned it up, and then released it to the public—and then re-released it to remove some directories. These emails passed through several domains to their current stage. We won't know why some emails were retained or even how many were deleted in the normal course of business. But again, *the data are in*.[15] But we must theorize this journey from production to our analysis.

Furthermore, just as different locations or authors may produce more texts than others, we must consider how domains and media also vary significantly in the quantity of text produced.

Text Data

Languages and Dialects

That there are languages (plural) is based mainly on the intersubjective notion of "mutual intelligibility." Typically, the difference between a language and a dialect is that the latter is a spoken difference (accent or pronunciation). To the extent "dialect" includes distinct grammar, vocabulary, and even spelling differences, we must ensure our tools take this into account.

Some tools, for instance, "correct" so-called misspelled words. As we discuss, this has the benefit of reducing complexity (while increasing homogeneity). We use scare quotes because there is no "correct" way to represent meaning with a set of characters, only more and less conventional ways.[16] The boundaries between those who adhere to these conventions are also fuzzy and overlapping, given that people can often switch or mix dialects (as well as languages).

People also deliberately "misspell" for a variety of ends, such as creating portmanteaus, like smartphone, or humorous and satirical misspellings (i.e., cacography) of, say, politicians' names. Alternative spellings even emerge in response to the automated procedures we'll discuss—for example, 1337 sp34k (or leet speak) popularized by gamers originally grew out of the 1990s hacker community (McKean 2002) to avoid (real or imagined) content moderation and surveillance.[17] In other words, what

[15] We cannot, for example, go back in time to prevent the accountants at Arthur Andersen from deleting emails or shredding their audits of Enron.

[16] A sentiment shared by Mark Twain: "I don't see any use in having a uniform and arbitrary way of spelling words. We might as well make all clothes alike and cook all dishes alike. Sameness is tiresome; variety is pleasing" (Paine 1912:541).

[17] "[Porta (1653)] suggests using misspellings to evade surveillance: 'For it is better for a scribe to be thought ignorant than to pay the penalty for the detection of plans'" (Kahn 1996:139).

[18] Of course, there are unintended misspellings as well as errors arising from optical character recognition (see **Acquiring Texts**) and encoding problems (see **Wrangling Words**).

[19] As Derrida (1980) explains: "Every text participates in one or several genres, there is no genreless text."

[20] Aristotle (1907:35) states: "The work of Herodotus might be put into verse, and it would still be a species of history, with meter no less than without it.... Poetry, therefore, is a more philosophical and a higher thing than history: for poetry tends to express the universal, history the particular."

may look like an "error" to some is intentional and thus meaningful to that language community.[18]

Genres and Topics

As we delimit further, we arrive at more specific conventions regarding the *content* of a given text. Knowing that a given selection is science fiction, for instance, we can make inferences about the content of the text, but likely not the media—this could be subtitles of a popular streaming series or chapters from a book series. At the level of genres and topics, we no longer attempt to impose a mutually exclusive classification scheme atop our text. Any selection of text may be placed in multiple genres or engage with several topics at once (Fowler 1982:37).[19]

Even within this dimension of variation are levels of generality. Fiction and non-fiction are among the most general. Philosophers and literary theorists have debated this distinction for millennia, but it still provides useful guardrails when building a corpus.[20] This is because genres and topics tell us something about the community and context of a text—hints about the intents and desires of authors and audiences. They inform the "substantive hunch" (Martin 2001) that animates our analysis.

Registers and Styles

In the same way as genres and topics cut across media, domain, etc., so do register and style. Register is commonly equated with formality. For example, in Turkish and French it is common to speak in the plural to indicate a level of social distance, and in Shakespeare, "thou" is informal and singular while "you" is formal and plural. In addition to formality, register typically includes perspective—first-, second-, third-person, but may also incorporate broader linguistic elements such as grammar and vocabulary.

The sociologist Basil Bernstein studied the distinct class-related "registers" of talk, which he divided into elaborated and restricted "codes." In extreme cases of restricted codes of talk, what is being said is "wholly predictable for speakers and listeners" (2003:126). His examples here are religious services or types of storytelling. He argued that the identity of working-class folk in London in the 1950s was so thoroughly shared—because "of their common occupational function and social status"—this "reduces the need to verbalize intent so that it becomes explicit" (2003:111–3). Speaking is fast and condensed. So, he concludes that working-class people speak in a more restricted register than those in the middle class.

What is the difference between register and style then? To simplify a large literature: style is usually reserved for the more idiosyncratic linguistic regularities associated with an author—or perhaps an organization or other collective producer.

REDRAWING BOUNDARIES

Depending on our research query, and the sources of variation we are using to balance or delimit, it is perfectly reasonable to redraw the boundaries of existing corpora by removing documents or including documents from multiple sources (see Tables 2.1 and 2.2). This highlights the place of inference in scholarly text analysis.

Table 2.2: Selection of Text Sources

News and Online Media	Political, Legal, Scholarly	Non-Fiction and Fiction
NYT's annotated corpus	State of the Unions	Movie subtitles
NYT California Digital Newspapers	European Parliament	Google Books N-Grams
Lexis Nexus and ProQuest	Campaign speeches	Hathi Digital Trust
All the News Corpus	Caselaw Access Project	North American Slave Narratives
Reddit, Twitter, Facebook	PubMed	Malawi Diaries
blogs, forums, emails	JSTOR	Woman Suffrage Movement Biographies
Wikipedia, Fandom, SongGenius	arXiv, SocArxiv, PsyArxiv	US Novel corpus

Say we randomly sample US TV scripts in the 2000s. We find Asian and Pacific Islander Americans (APIAs) characters have fewer speaking roles. We could, perhaps, infer this to all US TV scripts in the 2000s. If, instead, we are interested in the depictions of APIAs characters in US media, such as the "model minority myth," we may restrict our selection to shows with "recurring [APIAs] characters that develop in depth and complexity over time" (Deo et al. 2008:150). If we wish to focus on *influential* depictions, we may further delimit our selection to the most popular shows airing during "primetime." This is not a random sample. This is a purposive selection. The first follows a similar logic to that of sampling in traditional survey research, while the second follows the approach common to case studies.[21]

When setting the boundaries for what is inside and outside our case (or inside/outside the *sampling frame* from which we then derive a sample), we also establish the scope conditions of our *inferences* about the processes producing and preserving those texts. We'll always be studying a subset of texts. In this sense, **corpus building is sampling**. But first,

[21] Small (2009), drawing on, Mitchell (1983), Yin (2009) and Znaniecki (1934), calls this **statistical inference** as contrasted with **logical inference**.

we must consider how a given source relates to our research question. In this sense, **corpus building is selecting a case**. In practice, this is an ouroboros, with no clear start and finish (Nelson 2020; Brandt and Timmermans 2021; Wagner-Pacifici et al. 2015; Pardo-Guerra and Pahwa 2022; Ignatow and Mihalcea 2016:25–27). Luckily, computational methods are perhaps uniquely suited for the **iteration** that text analysis demands.

Part II

Prerequisites

Part II

Prerequisites

3
Computing Basics

The Analytical Engine has no pretensions whatever to originate anything. It can do whatever we know how to order it to perform. —A. Lovelace

COMPUTING is about conventions more than numbers. Here, we present those conventions, explain computing concepts, define some jargon we'll use, and highlight common errors. This chapter will also give those without programming experience a place to start. For those already familiar with R , we also lay out all the packages we'll need to install.

BRASS TACKS

Computers are simple creatures. Ambiguity is the computer's natural enemy. Code is a set of instructions designed to stamp out ambiguity. The computer follows our instructions and, if all is clear, it performs whatever task we intended. Like natural languages, programming languages have family trees, meaning they are related to, and draw on, earlier languages.[1]

We can classify programming languages by their general features. R is an *object-oriented, procedural, and functional* programming language: we perform procedures on objects using functions. These objects are different **data types** arranged in **data structures**. **Functions** are either included in base R , created during the session, or available in "packages." **Packages** must be installed on our machines and loaded during each session.

[1] For example, R (Team 2021) is the open-source progeny of S , itself influenced by Fortran and Scheme (of the Lisp family).

Coding Environments

Computers comprise three "layers." At the top is the GUI or Graphical User Interface. Whenever we point and click with our touchpad, mouse, or touchscreen, we interact with the GUI. Binary—zeros and ones— is at the bottom; computer hardware understands this layer. Several intermediaries exist between these two layers. Most programming languages used by social scientists and other computational scholars, like R or Python , are called "high-level" because they sit closer to the GUI.

Mapping Texts: Computational Text Analysis for the Social Sciences. Dustin S. Stoltz and Marshall A. Taylor, Oxford University Press. © Oxford University Press 2024.
DOI: 10.1093/oso/9780197756874.003.0003

[2] As are common file formats like XML, HTML, CSV, and TXT files.

Figure 3.1: The RStudio IDE.

These languages are written in **plain text**[2] and we call the resulting files "scripts."

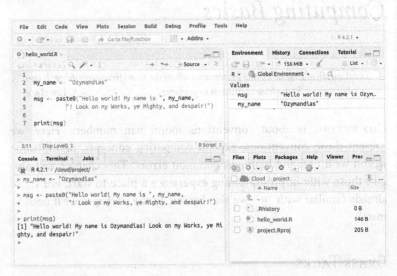

We write our scripts in plain text to *organize* it. To "run" the script, though, we need to "send" it to a program that can "interpret" its conventions and produce the desired output. In our case, this program is R . We could do this directly from a *console*. For this book, though, we'll assume you're using an **Integrated Development Environment** (IDE), a beefy plain-text editor.[3]

[3] Microsoft Word is a word processor, while Notepad is a plain-text editor and Mac's TextEdit has the option to be a plain-text editor.

In addition to RStudio, popular IDEs include VS Code, VSCodium, Sublime, Vim, Emacs, and Notepad++.

RStudio (Figure 3.1) is a dedicated R IDE with many point-and-click features that make our life easier (Team 2020). The free and open-source version of RStudio is sufficient for most.

IDEs, like RStudio, include a *script editor* and a *visual directory* (respectively, left top and right bottom panels in Figure 3.1). Our scripts and data files are in these directories. We must "tell" R where those files are. Directory errors are common; unintentional typos are often the culprits. Finally, IDEs will include a *console*.[4] We send code from the editor to the console to "run" it and the "output" of that code appears in real-time (bottom left in Figure 3.1). We can also see any "objects" we've created during that R session in our *environment* (top right in Figure 3.1).

[4] There are differences, but console, terminal, shell, and command line are often used as synonyms.

If new to R , we suggest using a free RStudio Cloud account.[5] For each section in this book, create a new session in R and open a new R script. Any packages required will be in a margin note with the heading "This Section Needs" and should be loaded at the top of the script. Then, copy each subsequent "code chunk" into this script. Finally, run this code

[5] RStudio Cloud is an online IDE at posit.cloud. We can use RStudio Cloud for nearly all examples in this book. Some examples in the Extended chapters require more computational resources than the free plan offers.

Mapping Texts: Computational Text Analysis for the Social Sciences. Dustin S. Stoltz and Marshall A. Taylor, Oxford University Press. © Oxford University Press 2024. DOI: 10.1093/oso/9780197756881.003.0003

to see the output in the console. A few general reminders (that will make more sense as we go):

- Run the code in the order it appears in each section.
- Creating new objects will overwrite objects of the same name.
- Object names should be short but descriptive.[6]
- Be sure to close any parentheses, brackets, and quotes.[7]

Data Objects, Types, and Structures

Data structures are how we organize our data. In R , these include **vectors**, **lists**, **matrices**, and **dataframes** (Table 3.1). Vectors and lists are similar because they are *flat* (think of a grocery list, a record of cattle weights, or a tally of coin flips). Matrices and dataframes, on the other hand, are squares with rows and columns (e.g., Excel spreadsheets or gradebooks).

Table 3.1: Basic Data Structures

Structure	Different Types?	Rows and Columns?
Vector	NO	NO
List	YES	NO
Matrix	NO	YES
Dataframe	YES	YES

Typically, we'll use "dimensions" to refer to how many rows or columns dataframes and matrices have, or the length of vectors and lists.

With vectors and matrices, all the elements must be the same *type*. Lists and dataframes, however, can be collections of different *types* of elements. Types tell R what can be done with the objects—it sets expectations. There are four basic types, from most to least encompassing: character , numeric or double ,[8] integer , logical (see Table 3.2). R automatically picks the type that can encompass all the elements in a vector. Here are some quick examples (outputs in the margin). We'll "combine" elements with c() to create vectors.

```
words <- c("space", "is", "big")
typeof(words)
```

```
nums <- c(1.2, 2.8, 2)
typeof(nums)
```

```
[1] "double"
```

Notice the `L` in the code below. This forces `R` to treat a number as `integer` rather than a `double` .

```
ints <- c(1L, 3L, 2L)
typeof(ints)
```

```
[1] "integer"
```

```
lgcl <- c(TRUE, FALSE, TRUE, TRUE)
typeof(lgcl)
```

```
[1] "logical"
```

Table 3.2: Basic Data Types

Type	Words/Punctuation	Decimals	Integers
character	YES	YES	YES
numeric or double	NO	YES	YES
integer	NO	NO	YES
logical	NO	NO	NO

The above are the basic building blocks of `R` objects. We can combine them to create a *class*. Like type, this sets `R`'s expectations for the object. The simplest class is a `factor` , which combines `character` and `numeric` types by pairing labels to levels.[9]

[9] Factors are often used for ordinal variables (e.g., "Disagree" to "Agree"). They also force labels into a specific order, which is handy when visualizing.

```
labels <- c("Okay Idea", "Good Idea", "Bad Idea", "Good Idea")
levels <- c("Bad Idea", "Okay Idea", "Good Idea")

fac <- factor(labels, levels)
```

```
typeof(fac)
class(fac)
```

```
[1] "integer"
[1] "factor"
```

Matrices are also a class. The `c()` function combines elements into a vector, and `cbind()` "column binds" the vectors. The result is a `matrix` class object.[10]

[10] **Arrays** include our two-sided matrix, but also objects with more than two sides—like a cube or tesseract. These show up once in this book.

```
c1 <- c(1.2, 2.8, 3)
c2 <- c(0, 4, 2)

mat <- cbind(c1, c2)
```

The `typeof` is a "double" because it is the type that can represent both whole numbers and decimals.

```
class(mat)
typeof(mat)
```

```
[1] "matrix" "array"
[1] "double
```

Finally, highlight the object name (`mat`) and click "run" or type CTRL + ENTER or CMD + ENTER. It will print the contents of the object to the console (output in margin).

```
mat
```

Below `cbind()` creates `matrix`, but now it's `character` as that is the type encompassing both numbers and words (output in margin).

```
d4 <- c(0, 4, 2)
d5 <- c("space", "is", "big")
mat2 <- cbind(d4, d5)
typeof(mat2)
```

```
     c1 c2
[1,] 1.2  0
[2,] 2.8  4
[3,] 3.0  2
```

```
[1] "character"
```

We can tell because double quotes surround each element. When we use `data.frame()`, though, one column is `numeric`, and the other is `character`, creating an object of class `data.frame`. Technically, a data.frame is a set of (vertical) lists of the same length. Each list retains its data type.

```
cbind(mat2)
```

```
     d4  d5
[1,] "0" "space"
[2,] "4" "is"
[3,] "2" "big"
```

```
data.frame(d4, d5)
```

```
  d4  d5
1  0 space
2  4   is
3  2  big
```

To help us navigate these objects, whenever we have a *named* list or dataframe, we can use the `$` operator to call that element by name. Let's create a list

```
lrrrs_list <- list(first = "fireman",
               second =  "math teachers",
               third = "and so on in that fashion")
names(lrrrs_list)
```

```
[1] "first"  "second" "third"
```

To access the element named `third`, we would:

```
lrrrs_list$third
```

```
[1] "and so on in that fashion"
```

Most data structures we encounter are variations on the above. Specifically, objects can be within other objects: for example, a list where the elements are lists (or even lists of lists of lists, and so on in that fashion).

Dialects of R

There are two *dialects* of `R` which we label *nesting* and *chaining*.[11]

- Nesting: An object is transformed by an inner function, then sent to the next *outward* function.
- Chaining: An object is transformed by a function, then sent to the next *right* function.

[11] For a comparison, see Tavares (2018). For a critique of chaining, see Matloff (2020); for the contrary, see Robinson (2017).

First, let's create a dataframe:

```
df <- data.frame(x = c(1031:1032), y = c(2, 2))
```

Let's do several procedures (output in margin), one at a time:

```
df$z <- df$x^df$y # create new column as the x^y
df$a <- df$z / sqrt(df$z) # z divided by square root of z
sum(df$a) # sum the column
```

`[1] 2063`

We can do each of the above operations at the same time by nesting them:

```
sum((df$x^df$y) / sqrt(df$x^df$y))
```

`[1] 2063`

[12] The base R pipe requires version 4.1 or later. Check with R.Version. We can also use %>% from magrittr.

We can also do the same operations by chaining them with the `|>` or "pipe" operator.[12] This dialect was popularized by the packages in `tidyverse`. Below `mutate()` and `select()` are from `dplyr`, which we make available when loading `tidyverse` with `library()`.

```
library(tidyverse)

df |>
  mutate(z = x^y) |>
  mutate(a = z / sqrt(z)) |>
  select(a) |>
  sum()
```

`[1] 2063`

Control Processes: Functions, Loops, and Apply

A key strength of computational tools is their capacity to **iterate**. Let's say we want to print "Hello _____!" to two animals: Axolotl and Capybara. We can plain code these:

```
msg1 <- "Hello Axolotl!"
msg1 <- "Hello Capybara!"
```

One simple rule: Write a function when we need to do something twice. Below, `name` is the only "argument" in our new function `wave()` (output in margin).

```
wave <- function(name) {
    paste0("Hello ", name, "!")
}

wave("Axolotl")
wave("Capybara")
```

`[1] "Hello Axolotl!"`
`[1] "Hello Capybara!"`

We made a small investment initially, but now we have a flexible process to say hello to any animal we can conjure!

Now, imagine we had a list of thousands of animals. Typing the name into the function would get tedious. Can we "loop through" the names to save time? There are two generic methods for this: `for loop` and apply() . Below is a `for loop` . The variable `i` [13] is assigned an element from our vector `names` , uses the function on that element, then moves on to the next element (output in margin).

```
names <- c("Axolotl", "Capybara")
for (i in names) {
  print(wave(i))
}
```

```
[1] "Hello Axolotl!"
[1] "Hello Capybara!"
```

Finally, there is the `apply` family. We'll primarily use `lapply()` . This function takes a list, *applies* a function to each *element* of that list, and then returns the transformed objects as elements of a new list (output in margin).

```
lapply(names, wave)
```

```
[[1]]
[1] "Hello Axolotl!"

[[2]]
[1] "Hello Capybara!"
```

There are more complex control processes, but creating functions and using `for loops` and `apply()` are our primary tools in this book.

Installing and Loading Packages

While `R` 's base is extensive, the techniques in this book require additional packages. A thriving community of `R` enthusiasts and developers extend `R` 's functionality by developing packages. Two common errors occur either because we did not install or load packages in the current session:

```
foo(df)
```

```
Error in foo(df) : could not find function "foo"
```

```
library(foo)
```

```
Error in library(foo) : there is no package called 'foo'
```

The first error means we need to **load the package** containing this function. The second error means we need to **install the package**.[14]

Developers host these packages on *repositories*. CRAN is the official `R` repository where anyone can submit a package that meets certain quality and licensing requirements. Developers host their packages-in-progress on R-Forge, GitLab, GitHub, Codeberg, or Bitbucket. To install `text2map` , we'd use the following code:

```
install.packages("text2map")
```

We only have to install a package once on a machine, but we'll need to "load" them during each new `R` session with `library()` . The following code loads the `text2map` package. This provides access to all its functions during this session.

```
library(text2map)
```

To explore those functions and to get further documentation, use:

```
?text2map # main package page
help(package = text2map) # lists all functions
browseVignettes("text2map") # loads any "vignettes"
```

For this book, we'll need several packages (see **Appendix**). Install them now.[15] The following are all the packages we'll need that are available from CRAN:

[15] We'll never load them all at once! The last loaded packages' functions will "mask" any other functions with the same name. So, only load packages you need. We can also be explicit by using the double colon `::` between the package name and the function.

```
cran_pkgs <- c(
"backbone", "caret", "factoextra", "gender", "ggpubr", "ggraph",
"ggrepel", "ggtern", "glmnet", "gmodels", "googleLanguageR",
"guardianapi," "gutenbergr", "hunspell", "igraph", "irr",
"lexicon", "lsa", "marginaleffects","Matrix", "network", "proustr",
"qdapDictionaries", "quanteda", "quanteda.textmodels", "remotes",
"reshape2", "reticulate", "rsample", "rsvd", "rtrek",
"semgram", "sentimentr", "sna", "stm", "stminsights",
"stringi", "tesseract", "text2map", "text2vec", "textclean",
"textstem", "tidygraph", "tidymodels", "tidyquant", "tidytext",
"tidyverse", "tokenizers", "topicdoc", "topicmodels", "udpipe"
)

install.packages(cran_pkgs)
```

The following packages are hosted on repositories other than CRAN. We'll first install those hosted on GitHub. To install them, we need `remotes`.

```
library(remotes)

install_github("trinker/entity")
install_github("trinker/tagger")
install_github("trinker/termco")
install_github("trinker/coreNLPsetup")
install_github("quanteda/quanteda.corpora")
install_github("lmullen/genderdata")
```

We also wrote specialized text analysis packages to support this work, hosted on GitLab. Install them by running the following:

```
repo <- "culturalcartography/"
pcks <- c("text2map.theme", "text2map.corpora",
          "text2map.pretrained", "text2map.dictionaries")
gl_pcks <- paste0(repo, pcks)

install_gitlab(gl_pcks)
```

Using Python in R

A few `R` functions we'll use depend on packages written in `Python` — another popular programming language. To deal with this, we'll install

`Python` packages in a "virtual environment." This means we need to "call" this virtual environment whenever using these packages. Let's set that up now.

First, install the following `R` packages:

```
pkgs <- c("reticulate", "keras", "spacyr")
install.packages(pkgs)
```

The virtual `Python` environment manager we'll use is called "miniconda" or "conda." We'll create this with `reticulate` . We can name our environment anything, but we'll need to remember that name to reuse it later.

```
library(reticulate)
install_python()
#
miniconda_uninstall()
install_miniconda()

conda_create(envname = "myenv")
```

After we create the environment, we'll install a few Python packages in it.

```
py_pkgs <- c("tensorflow", "spacy", "keras")
conda_install(envname = "myenv", packages = py_pkgs, pip = TRUE)
```

We reactivate this virtual environment whenever we need to access these packages with `use_condaenv()` .

```
use_condaenv(condaenv = "myenv")
```

Data Visualization

We include any packages used in a section in a margin note next to the heading (see margin). When we see this, create a new `R` session (to clear previous packages and objects) and then load these packages before beginning this section using `library()` like this:

```
library(ggplot2)
library(ggpubr)
library(remotes)
```

We'll make many visualizations in this book. `R` is great for this, especially because of the `ggplot2` package which builds on a consistent "grammar of graphics" (Wickham 2010).[16] First, `ggplot()` prepares the **data**, often applying a **stat** (or statistical transformation). Second, `aes()` designates the **aesthetics** of the plot. Next, we'll add different

THIS SECTION NEEDS:

- `ggplot2`
- `ggpubr`
- `remotes`

[16] We rely on Healy's *Data Visualization* (2018a), which offers a deep dive into design principles.

layers called `geoms` (geometric objects) which roughly correspond to kinds of plots, such as dot plots, bar charts, line graphs, etc.

The default aesthetics of `ggplot2` are pretty good. The code can get pretty complex as we fine-tune our visualization. To replicate this book's plots exactly, we built a custom `theme`. To set the theme, install the `text2map.theme` package from GitLab:

```
install_gitlab("culturalcartography/text2map.theme")
```

Then, each time we load a new session of `R`, run this:

```
text2map.theme::set_theme()
```

Let's generate two plots (see Figure 3.2). We'll add a "grouping" variable to specify `color` (for the borders) and/or `fill` (for the insides) for each `geom()`. We'll also perform operations on one of our variables using `mutate()` before passing the data to `ggplot()` in a chain. Next, we'll create the two different plots and print them together using `ggarrange()`.[17]

```
p3 <- mtcars |>
    mutate(cyl = paste(cyl, "cylinders")) |>
    ggplot(aes(x = wt, y = mpg, color = cyl))

p3.a <- p3 + geom_point()
p3.b <- p3 + geom_boxplot(aes(fill = cyl))

ggarrange(p3.a, p3.b, ncol = 2)
```

Our theme builds on the Urban Institute's. We use colors from `viridis`, which is optimized for data representation (i.e., perceptually uniform), easier to read for those with colorblindness, and translates to grayscale. *Open Sans* and *Lato* are both good fonts for data visualizations because they have high readability at small sizes and even spacing.

[17] Note the `+` operator. This operates like a pipe `|>`, but is only used with `ggplot` objects and functions.

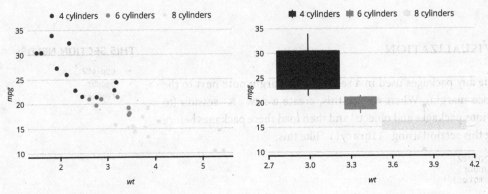

Figure 3.2: Example Data Visualization.

We'll use data visualizations similar to this throughout the book. Visualizations are powerful tools for "seeing" our data and the transformations of our data that mapping entails.

WHERE TO FROM HERE

This chapter offered the basics of computing with R that we'll need for the techniques in this book. We can always return when we have questions about coding procedures or need a refresher on terminology.

We only provide a brief overview as there are many detailed and accessible resources (and many are free). We recommend reading each R package's official documentation on CRAN.[18] The *Official Introduction to R* (Venables et al. 2021) is an indispensable guide, as is Wickam and Grolemund's *R for Data Science* (2016)[19] Two more specialized references are Bryan and Hester's *What They Forgot to Teach You About R* (Bryan and Hester 2019) and Healy's *Data Visualization* (Healy 2018a). Finally, there are many forums for posting coding errors to get potential solutions from experienced programmers—like Stack Overflow, community.rstudio.com, and various Subreddits and Discord servers. These are invaluable resources.

[18] For instance, text2map 's manual is here: cran.r-project.org/package=text2map

[19] There are also several "cheatsheets" at rstudio.com/resources/cheatsheets

4
Math Basics

Mathematics compares the most diverse phenomena and discovers the secret
analogies that unite them   —J. Fourier

COMPUTATIONAL text analysis involves math. No surprises there!
Luckily, a little math goes a long way. Below is an overview of some
mathematical concepts and measures we'll use.[1] Anyone with at least
high school math and this chapter should be able to complete the analyses
in this book. This chapter is an introduction, refresher, and cheatsheet
we'll continually reference.

[1] We promised no equations, and we're sticking to it.

THE FUNDAMENTALS

Quantification begins with the **scalar**: a single number. **Integers** or
"whole numbers" are one kind of scalar, and **real numbers** or "whole
numbers with decimals" are another kind of scalar. A **vector** is a list of
scalars where the order matters.

```
## Scalars
a_intg <- 8 # integer
a_real <- 6.5 # real number

## Vectors
a_vec <- c(8, 6.5)
```

Adding scalars is as simple as two plus two equals four. When we add
vectors, though, we have to account for all the numbers *and their order*
(output in margin).

```
## adding scalars
scal1 <- 1
scal2 <- 15
scal1 + scal2
```

[1] 16

```
## adding vectors
vec1 <- c(1, 4, 4, 5)
vec2 <- c(0, 5, 1, 4)
vec1 + vec2
```

[1] 1 9 5 9

We added the numbers in the same position in each vector. Subtracting vectors from vectors works the same. What happens if we add a scalar
to a vector? Each number in the vector is increased by the amount of the
scalar. Subtracting scalars from vectors works in the same way.

Mapping Texts: Computational Text Analysis for the Social Sciences. Dustin S. Stoltz
and Marshall A. Taylor, Oxford University Press. © Oxford University Press 2024.
DOI: 10.1093/oso/9780197756874.003.0004

Often we'll summarize the numbers in a vector to create a single number (i.e., a scalar). The most common is the average or mean, which we get by summing all the numbers and dividing by how many numbers there are. We'll also encounter the **norm** of the vector.[2] The $L1$-norm involves adding the absolute values of all the numbers in the vector. The $L2$-norm results from squaring all the numbers, adding them, and getting the square root.[3]

[2] Depending on context, this is sometimes called the length, magnitude, or distance from the origin.

[3] The Pythagorean Theorem is a famous version of this formula, but we're using it for more than just measuring triangles and spreading fava bean propaganda.

```
vec1 <- c(1, 4, 4, 5)

avg <- vec1 / sum(vec1)

l1n <- sum(abs(vec1))
l2n <- sqrt(sum(vec1^2))
```

Sometimes we subtract the mean from the vector, which shifts each number by precisely the amount of the mean. This is **centering**. One reason we might center is to make two vectors more easily compared. In the code below, after centering `vec1` and `vec2` , they now have the same means (at zero), and lower bound (at -2.5). This tends to make the math easier.

```
vec1 <- c(1, 4, 4, 5)
vec2 <- c(0, 5, 1, 4)
## centering vectors
vec1 - mean(vec1)
vec2 - mean(vec2)
```

```
[1] -2.5  0.5  0.5  1.5
[1] -2.5  2.5 -1.5  1.5
```

In other cases, we'll want to **normalize** or **norm** (as a verb) a vector, which involves changing our vector, so its norm equals one, i.e., a *unit vector*. We accomplish this by dividing the vector by a respective norm. The two most common are the $L1$- and $L2$-norms.

```
vec1 <- c(37, 42, 47, 1138)
# Normalize by L1 Norm
norm1 <- sum(abs(vec1))
vecL1 <- vec1 / norm1

## Normalize by L2 Norm
norm2 <- sqrt(sum(vec1^2)) # L2 norm
vecL2 <- vec1 / norm2

# respective norms now equal 1
sum(abs(vecL1))
sqrt(sum(vecL2^2))
```

```
[1] 1
[1] 1
```

COMPARING VECTORS

In computational analysis, we often compare two vectors: Is this list of numbers different from another list of numbers, and if so, how different? Say we asked three people how many years they've worked at their job and how much they make per hour. We'll have a list of years and a list of wages.

```
years <- c(31, 41, 5)
wages <- c(92, 65, 35)
```

The order matters because each person's answers must align. Response in the first position on the `years` vector should align with the response in the first position on the `wages` vector. When we compare the two, we'll want to know if the numbers seem to go up in the same positions and down in the same positions. In our example, this helps us see patterns in how people's wages relate to their years of experience.

Dot Product

[4] This is also called the inner product or scalar product.

[5] Note the $L2$-norm is the square root of the dot product of a vector with itself.

The cornerstone of methods for comparing vectors is the **dot product**.[4] The dot product of two vectors involves multiplying each number in the first vector with its corresponding number in the second vector. Then we sum them to get a scalar. If we square a single vector and then sum all its elements, this is the dot product of a single vector with itself.[5]

```
vec1 <- c(1, 2, 4, 2)
vec2 <- c(2, 3, 1, 1)

dt1 <- sum(vec1 * vec2)
dt2 <- 1 * 2 + 2 * 3 + 4 * 1 + 2 * 1

all.equal(dt1, dt2)
```

```
[1] TRUE
```

[6] Y to the sky! X to the left!

Vectors are lists of numbers where the order matters, and we can think of them as coordinates in a space or the address on a map. As is tradition, on a flat plot with a vertical and horizontal number line, the side-to-side line is called x, and the vertical line is called y.[6] Because we only have two number lines, we can know precisely where any point is with two numbers. Say we have three points. Call them Gallifrey, Magrathea, and Trisolaris. The first vector is $[1, 2]$, the second $[3.5, 1]$, and the third $[2.5, 3.5]$. Plotting these points gives us a **vector space** (see Figure 4.1).

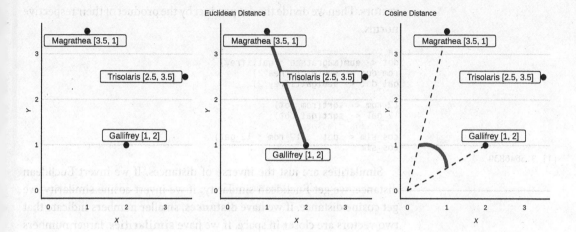

Figure 4.1: Vectors in a Two-Dimensional Vector Space.

Euclidean Distance and Cosine Similarity

The similarity between two vectors is now about space: What is the **distance** between each point? We primarily measure distances in two ways: Euclidean and cosine. Euclidean distance is the shortest line between two points. This metric ranges from 0 (identical points) to some unknown upper bound that varies from dataset to dataset. Cosine—or **cosine similarity**—is the angle formed when drawing a line from each point to the origin $[0, 0]$. This ranges from 1 (identical points) to either 0 or -1, depending on the data.[7]

The key to both is the *dot product*. To find the Euclidean distance, we'll first subtract the two vectors. This result is a vector of the differences between the original two vectors. Next, we'll square this difference vector, sum it, and then find the square root. In the case of a single vector, this is the square root of the dot product of the vector with itself—that is, the $L2$- norm (output in margin).

[7] We'll compare Euclidean and cosine metrics in more detail in **Core Inductive**.

```
magrathea <- c(3, 1)
gallifrey <- c(3.5, 1)
## Difference vector
dif <- magrathea - gallifrey
## Dot product
dif_dot <- sum(dif^2)
## Square root
euc_dist <- sqrt(dif_dot)

euc_dist
```

[1] 0.5

To find the cosine similarity, we'll first find the dot product between the two vectors. We'll then find the $L2$-norms for both the original vectors. Then we divide the dot product by the product of their respective norms.

```
## Dot products
dot <- sum(magrathea * gallifrey)
rom_dot <- sum(magrathea^2)
gal_dot <- sum(gallifrey^2)
## L2 norms
l2_rom <- sqrt(rom_dot)
l2_gal <- sqrt(gal_dot)
## Cosine similarity
cos_sim <- dot / (l2_rom * l2_gal)
cos_sim
```

[1] 0.5646839

Similarities are just the inverse of distances. If we invert Euclidean distance, we get Euclidean similarity; if we invert cosine similarity, we get cosine distance. If we have **distances**, smaller numbers indicate that two vectors are closer in space. If we have **similarities**, larger numbers indicate vectors are closer.

Correlation

Perhaps the most common method to compare two vectors is **correlation** (de Mesquita and Fowler 2021:13–36).[8] Again, the cornerstone of this measure is the *dot product*. A correlation is the cosine of two vectors, only we first subtract the means from the vectors (i.e., center).[9] Let's use the same example vectors as before. Let's walk through calculating correlation by hand.

```
Magrathea <- c(3.5, 1)
gallifrey <- c(1, 3)

## Center vectors
c_rom <- Magrathea - mean(Magrathea)
c_gal <- gallifrey - mean(gallifrey)
## Dot products
dif_dot <- sum(c_rom * c_gal)
rom_dot <- sum(c_rom^2)
gal_dot <- sum(c_gal^2)
## L2 norms of centered vectors
l2_rom <- sqrt(rom_dot)
l2_gal <- sqrt(gal_dot)
## Cosine distance
res1 <- dif_dot / (l2_rom * l2_gal)
```

Now, calculate correlations with R 's function cor() and see if the two results are identical with all.equal() (output in margin).

```
res2 <- cor(Magrathea, gallifrey)
```

```
all.equal(res1, res2)
```

[1] TRUE

In our example, there was a perfect negative association: when a number is low in one vector, it is high in the other vector, and vice versa. With correlations, we quantify the degree two vectors vary together and

[8] Specifically, we'll discuss the most common: Pearson correlation.

[9] If we center, but skip norming, we'd get the **covariance**.

the direction of this association.[10] However, correlations cannot tell us *how much* one vector increases with every increase in another vector. For instance, how much do wages tend to increase with an additional year of experience? For this, we need another tool called regression.

Regression

Regression is a family of methods that summarizes the variation in our data (de Mesquita and Fowler 2021:74–93). We'll discuss the bread-and-butter technique known as **Ordinary Least Squares** (OLS) regression (Tufte 1974:65–134). With OLS, we want a line through our data that "fits" with minimal errors.[11]

Recall that the correlation between two vectors is their cosine, but first, we center the vectors by subtracting their means. Also, recall that cosine is the dot product of two vectors divided by the product of their $L2$-norms. Standard OLS makes a critical alteration to these steps: we only center and norm *one of* our vectors.

With regression, one vector is an *outcome* variable,[12] that is, the Y, and one or more vectors are *predictor* variables,[13] that is, Xs. We are interested in the extent a change in the outcome variable is associated with a change in the predictor variable. With OLS, we *won't* norm or center the Y (the outcome variable). Let's use a fictitious survey of how many puppies people have (predictor) and their happiness level (outcome).

```
x_puppy <- c(0, 1, 4, 3, 2)
y_happy <- c(1, 3, 6, 7, 5)

c_puppy <- x_puppy - mean(x_puppy) # center our predictor(s)
dot <- sum(y_happy * c_puppy) # dot product
dot_pup <- sum(c_puppy^2) # dot product
l2_pup <- sqrt(dot_pup) # L2 norm of predictor(s)

coef1 <- dot / (l2_pup * l2_pup) # calculate OLS
```

Let's compare our step-by-step OLS with base R 's OLS function. We must bind our two vectors into a dataframe to work with lm() .

```
dfa <- data.frame(puppy = x_puppy, happy = y_happy)
ols <- lm(happy ~ puppy, data = dfa)
coef2 <- coef(ols)["puppy"]

all.equal(coef1, coef2, check.attributes = FALSE)
```

Both give us the same answer: 1.4. What does this mean? Since we didn't transform our outcome variable (the Y), the number is *in the same metric* as that outcome: for every one unit increase in puppies, we expect our respondents' happiness level to increase by 1.4 units.[14]

[10] This is true whether we are comparing locations in a vector space or years of experience with wages.

[11] We often call regression and similar techniques "fitting a model."

[12] Also called *dependent* or *response* variables.

[13] Also called *independent* or *explanatory* variables.

[1] TRUE

[14] This number is called the slope, coefficient, estimate, or beta.

There are many extensions to this model. *Multiple OLS regression*, where we have more than one predictor (Tufte 1974:135–163), allows us to explore how happiness is related to both how many puppies people have and, say, how noisy their homes are.

```
x1_noise <- c(2, 4, 2, 1, 1)
x2_puppy <- c(0, 1, 4, 3, 2)
 y_happy <- c(1, 3, 6, 7, 5)

## center our predictors
c1_noise <- x1_noise - mean(x1_noise)
c2_puppy <- x2_puppy - mean(x2_puppy)
## dot products
dot_x1   <- sum(c1_noise^2)
dot_x2   <- sum(c2_puppy^2)
doty_x1  <- sum(y_happy * c1_noise)
doty_x2  <- sum(y_happy * c2_puppy)
dot_x1x2 <- sum(c1_noise * c2_puppy)
## beta 1
beta1 <- ((dot_x2 * doty_x1) - (dot_x1x2 * doty_x2)) /
         ((dot_x1) * (dot_x2) - (dot_x1x2)^2)
## beta 2
beta2 <- ((dot_x1 * doty_x2) - (dot_x1x2 * doty_x1)) /
         ((dot_x1) * (dot_x2) - (dot_x1x2)^2)

beta1
beta2
```

```
[1] -0.3529412
[1] 1.294118
```

Let's double-check using base R 's own OLS estimates.

```
df <- data.frame(noise = x1_noise, puppy = x2_puppy, happy =y_happy)
ols <- lm(happy ~ noise + puppy, data = df)
coef(ols)[c("noise", "puppy")]
```

```
     noise
-0.3529412
     puppy
 1.2941176
```

Checks out! A one-unit increase in noisiness is associated with a 0.35 *decrease* in happiness. Notice that our puppy coefficient is still positive but not the same as the previous "fit." Here, for every additional puppy we expect a 1.29 unit increase in happiness *conditional on noisiness*. Table 4.1 lists some of the common vector measures we've reviewed here.

There are assumptions OLS expects and which our data do not always meet. We won't go into detail, but OLS is a "linear model," or LM. Extensions to this are called "generalized linear models" or GLMs. For example, one GLM we'll encounter in this book is **logistic regression** which is appropriate when our outcome variable is categorical, like "yes" or "no."[15]

Like regular OLS regression, logistic regression predicts an outcome using some predictors. Here, we'll assume our outcome has two values: yes or no. Logistic regression is especially suited for this scenario. Technically, our outcome is whether an observation is a 1 or a 0, but we'll model the *probability* of getting a 1 or 0.

With OLS regression, the outcome and predictors can (in theory) range from positive infinity to negative infinity. For reasons we won't

[15] If the outcome is categorical but ordinal, then we would probably want what is called **ordered logistic regression**. If the outcome is categorical and consists of three or more unordered categories, then we probably want **multinomial logistic regression**.

Table 4.1: Common Vector Measures

Measure	Explanation
Dot Product	sum of the product of two vectors or sum of the square of one vector
L2-Norm	square root of the dot product of vector to itself
Difference Vector	result of subtracting two vectors
Cosine	normed dot product of two vectors
Correlation	normed/centered dot product of difference vector
OLS	dot product of two (or more) vectors, but one vector is *not* normed/centered

discuss, this makes the math simple. With logistic regression, we want something with the same bounds—but how? We first "trick" our model by taking the probability over one minus the probability. This is called the odds. Here our range is now between 0 and positive infinity—halfway there! We then take the logarithm of those odds, giving a range between negative infinity and positive infinity. *Then* we can treat it more like a bread-and-butter OLS regression.[16] Whenever we're trying to find the probability some observation falls into a category, logistic regression is a good place to start.

COMPARING DISTRIBUTIONS

Sometimes we just care about the numbers in our vector, and not so much the order. In other words, we care about the **distribution** of the numbers in our list.[17] For instance, how many people have one puppy? Two? Three? There are three things we'll need to summarize a distribution: **central tendency**, **dispersion**, and the **type of distribution**.

Central Tendency

Recall that sometimes we'll find a single number (i.e., scalar) that summarizes a vector. Measuring the *central tendency* in our list of numbers is one way of doing this. We already discussed the mean, which generally refers to the *arithmetic mean*: summing the numbers and dividing that by how many numbers there are. Two other common central tendencies are *median* and *mode*. The former is the middle value separating the lower half of our list from the upper half. The latter is whichever number occurs the most frequently.

[16] The log of the odds is also called a *logit*. Logits are not very intuitive and we have to do a little math to convert our results *back* into probabilities.

[17] If the numbers in our vector sum to 1, we'll often call this a *probability distribution*.

Dispersion

Another way to summarize our vector is to measure how spread out or dispersed our numbers are. Measures of dispersion include the **range** and the **variance**. The first is the difference between the smallest and biggest number. The second involves subtracting the mean from our vector, then squaring and summing that vector (that's right, *dot product* again) and then dividing by the number of observations.[18]

Finally, the **standard deviation** is the square root of the variance. The standard deviation has the benefit of being interpreted in the metric units of the variable: for example, if we measured a sample of Muppets on *Sesame Street* and find a mean of 24 inches and a standard deviation of 9 inches, then Muppet's heights in this sample deviate from the mean of 24 inches by, on average, about 9 inches.[19]

Types of Distributions

Statistics, as used in the social sciences, often begins with the assumption that when we measure something in the world, it will have a *normal (or Gaussian) distribution*.[20] So, let's start there.

Our list is normally distributed if the numbers are symmetrical above and below the mean. Here, we'll simulate two vectors with normal distributions, slightly different means, and one with different standard deviations. These distributions are shown in Figure 4.2.

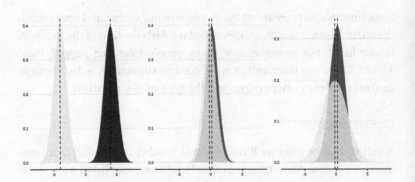

There are also many non-normal distributions—too many to elaborate here. We should not assume our data follow a normal distribution.[21] When comparing the two vectors, it is not enough to determine if their central tendencies differ, but also their overall dispersions and the form of their distributions.

[18] We might also divide by the number of observations *minus one*, which is common when we are working with samples as opposed to a full population.

[19] Elmo and Kermit are precisely 24 inches while Big Bird is at 98 inches!

[20] Or, that the distribution of means from repeated samples of that "something" will be normal when the sample sizes are sufficiently large. This is known as the **Central Limit Theorem**.

Figure 4.2: Normal (Gaussian) Distributions.

[21] We'll encounter plenty of non-normal distributions in this book.

Our Dear Friend, the Matrix

We'll end this primer with the **matrix**,[22] which is a collection of vectors stacked on top of each other or side by side. What's handy about a matrix is that we can work on several vectors simultaneously.

First, let's create an example matrix by building vectors and then "binding" them as rows.

```
vec1 <- c(1, 2, 4, 2)
vec2 <- c(3, 3, 3, 1)
vec3 <- c(4, 4, 4, 1)
mat <- rbind(vec1, vec2, vec3)
mat
```

```
     [,1] [,2] [,3] [,4]
vec1   1    2    4    2
vec2   3    3    3    1
vec3   4    4    4    1
```

We'll often need to **transpose** a matrix, which tips-and-flips it, so the rows become the columns and vice versa:

```
t(mat)
```

```
     vec1 vec2 vec3
[1,]   1    3    4
[2,]   2    3    4
[3,]   4    3    4
[4,]   2    1    1
```

A matrix is a mathematical object like any other, which means we can also do arithmetic with them, but again we'll need to work with *all the numbers* and keep track of their *positions* in our matrix. Let's create two small matrices and add them.

```
mat1 <- matrix(c(1:4), ncol = 2)
mat2 <- matrix(c(5:8), ncol = 2)
mat1 + mat2
```

```
     [,1] [,2]          [,1] [,2]         [,1] [,2]
[1,]   1    3    +  [1,]   5    7    =  [1,]   6   10
[2,]   2    4       [2,]   6    8       [2,]   8   12
```

We added the numbers in the corresponding row-column position (i.e., cell) in each matrix. What happens if we add a scalar to our matrix? Every cell increases by the amount of that single number.

This gets more complicated when the matrices are not the same shape. We cannot add or subtract them, but we can multiply matrices of differing shapes. **Matrix multiplication** is a little different than regular multiplication, and instead of using `*` in `R`, it requires a particular

[22] Matrix comes from Latin for womb or mother: "I have... defined a 'Matrix' as a rectangular array of terms, out of which different systems of determinants may be engendered as from the womb of a common parent" (Sylvester 1851:247).

operator, %*% (output in margin). It's central to much of what we'll do later.

```
mat1 %*% mat2
```

```
      [,1] [,2]
[1,]   23   31
[2,]   34   46
```

Here, we find the sum of each cell-by-cell product between each *row vector* in the first matrix and each *column vector* in the second. In other words, we found the *dot product* of two vectors. These two vectors, though, are not the corresponding rows in the matrices. The first result is the dot product of the first row in the first matrix with the first column in the second matrix, etc. (output in margin).

```
sum(mat1[1, ] * mat2[, 1])
sum(mat1[2, ] * mat2[, 1])
sum(mat1[1, ] * mat2[, 2])
sum(mat1[2, ] * mat2[, 2])
```

```
[1] 23
[1] 34
[1] 31
[1] 46
```

We can multiply matrices of different shapes, but their dimensions must be compatible: the number of rows of one matrix *must* equal the number of columns of the other matrix. The output is a square matrix: a matrix with the same number of rows and columns.

Matrix Projection

A common scenario where we need matrix multiplication is when conducting **projection** (Breiger 1974; Everett and Borgatti 2013). Sometimes, the rows and columns of our matrix are the same kinds of things. A typical example is a friendship network,[23] where we line the same people along the rows and columns, and if two people are friends, we'd place a "1" wherever their respective rows and columns intersect. We call this a *one-mode* matrix. Often our matrix rows are different kinds of things than our columns. Say we ask people what fruits they ate for lunch. We'd place a "1" at the intersection of a person's row and a food's column. We call this a *two-mode* matrix.

[23] More on networks in a bit.

```
fruits <- c("huckleberry", "guava", "mango", "fig", "cherry")
titania <- c(1, 0, 0, 1, 0)
oberon <- c(0, 1, 0, 1, 1)
puck <- c(1, 0, 1, 1, 0)

two_mod <- rbind(titania, oberon, puck)
colnames(two_mod) <- fruits

two_mod
```

```
        huckleberry guava mango fig cherry
titania           1     0     0   1      0
oberon            0     1     0   1      1
puck              1     0     1   1      0
```

Often we'll convert this two-mode into a one-mode matrix, and we call this *matrix projection*. Projection involves matrix multiplication with one extra step: *we transpose one matrix*. Recall the dimensions of the resulting matrix depend on which matrix is first. If the transposed matrix is first in the order of operations, then we get a food-by-food matrix. If the transposed matrix is second, then we get a person-by-person matrix. Let's see this in action.

```
two_mod %*% t(two_mod)

        titania oberon puck
titania       2      1    2
oberon        1      3    1
puck          2      1    3


t(two_mod) %*% two_mod

          huckleberry guava mango fig cherry
huckleberry         2     0     1   2      0
guava               0     1     0   1      1
mango               1     0     1   1      0
fig                 2     1     1   3      1
cherry              0     1     0   1      1
```

In the first projection, the numbers are how many fruits the row person had in common with the column person. Titania and Puck both ate huckleberries and figs, for example. In the second projection, the numbers are how many people the row fruit and the column fruit had in common. One person who ate a fig also ate a mango, for example. Base R provides two efficient functions[24] for this:

```
## row-by-row matrix: two_mod %*% t(two_mod)
tcrossprod(two_mod)
## column-by-column matrix: t(two_mod) %*% two_mod
crossprod(two_mod)
```

[24] A few operations are called "cross product." Here, it refers to the inner product of the row vectors of a matrix and the column vectors of its transpose (Williams 2010:768).

Matrices help us organize our data, but they also correspond to two other mathematical objects: spaces and graphs. Both are intuitive ways of representing the patterns in our data. Let's briefly discuss how matrices are related to spaces with singular value decomposition before discussing how they relate to graphs.

Vector Spaces and Singular Value Decomposition

What does it mean to "reduce" the dimensionality of a matrix? The most common methods involve singular value decomposition, or SVD (Martin and Porter 2012). To understand SVD, we can think about how a matrix has a corresponding geometric interpretation. We call the columns of our matrix *dimensions* because they define positions along the dimensions of a vector space.

A *linear transformation* is when we change the space in some way that a straight line before the transformation stays a straight line after. For example, imagine holding a mirror to our space: any straight lines in the space are still straight in the reflection. What's useful is that any stretching, compressing, flipping, or shearing[25] of the space is a linear transformation *if we first rotate the space correctly.*

Say we have a two-column matrix and so a two-dimensional space. We can draw a square in this space using the axes, origin, and a single point (Figure 4.3, left panel). When we apply SVD, we are converting our square into a rectangle. But, we're trying to compress, stretch, flip, and rotate it such that one side of our rectangle *is as long as possible.* The lengths of the sides of our rectangle are the **singular values**, and the first singular value is the longest side.[26] As the right panel in Figure 4.3 shows, singular values describe how much the space is "stretched" in any direction. The coordinates of the new point are the **singular vector**. Significantly, we can "recover" our original data by reversing those same linear transformations.

[25] This means turning a square into a rhombus by pushing on the top corner.

[26] This generalizes to a space with any number of dimensions, but we lose the ability to visualize it.

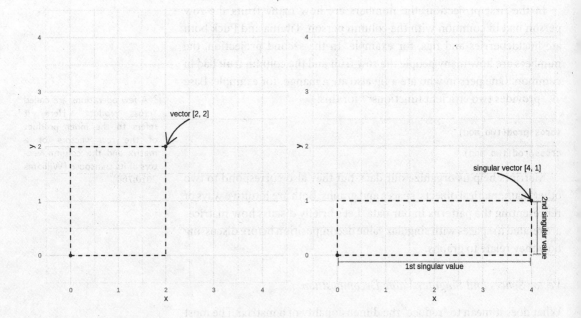

Figure 4.3: Hypothetical Vector Space and SVD.

More technically, SVD finds three matrices. If we multiply these matrices together, it recovers the original matrix. There are several steps to getting these three matrices—called U, D, and V – and luckily, there

are functions for this. We'll do this step by step and then compare it to
`svd()` . Let's create a matrix, A.

```
A_mat <- matrix(c(1, 1, 1, 1, 1, 1,
                  1, 1, 1, 1, 1, 1,
                  0, 0, 0, 0, 0, 0,
                  2, 1, 1, 1, 0, 0),
                6, 4)
```

SVD involves finding the *eigenvalues* and *eigenvectors* of the two matrix
projections of A, which we call AA^T and A^TA. The eigenvectors of the
first (AA^T) are the columns of U, and the eigenvectors of the second
(A^TA) are the columns of V.[27] The vectors are only as long as the shortest
rows and columns of A (in our case, 4). So, we need to trim the output of
AA^T.

```
AAT <- tcrossprod(A_mat)
ATA <- crossprod(A_mat)

U_mat <- eigen(AAT)$vectors[, seq_len(4L)]
V_mat <- eigen(ATA)$vectors
```

Next, the singular values (D) are the square root of the eigenvalues.
Note that the eigenvalues for both AA^T and A^TA are the same (but AA^T
has more zeros).[28]

```
round(eigen(AAT)$values)
round(eigen(ATA)$values)

[1] 17  2  0  0  0  0
[1] 17  2  0  0
```

```
D_mat <- sqrt(round(eigen(ATA)$values))
round(D_mat, 3)

[1] 4.123 1.414 0.000 0.000
```

Let's compare this to `svd()` .

```
UDV <- svd(A_mat)
round(UDV$d, 3)

[1] 4.123 1.414 0.000 0.000
```

We can ignore the numbers for now. Note that D is a list of numbers,[29]
and the numbers are in descending order (this is important). These are
our *singular values*.

The singular values are the "relative importance" of each row and
column in U and V in "explaining" the original matrix. Let's calculate
the "variance explained" by each:

[27] For technical reasons, the signs will not be the same between `eigen()` and `svd()` , but we can ignore this.

[28] We'll round them because the zeros will often be *almost* zero, and sometimes negative, for example, -0.000000000013.

[29] Usually, these numbers are the diagonal of a matrix with zeros on either side.

```
prop.table(UDV$d^2) |> round(2)
```

```
[1] 0.89 0.11 0.00 0.00
```

The first singular value explains roughly 89% of the variance in the original matrix. We can use this singular value to create the approximation of the original matrix using the following.

```
# prepare the first component matrices
u1 <- UDV$u[, 1, drop = FALSE]
v1 <- UDV$v[, 1, drop = FALSE]
d1 <- diag(UDV$d)[1, 1, drop = FALSE]
# approximate the original
A1 <- u1 %*% d1 %*% t(v1)
A1
```

```
       [,1]  [,2] [,3]  [,4]
[1,]  1.333 1.333    0 1.333
[2,]  1.000 1.000    0 1.000
[3,]  1.000 1.000    0 1.000
[4,]  1.000 1.000    0 1.000
[5,]  0.667 0.667    0 0.667
[6,]  0.667 0.667    0 0.667
```

[30] This is the motivation behind all dimension reduction techniques.

If we include more than the first singular value, we'd more precisely reproduce the original matrix. We can also create a "reduced" matrix to approximate the original.[30] The rows of our original matrix are vectors of four dimensions. Only two singular values are not zero, though. So, let's reduce the matrix to two.

```
k_seq <- seq_len(2L)

v_r <- UDV$v[, k_seq, drop = FALSE]
d_r <- diag(UDV$d[k_seq])

u_reduced <- A_mat %*% v_r %*% d_r
round(u_reduced, 2)
```

```
       [,1]  [,2]
[1,] -9.52  1.16
[2,] -7.14  0.00
[3,] -7.14  0.00
[4,] -7.14  0.00
[5,] -4.76 -1.16
[6,] -4.76 -1.16
```

This may not be intuitive just yet, but we'll return to the idea of dimension reduction several times throughout this book.

Graphs and Matrix Projection

THIS SECTION NEEDS:

- ggraph

Many patterns in the world are the *relations* between elements (Emirbayer 1997). A **network** is the structure of elements and the relations between them. Many phenomena are networks: for example, disease contagion, genealogies, the diffusion of market products, and our nervous system. We cannot understand these processes without considering the relations between elements. Every network comprises *nodes* (or *vertices*) and *ties* (or *edges*, or *links*). We get this jargon from *graph theory*, and often call networks *graphs*.[31]

What these nodes and ties comprise varies—really, we are constrained only by our imagination. In a *social* network, nodes are usually social actors—individuals, groups, organizations, etc. Ties are whatever connects these social actors—say, friendship, cohabitation, similar tastes, etc. Using graph theory, we can analyze the "structural" properties of those patterns. For instance, we could assess gossip flowing through a network of company emails or find brokers in an organizational hierarchy.

A matrix can represent any graph. As such, networks lead a double life: as graphs and matrices.[32] Let's consider a real-world social network, both as a matrix and graph. Below is the matrix representation of the Florentine Families data (Padgett and Ansell 1993). This dataset comprises marriages between 16 families in Renaissance-period Florence, Italy. We'll only look at the first five rows and five columns.

```
data("flo", package = "network")
flo[1:5, 1:5]
```

	Acciaiuol	Albizzi	Barbadori	Bischeri	Castellan
Acciaiuol	0	0	0	0	0
Albizzi	0	0	0	0	0
Barbadori	0	0	0	0	1
Bischeri	0	0	0	0	0
Castellan	0	0	1	0	0

In the matrix, an ij (row-column) pair gets a 1 if there was at least one marriage between those two families and a 0 if not. We typically call these *adjacency matrices*. When they are unweighted like this (just 0s and 1s), we call them *binary matrices*, and when they are *symmetric* (i.e., the rows and columns are the same entities and a tie has either no direction or is bidirectional), we call them *undirected matrices*.

Let's look at it in graph form (see Figure 4.4), using `ggraph` .[33]

```
set.seed(59812) # set a seed to make layout reproducible

flo |>
  ggraph(layout = "fr") +
  geom_edge_link() +
  geom_node_label(aes(label = name)) +
  theme_graph()
```

[31] Graphs and networks are not strictly synonyms, but we'll still use them interchangeably. Sorry, mathematicians!

[32] Network science, then, is a fusion of graph theory and matrix algebra.

[33] The network itself is an igraph object. igraph is the most popular network analysis packages in R . ggraph is preferred for creating visualizations of graphs inline with the ggplot2 grammar.

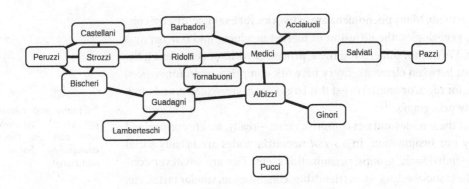

Figure 4.4: Florentine Family Network as a Graph.

[34] The layout of this graph uses the Fruchterman-Reingold force-directed algorithm (Fruchterman and Reingold 1991). There are numerous layouts to choose from.

The row and column names of the matrix are the nodes and the cell entries are the ties. Since this network is unweighted, the presence of a tie corresponds to a "1" in the matrix and the absence of a tie is a "0" in the matrix. The network is also undirected; thus, the absence of arrows indicating the "flow" of the tie.[34]

This is an example of a *unipartite graph*, and the corresponding matrix is a *unimodal matrix*. We know this because the nodes are all the same kinds of things, here families. We'll also work with *bimodal matrices*: the row and column entities are different. An example from network analysis is the Southern Women dataset (Davis et al. 1941), documenting which of 14 social events (columns) 18 women in a Mississippi town (rows) attended.

Recall the *one-mode projection*. A bimodal matrix has two projections (i.e., two possible "modes"): the row-level projection and the column-level projection. Since graphs and matrices are two ways to represent the same network, projecting a bipartite graph into two unipartite graphs is equivalent to projecting an *incidence* matrix into two *adjacency* matrices.

A LITTLE MATH GOES A LONG WAY

[35] For an accessible introduction to this branch of mathematics, see Strang (2020).

Unlike the mathematics that many encounter in statistics courses, this chapter approaches quantification first from the perspective of *linear algebra*.[35] Most of what gets called "Artificial Intelligence" and "machine learning" are built with basic linear algebra operations like the dot product, matrix multiplication, and singular value decomposition. This is a simplification, of course, but not an inaccurate one. Whenever a technique in this book uses a mathematical tool covered in this chapter, we'll refer readers back in a margin note.

Part III

Foundations

5

Acquiring Text

One book after another, one invention after another, one work of art after another
all add up to an endless, formless mass... —G. Simmel

MOUNTAINS and deltas, narrow creeks and vast canyons, sprawling
neighborhoods and cramped cities can all be mapped. And, the same
place can foment a diversity of maps—political, topographic, cadastral.
But, mapping a place begins, of course, with the choice of a place.

Just as any place can be mapped, we can use *any piece of text*: interviews,
fieldnotes, archival documents, webpages, books, magazines, speeches,
journal articles, social media posts, meeting minutes, a collection of
notes passed in class—*any text will do*. But, mapping a text begins, of
course, with the acquisition of text. This chapter considers locating texts,
collecting them, and making them useable in R . We'll end the chapter
by considering the ethical implications of collecting these data.

Regardless of how the document is produced, it must be in a *machine-
readable* form (which is increasingly less of a hurdle). Our strategy for
making it machine-readable depends on the text. Here, we review five
methods: (1) public datasets, (2) optical recognition of images, (3) automated transcription of audio files, (4) application programming interfaces (APIs), and (5) Web scraping.

PUBLIC TEXT DATASETS

The easiest way to acquire text is to use one of the numerous publicly available text datasets. The most accessible are provided with R
packages. For example, both the text2map.corpora package hosted on
GitLab and the quanteda.corpora package hosted on GitHub contain
several.[1]

```
install_github("quanteda/quanteda.corpora")
install_gitlab("culturalcartography/text2map.corpora")
```

After installing once, we can use the data() function to load a
dataset from a specified package. Let's load the US State of the Union
Address (SOTU) corpus from quanteda.corpora .

THIS SECTION NEEDS:

- remotes
- tidyverse
- tidytext

[1] CRAN—the official
repository for R packages—
caps package sizes. Packages
hosted on GitHub or GitLab
can be much larger and thus
include larger datasets.

Mapping Texts: Computational Text Analysis for the Social Sciences. Dustin S. Stoltz
and Marshall A. Taylor, Oxford University Press. © Oxford University Press 2024.
DOI: 10.1093/oso/9780197756874.003.0005

```
data("data_corpus_sotu", package = "quanteda.corpora")
```

tidy() turns the corpus into a more intuitive data structure. We'll then use mutate() to find the length of each speech.

```
df_sotu <- tidy(data_corpus_sotu)
# have a quick look:
head(df_sotu)
```

Using str_count , create a new column with word count for each speech. Next, pass the dataframe to ggplot() .[2] str_count counts matches to a pattern \w+. This pattern is a "regular expression" or "regex".[3] The word counts over time are visualized in Figure 5.1.

[2] Recall, for the same plot aesthetics load settheme() from text2map.theme .

[3] See **Wrangling Words.**

```
df_sotu <- df_sotu |> mutate(Length = str_count(text, "\\w+"))

df_sotu |>
ggplot(aes(x = Date, y = Length)) +
    geom_path()
```

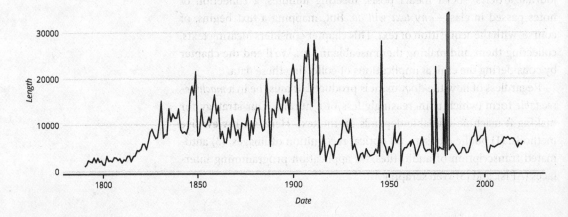

Figure 5.1: Length of US SOTUs, 1790–2020.

We'll often save datasets or objects we create in R as .Rds files. Other data formats require wrangling to import into R and convert into a usable form. Two common formats for corpora are **plain-text format** files (.txt) or as cells in **comma-separated values** (.csv). Below are examples of importing data saved in these formats. Like everything in R , there are many ways to import files, and the output depends on the functions used (but usually a dataframe or list).

```
# if our corpus is a column in a csv
my_corpus <- read.csv(file = "my_corpus.csv")
# from library(tidyverse)
my_corpus <- read_csv(file = "my_corpus.csv")
```

```
# if our corpus is a single .txt file
my_corpus <- read.table(file = "my_corpus.txt")
# from library(readtext)
my_corpus <- readtext(file = "my_corpus.txt")

# if our corpus is a folder of .txt files
txt.files <- list.files(pattern = "\\.txt$", full.names = TRUE)

my_corpus <- lapply(txt.files, read.table)
# from library(readtext)
my_corpus <- lapply(txt.files, readtext)
```

OPTICAL CHARACTER RECOGNITION

If our documents are not (yet) digital, such as might be the case with archival documents, we'll be scanning or photographing them. These images can be saved in many formats, like pdf or png . We might also acquire online documents in pdf or png form. With these formats, the goal is to wrangle our words into txt files or as cells in csv files, or to save them as Rds files. To do this, we'll use optical character recognition (OCR) software.

THIS SECTION NEEDS:
- tesseract

are my refuge. I have wandered here many days; the caves of ice, which I only do not fear, are a dwelling to me, and the only one which man does not grudge. These bleak skies I hail, for they are kinder to me than your fellow-beings. If the multitude of mankind knew of my existence, they would do as you do, and arm themselves for my destruction. Shall I not then hate them who abhor me? I will keep no terms with my enemies. I am miserable, and they shall share my wretchedness. Yet it is in your power to recompense me, and deliver them from an evil which it only remains for you to make so great, that not only you and your family, but thousands of others, shall be swallowed up in the whirlwinds of its rage. Let your compassion be moved, and do not disdain me. Listen to my tale: when you have heard that, abandon or commiserate me, as you shall judge that I deserve. But hear me. The guilty are allowed, by human laws, bloody as they are, to speak in their own defence before they are condemned. Listen to me, Frankenstein. You accuse me of murder; and yet you would, with a satisfied conscience, destroy your own creature. Oh, praise the eternal justice of man! Yet I ask you not to spare me: listen to me; and then, if you can, and if you will, destroy the work of your hands."

"Why do you call to my remembrance," I rejoined, "circumstances, of which I shudder to reflect, that I have been the miserable origin and

Figure 5.2: Page from Mary Shelley's *Frankenstein*.

Let's use a single image (Figure 5.2): a page from Mary Shelley's *Frankenstein* (1888:138). We'll use tesseract , which uses the open-source Tesseract engine pretrained to recognize over 100 languages. If this is our first time using it, we need to first install the engine on our operating system outside of R and also in R.[4] Once installed and loaded into the R session, we direct ocr() to the location of the image.

[4] tesseract-ocr.github.io/
tessdoc

```
my_text <- ocr("images/img_shelley.png")
```

```
## __OCR of a page from Shelley's *Frankenstein*__:
## are my refuge. Ihave wandered here many days;
## the caves of ice, which I only do not fear, are a
## dwelling to me, and the only one which man does
## not grudge. These bleak skies I hail, for they are
## kinder to me than your fellow-beings. If the
## multitude of mankind knew of my existence, they
## would do as you do, and arm themselves for my
## destruction. Shall I not then hate them who abhor
## me? I will keep no terms with my enemies. I
## am miserable, and they shall share my wretched-
## ness, Yet itis in your power to recompense me,
## and deliver them from an evil which it only remains
## for you to make so great, that not only you and
## your family, but thousands of others, shall be
## swallowed up in the whirlwinds of its rage. Let
## your compassion be moved, and do not disdain me.
## Listen to my tale: when you have heard that,
## abandon or commiserate me, as you shall judge
## that I deserve. But hear me. The guilty are
## allowed, by human laws, bloody as they are, to
## speak in their own defence before they are con-
## demned. Listen to me, Frankenstein. You accuse
## me of murder ; and yet you would, with a satisfied
## conscience, destroy your own creature. Oh, praise
## the eternal justice of man! Yet I ask you not to
## spare then: listen to me; and then, if you can, and
## if you will, destroy the work of your hands."
## "Why do you call to my remembrance," I rejoined,
## "circumstances, of which I shudder to reflect,
## that I have been the miserable origin and
```

tesseract converted the image of printed text into characters which R can understand. What about a picture of handwritten documents? The principles are the same; however, there is much more variation with handwriting. This requires fine-tuning tesseract on a handwriting sample. This also entails building a **labeled** dataset, where researchers manually associate handwriting samples with correct words (Rakshit et al. 2010).[5] Similarly, if researchers use tesseract with a language not pretrained, they can train the engine using hand-labeled samples (Clausner et al. 2020).

[5] See **Core Deductive**.

AUTOMATED AUDIO TRANSCRIPTION

THIS SECTION NEEDS:

• googleLanguageR

We may also have audio data—for example, interviews or news broadcasts. While we could hand-transcribe these, automated transcription is accurate and fast. We can even import the audio file and transcribe it directly in R , but this can get complicated.

As a brief demonstration, let's use Google's Speech-to-Text API (see the next section for more details on APIs), using gl_speech() , on a famous excerpt from President John F Kennedy's (JFK) Rice University Speech (Kennedy 1962)—hereafter referred to as the JFK Speech. The wave file is in a special folder in text2map.corpora .

```
folder <- system.file("extdata", package = "text2map.corpora")
audio_file <- paste0(folder, "/jfk.wav")
```

As we'll discuss, Google places various restrictions on its APIs. Longer audio files must be uploaded to Google Console Storage, and after a certain amount of use (~60 minutes/month), we need to pay.[6] Before we use gl_speech() , we need permission to connect to Google's Speech-to-Text API.

[6] cloud.google.com/speech-to-text/pricing

```
# load authentication in the environment
gl_auth("my_authentication_file.json")

# call the Speech-to-Text API
# the API requires a mono, non-extensible .wav file
jfk <- gl_speech(audio_file,
  sampleRateHertz = 44100L,
  language = "en-US"
)

jfk_text <- jfk$transcript$transcript
```

The function uses pauses to break the text into "lines." Below let's concatenate the transcript and see how it looks:

```
cat("__Kennedy's Rice University Speech__:\n","\n", jfk_text,"\n")
```

```
## __Kennedy's Rice University Speech__:
##
## we choose to go to the moon
## we choose to go to the moon
## we choose to go to the moon in this decade and
## do the other things not because they are easy but
## because they are hard because they measure the best
## of our energies and skills because that challenge is
## one that we're willing to accept one we are unwilling
## to postpone and one we intend to win
```

Not bad! We could get similar outputs from services like Otter.ai, Temi, or Trint. These services produce accurate transcriptions and provide a user interface to fix any errors by hand. When exporting from these services, the best file format for these transcripts is a `.txt` plain-text file (and not, e.g., a Word document or HTML file).

APPLICATION PROGRAMMING INTERFACES (APIs)

Web scraping identifies and collects content from pages hosted on the World Wide Web (Ignatow and Mihalcea 2017:82). Three common targets of scraping are news media, social media, and crowdsourced websites. Using *news media* in scholarly research goes back to the foundations of quantitative text analysis over a century ago (Speed 1893) and communications research in the 1940s (Lazarsfeld 1940). News was studied both for its potential influence on readers (Fenton 1910), and as a way to track the "social weather" of a region (Tenney [1912] 2008). *Social media* is the star of recent "Big Data" efforts in the social sciences. Projects using social media data range from studies on misinformation diffusion (Bail et al. 2020) to friendship formation (Wimmer and Lewis 2010) and the impact of legislation on online sentiment (Flores 2017). These data are cheaper than surveys and are relatively immediate—and *potentially* less moderated[7]—thoughts and feelings. Lastly, there are *crowdsourced* websites, where volunteers—often driven by passion—contribute information. This includes Wikipedia, Song Genius, and Fandom. Such sites are valued both for their ability to produce semi-structured datasets—for example, categorizing every Marvel superhero's powers (Muscio 2023)— and loci of well-documented collective production and governance (Adams and Brückner 2015; Konieczny 2009).

To scrape such sites, we'll interact with an *application programming interface* (API). When typing the URL for a website, our browser sends a request to a server. The server then "responds" to the browser— hopefully, by returning the requested webpage. The portion of the server responsible for processing and making requests is the API (Gazarov 2016). An API is an intermediary that allows applications to "talk" to each other and defines the standardized "terms of engagement." This interface is commonly written in `XML` or `JSON` .[8] Think of an API as a "user interface." Instead of human users, though, it makes navigation easier for client software (i.e., software on our "data-requesting" computer) (Berlind 2015; McLevey 2021:63–87).

Those more familiar with `R` can interact directly with these markup languages. Luckily, "wrappers" exist to make this easy, for example, `academictwitteR` , `rtimes` , `geniusr` , `WikiediR` and many more.[9] Many websites have separate APIs specifically for automated interaction.

[7] As the pop-culture Cuisinart Alfred Yankovic states, "As it turns out, there is a thing called the Internet, and stuff does go out there whether the suits like it or not" (Press 2007).

[8] These are markup languages—like `HTML` —for storing and representing datasets.

[9] Wrappers are at the mercy of the organization offering the API (Freelon 2018). In fact, volatility is why we removed a Twitter example. If the following code breaks, be patient! Explore the recent documentation for the wrapper.

To use these, however, we need (1) *developer* accounts with the host and (2) *tokens* or *keys* that allow access. We will walk through an API for *Yahoo! Finance* which does not require a key, and the API for *The Guardian* which does.

Using Yahoo! Finance *API and* The Guardian *API*

```
library(tidyverse)
library(tidyquant)
library(guardianapi)
library(rtweet)
```

THIS SECTION NEEDS:

- tidyverse
- tidyquant
- quardianapi
- rtweet

In late 2020, GameStop ($GME) was a company in decline, with big investors betting against the company (i.e., short selling). On January 1, 2021, it was trading around US$19 per share; it then jumped to over US$300 per share. Using tidyquant we'll pull financial information from *Yahoo! Finance* and visualize it (Figure 5.3).

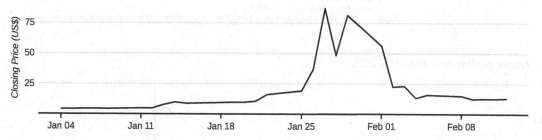

Figure 5.3: GameStop Stock Price.

```
gme <- tq_get("GME", get = "stock.prices",
              from = "2021-01-01", to = "2021-02-15")

gme |>
  ggplot(aes(x = date, y = close)) +
  geom_line() +
  labs(subtitle = "Jan 1st to Feb 15th, 2021",
       y = "Closing Price (US$)", x = NULL)
```

Users of a Reddit forum coordinated the purchase of GameStop stock, performing what is known as a "short squeeze," which dramatically increased the stock's price. Say we want all *The Guardian* articles in the months preceding and succeeding the short squeeze. First, we need to get a developer key from *The Guardian* Open Platform API.[10] Select "Register for a developer key." Next, we'll need to submit a short form, verify our

[10] open-platform. theguardian.com

email address, and shortly thereafter, we'll receive another email with our API key: random alphanumeric strings.[11]

Run the following function, paste the key into the console after the prompt, then press `enter` .

```
gu_api_key()
```

```
Please enter your API key and press enter:
```

Now, we'll use `gu_content()` to grab all the content with the word "gamestop" between May 1, 2020, and May 1, 2021.

```
df_gme <- gu_content(query = "gamestop",
                     from_date = "2020-05-01",
                     to_date = "2021-05-01")

df_gme_daily <- ts_data(df_gme, "1 day")
```

```
df_gme |>
mutate(Date = as.Date(first_publication_date)) |>
ggplot(aes(Date)) +
  geom_bar() +
  labs(x = NULL, y = NULL,
    subtitle = "Articles per Day, May 2020 - May 2021")
```

Figure 5.4: Articles References GameStop.

We see in Figure 5.4 that almost no articles on GameStop before the short squeeze in late January, and then it shoots to the moon, peaking at fifteen articles in one day!

Using developer APIs with `R` wrappers, like `guardianapi` and `tidyquant` , is an indispensable method for collecting Web-based data. Searching for developer APIs is an excellent place to start when we need data from a website or platform.

Automated Web Scraping

Many websites with APIs have no `R` wrappers and no public API. Sometimes those with APIs and wrappers are too restrictive, too expensive, or are suddenly deprecated (Freelon 2018). In these scenarios, we'll turn to custom scrapers.[12]

`rvest` is a popular package for building scrapers. First, we'll need a URL of a webpage to scrape. Let's scrape some data from arXiv—a free repository of scientific "e-prints" (digital preprints and postprints) of scientific articles.[13] Say we want all papers uploaded to arXiv with the statistics classification. Let's go to arxiv.org in our Web browser, click on "Advanced Search," check the "Statistics (stats)" subject box, ensure that the "All Dates" is checked, and then click "Search."

As of June 2022, this search returns 82,286 results. Figure 5.5 (left panel) is a screenshot of the results page. This page gives useful information for each paper: the arXiv ID, subject tags, title, authors, abstract, abstract date, and announcement date. We want to collate this information into a dataframe. Here's where `rvest` comes in.

First, we need the base URL for this search. Copy the URL from the Web browser's search bar. Assign it to an object in `R` (ensure there are no spaces). It is long, so we'll break ours into pieces and paste them together. The link should end with "-announced_date_first".

```
url <- paste0(
  "https://arxiv.org/search/advanced?advanced=&",
  "terms-0-operator=AND&terms-0-term=&",
  "terms-0-field=title&",
  "classification-physics_archives=all&",
  "classification-statistics=y&",
  "classification-include_cross_list=include&",
  "date-filter_by=all_dates&date-year=&",
  "date-from_date=&date-to_date=&",
  "date-date_type=submitted_date&",
  "abstracts=show&size=50&",
  "order=-announced_date_first"
)
```

We need to know how many pages we could scrape but arXiv doesn't tell us. So, we need to guess.[14] Each page displays 50 papers, for example, page two displays papers 51–100. With about 85,000 papers (see Figure 5.5, left panel), that would be around 1700 pages—that's too many for our demonstration! Let's grab the first 5,000 papers.

This code produces a string of numbers, from 0 to 4,950 (with the first page starting at 0 and the 100th page starting at 4,950 for a total of 5,000 returned papers and 100 total pages).

THIS SECTION NEEDS:

- `tidyverse`
- `lubridate`
- `rvest`

[12] There are downsides to scrapers. We need to tailor them for each site and minor updates could "break" the scraper. However, the skillset is highly transferable across sites.

[13] arxiv.org *does* offer an API, a point we'll return to in the next section.

[14] It is also possible to click the "Next" button using `follow_link` in `rvest`.

```
paper_number <- seq(0, 4950, by = 50)
```

With rvest , reading the raw HTML of a webpage into R is straight-forward. The console would get overwhelmed by the raw HTML printed, so rvest truncates it.

```
read_html(url)
```

```
{html_document}
<html lang="en">
[1] <head>\n<meta http-equiv=...
[2] <body>\n \n \n <header>...
```

We are technically building an automated "bot." So, we might get blocked. Let's "create a session" so it looks a bit more like we are using a Web browser:

```
uast <- paste0(
    "Mozilla/5.0 (Windows NT 6.1) AppleWebKit/537.36 ",
    "(KHTML, like Gecko) Chrome/41.0.2228.0 Safari/537.36"
)

sess <- session("https://arxiv.org/", httr::user_agent(uast))
```

Now use this session to "jump to" the pages we need. HTML content is organized in a nested hierarchy. Each section in that hierarchy has a unique identifier called a node or element. As we don't need most of the HTML , rvest provides a handy function, html_elements() , to grab specific content using these identifiers. Let's see how many unique elements are on the page:

```
url |>
  session_jump_to(x = sess) |>
  html_elements("*") |> # asterisk matches any string
  unique() |>
  length()
```

```
[1] 1766
```

That's a lot! Narrow this down by getting the unique IDs or "tags" for elements containing the content we're interested in scraping. To find these, we could inspect the raw HTML of the page,[15] or we can use browser extensions like SelectorGadget (for Google Chrome) or SelectorsHub (on Firefox).

Assuming we want the full abstracts, we first need to click the "More" button for one of the abstracts on the page before using SelectorGadget—that way we can get the identifier for the full abstract and not the "short" abstract. As we see in the screenshot below (Figure 5.5, right panel), ".abstract-full" is the tag for the full abstracts.[16]

[15] Use CTRL+SHIFT+I on Google Chrome and Mozilla Firefox on a PC, and OPTION+COMMAND+U for Mac users.

[16] The tag for the reduced abstract is ".abstract-short".

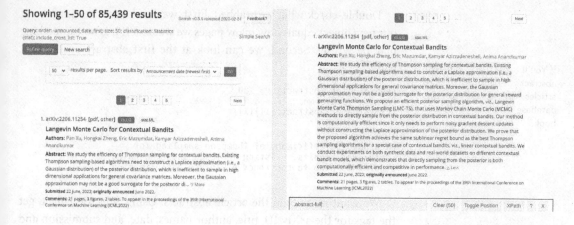

Figure 5.5: arXiv Search Results and SelectorGadget.

Feed that tag into `html_elements()` and then use `html_text()` to remove the extra `HTML` tags, keeping only the text. Below is a "chained" version using the pipe `|>` .

```
web_page <- url |>
    session_jump_to(x = sess)

paper_abstract <- web_page |>
    html_elements(".abstract-full") |>
    html_text()
```

That gave us text for all the abstracts on a *single page*—but we want all the reviews on a hundred pages! We'll use `lapply()` . First, create a list of URLs for each page using our sequence of paper numbers, then we create a session for each (similar to 100 tabs open in our Web browser).

```
# Create a list of all the URLs
url_list <- paste0(url, "&start=", paper_number)

# Create a list of webpages
page_list <- lapply(
    url_list,
    function(page) {
        Sys.sleep(5)
        return(session_jump_to(page, x = sess))
    }
)
```

We'll loop through those sessions, collecting the abstracts from each.

```
paper_abstract <- lapply(
    page_list,
    function(page) {
        page |>
            html_elements(".abstract-full") |>
            html_text()
    }
)
```

Double-check what we grabbed. First, we check that the `length` of our new object equals how many pages we wanted. If it is not, something may be wrong. Second, we can look at the first abstract on the first page.[17]

[17] You'll see a different abstract because more articles are added to this database since we wrote this book.

```
length(paper_abstract) == 100
# remove extra white space with trimws
trimws(paper_abstract[[1]][1])
```

```
We study the efficiency of Thompson sampling for
contextual bandits. Existing Thompson sampling-based
algorithms need to construct a Laplace approximation...
```

We want more than the article abstracts. Using SelectorGadget, get the tags for the arXiv ID, title, author names, date, and submission and announcement dates. The procedure is nearly identical; we only change the element being isolated.

```
paper_id <- lapply(
    page_list,
    function(page) {
        page |>
            html_elements(".is-inline-block > a") |>
            html_text()
    }
)
```

```
paper_title <- lapply(
    page_list,
    function(page) {
        page |>
            html_elements(".is-5") |>
            html_text()
    }
)
```

```
paper_authors <- lapply(
    page_list,
    function(page) {
        page |>
            html_elements(".authors") |>
            html_text()
    }
)
```

```
paper_subj <- lapply(
    page_list,
    function(page) {
        page |>
            html_elements(".tags.is-inline-block") |>
            html_text()
    }
)
```

```
paper_date <- lapply(
    page_list,
    function(page) {
        page |>
            html_elements(".mathjax+ .is-size-7") |>
            html_text()
    }
)
```

The above gives six lists. Each list should be the same length and in the same order (i.e., the first `paper_abstract` matches the first `paper_id`, etc.). This makes it easy to put into a dataframe. We also want to include the date we scraped the data using `Sys.Date()` (if interested in the time, we can use `Sys.time()`).

```
df_arxiv <- data.frame(
    id = unlist(paper_id),
    authors = unlist(paper_authors),
    title = unlist(paper_title),
    abstract = unlist(paper_abstract),
    tags = unlist(paper_subj),
    paper_date = unlist(paper_date),
    scrape_date = Sys.Date()
)

# look at our work
head(df_arxiv)
```

We have 5,000 rows—one per paper.[18] This is what we expected. Some variables are not as tidy as we need. For example, each statistic paper is "tagged" with keywords about its content. For example, "cs.AI" is Computer Science-Artificial Intelligence.[19] Let's say we are interested in paper submissions over time for different tags.

Right now, several tags are grouped into a single column, separated by whitespace. To count each tag separately, we need to expand those into their own columns.

We first trim the excess whitespace in the variable and then count how many tags are in each row by counting every one or more non-space characters.

```
df_arxiv <- df_arxiv |>
    mutate(tags = str_squish(tags))

maximum <- max(str_count(df_arxiv$tags, "\\S+"))
```

Now that we know how many columns we need, we can separate each tag per paper into a column using `separate()`:[20]

```
df_arxiv <- df_arxiv |>
    separate(tags, paste0("tag_", seq_len(maximum)),
        extra = "merge", sep = "\\s+", fill = "right")
```

[18] We won't print it here for space, but you may be curious about \n in the output? See **Wrangling**.

[19] See the rest here: arxiv.org/category_taxonomy

[20] This code is inspired by stackoverflow.com/a/56356703.

Since we are interested in submissions *over time* per tag, we need to wrangle the `paper_date` column so only the submission date remains. We'll use `gsub()` and `parse_date_time()` to do so below.

```
df_arxiv$submit_date <- gsub("^.*Submitted\\s*|\\s*;.*$",
                              "", df_arxiv$paper_date)

df_arxiv$date_new <- parse_date_time(df_arxiv$submit_date,
                        orders = c("dmy"))
```

We will "melt" or "pivot" our `df_arxiv` dataframe so each row is a date by tag. This makes plotting easier and involves turning a wide dataframe into a long dataframe.

```
melt_arxiv <- df_arxiv |>
    select(date_new, tag_1:tag_6) |>
    pivot_longer(!date_new)
```

There are over a hundred unique tags; since we focused on statistics papers, we'll filter out non-statistics tags. Then, rename them with more meaningful labels. Finally, we use `group_by()` to count each time a tag occurs on each date.

```
melt_arxiv <- melt_arxiv |>
    filter(grepl("stat.", value, fixed = TRUE)) |>
    mutate(stats = recode(value,
        "stat.AP" = "Applications",
        "stat.CO" = "Computation",
        "stat.ME" = "Methodology",
        "stat.ML" = "Machine Learning",
        "stat.OT" = "Other Statistics")) |>
    group_by(stats, date_new) |>
    summarize(count = n())
```

Using `ggplot()`, we'll divide our data into separate plots using `facet_wrap()` and fit a line that summarizes the data.[21] We see in Figure 5.6 that "Machine Learning" dominates the statistics papers on arXiv with 30 submissions on average per day.[22]

```
melt_arxiv |>
    ggplot(aes(x = date_new, y = count)) +
    geom_smooth() +
    labs(x = "Date", y = "Average",
        subtitle = "Papers per Stats Category") +
    facet_wrap(~stats, nrow = 1)
```

By building this custom scraper, we have an "infrastructure" that can expand to include, for example, all 85,000+ statistics papers or continually update our corpus as new papers are submitted. Building scrapers takes time and effort, but the more difficult-to-reach communities and troublesome datasets may lead to new insights precisely because fewer scholars have the opportunity to analyze them (cf. Martin 2017:218).

[21] Using smoothed conditional means.

[22] Of course, we cannot conclude that this pattern characterizes statistics in general. There is quite possibly an affinity between submitting papers to arXiv and studying machine learning—see **Corpus Building**.

Papers per Stats Category

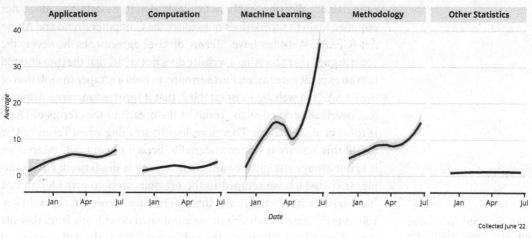

Collected June '22

Figure 5.6: arXiv Papers with a Statistics Classification.

LEGAL AND ETHICAL SIDE OF SCRAPING

Let's reflect on the ethics of data acquisition before we move on.

By social science standards, much text data is easy to get. We (usually) access it publicly via the Internet and thus require no interviewees, survey respondents, experiment participants, consent forms, expensive sampling designs, or even much time. Ease, however, does not mean fair game—even when the data exist, ostensibly, in the public sphere.

We'll address three ethical dilemmas we might encounter related to (1) terms of service, (2) intellectual property, and (3) individual and organizational privacy. This discussion is informed heavily by the ethical/legal framework for Web scraping proposed by Krotov, Johnson, and Silva (2020:549).[23]

Terms of Service

In the case of developer APIs, we typically enter a formal agreement constraining how we use the service. The services R interacts with often block activity that violates this agreement: for example, requesting too much material too quickly. When building a custom scraper things get more complicated. Generally, publicly available text—that is, text that does not require a login to access—is fair game for scraping, at least legally.

[23] Our discussion is not an exhaustive review of this framework. The authors also cover issues with Web-scraped data for decision-making (p. 549), how scraping can negatively impact the value of websites' services (p. 549), and how parties engaged in scraping might be liable for any material damage to a website or server (p. 546). We do not discuss these points here.

In 2019, the Ninth Circuit Court of Appeals upheld a lower court ruling that collecting publicly available data (i.e., data that does not require a login to access) does not violate the Computer Fraud and Abuse Act (CFAA). Websites have "Terms of Use" agreements; however, the court argued that accessing a website does not signal that the user entered into an explicit agreement. Furthermore, to hold a scraper in violation of the CFAA, "the website must establish that it incurred material damages (i.e., overload servers) as the result of the breach of the 'Terms of Use'" (Krotov et al. 2020:563). Therefore, legally, scraping when Terms of Use forbid this activity is not considered a "breach of contract." Moreover, it is not always straightforward what activity is disallowed. For example, arXiv (which we scraped in the previous section) provides an API "to maximize its openness and interoperability"; however, the websites' robots.txt[24] states: "Indiscriminate automated downloads from this site are not permitted." While we strongly suggest using the API, we leave it as a task for the reader whether our scraping example is "indiscriminate" downloading.

Whether one should follow the Terms of Use (or robots.txt rules) depends on the researchers' judgment and whether the research justifies going against the website owner's will. Researchers doing noncommercial studies for the public good and exploring issues of social significance should be allowed access to public resources on the Web, provided that access does not create material damages (Vaccaro et al. 2015).

Intellectual Property

Text data may be copyrighted. As such, using such data might be subject to any copyright law within the researchers' locale. Much text data of interest are not usually "owned" by the hosting website—for example, social media sites such as Twitter or Facebook.[25] But what if we scrap texts that *are* copyrighted, like books or song lyrics? Even in these cases, scraping the texts themselves might not constitute copyright infringement; rather, *publishing* the texts in "some tangible medium" (US Copyright Office 2022b)—for example, an academic article—might lead to issues (Krotov et al. 2020:546). This is especially problematic if the author receives any financial or material benefits from the republished work.

In the US, researchers often rely on "Fair Use" legal doctrine to argue that their uses of copyrighted materials are not subject to claims of copyright law violations. "Fair Use" is laid out in the Copyright Act of

[24] This is a de facto standard for telling "robots" like search engine crawlers how they should interact with the site. The initial impetus was to prevent overloading a website.

[25] Even this point is contentious. Both Twitter's and Facebook's Terms of Service claim the end-user owns their content. But, in *People of the State of New York v. Malcolm Harris*, the court concluded that Twitter had to surrender user data for Malcolm Harris—an Occupy Wall Street protester (Jeong and Hoven 2012).

1976, Section 107, and is meant to carve out the space to use certain amounts of copyrighted material without the need for licensed approval. Research is one area for which "Fair Use" is meant to apply, including "criticism, comment, news reporting, teaching, [and] scholarship" (US Copyright Office 2022a). But this provision is not meant to be a Get Out of Jail Free card; people using a work under the auspices of any of these types of uses can still have a copyright infringement claim bought against them. Per the 1976 Copyright Act, users (and, if the situation arises, courts) are to use the following factors when determining whether a use is "protected" by the "Fair Use" doctrine (US Copyright Office 2022a):[26]

1. **Purpose and character of the new use.** Is the new use going to generate a profit or some sort of revenue? How different is the new use from the copyrighted work? Is it purely "derivative," or is it "transformative"?

2. **Nature of the original work.** How "creative" is the original work? Is it, say, a novel, or a newspaper article? Since copyright law is meant to protect creative activity from exploitation, the former sets a higher bar for meeting "fair use" than the latter.

3. **Amount.** How much of the original copyrighted work is being used in the new use? Regardless of the quantitative amount, is the "essence" of the copyrighted work being copied?

4. **Effect on the market for the original work.** Is the new work going to directly or indirectly harm the original work's ability to generate any profit or revenue?

So, if a researcher is analyzing a collection of murder mystery novels and prints multiple pages of a book's content and includes a portion that gives away a major plot spoiler, then the original copyright holder for the book might have grounds to bring an infringement claim. As in many legal contexts, "it depends."

Importantly, copyright law protects the material medium within which an idea is fixed—not the idea itself (Krotov et al. 2020). So, in theory, an analysis of a collection of texts is fair-game if no excerpts are provided—for example, the data is transformed into a document-term matrix (as discussed later). But, social science audiences often want to see *some* text to support the researchers' claims. This is a reasonable request, but it also means that researchers should be mindful of how they are pulling from the copyrighted material.[27]

[26] Copyright laws vary by country. For example, "Fair Use" is not understood as broadly in European countries as in the US. Furthermore, this is not as harmonized across European Union member countries as are other areas of copyright law (Bently and Aplin 2019). To avoid copyright infringement, researchers are encouraged to explore copyright law in their own locale.

[27] If researchers decide to use, say, a company logo in their work, they may also be subject to trademark law.

Individual and Organizational Privacy

One great thing about automated scraping is that we can collect, in a short period, far more webpages than we could read. Often we may not know whether it includes sensitive information. This is true even with ostensibly anonymized text, as was the case when the research arm of AOL released search data for 650,000 users, but without identifying the users. Nevertheless, *The New York Times* showed how easy it was to identify one user from their search queries alone (Barbaro and Zeller 2006). Recall, also, text acquired from the Internet is "readymade."[28] Therefore, "it is best to assume all data are potentially identifiable and potentially sensitive" (Salganik 2019:314).

Furthermore, automated collection from multiple sources, especially if we're merging them, could lead to "de-anonymization." For example, say we are scraping Reddit, and we collect posts from a Redditor using a pseudonym. We might extract enough details from their Reddit posts—however vague—to learn their general occupation, general location, marital status, and perhaps some interests they prefer to keep secret. Perhaps one post from several years ago links to their Twitter account where, at one point, they posted a link to a job opening at their place of employment. With this information, we could de-anonymize their activity on Reddit. This hypothetical scenario shows how expectations of privacy are not always clear. As Nissenbaum (2009:2) argues, "What people care most about is not simply restricting the flow of information but ensuring that it flows appropriately."

When scraping, the website owners are not the only parties whose expectations of privacy may be compromised. For academics, some considerations are addressed by the institutional review board (IRB); but as Salganik (2019) argues, the IRB is a floor and not a ceiling. Privacy considerations neither begin and end with IRB approval, when scraping is completed, nor even when we publish our research. It is instead a *continuous* process. When we scrape text and structure it into an organized dataset, we become the stewards of the data, and also the stewards of those who produced, and are represented by, the text. We should continually revisit privacy issues and evaluate how our data—and transformation or publication of that data—may breach expectations.

[28] The producers did not create the text thinking of how it would contribute to our research projects—it is "unprompted" (Ignatow and Mihalcea 2016:13).

6
From Text to Numbers

A map is not the territory it represents, but, if correct, it has a similar structure to the territory, which accounts for its usefulness. —A. Korzybski

HUMANS started etching stone, ceramics, and metals over ten millenia ago. Ever since, writing proliferates, accumulating into a vast stock of human intentions, and resulting in a fundamental complication: *How do we find a specific writing among all the other writings?* This question blurs three technical considerations: (1) How do we represent texts efficiently? (2) How do we summarize the contents of a text? (3) How do we retrieve a text based on its contents? Many text analysis tools emerged to answer these very questions about **information retrieval**.

The computer-assisted representation of textual data has remained a relatively niche suite of social scientific methods until the last two decades (e.g., Franzosi 2004; Weber 1984; Roberts 1989; Carley 1993; Mohr 1994), but scholars often used computer programs to *retrieve* relevant literature.

For a long time, researchers melded representation and retrieval. Dewey, for example, a librarian at Amherst College in the 1870s, represented books' content by an index. This index also designated the location of the books on the shelves. Later, several automated "retrieval" systems were developed that relied on microfilm—such as Vannevar Bush's hypothetical "Memex" (Bush 1945). Although processing power increases yearly, increasing computerization exacerbates retrieval problems as we accumulate text. Cumbersome top-down classification schemes like Dewey's soon gave way to the *automated* representation of documents' contents.

In addition to information retrieval research, we rely on tools developed in **corpus linguistics**. This pragmatic—and staunchly anti-Chomskyian—approach emerged in the 1950s, aided by computerization. This field explored the frequency distribution of words, syllables, phrases, or grammatical features, as well as the "collocation" or the extent linguistic features co-occur in particular contexts (Firth 1957; McEnery and Hardie 2011).

Mapping Texts: Computational Text Analysis for the Social Sciences. Dustin S. Stoltz and Marshall A. Taylor, Oxford University Press. © Oxford University Press 2024.
DOI: 10.1093/oso/9780197756874.003.0006

We'll draw extensively on these two fields—information retrieval and corpus linguistics. The first step in our journey involves *turning words into a structured dataset with useful numeric quantities*.

We'll rely on two generic data structures as the primary cartographic tools: the (1) **document-term matrix** (DTM)[1] and the (2) **term-context matrix** (TCM). The former is a tabular structure where the rows are our documents and the columns are the contexts in which a word appears. The latter is also a tabular structure, but the rows are terms and the columns may be the documents in which the terms appear (i.e., a rotated DTM) or the other terms a target term occurs alongside (a term-co-occurrence matrix) within a given window. We'll continue to use these text matrices throughout this book.

[1] A DTM is a common type of *document-feature matrix* (DFM), where the terms are our features.

Units of Analysis

Documents are any collection of words, ranging from short social media posts or paragraphs to book chapters or full books. **Features** are sub-document units. Typically, this means characters, words, terms, or phrases, which we often call "tokens" and sometimes, n-grams. We may transform, summarize, or collapse tokens into more complex features, such as lemmas, syntax, topics, concepts, etc. By **authors**, we mean individuals, groups, or organizations responsible for the production of a document. Finally, a **corpus** is any collection of documents. For example, if we study the extent each play in Shakespeare's First Folio engages with the concept of death,[2] each play is a *document*, the First Folio is a *corpus*, and we assume Shakespeare is the *author*. If we are instead interested in how a character's gender in *The Comedy of Errors* influences what they say (e.g., Hota et al. 2006), each speaking part is a *document* and the single play becomes our *corpus*.

THIS SECTION NEEDS:

• tidyverse
• tokenizers

[2] As we do in **Extended Deductive**.

Generally, researchers want to make inferences about the documents or the authors by extracting patterns in their use of words. Say we collect tweets posted during the Fukushima Disaster. We may want to know which tweets are "conversational" and which are "informational" (Truong et al. 2014) or which authors experienced the disaster. We also want to make inferences about the meanings of the words themselves. These may, in turn, facilitate inferences about documents and authors. For example, "clean up" means something slightly different in tweets about the Fukushima disaster than those about restaurants. The first step, though, is to **tokenize**.

Tokenizing

We often break a document into smaller units to represent the content of that document. The smallest units are called **tokens** and the process is called tokenizing.[3] These sub-document units are typically what's in mind when we think of a "word"; however, we can tokenize a document into more complex units, such as n-grams—for instance, bigrams (every two sequential words) or trigrams (every three sequential words).[4] We could also tokenize by character n-grams—for example, every two sequential characters.

The simplest way to proceed is to assume that a "word" is our token. But trying to come up with a clear "rule" to tell an algorithm where each word begins and ends can be tricky. Again for simplicity, let's say that all words are cleanly separated on either side by a single *whitespace*. This assumption fits best with Latin-based scripts, like English.[5] Even then, it is easy to find exceptions to our rule. Is "New York City" or "merry-go-round" or "to and fro" one or three tokens? Is "I've" and "don't" one or two?

Let's work through a demonstration. We prepared television scripts for *Star Trek: The Next Generation* using `rtrek`. The season 5 scripts are available in `text2map.corpora`. Below we'll tokenize the seventeenth line of the season premiere (titled "Redemption, Part 2"). We'll tokenize using the literal space between characters. In any tokenizing process, this is typically the fastest option.

```
data("corpus_tng_season5", package = "text2map.corpora")
df_trek <- corpus_tng_season5 # rename so it's tidier
dim(df_trek) # how many rows and columns
```

This will tokenize by splitting into words on the *single space* (fixed = TRUE tells `R` this is literal characters).

```
strsplit(df_trek$line[17], " ", fixed = TRUE)
```

```
[[1]]
 [1] "Captain's"      "log,"
 [3] "stardate"       "45020.4."
 [5] "We"             "have"
 [7] "arrived"        "at"
 [9] "Starbase"       "Two-thirty-four,"
[11] "where"          "I"
[13] "have"           "taken"
[15] "the"            "opportunity"
[17] "to"             "make"
[19] "a"              "proposal"
[21] "to"             "Fleet"
[23] "Admiral"        "Shanthi."
```

[3] As discussed previously, that language in general, and text in particular, can and should be segmented is an assumption (Aronoff 1992), but a necessary one for computational text analysis.

[4] A single word is often called a unigram.

[5] Tokenizing for Arabic scripts is particularly complex because characters may change depending upon their positions in a word. A word can be realized as four distinct tokens and requires morphological analysis before tokenizing (Attia 2007; Farghaly and Shaalan 2009).

```
[1] 10834      5
```

The backslash \ is used to either make a literal character into a special one, or make a special character literal (often called "escaping"). As `R` *also* uses the backslash to "escape," this can get complicated. We must use two backslashes so `R` passes just one backslash to the regex engine—this also means we need four backslashes to match one literal backslash!

That worked pretty well. However, words are separated by characters other than a single space. For example, there are double-spaces, tabs (\t), returns (\r), and newlines (\n). To make sure we split on *any* whitespace between characters, we can use the **regular expression** (regex)[6] \s and add a + to match one or more. Because we are now using a regex pattern rather than the literal character, we remove `fixed = TRUE` .

```
# tokenize by splitting into words by regex whitespace
strsplit(df_trek$line[17], "\\s+")
```

Instead of whitespace, we can use regex patterns to tokenize on any non-word character (\W).[7] We can also *negate* a match by putting characters in brackets beginning with the caret ([^]). For example, a-z matches all lowercase English letters, A-Z matches the uppercase, and 0-9 matches numerals, the following matches any string of characters that is *not* within these sets: [^a-zA-Z0-9]+ .

```
# tokenize by splitting on non-word characters
strsplit(df_trek$line[17], "\\W")
# tokenize by splitting on non-alphanumerics
strsplit(df_trek$line[17], "[^a-zA-Z0-9]+")
```

We can continue to customize our pattern—say, for example, if treating dashed words like "two-thirty-four" as a single token—or we can use a pre-developed solution for tokenizing with tokenizers . This package follows a list of over a dozen rules to define word boundaries.[8] Notice that tokenize_strings() removed capitalization and punctuation as part of the tokenizing process.

```
tokenize_words(df_trek$line[17])
```

```
[[1]]
  [1] "captain's"    "log"
  [3] "stardate"     "45020.4"
  [5] "we"           "have"
  [7] "arrived"      "at"
  [9] "starbase"     "two"
 [11] "thirty"       "four"
 [13] "where"        "i"
 [15] "have"         "taken"
 [17] "the"          "opportunity"
 [19] "to"           "make"
 [21] "a"            "proposal"
 [23] "to"           "fleet"
 [25] "admiral"      "shanthi"
```

We may also want to treat otherwise separate words as a single piece. For example, perhaps we want to divide our documents into every two-word sequence, or bigram, in a text. We could include phrases on up to any n-sized n-**gram**.[9]

[6] **Regular expressions** are special sequences matching a *pattern* of characters, rather than literal (i.e., fixed) characters. The Unix operating system popularized regex and is now used across programming languages. There are different regex "flavors" and these patterns are often hard to read without a lot of practice.

[7] Capitals in regex often mean "not," meaning the \w pattern matches word characters and \W matches non-word characters.

[8] These rules were developed by the International Components for Unicode (site.icu-project.org).

[9] A related, but less common, way of tokenizing is the **skip** *n*-gram, where we allow a certain number of words to be between two or more words.

```
# tokenize into bigrams
tokenize_ngrams(df_trek$line[3], n = 2L)

# tokenize into unigrams and bigrams
tokenize_ngrams(df_trek$line[3], n = 2L, n_min = 1L)

[[1]]
[1] "aft shields" "shields are"
[3] "are gone"

[[1]]
[1] "aft"        "aft shields"
[3] "shields"    "shields are"
[5] "are"        "are gone"
[7] "gone"
```

Finally, we can also go the opposite direction by tokenizing with *characters* rather than full words or phrases, by breaking words into phonemes/morphemes or even single letters. Character-based n-grams are sometimes used with logographic scripts like those used with Chinese or Korean (Lee and Ahn 1996; Nie and Ren 1999).

```
# tokenize by each character
tokenize_characters(df_trek$line[3])

# tokenize by clusters of 3 characters
tokenize_character_shingles(df_trek$line[3],
    n = 3,
    n_min = 3
)

  [[1]]
   [1] "a" "f" "t" "s" "h" "i" "e" "l" "d" "s"
  [11] "a" "r" "e" "g" "o" "n" "e"

  [[1]]
   [1] "aft" "fts" "tsh" "shi" "hie" "iel"
   [7] "eld" "lds" "dsa" "sar" "are" "reg"
  [13] "ego" "gon" "one"
```

Any computational text analysis begins with tokenizing regardless of which rules are used to tokenize. The output of tokenizing is a list. Typically, this is a list of lists, where the first-order list is each "document," and the second-order list is each token. This list of lists is often a necessary, but *intermediary*, data structure.

Chunking

As discussed, our "documents" can be any length of text. Often, we take documents in the form we collect them: each tweet, article, or book is a document. The contexts of the text's production dictate where such documents begin and end. Sometimes, though, we'll extract a chunk of text from a large work. Perhaps we have an entire book, but we need chapters or even paragraphs as our documents or want to standardize the size of our texts to facilitate comparison.

Just as we used regex patterns to tokenize texts, we can use regex patterns to split our larger documents into smaller chunks. For example, we could use punctuation to divide text into sentences, or we could use those special characters for different kinds of whitespace—tabs (\t), returns (\r), and newlines (\n). We may also chunk documents by a certain token count.

```
# chunk by punctuation
strsplit(df_trek$line[17], "[!.,]")

# chunk by newlines
strsplit(df_trek$line[17], "[\n]")

# chunk by every N tokens
chunk_text(df_trek$line[17], chunk_size = 10)
```

Finally, sometimes we want a "moving window"—that is, a **shingle**—where each chunk of text is partially overlapping with the previous. This is equivalent to tokenizing by n-grams discussed above. The difference is how we intend to use the output. When tokenizing, we are looking for ways to represent the *content* of our documents, whereas with chunking we are, in effect, creating our documents.

```
# chunk text into a moving window of 3 tokens
tokenize_ngrams(df_trek$line[17], n = 3L, n_min = 3L)
```

```
[[1]]
 [1] "captain's log stardate"  "log stardate 45020.4"
 [3] "stardate 45020.4 we"     "45020.4 we have"
 [5] "we have arrived"         "have arrived at"
 [7] "arrived at starbase"     "at starbase two"
 [9] "starbase two thirty"     "two thirty four"
[11] "thirty four where"       "four where i"
[13] "where i have"            "i have taken"
[15] "have taken the"          "taken the opportunity"
[17] "the opportunity to"      "opportunity to make"
[19] "to make a"               "make a proposal"
[21] "a proposal to"           "proposal to fleet"
[23] "to fleet admiral"        "fleet admiral shanthi"
```

Alternatively, instead of breaking larger pieces of text into chapters, paragraphs, sentences, n-gram windows, etc., we may want to *aggregate* up from these smaller chunks. For example, perhaps we have sentences, but we want paragraphs or even a full book. For example, rtrek gives lines, but we want an episode's full script instead. First, we group all lines by the episode number, then "summarize" this grouping. Second, we collapse the lines using paste0() and the whitespace character indicating a newline (\n). We should now have one row for each episode.

```
df_trek <- df_trek |>
  group_by(number) |>
  summarize(text = paste0(line, collapse = "\n"),
            doc_id = first(title),
            airdate = first(airdate))

dim(df_trek) # how many rows and columns now?
```

    [1] 26 4

DOCUMENT FEATURES

What a *feature* refers to depends on how we tokenize the document and how we categorize or summarize those tokens. As we mentioned earlier, the most common document-feature matrix is a document-term matrix (DTM). This represents documents by a vector of term counts and the positions in the vector are types of words.

Once tokenized, each document is a list of tokens. We then count how often each *unique* token[10] occurs in each document. With a single document, we represent its content as a vector of numbers. The position in the vector references a unique type. The number is how often that type occurs in that document.

There are two things to note when transforming a token list into a token-count list. First, we won't retain the *order of the words* in a document. Second, we collapse tokens that are *precisely* the same characters. For example, "The" and "the" would be counted as distinct tokens, as would "Raúl" and "Raul." Let's use an excerpt from Mary Shelley's *Frankenstein*.

```
doc <- "nothing is so painful to the human mind
        as a great and sudden change the sun might
        shine or the clouds might lower but nothing
        could appear to me as it had done the day
        before a fiend had snatched from me every
        hope of future happiness no creature had ever
        been so miserable as I was so frightful an
        event is single in the history of man"
```

We'll tokenize using `strsplit()` and the regular "space." The output of this function is a **token list**. Next, we'll use `table` to count how many times each unique token occurs in the document, creating a **token-count list**.

```
# tokenize by splitting into words by space
docs_tokens <- strsplit(doc, " ", fixed = TRUE)
```

```
# get word frequencies
docs_freqs <- table(docs_tokens)
```

THIS SECTION NEEDS:

- tidyverse
- tidytext
- tokenizers
- reshape2
- quanteda
- text2map

[10] This is called a **type** in contrast to a **token**.

```
# look at the first few
docs_freqs[1:5]
```

```
  a    an  and appear    as
  2     1    1      1     3
```

Imagine that we have multiple documents, each represented as a vector of token counts. We'll "stack" each vector on top of each other to make a DTM. Let's use a sample of the first 5,000 sentences from the Europarl Corpus[11] in French and the same first 5,000 sentences in English, which is in `text2map.corpora`.

[11] The Europarl Corpus is a collection of European Parliament Proceedings from 1996 to 2011 (Koehn 2005).

```
data("corpus_europarl_subset", package = "text2map.corpora")

df_europarl <- corpus_europarl_subset |>
                rowid_to_column(var = "doc_id")
```

```
df_europarl <- df_europarl |>
  mutate(
    text = tolower(text), # lowercase
    text = gsub("[[:punct:]]", " ", text), # remove punctuation
    text = gsub("[[:digit:]]+", " ", text), # remove numbers
    text = gsub("[[:space:]]+", " ", text) # remove excess space
  )
```

Above, we loaded our text dataset and transformed the text by low-ercasing, removing punctuation, removing numbers, and removing any double spaces.[12] Now each sentence looks like one long string of lower-cased non-numeric character sets with single whitespaces between them. Next, we'll *tokenize* each document by turning each into a list of tokens, this time using `tokenizer`.

[12] See **Wrangling Words**.

```
docs_tokens <- tokenize_words(df_europarl$text)
```

Once we have our documents represented as token lists, the next step is to count the times each unique token (a.k.a. type) occurs in each document. Computationally, this involves determining which elements are exact matches. `table()` takes care of this matching and counting. Below we use it with `lapply()` which "applies" a function to each element of the list (i.e., each document).

```
docs_freq <- lapply(docs_tokens, table)
```

The final output is a list of lists. Recall, the first-order list is each document, and the second-order list is the token-counts for each document. Using `melt()`, we turn this into a "triplet" dataframe consisting of three columns: term, count, and document id. Both `tidytext` and `udpipe`, discussed below, use this as a primary data structure.

```
df_triplet <- melt(docs_freq)
colnames(df_triplet) <- c("term", "freq", "doc_id")

length(unique(df_triplet$doc_id)) # should equal N documents

tail(df_triplet) # have a quick look at the bottom
```

```
          term freq doc_id
228725     not    1  10000
228726  should    1  10000
228727   there    1  10000
228728    this    1  10000
228729    want    1  10000
228730      we    1  10000
```

Instead of a triplet dataframe, we can put each token-count list into a *matrix*, where rows are all the documents and the columns are the unique words in the corpus. Below is a base R method for this.

First, we need all the unique tokens. Next, we'll create an empty matrix with our document IDs as row names and the corpus vocabulary as column names. Finally, we'll use a for loop to fill the matrix whenever the tokens in our token-count list match a column name.

The first step is to get a list of all the unique tokens.[13] Optionally, we can sort alphabetically.

[13] A unique token is called a **type** and the collection of types is the vocabulary, **vocab**, or V.

```
vocab_unique <- sort(unique(unlist(docs_tokens)))
```

The second step is to initialize an empty matrix with the correct dimensions, column names, and row names.

```
dtm <- matrix(
    data = 0,
    ncol = length(vocab_unique),
    nrow = length(docs_freq),
    dimnames = list(df_europarl$doc_id, vocab_unique)
)
```

Finally, we'll fill the empty cells whenever a word in a document's token list matches a word in the column. Using a loop, we'll replace that cell with how many times we find a match.

```
for (i in seq_along(docs_freq)) {
    freqs <- docs_freq[[i]]
    words <- names(freqs)
    dtm[i, words] <- as.integer(freqs)
}
```

Check the dimensions of our matrix. The first number is the rows (i.e., documents) and the second is the columns (i.e., vocabulary).

```
dim(dtm)
```

Now let's look at a selection from our DTM (drawing from the first five English sentences).

```
selection <- c("resumption", "session", "european", "you")
dtm[5001:5005, selection]
```

```
     resumption session european you
5001          1       1        0   0
5002          0       1        1   2
5003          0       0        0   1
5004          0       1        0   1
5005          0       0        1   0
```

The DTM is a structured and efficient method for representing the content in our documents and also easily comparing each document by standardized features (here, each unique term in the corpus).

Sparsity

There are several functions dedicated to building DTMs. These functions produce slightly different objects than our base R matrix, though. This is because DTMs are matrices with lots of zeros or words in the vocabulary that do not appear in a document. Let's calculate the "sparsity" of a matrix (i.e., the percent of cells that are zeros) and how many words show up only once in our corpus.

```
# calculate the overall sparsity of a matrix:
total_cells <- ncol(dtm) * nrow(dtm)
zero_cells <- sum(dtm == 0)
zero_cells / total_cells
```

```
[1] 0.9985835
```

```
# how many terms in our vocabulary occur just once?
total_vocab <- ncol(dtm)
total_hapax <- sum(colSums(dtm) == 1)
total_hapax / total_vocab
```

```
[1] 0.3944386
```

Over 99% of the cells are empty! Over a third of the unique words only occur once in any document, that is, only one row in the column would have a non-zero value.[14] This is not unique to European Parliament sentences but is a standard feature of any corpus.

A sparse matrix is also a *class* of R objects designed for matrices with high sparsity. Instead of allocating memory for the number zero, sparse classes assume zero is wherever memory is *not* allocated. How much more memory-efficient sparse classes are depends on the sparsity of the matrix and the type of representation (integer, real number, or logical). For example, our DTM as a base R dense matrix is around 1200 Mbs (1.2 Gb), but as a Matrix sparse matrix, it shrinks to 4.4 Mbs.[15]

[14] In corpus linguistics, any word that only appears once in a corpus is called *hapax legomenon*. If a type occurs just twice, it is *dis legomenon*.

[15] As an R object, these special matrices are class dgCMatrix , dgTMatrix , lgCMatrix , if built with Matrix , or simple_triplet_matrix if built with slam .

```
# convert our regular dense dtm into a sparse matrix:
dtm_sparse <- as(dtm, "sparseMatrix")
# convert our sparse dtm back into a dense matrix:
dtm_dense <- as.matrix(dtm_sparse)

# compare the sizes of the two objects:
print(object.size(dtm_dense), units = "auto")
print(object.size(dtm_sparse), units = "auto")
```

```
1.2 Gb
4.4 Mb
```

Most dedicated text analysis packages rely on matrices represented as these special sparse classes (and when working on large corpora, we often *need* them). To grasp the benefit, imagine working with hundreds of thousands or millions of documents.[16] The downside to the sparse matrix format, however, is that we lose the intuitiveness of a base R matrix, and we sometimes need to use special functions to perform regular matrix operations.

[16] As dense matrices, this would require 5 to 10 times more RAM than most personal computers have today.

Dedicated DTM Functions

Previously, we used a base R method to create a DTM. Usually, we'll use a dedicated text analysis package instead (see Table 6.1). Keep in mind: many functions create objects tagged as "special" classes. Underneath them, though, are the basic data structures we're already familiar with: lists, dataframes, and matrices.

Table 6.1: Packages with DTM Functions

quanteda	tm	text2vec	tidytext
text2map	udpipe	qdap	koRpus
corpustools	textmineR	gofastr	textTinyR

Below we outline a few packages.[17] There is much overlap in the functionality of these packages, and when we inspect the outputs of each, we see they produce similar R objects.

quanteda is a popular text analysis package. To create a DTM with quanteda , we use dfm() . But first, we need to turn each document into a **token list** and we'll use quanteda 's tokens() to do so.[18]

[17] These packages tend to use similar nomenclature. To prevent clashes, we can be explicit by using the double colon :: between the package name and the function.

[18] By default, the output is the class dfm , but it is a Matrix class sparse matrix.

```
tokns <- quanteda::tokens(df_europarl$text)
dtm_quanteda <- quanteda::dfm(tokns)

# what kind of object is it?
class(dtm_quanteda)
is(dtm_quanteda, "Matrix")
```

Alternatively, `text2map` 's `dtm_builder()` also produces a DTM of class `dgCMatrix` .

```
dtm_text2map <- df_europarl |> dtm_builder(text, doc_id)

# what kind of object is it?
class(dtm_text2map)
is(dtm_text2map, "Matrix")
```

[19] This creates a tibble , a kind of "enhanced" dataframe.

Another popular method for creating DTMs involves creating a token-count dataframe using `tidytext` .[19] After using `unnest()` , the dataframe is in a *narrow* format with two columns: one for the document name, one for each token in each document. At this point, all the tokens and the order they occur in each document are retained. Next, we'll use `count()` to sum each time a unique token occurs in each document. The result is a triplet dataframe, with three columns: document, token-type, and token-count.[20]

[20] This dataframe can also be "cast" into the several kinds of DTMs output by the packages above.

```
# this creates a triplet dataframe
df_tidy <- df_europarl |>
    unnest_tokens(word, text) |>
    count(doc_id, word, sort = TRUE)

dtm_quanteda <- df_tidy |> cast_dfm(doc_id, word, n)
dtm_sparse <- df_tidy |> cast_sparse(doc_id, word, n)
```

Lastly, sometimes there is the need to convert these sparse matrices to a standard base R dense matrix. This is usually accomplished with `as.matrix()` . This likely increases the memory required. The following are all equiavalent.[21]

[21] These new matrices have the same dimensions, but the packages order the columns (vocab) differently, some alphabetically and some by overall frequency.

```
dtm_base2 <- as.matrix(dtm_quanteda)
dtm_base3 <- as.matrix(dtm_sparse)
dtm_base4 <- as.matrix(dtm_text2map)
```

TOKEN DISTRIBUTIONS

[22] See **Math Basics**.

Using the DTM, it is simple to get basic statistics about the terms in our corpus. Here, we'll learn one of the most fundamental insights from corpus linguistics: *words are not distributed normally.*[22] This has widespread implications for text analysis. For instance, most documents will share most of their words, even if they're about very different topics. Let's explore these distributions.

First, say we need to know the document lengths. We'd sum the rows of our matrix. Second, we might be interested in each term's frequency (which terms occur a lot or a little in the corpus). We'd sum the columns of the matrix.[23]

```
dtm <- df_europarl |> dtm_builder(text, doc_id)

doc_length <- rowSums(dtm)
term_freqs <- colSums(dtm)
```

To get the total words in the corpus, we can sum either the document lengths or the term frequencies.

```
total_words <- sum(doc_length)
total_words <- sum(term_freqs)
```

We should report these corpus statistics in published research. They can also help diagnose issues in our corpus. To facilitate this, dtm_stats() gets these quantities for any DTM. Here is a portion of the output for our Europarl DTM (in the margin). We can see each line has an average of 26 words, and a few lines have no words! Empty documents won't be an issue for this chapter, but they are typically unintended byproducts of data collection and preparation.

```
dtm_stats(dtm)
```

We can also explore frequently occurring words in our corpus with the following script.

```
# sort terms in descending order
term_freqs <- sort(colSums(dtm), decreasing = TRUE)
# total words in the corpus
total_words <- sum(term_freqs)
```

What is the proportion of terms occurring at least 3 times (output in margin)?

```
sum(term_freqs >= 3) / length(term_freqs)
```

And, what are the 10 most frequent terms (output in margin)?

```
term_freqs |>
    data.frame() |>
    slice_max(term_freqs, n = 10)
```

These words do not seem insightful: "the," "of," and "and," etc., and their French counterparts "la"/"le," "de," and "et"—we'll discuss this below (see also **Wrangling Words**). For now, the point is to get used to working with the DTM and answering basic frequency questions.

[23] If we built our DTM using quanteda or text2map, the output is a sparse matrix using the Matrix format. So, we'll need tools from these packages to perform the above operations on our matrices. Loading Matrix replaces the necessary base R functions for this session. Both quanteda and text2map load Matrix. If not loaded, we'll see the error: "'x' must be an array of at least two dimensions."

Term Distribution

	Measure	Value
1	Min Types	0
2	Min Tokens	0
3	Max Types	95
4	Max Tokens	141

Central Tendency

	Measure	Value
1	Mean Types	22.87
2	Mean Tokens	26.74
3	Median Types	21
4	Median Tokens	23

```
[1] 0.446151
```

	term_freqs
the	9767
de	7205
la	4884
of	4676
to	4473
and	3488
le	3298
et	3238
l	3135
in	3125

Zipf's Law and Herdan-Heaps' Law

Looking at the distributions of term frequencies, we'll see an important property of language: words are not evenly (or evenly normally) distributed. Rather, they follow a long tail distribution, where a few words occur a lot, and most words occur few times or even just once. This is **Zipf's Law**, where the frequency of a word is inversely proportional to its rank among word frequencies.[24] In large English corpora—say several billion tokens—the word "the" is most frequent and occurs twice as often as the second most common word "of." Even with our medium-sized corpus of a couple of million tokens (with the Europarl sentences), we see roughly the same distribution—across two different languages! We can even visualize Zipf's Law by generating a frequency-rank plot with our DTM and see how closely the slope fits −1. Let's do this for the English and French sentences separately. We should expect the plots to look virtually identical across the two languages.[25]

```
#the first 5000 lines are French, the last 5000 are English
term_freqs_fr <- sort(colSums(dtm[1:5000,]),
                      decreasing = TRUE)
freq_rank_fr <- data.frame(
    freq = term_freqs_fr,
    rank = seq_along(term_freqs_fr),
    lang = "French"
)

term_freqs_en <- sort(colSums(dtm[5001:nrow(dtm),]),
                      decreasing = TRUE)
freq_rank_en <- data.frame(
    freq = term_freqs_en,
    rank = seq_along(term_freqs_en),
    lang = "English"
)

freq_rank <- rbind(freq_rank_fr, freq_rank_en)


freq_rank |>
    ggplot(aes(x = rank, y = freq+1)) +
    geom_point(alpha = .2) +
    scale_x_log10() +
    scale_y_log10() +
    geom_smooth(method = "lm", linetype = 2, se = FALSE) +
    labs(x = "Rank", y = "Count",
         subtitle = "Terms' Rank by Frequency") +
  facet_wrap(~lang)
```

Figure 6.1 (top row) shows these plots. The slopes are negative and seem close to a 45-degree angle, suggesting a slope near −1.[26]

Another feature of word distributions to remember is the fact that total unique words in a document (or corpus) increase as the length of that document (or corpus) increases. This is **Herdan-Heaps' Law**.

[24] There are several theories (e.g., Mandelbrot 1953; Miller 1957) as to why we see this. For example, Zipf (1949) considered the reason the "principle of least effort."

[25] We add a 1 to the frequencies before logging them to avoid taking the log of zero, which is undefined.

[26] If we ran OLS models (see **Math Basics**) on these data, we would find that the slopes are, indeed, nearly −1 as expected.

To show this, first, we'll *binarize* our DTM, which means creating a matrix with only ones and zeros (or `TRUE` and `FALSE`), where a one indicates that the word occurs at least once in a document.

```
# 4 ways to create a binary matrix
bin_dtm <- dfm_weight(dtm_quanteda, scheme = "boolean")
bin_dtm <- as(dtm, "lMatrix")
bin_dtm <- ifelse(dtm > 0, 1, 0)
bin_dtm <- dtm[] > 0
```

When we sum the rows of our binarized DTM, we'll get the number of types in each document. We then divide that by the total number of tokens in each document (the document length)—this is the *type-token ratio*.

```
doc_types <- rowSums(bin_dtm) # get number of types
doc_lengths <- rowSums(dtm) # get number of tokens in each document


type_token <- data.frame(
    types = doc_types,
    tokens = doc_lengths,
    lang = c(rep("French", 5000),
            rep("English", 5000))
)


type_token |>
    ggplot(aes(x = tokens, y = types)) +
    geom_point(alpha = .2) +
    labs(x = "Tokens", y = "Types",
            subtitle = "Total Tokens by Total Type") +
  facet_wrap(~lang)
```

The plots are in the bottom two rows of Figure 6.1. There are, once again, striking similarities across the languages—as we would expect.

These two intertwined laws—Zipf's and Herdan-Heaps'—hold for virtually any *n*-grams. They are a feature of corpora in most—*possibly all*—languages (Yu et al. 2018). This is the case even in "artificial" languages like Esperanto and Klingon (Smaha and Fellbaum 2015)! Regardless of the language we're working with, then, *most documents will share most of their words.*

Weighting and Norming

Up to this point, we have primarily been working with DTMs where the cells are the raw frequency counts of unique terms, typically called *term frequencies* or *tf* (1975:4). Information retrieval researchers argued that "the frequency of word occurrence in an article furnishes a useful measure of word significance" (Luhn 1958:160).

THIS SECTION NEEDS:

- tidyverse
- tidytext
- quanteda
- text2map
- ggpubr

Figure 6.1: Visualizing Zipf's and Herdan-Heaps' Laws.

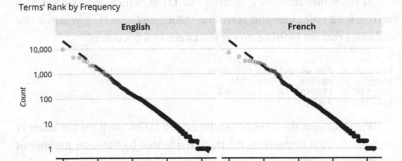

Terms' Rank by Frequency

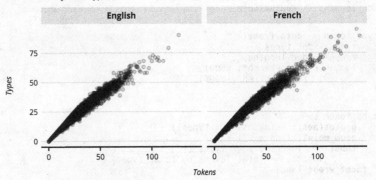

Total Tokens by Total Type

However, there is an established relationship between raw counts of types, on one hand, and the total number of tokens in a collection, on the other. The more total words, the more likely we encounter a new type of word—Herdan-Heaps' Law! Therefore, it is common practice to *re-weight* the DTM to shift the importance we place on different features of our DTM.

Relative Term Frequency

The most common DTM weighting scheme is to *norm* the DTM by dividing these raw counts by the document lengths (i.e., the row sums of our matrix).[27] This is extremely common and is often called *relative frequency*, or *rf*. To show how, we'll weight our DTM by each document's length. Let's use Europarl again, but this time only use the English sentences.

[27] As term frequencies are necessarily vectors of positive integers, this is, in effect, the L_1-norm (see **Math Basics**).

```
data("corpus_europarl_subset", package = "text2map.corpora")

df_europarl <- corpus_europarl_subset |>
  filter(language == "English") |>
  rowid_to_column(var = "doc_id") |>
  mutate(
    text = tolower(text),
    text = gsub("[[:punct:]]", " ", text),
    text = gsub("[[:digit:]]+", " ", text),
    text = gsub("[[:space:]]+", " ", text)
  )

dtm <- df_europarl |> dtm_builder(text, doc_id)

doc_lengths <- rowSums(dtm)
dtm_rf <- dtm / doc_lengths
# inspect our DTM
dim(dtm_rf)
```

Let's grab the first five English sentences and inspect the first five words.

```
dtm_rf_sub <- dtm_rf[seq_len(5), ]
# keep columns with non-zero values
dtm_rf_sub <- dtm_rf_sub[, colSums(dtm_rf_sub) != 0]
# inspect the first five words
round(dtm_rf_sub[, seq_len(5)], 3)
```

```
  resumption   of   the  session    i
1       0.25 0.250 0.250    0.250    .
2        .   0.028 0.083    0.028 0.056
3        .   0.065 0.065      .      .
4        .   0.050 0.100    0.050    .
5        .   0.100 0.125      .   0.025
```

The relative frequency DTM is the same dimensions, but the cells are no longer integers. Now they are *proportions*—real numbers that cannot be greater than one or less than zero.[28]

If a cell has a 1, this would mean that *all the words* in this document are the same word. If a cell had a 0.5, this would mean half of the words in this document are this word. And, if summing all the rows, they each will equal 1 (output in margin).

```
rowSums(dtm_rf_sub)
```

Below we walk through how to get a relative frequency DTM using a dedicated text analysis package—namely, quanteda .

```
tokens <- tokens(df_europarl$text)
dtm_quanteda <- dfm(tokens)
quanteda_rf_dtm <- dfm_weight(dtm_quanteda, "prop")
```

[28] There are two drawbacks to storing our documents in a relative frequency DTM. First, we cannot recover the raw counts unless we retained the document lengths. Second, storing "real values" consumes more memory. In R , integers (and logicals) consume 4 bytes, while real values consume 8 bytes.

```
1 2 3 4 5
1 1 1 1 1
```

Term Frequency/Inverse Document Frequency

Words occurring infrequently within a corpus may still be distinctive for a particular document if it *only* occurs in that document (or in very few documents). Similarly, Sparck Jones (1972) argued that a word's frequency in a corpus (or **document frequency**) was inversely proportional to its significance. This was because less frequent words referred to more specific ideas. Her work introduced the idea of **inverse document frequency**, or *idf*. Roughly, this is the number of documents in a corpus, divided by the total documents in which a term appears. This allows us to identify words that are surprising to find in a document and thus potentially insightful.

We can use this to weight DTM cells by multiplying the term frequency within a document with the inverse of the term's document frequency in the corpus (i.e., *tf-idf*). This increases the weight of a word according to the times it occurs in a document *relative to* its frequency in the corpus. Below is a method to weight our DTM by *tf-idf* in base R .[29]

[29] We'll use the base 10 logarithm in our calculation of the *idf* scores. This is also the default in quanteda 's dfm_tfidf(). Different papers and packages use different bases, though. For example, Salton (Salton 1975:29) uses base 2 in his classic essay on indexing, and so does tm .

```
# we already have term frequencies
# assign it to a new object for clarity
tf <- dtm
# this calculates inverse-document frequencies
idf <- log10(nrow(dtm) / colSums(dtm != 0))
dtmtfidf <- tf * idf
```

Several packages have functions to weight DTMs by *tf-idf*—and can be faster. For example, this is how we'd re-weight a matrix using quanteda .

```
dtm_quanteda <- tokens(df_europarl$text) |> dfm()
dtmtfidf <- dfm_tfidf(dtm_quanteda)
```

Let's compare terms with high counts and relative frequencies with those terms that have high *tf-idf* scores. For this, let's use the US State of the Union addresses (SOTUs). See Figure 6.2.

We'll subset the DTMs by Richard Nixon's and John F. Kennedy's addresses. We need to divide our DTMs by which documents correspond to which president.

```
idx_nixon <- text_sotu$President == "Nixon"
idx_kennedy <- text_sotu$President == "Kennedy"

df_nixon <- data.frame(
        tf = colSums(dtm[idx_nixon, ]),
        rf = colSums(dtm_rf[idx_nixon, ]),
        tfidf = colSums(dtmtfidf[idx_nixon, ]),
        President = "Nixon",
        Term = colnames(dtm)
)
```

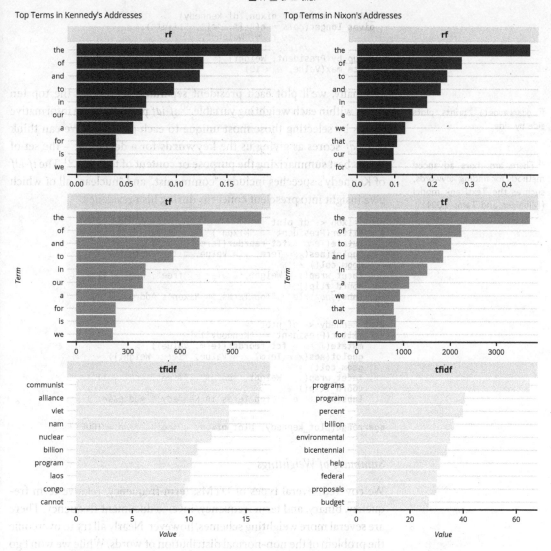

Figure 6.2: Comparing Term Weightings.

```
df_kennedy <- data.frame(
      tf = colSums(dtm[idx_kennedy, ]),
      rf = colSums(dtm_rf[idx_kennedy, ]),
      tfidf = colSums(dtmtfidf[idx_kennedy, ]),
      President = "Kennedy",
      Term = colnames(dtm)
)
```

```
df_plot <- rbind(df_nixon, df_kennedy) |>
  pivot_longer(cols = c("tf", "rf", "tfidf"),
               names_to = "Weight",
               values_to = "Value") |>
  group_by(President, Weight) |>
  slice_max(Value, n = 10)
```

[30] ggarrange() prints plots side by side.

[31] There are more advanced methods for finding keywords, such as the TextRank model (Mihalcea and Tarau 2004).

Finally, we'll plot each president separately and select the top ten terms within each weighting variable.[30] *tf-idf* provides more informative words by selecting those most unique to each president. We can think of *tf-idf* scores as giving us the **keywords** for a document – the set of words best summarizing the purpose or content of that text.[31] The *tf-idf* of Kennedy's speeches includes "communist," and "nuclear," all of which give insight into prescient concerns during his presidency.

```
plot_nixon <- df_plot |>
  filter(President == "Nixon") |>
  mutate(Term = fct_reorder(Term, Value)) |>
  ggplot(aes(x = Term, y = Value, fill = Weight)) +
  geom_col() +
  facet_wrap(. ~ Weight, scales = "free", ncol = 1) +
  coord_flip() +
  labs(subtitle = "Top Terms in Nixon's Addresses")
```

```
plot_kennedy <- df_plot |>
  filter(President == "Kennedy") |>
  mutate(Term = fct_reorder(Term, Value)) |>
  ggplot(aes(x = Term, y = Value, fill = Weight)) +
  geom_col() +
  facet_wrap(. ~ Weight, scales = "free", ncol = 1) +
  coord_flip() +
  labs(subtitle = "Top Terms in Kennedy's Addresses")
```

```
ggarrange(plot_kennedy, plot_nixon, common.legend = TRUE)
```

Summary of Weightings

We covered several types of DTMs: term frequency, relative term frequency, binary, and term frequency/inverse document frequency. There are several more weighting schemes, however. Nearly all try to overcome the problem of the non-normal distribution of words. While we won't go over all of these here, Table 6.2 contains additional weighting schemes that we can explore on our own.

Table 6.2: Selection of DTM Weighting Schemes

Weighting	Description
Term Frequency (TF)	Term's count in a document
Relative TF (RF)	Divide TF by total terms in a document
Binary or Boolean	Zero cells are 0 (FALSE); otherwise, 1 (TRUE)

Document Frequency (DF)	Total documents in which a term occurs
Inverse DF (IDF)	Log of the total documents divided by the DF
Relative DF	Term's corpus count divided by term's DF
TF-IDF	Multiply RF with the IDF
Pointwise Mutual Information (PMI)	log2 of TF divided by expected count
Positive PMI (PPMI)	Same as PMI, but negative values set to 0

TERM FEATURES

In addition to mapping the meaningful patterns in documents, we often want to summarize ways tokens are used. Broadly, we do this by looking at a token's **context**. At the simplest, we can consider the "dispersion" or locations of tokens within a text (Carpena et al. 2009; Ortuño et al. 2002). Not only are some words much more frequent in a corpus, but some words are also much more evenly distributed within documents than others. To see this, let's create a "lexical dispersion" plot.

The first step is associating a given token with a given location in a document or corpus. Let's use *Star Trek* scripts and see how words are dispersed over each episode.

THIS SECTION NEEDS:

- tidyverse
- text2map
- quanteda
- text2vec
- tidytext
- tokenizers
- Matrix
- ggraph
- tidygraph

```
data("corpus_tng_season5", package = "text2map.corpora")
```

Let's pick keywords that occur with roughly the same frequency but have different *dispersions*. Here, "vulcan" occurs 72 times; "every" occurs 72; "romulan" occurs 78; and "klingon" occurs 84 times in the season.

```
key_words <- c("vulcan", "romulan", "klingon", "every")

df_token_position <- corpus_tng_season5 |>
    unnest_tokens(word, line) |>
    mutate(position = 1:n()) |>
    filter(word %in% key_words)

df_token_position |>
    ggplot(aes(x = position, y = 1)) +
    geom_segment(aes(xend = position, yend = 0)) +
    facet_grid(word ~ .) +
    labs(y = NULL, x = "Position") +
    theme(panel.grid.major.y = element_blank(),
        axis.ticks.y = element_blank(),
        axis.text.y = element_blank())
```

In Figure 6.3, we interpret concentrated terms, like "klingon," as significant to the show's plot. We can glean that earlier in the season, "vulcan" was important.

We can efficiently represent the features of a term's context with a **term-context matrix** (TCM). Whereas the DTM represents the content

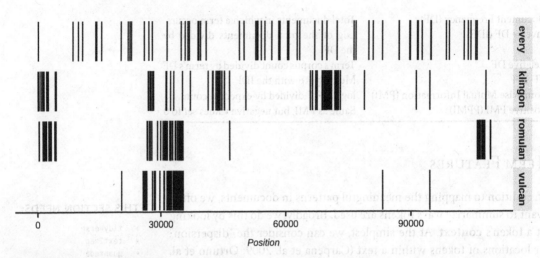

Figure 6.3: Lexical Dispersion Plot.

of documents in a corpus, the **TCM** shows how terms are used in a corpus. Here, the rows of the TCM are target words, and columns are **contexts** to which the target term is associated. In the example above, the context is simply a word's *position* in a string of words. We could also rotate a DTM to get a *term-document matrix*, where the document is the term's context. Finally, in a term co-occurrence matrix, each row is a term, i, and each column is also a term, j, that i appears alongside. These are all TCMs; their "contexts" vary by scale—as if zooming in and out of a map.[32]

Term co-occurrence matrices capture two kinds of word *associations*. First, we get **syntagmatic** similarities: two words are literally used together. Second, we get **paradigmatic** associations: two words can be used in similar places but might never co-occur.

Let's explore this with Taylor Swift's songs from her first ten albums. We'll again do minimal preprocessing (lowercase, remove punctuation).

32 We'll add considerable complexity to TCMs in **Extended Inductive**.

```
data("corpus_taylor_swift", package = "text2map.corpora")

df_swift <- corpus_taylor_swift |>
    mutate(text = tolower(song_text),
        text = gsub("[[:punct:]]", " ",text),
        text = trimws(text))
```

Then, we'll create a DTM where each row is a song.

```
dtm <- dtm_builder(df_swift,text, song_id)
dim(dtm) # 120 songs and a vocab of 3240
```

Next, we'll transpose the DTM, which tips and twists it, so the dimensions are flipped.

```
tdm <- t(dtm) # transpose the dtm to get a tdm
dim(tdm) # A vocab of 3240 and 120 songs
```

In this TCM, the *features* summarizing each token are the *songs* in which they occur and do not occur. With a feature matrix like this, we can compare how associated any two terms are by comparing their vectors (i.e., their respective rows in the TCM). There are many methods to measuring similarity between rows in a matrix—for example, the Jaccard index, Euclidean distance, cosine similarity, and Pearson's correlation. Here, we'll cover the most common in text analysis, cosine similarity.[33]

Cosine similarity treats the rows of our TCM as vectors representing the *uses* of terms and the *locations* of these terms in an abstract metric "space." This space is more than three dimensions, so it is difficult to imagine, but we'll compare the "angle" between these two vectors using cosine. If two vectors are similar—that is, they have similar counts in the same positions—they'll have a smaller angle.[34] Let's create our own cosine similarity function.

```
cos_sim <- function(A, B) {
    sum(A * B) / sqrt(sum(A^2) * sum(B^2))
}
```

```
# get select the rows by word
vec1 <- as.vector(tdm["shake", ])
vec2 <- as.vector(tdm["love", ])
vec3 <- as.vector(tdm["alone", ])

cos_sim(vec1, vec2) # "shake" and "love"
cos_sim(vec2, vec3) # "love" and "alone"
cos_sim(vec3, vec1) # "alone" and "shake"
```

```
[1] 0.0006406371
[1] 0.05576185
[1] 0.001531841
```

With cosine *similarity*, a "1" means the vectors are the same. So, "love" and "alone" are more similar to each other than either is to "shake." Remember, perfect similarity here means two words are present in the same songs and absent from the same songs. This gets at syntagmatic associations between words.

Using matrix multiplication,[35] we can project the DTM to a **term-co-occurrence matrix** (TCM), showing which words "co-occur" with other words in a document (here, a song). First, we transpose the DTM to get a term-document matrix (TDM). Second, we "project" our rectangular matrix into one of two square matrices using matrix multiplication.

[33] See also **Core Inductive** for a bit more detail on Euclidean distances and cosine similarities.

[34] Using cosine to measure similarity between two rows of a text matrix comes from the **vector space model** (Salton et al. 1975).

[35] See **Math Basics**.

```
# we can also create a TCM with the cross product
#column by column (i.e., term by term) matrix
tcm <- crossprod(dtm)

# this creates a document-similarity matrix
# row by row (i.e., document by document) matrix
dsm <- tcrossprod(dtm)
```

We'll either get a matrix of document-by-document similarities (DSM), or a term-by-term co-occurrence matrix (TCM). The output is a square $N \times N$ matrix, where N is either the size of the vocabulary or N is the number of documents in the corpus. In a TCM, the *features* are now the *context terms* with which a *target term* tends to co-occur within a sequence (here, an entire song). Now, cosine similarities will measure paradigmatic associations between words.

```
vec1 <- as.vector(tcm["shake", ])
vec2 <- as.vector(tcm["love", ])
vec3 <- as.vector(tcm["alone", ])

cos_sim(vec1, vec2)
cos_sim(vec2, vec3)
cos_sim(vec3, vec1)
```

```
[1] 0.4689983
[1] 0.862345
[1] 0.5598621
```

The magnitudes have changed considerably, but the rank of similarities has not changed. "Alone" and "love" remain the most similar.

Often the document is too large to provide an informative context for each term, or there is too much variation in document lengths. We can refine the TCM by changing the size of the "context." Rather than an entire document, the context might be paragraphs, sentences, or a moving window (i.e., a skipgram or shingle) of a certain number of words.

We'll create a TCM with a context window of five tokens for Swift's songs using `fcm()` (i.e., feature co-occurrence matrix). Let's also include a corpus of Beyoncé's songs to compare.

```
data("corpus_beyonce", package = "text2map.corpora")

df_beyonce <- corpus_beyonce |>
  mutate(text = tolower(song_text),
         text = gsub("[[:punct:]]", " ",text),
         text = trimws(text))
```

[36] Linguists debate this distinction (Bybee et al. 1994). Another way of thinking about the difference is a spectrum from more specific meaning (semantic) to more generic meanings (syntatic) (Sweetser 1988).

As a loose rule, smaller windows (e.g., one to three words) are more "syntactic," while larger windows (e.g., four- to ten-word windows) are more "semantic."[36] Since we're using songs, let's set the window to four.

```
tkns_ts <- tokens(df_swift$text)
tkns_be <- tokens(df_beyonce$text)

tcm_ts <- fcm(tkns_ts, context = "window", window = 4L, tri = FALSE)
tcm_be <- fcm(tkns_be, context = "window", window = 4L, tri = FALSE)
```

In corpus linguistics, the TCM formalizes Firth's (1957:11) famous quip "you shall know a word by the company it keeps." If the context window is relatively small, the TCM captures a special kind of co-occurrence called **collocation**. This refers to words that are often right next to each other, for example, "fast food," or "european union." One use for collocations is determining which n-grams we may want to retain during tokenization.

How do we measure whether two (or more) terms co-occur an *unusual amount* in a corpus? We find the probability a target term occurs with a context term *controlling for* the probability of those terms appearing on their own. If we take the natural log of this, then we have the **pointwise mutual information** (PMI).[37] Although there are packages for this, let's build a function step-by-step (adapted from `text2vec`'s `coherence()`).

[37] A TCM weighted by PMI is foundational to "word embeddings" (Levy and Goldberg 2014); see **Extended Inductive**.

```
get_ppmi <- function(tcm, tkns) {

    # how big of context windows did we use
    n_windows <- round(sum(lengths(tkns)) / 4L)
    # small constant to avoid a logarithm of zero
    constant <- 1e-10
    # get overall probabilities
    tcm_pmi <- (tcm / n_windows) + constant
    # get the diagonal: how many times a word occurs at all
    tcm_diag <- diag(tcm_pmi)
    # divide the cells by the diagonal
    tcm_pmi <- tcm_pmi / tcm_diag
    # fix the diagonal and log
    tcm_pmi <- tcm_pmi %*% diag(1 / tcm_diag)
    tcm_pmi <- log(tcm_pmi)

    # convert it to a base R matrix
    tcm_pmi <- as.matrix(tcm_pmi)
    colnames(tcm_pmi) <- rownames(tcm_pmi)
    return(tcm_pmi)

}
```

After running our function, we can use it to weight our TCMs.

```
tcm_pmi_ts <- get_ppmi(tcm_ts, tkns_ts)
tcm_pmi_be <- get_ppmi(tcm_be, tkns_be)

# have a look
tcm_pmi_ts[1:3, 1:3]
tcm_pmi_be[1:3, 1:3]
```

```
               i      blew     things
i       1.723724  16.46247   3.281868
blew   16.462466  23.02585  20.946410
things  3.281868  20.94641   7.306280
```

```
            certified  quality         a
certified   23.02585  36.81142  16.894625
quality     36.81142  23.02585  16.894625
a           16.89463  16.89463   3.109061
```

If two terms have a high PMI, this means whenever we see one term, we'll probably see the other term nearby (again, *syntagmatic* associations). For example, in Beyoncé's songs, if we see "certified," we'll likely see "quality." Let's look at only the row for the terms with the highest PMI to "winning" in our Swift TCM (output in margin).

```
df_winning <- data.frame(
    pmi = as.vector(tcm_pmi_ts["winning", ]),
    terms = names(tcm_pmi_ts["winning", ])) |>
    arrange(desc(pmi))

head(df_winning, n = 3)
```

```
      pmi     terms
1  36.88908   smile
2  36.88908    ring
3  36.88908  suburban
```

[38] This checks out when we look at lyrics from "Coney Island": "...the gift-wrapped suburban dreams.... Sorry for not winning you an arcade ring."

We can conclude that whenever we see "winning" in Swift's songs, we'll likely see "smile," "ring," or "suburban" nearby![38]

After weighting the TCM by pointwise mutual information, let's again use cosine to compare terms (i.e., get *paradigmatic* associations). Below, we'll compare all the shared words in Beyoncé and Swift's songs using an anchor term, "sorry." Below, we'll subset both TCMs so they have the same vocabulary.

```
vocab <- intersect(colnames(tcm_pmi_be), colnames(tcm_pmi_ts))
tcm_pmi_be <- tcm_pmi_be[vocab, vocab]
tcm_pmi_ts <- tcm_pmi_ts[vocab, vocab]
```

[39] In addition to sim2() and dist2() in text2vec, we could use dist() in base R to compare row vectors. quanteda has similar functions.

We'll use a faster function from text2vec.[39]

```
sim_be <- sim2(tcm_pmi_be["sorry", , drop = FALSE],
               tcm_pmi_be, method = "cosine")
sim_ts <- sim2(tcm_pmi_ts["sorry", , drop = FALSE],
               tcm_pmi_ts, method = "cosine")

df_compare <- data.frame(
    term = rownames(tcm_pmi_be),
    swift = as.vector(sim_be),
    beyonce = as.vector(sim_ts)
)
```

Finally, let's plot all the shared words by their cosine similarity to "sorry" in Beyoncé's songs and "sorry" in Swift's songs (Figure 6.4).

```
df_compare |>
    ggplot(aes(x = swift, y = beyonce)) +
    geom_abline(intercept = 0, slope = 1, linetype=2) +
    geom_label(aes(label = term)) +
    labs(x = "Cosine to 'Sorry' in Taylor Swift's Songs",
         y = "Cosine to 'Sorry' in Beyonce's Songs")
```

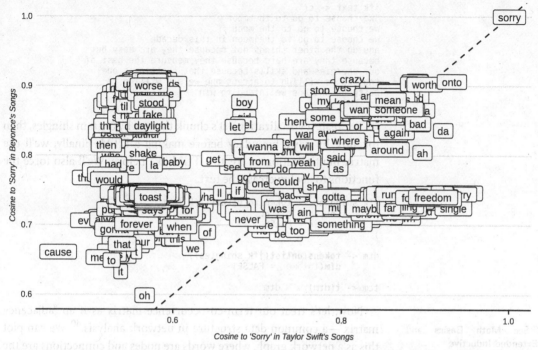

Figure 6.4: Term Similarities with PMI-Weighted TCMs.

We added a diagonal line where terms above it are more similar to "sorry" in Beyoncé's songs and terms below are more similar to "sorry" in Swift's songs. "Single" is more similar in Swift's corpus, while "fake" is more similar in Beyoncé's.

What jumps out when we see this scatter plot, though, is that the words are kind of a mess. Language is high-dimensional or feature-rich. Songs, like any other text, have multiple levels of meanings (Barthes and Duisit 1975). To map these meanings, we often *reduce these dimensions* to facilitate interpretation.

DIMENSION REDUCTION

The matrices we use to represent document- and term- features are often "high dimensional." In plain terms, this means our matrices have lots of columns. Consider, for example, the co-occurrences of words in a short piece of text: the excerpt from Kennedy's Rice speech we previously auto-transcribed. It contains 35 unique types.

```
jfk_text <- c(
"We choose to go to the moon
We choose to go to the moon
We choose to go to the moon in this decade
and do the other things not because they are easy but
because they are hard because they measure the best of
our energies and skills because that challenges one
that we're willing to accept one we are willing to
postpone and one we intend to win"
)
```

To create a visualization, let's chunk the text by 5-gram shingles, then tokenize by word boundary before making a DTM. Finally, we'll use matrix multiplication to create a TCM like before. We'll also force the functions to *not* lowercase the text.

```
jfk_shingles <- tokenize_ngrams(jfk_text,
    n = 6L, n_min = 6L,
    lowercase = FALSE
)

dtm <- tokens(unlist(jfk_shingles)) |>
    dfm(tolower = FALSE)

tcm <- t(dtm) %*% dtm
```

Now, let's treat our term-co-occurrence matrix as if an "adjacency matrix"—a common data structure in network analysis.[40] We can plot this as a network graph, where words are nodes and connections are the co-occurrences between words.[41] The graph is shown in Figure 6.5.

```
gr <- tcm |>
    as.matrix() |>
    as_tbl_graph(directed = FALSE) |>
    mutate(fon = ifelse(name %in% c("We", "we"), 4, 1))

ggraph(gr, layout = "grid") +
    geom_edge_arc(aes(alpha = weight), strength = .04) +
    geom_node_label(aes(label = name, fontface = fon)) +
    theme_void() +
    theme(legend.position = "none")
```

Even with this short text, our graph is on the verge of being unruly. We'll discuss strategies to *reduce these dimensions* or *limit the feature space* later. Many of these strategies, however, are not typical dimension reduction techniques, but are better understood as such. For example, when we didn't lowercase our texts, this is telling our scripts to treat "We" and "we" as distinct types instead of the same type. If we rerun the above script but allow the functions to lowercase our text, this would reduce the dimensions of our matrices. In our example, the DTM had 36 columns. Had we lowercased first, it would be 35 columns. This doesn't seem like much, but in larger corpora, lowercasing can significantly reduce columns. Information is also lost when we remove the distinction

[40] See **Math Basics** and **Extended Inductive**.

[41] For this, we need specialty packages: tidygraph and ggraph .

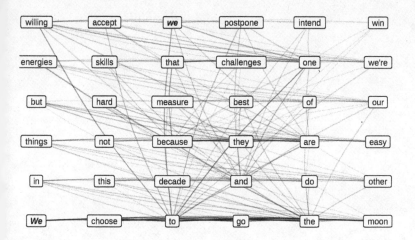

Figure 6.5: Term Adjacency Network.

between upper and lowercase letters. Whether the trade-off is worth it always depends on the research question.

There are also more practical reasons we might want to reduce the dimensionality of our text data: memory and time. It is increasingly straightforward to download immense corpora. For example, Wikipedia provides its "data dump"[42] of all articles at a given time. This is dozens of gigabytes of data, millions of unique word types, and billions of tokens. Even if represented as a sparse DTM, such a corpus could surpass the memory capacity of even high-end personal computers. Another consideration relates to time. Even with fast processors, certain computations take a long time (days, weeks, or longer). *Parallelization*, where more than one processor or core performs computations on different pieces of the dataset, is one way to increase speeds. Reducing the dimensions of our dataset beforehand, through preprocessing, also reduces the time required to perform operations on our text data. Therefore, we often discard information not because it is useless but because we could not perform the analysis otherwise.

An overarching theme in text analysis relates to how we reduce the columns of our matrices (i.e., dimensions or features) without losing information relevant to our questions. At each point in our analysis, it is crucial to remember that *there are no dimension reduction methods that we should always use*. Which method is the best is always related to the questions we wish to answer: how do we intend to use our textual map. Regardless of these critical considerations, reduction will always involve a combination of *deletion*, *extraction*, *replacement*, and *summarization*. In the next chapter, we discuss "preprocessing" sub-document units as a valuable form of reduction.

[42] dumps.wikimedia.org/backup-index.html

Part IV

Below the Document

7
Wrangling Words

My spelling is Wobbly. It's good spelling but it Wobbles, and the letters get in the wrong places
—Winnie-the-Pooh

METAPHORS orient us. When mapping, we aim to simplify our texts to make their "patterns accessible for joint exploration" (Lee and Martin 2014:1). At this stage in our journey, we consider what must be *deleted*, *extracted*, *replaced*, and *summarized*. These procedures typically involve decisions made *before* constructing text matrices or more complex analyses. As a result, it's often called **preprocessing** or **cleaning**. These labels are somewhat misleading (Rawson and Muñoz 2016), though. They imply that our analysis has yet to begin, that researchers must always take these steps, or that some words are "dirt" we must sweep away. Just as deciding whether to include elevation, road labels, or political boundaries is part of mapping terrain, the techniques that tend to fall under the labels "preprocessing" or "cleaning" are part of the analysis—forms of simplification and distillation. We must scrutinize how each step relates to our research aim.

Below we discuss **text wrangling**: *systematically altering the characters of our text*. There are two ways to do this: (1) replacing and (2) removing. In both cases, we use **rules**[1] and **dictionaries**.[2] Both rules and dictionaries rely on *matching strings* in our text. So, *the order we process our text matters*. This also means that we must think through possible *mismatches*.

A useful cautionary tale is when content moderation systems unintentionally remove content. An online forum operator, for example, wants to stop people from using profanity and so they construct a dictionary of profane terms. If any words match this dictionary, the post is blocked. But, sometimes profane words are spelled like nonprofane words (i.e., homonyms) and may even occur *inside* mundane words. If we look for exact matches, we'll find many false positives. This is called the Scunthorpe problem.[3] Examples include Facebook banning a Belgian political candidate named Luc Anus or forums preventing discussion of cocker spaniels or Alfred Hitchcock. A variation on this, dubbed the Clbuttic Mistake, occurs when we replace matched words with a

[1] A **rule** is a basic operation of the form "if this, then that," and primarily involves regular expressions.

[2] A **dictionary** is a data structure involving a collection of pairs, typically a **key** and a **value**. Each key is unique but can be any collection of characters. When we find a match for a key, the dictionary returns the associated value, which may be a string or a number.

[3] In 1996, the Internet provider AOL prevented the residents of Scunthorpe (among other towns) from creating accounts because the town name contained a word in the banned list.

Mapping Texts: Computational Text Analysis for the Social Sciences. Dustin S. Stoltz and Marshall A. Taylor, Oxford University Press. © Oxford University Press 2024.
DOI: 10.1093/oso/9780197756874.003.0007

new, presumably less profane, word. Like when "assassinate" becomes "buttbuttinate" (Moore 2008).

The reasons to alter our text include: (1) fixing technical errors and (2) simplifying our texts. The first addresses unintended misalignments between the human-readable and machine-readable forms of a text. For example, when using automated transcription and optical character recognition, words that look or sound alike may be mixed up. Or, in the case of encoding errors, the text may be garbled as presented to the human reader. For the second, we may want to collapse two or more word forms into a single word. This could include removing capitalization or replacing a "misspelled" word with the canonical form. While correcting technical errors is more aptly called "cleaning," whenever we simplify our texts, we are reducing the dimensionality of our corpus. This makes our corpus easier to analyze and share with other researchers as well as reduces the memory and processing requirements.

CHARACTER ENCODING

The smallest sub-document unit is typically called a **character**. This includes, for example, Arabic numerals; letters of the Latin, Cyrillic, Arabic, and Mkhedruli alphabets; Chinese logographics; alphasyllabary abugidas like the Devanagari; featural alphabets like Korean Hangul; syllabaries like the Japanese Kana and Cherokee—and more! Characters also include punctuation, mathematical symbols, and a range of "non-printing characters" such as the space, tab, newline, and return.[4] Now, we're about to get technical.

When our texts are digital, each unique character in our texts must be "encoded"—or associated with a unique numerical sequence (i.e., code). This allows our operating systems, browsers, etc., to distinguish between each character and spit out the correct character to a user's screen. Perhaps the most famous character "encoding" is Morse code, where unique strings of short sounds and long sounds are matched to each letter of the English alphabet.

As it relates to modern computing, the most well-known character encoding system is ASCII (American Standard Code for Information Interchange), developed in the 1960s out of several projects attempting to standardize data processing (Mackenzie 1980). These codes represented commonly used characters in English writing. For example, the space is

[4] The term **character** is a holdover from early computer programming of the 1950s and 1960s. Functionally, it corresponds to the linguistic concept **grapheme**, but not precisely (Haralambous and Dürst 2018). How best to *segment* a given writing tradition is an ongoing discussion, complicated by ligatures and cursivity. Furthermore, many *graphetic* qualities of writing, for example, fonts, are not encoded at the character level.

represented in binary as "010 0000" and capital A is "100 0001." "Latin 1" is another common encoding system, which extends ASCII and should cover most languages using a Latin script.

At the moment, though, the best encoding follows the Unicode standard, specifically UTF-8. The benefit of UTF-8 is that it is the default encoding on most machines and *locales*[5] and supports a much larger range of characters than does ASCII or Latin 1—including non-English Latin scripts, as well as non-Latin scripts.

Furthermore, all ASCII and Latin 1 encodings are compatible with UTF-8. The reverse, however, isn't true and can lead to some weird outputs. If, for example, a character cannot be converted into ASCII, this character is often replaced with its Unicode equivalent "U-code."

Let's work with an example. The first sentence has special "curved" double quotation marks (called smart quotes). If we used `cat()` to print it, those quotation marks are replaced with U-codes, but with angle brackets `<>` on either side.

```
my_text <- c(' "Why do you call to my remembrance" ')
Encoding(my_text) <- "UTF-8"
cat(my_text)
```

```
<U+201C>Why do you call to my remembrance<U+201D>
```

What's happening? Before `cat()` is printing, there is a conversion going on behind the scenes: a UTF-8 string is input, then converted into the locale encoding, which here happens to be ASCII. ASCII doesn't have a way to encode curved quotation marks. So, a character string representing the U-codes with angle brackets (which do contain characters that can be represented in ASCII) takes their place. The string is then *re-encoded* into UTF-8, but the U-codes are now treated like *literal* characters.

```
# let's explicitly reproduce the example:
iconv(my_text, from = "UTF-8", to = "ASCII", sub = "Unicode")
```

Even worse is when text is decoded using an *unintended* character encoding protocol. Rather than replacing characters not represented by the encoding, it may still attempt to interpret the character, resulting in gibberish known as **mojibake** (*mo-ji bah-keh*). A commonly encountered example of mojibake is when UTF-8 is interpreted as Windows-1252 (a pre-Windows 10 Latin encoding system). The smart, right-side, double

[5] To check your system's locale run `Sys.getlocale()` in your R session or `sessionInfo()`. We can set the locale with `Sys.setlocale()`.

quote " (which is U+201D in UTF-8) is rendered as â€œ if we tried to use Windows-1252 encoding (see Table 7.1).

Table 7.1: Common "Mojibake" Encoding Errors

Expected	Mojibake	Unicode	Expected	Mojibake	Unicode
"	â€œ	U+201C	'	â€™	U+2019
"	â€☐	U+201D	—	â€"	U+2014
'	â€˜	U+2018	…	â€¦	U+2026

The above examples offer enough reason to become familiar with encodings, understand the encoding of our locale, and be consistent throughout our pipeline (as best we can). Doing so will mitigate unintended encoding errors in our corpus, making it less likely that we end up analyzing gibberish.

MARKUP CHARACTERS

THIS SECTION NEEDS:

- stringi
- quanteda
- tidytext
- tidyverse
- textclean
- tokenizers
- gutenbergr
- hunspell

When reading in a browser (like Mozilla Firefox or Apple Safari) or a word processor (like Microsoft Word or OpenOffice Writer), the text is "what you see is what you get" or WYSIWYG. We see different fonts and sizes, some words bold or italicized, words grouped into paragraphs or columns, etc. Behind the scenes is a range of characters that are not printed. Rather, the browser or word processor is *interpreting* those characters as formatting or style. These non-content characters are often called **markup**.

[6] For example, Microsoft Notepad, gedit on Linux, or the editors built into IDEs like RStudio or VS Code.

Unlike word processors or browsers, *plain-text editors*[6] do not interpret markup language. Rather, they operate as "what you see is what you mean" or WYSIWM. If we open a webpage HTML (Hypertext Markup Language) file in a plain-text editor, we see both content and markup characters. Aside from HTML, the most common markup languages include XML,[7] LaTeX, SGML, and Markdown. Within basic ASCII there are markup characters we'll encounter regularly. These are *non-printing characters* as they define whitespace formatting around the printed characters (see Table 7.2).

[7] The Microsoft Word "DOCX" format is a compressed archive (ZIP) of an XML file. We can "unzip" the DOCX and open the XML file in a plain-text editor.

The regularity of these markup languages can be a resource for wrangling text. Several packages can interpret markup and either remove it or use it to convert text into specific data structures. For example, `html_text()` in `rvest` removes all HTML markup tags.

Table 7.2: Common Non-Printing Characters

Description	Characters	
Tab	\t	
Newline	\n	
Carriage return	\r	
Space	\s	Includes \t \n \r
Line separator	\r\n	
Horizontal space	\h	
Vertical tab	\v	
Word boundary	\b	

We can also use the newline mark \n or carriage return \r encodings to break long pieces of text into lines and paragraphs. Let's use a selection from Kennedy's Rice speech. Below we arrange the speech as one long string, but after each line, we include \n to indicate a newline.

```
jfk_text <- c(
"we choose to go to the moon\nwe choose to go to the moon\n
we choose to go to the moon in this decade and\ndo the other
things not because they are easy\nbut because they are hard\n
because they measure the best of our energies and skills\n
because that challenge is one that we're willing to accept\n
one we are unwilling to postpone and one we intend to win"
)
```

We can turn this long string into separate strings for each line by splitting on the newline character. This will structure our lines as discrete units of analysis.

```
strsplit(jfk_text, split = "\\n")
```

```
[[1]]
[1] "we choose to go to the moon"
[2] "we choose to go to the moon"
[3] "we choose to go to the moon in this decade and"
[4] "do the other things not because they are easy"
[5] "but because they are hard"
[6] "because they measure the best of our energies and skills"
[7] "because that challenge is one that we're willing to accept"
[8] "one we are unwilling to postpone and one we intend to win"
```

REMOVING AND REPLACING CHARACTERS

It is often useful to replace one character with a similar alternative or a shared root character. This "collapses" two versions of what researchers consider the "same" token. Unlike character encoding errors, these are not "corrections." They are explicit reductions and thus should be motivated by our research aims.

We've already encountered an example: **case**. Certainly, not all languages have distinct upper (majuscule) and lower (minuscule) letters,[8] but many do. In English, we often use capitals to denote, for example, the beginning of a sentence, proper nouns, acronyms, or to convey anger or excitement—and "camelcase" may convey sarcasm. Lowercasing or uppercasing all words assures the same word with different cases is still treated as the same, although it also means that we lose the information that capitalizing conveys.

We may also want to change characters from one script to those in another—that is, **transliterate**. For example, accented characters are common among languages using the Latin script, such as "Raúl" and "Raül," where English would render it "Raul." Depending on the analysis, however, we may want to treat each of these names as equivalent. To do so, we could replace u, ú, or ü with one of the other two, to render them equivalent.

```
names <- c("Raul", "Raúl", "Raül")
# how many unique names?
length(unique(names))

names <- gsub("ú|ü", "u", names)
# now how many unique names?
length(unique(names))
```

We can do this with `stringi`, which uses dictionaries designating from and to a wide range of languages.[9]

We'll first transliterate from "any" character set to the broadest range of Latin characters, and then we'll transliterate this output to only those represented by one of the 128 "Basic Latin" characters of ASCII. Instead of being replaced by the U+codes, characters are replaced by their *nearest equivalent* in Basic Latin as determined by the dictionary.

```
in_str <- c(" キャンパス", "wylądować", "Дорога", "heiß", "brûlée")
Encoding(in_str) <- "UTF-8"

# compare
stri_trans_general(in_str, id = "Latin-ASCII")
stri_trans_general(in_str, id = "Any-Latin")
```

```
[1] "キャンパス" "wyladowac"  "Дорога" "heiss" "brulee"
[1] "kyanpasu" "wylądować" "Doroga" "heiß"  "brûlée"
```

To correctly transliterate all of these to Basic Latin, use:

```
stri_trans_general(in_str, id = "Any-Latin; Latin-ASCII")
```

```
[1] "kyanpasu"  "wyladowac" "Doroga"    "heiss"    "brulee"
```

---

[8] Curiously, Georgian is typically written without case (called the Mkhedruli) but has a separate script of all capitals (called the Asomtavruli). In the 1950s, a linguist made a vain attempt to popularize mixing Asomtavruli with Mkhedruli, as upper and lowercase, respectively (Unicode 2022).

[9] `stringi` uses dictionaries from the ICU (unicode-org.github.io/icu/). Use `stri_trans_list()` to see the full list of language transliterators.

In UTF-8, ASCII and Basic Latin form the first and second Unicode blocks, respectively. Characters outside this set consume more memory. For example, compare `charToRaw("su")` with `charToRaw("ス")`.

We may also want to replace some punctuation because ASCII only has a limited range of punctuation it can represent. Table 7.3 shows the punctuation represented in Basic Latin. Perhaps the most common punctuation needing replacement are the curved, curly, or smart quotes and apostrophes. They are so pesky that `textclean` has a function for replacing them: `replace_curly_quote()`.

In many cases, we'll strip punctuation from our corpus. For example, we usually want "wild." and "wild?" and "wild!" to be seen as the same token ("wild"). Without removing punctuation first, a tokenizer might assume they are distinct types (depending on what rules we use to tokenize).

Table 7.3: Punctuation Marks and Unicodes

Mark	Unicode	Description	Mark	Unicode	Description
	U+0020	space	:	U+003A	colon
!	U+0021	exclamation	;	U+003B	semicolon
"	U+0022	quotation	<	U+003C	less than
#	U+0023	number	=	U+003D	equal to
$	U+0024	dollar	>	U+003E	greater than
%	U+0025	percent	?	U+003F	question
&	U+0026	ampersand	@	U+003@	at
'	U+0027	apostrophe	[	U+005B	left square bracket
(	U+0028	left parenthesis	\	U+005C	backslash
)	U+0029	right parenthesis	]	U+005D	right square bracket
	U+002A	asterisk	^	U+005E	circumflex/caret
+	U+002B	plus sign	_	U+005F	low line/underscore
,	U+002C	comma	`	U+0060	grave accent
-	U+002D	hyphen/minus	{	U+007B	left curly bracket
.	U+002E	period/full stop	|	U+007C	vertical bar
/	U+002F	forward slash	}	U+007D	right curly bracket
/	U+002F	forward slash	~	U+007E	tilde
/	U+002F	forward slash			

All these procedures rely on **regex**—this is true regardless of the programming language. In `R`, most packages rely on base `R`'s suite of string matching functions—which are based on the Unix-based GREP—in addition to `stringi` and `stringr`, which are related (see Table 7.4).[10] The simplest way to remove punctuation is with the character class `[:punct:]`, which matches all ASCII punctuation. Let's work through an example.

[10] `stringr` builds atop `stringi` which uses ICU regular expressions.

Table 7.4: Basic String Functions

Operation	Base R	Stringr
Extract	regexpr() + regmatches()	str_extract(), str_match()
Detect	grep(), grepl()	str_which(), str_detect()
Substitute	gsub(), sub()	str_replace(), str_sub()
Locate	gregexpr(), regexpr()	str_locate()
Split	strsplit()	str_split()

```r
df_punct <- tibble(
  text = c("North_America! and South_America.",
           '"total bone-saw!"', "$1,000 more.", "upper_hand's? ",
           "#Cat's", "@Dog's!", "8:30 AM", "AT&T")
)
```

```r
gsub("[[:punct:]]", "", df_punct$text) # remove all punctuation
gsub("[[:punct:]]", " ", df_punct$text) # replace with space
```

We might want to remove some, but not *all* punctuation, at least not right away. *Intra-word* punctuation often denotes a single idea, like hyphenated phrases or contractions. Furthermore, it is common to represent n-grams with underscores between the grams, for example, "south_africa."

```r
# remove specific characters
gsub("[!#?]", "", df_punct$text)
# replace with space
gsub("[!#?]", " ", df_punct$text)
```

The next regex pattern captures punctuation between words as a group \\1 , including everything within the parentheses, and removing all other punctuation.

```r
pattern <- "(\\w+[[:punct:]]+\\w+)|[[:punct:]]+"
gsub(pattern, "\\1", df_punct$text)
```

Finally, this pattern captures dashes, underscores, commas, and apostrophes between words as a group \\1, and remove all other punctuation marks.

```r
pattern <- "(\\w+[-_',]+\\w+)|[[:punct:]]+"
gsub(pattern, "\\1", df_punct$text)
```

Some tokenizing functions strip punctuation by default. Others preserve *intra-word punctuation*. Furthermore, if punctuation at the end of a word is retained, like an exclamation mark, it is often treated as a unique token.

```
#stringi
stri_extract_all_words(df_punct$text)

#quanteda
tokens(df_punct$text)
tokens(df_punct$text, remove_punct = FALSE)
tokens(df_punct$text, remove_punct = TRUE, remove_symbols = TRUE)

#tidytext
unnest_tokens(df_punct, word, text)
unnest_tokens(df_punct, word, text, strip_punct = FALSE)

#tokenizers
tokenize_words(df_punct$text)
tokenize_words(df_punct$text, strip_punct = FALSE)
```

Finally, there is the question of numbers. It is common to remove the Arabic numerals (0, 1, 2, 3, 4, 5, 6, 7, 8, 9) and, like removing all punctuation, it is easy with base R .

```
string_numbers <- c("1,000", "4", "40-50 feral hogs",
                    "1st place!", "$20 million",
                    "£1,000", "11/16/1980", "8:30 PM")

# compare two ways to remove all numerals
gsub("[[:digit:]]+", "", string_numbers)
gsub("\\d+", "", string_numbers)
```

The implied goal of removing numerals is to limit the feature space. But, an alternative to deleting is to replace them with their alphabetic equivalents. One could build a dictionary to match each number and replace it with the appropriate word, but we may want to be careful to treat, ordinals, dates, or times differently. Luckily, textclean provides functions for replacing each with their written equivalents.[11]

[11] Under the hood, it is a lot of fancy regex.

```
replace_number(string_numbers)
replace_ordinal(string_numbers)
replace_money(string_numbers)
replace_date(string_numbers)
replace_time(string_numbers)
```

Beyond encoding, lowercasing, transliterating, punctuation, and numbers, we may encounter, on a case-by-case basis, a range of special characters specifically related to data obtained from the Web. If, for example, we get text data from Twitter, we need to deal with hashtags and usernames (e.g., #ReadBannedBooks, @levarburton) and emojis. If we scrape Web data, it often has HTML markup tags. rvest provides html_text() and textclean has replace_html() to remove HTML syntax, or we could use gsub() with a regex pattern to strip markup text.[12]

[12] For help with hashtags, handles, urls, emojis, and other unique cases, see textclean .

"Misspelled" Words

We often find "unconventional" terms. Perhaps they are rendered incorrectly (e.g., common with OCR), or have encoding issues. Other times, they are kerned (spaces between letters, "W H Y ?"), or elongated ("Whyyyyyyyy?"), use different regional spellings (e.g., color vs. colour), are slang words, nonsense words or catchphrases,[13] or are intentionally or unintentionally "misspelled" words.

Recall that part of the reason we are altering our text is to *limit our feature space* before the analysis. The question is, as always, what information are we losing when we reduce these spelling variations to a conventional form?

There are many tools for dealing with "non-standard" words. textclean offers functions that attempt to "fix" both kerning and elongation. Both use a combination of dictionaries and rules. The elongation function looks for characters (any case) repeated at least three times in a row. These words are replaced with their "canonical" form by dropping all consecutive letters but the first one, and then attempting to match it to the most common word form in Google's *n*-gram dataset.[14] The kerning function looks for 3 or more capital letters in a row with spaces between them.

```
elong <- c("l o o k", "moorley's!", "real coooool!",
           "heeeeere's Johnny!", "Khaaaaannn!", "as",
           "I'm liiiike whyyyy me?")

replace_word_elongation(elong)

kerned <- c("I'm", "a l l", "O U T", "O F", "B U B B L E G U M")

replace_kern(kerned)
```

textclean also provides a function for common misspellings. This uses hunspell on the backend—so let's look at this package instead. Hunspell[15] is the spell checker for a variety of common applications, like Mozilla Firefox and Google Chrome. Like most of the tools we've discussed, Hunspell uses a combination of rules and dictionaries to identify and deal with potential misspellings. First, the function tokenizes the text by unigrams. It then breaks these unigrams into "stems" and "affixes."[16] Next, the function compares the stem + affix combination with language-specific dictionaries. If there is no match, that token is considered potentially misspelled.

Let's use Lewis Carroll's works. We can download them from Project Gutenberg[17] using gutenbergr . The output is a dataframe with 3,907 lines—one for each line in each book.

[13] "Cowabunga," "pi-kapika," and "snoochie boochies" may be notorious blatherskite, but they're still words!

[14] storage.googleapis.com/books/ngrams/books/datasetsv2.html

[15] hunspell.github.io/

[16] We'll cover stemming later in this chapter.

[17] This is an online library of free ebooks founded by Michael Hart, the inventor of the ebook.

```
book_ids <- c(11, 12, 13, 620, 651)
my_mirror <- "http://mirrors.xmission.com/gutenberg/"

carroll <- gutenberg_download(book_ids,
                                 meta_fields = "title",
                                 mirror = my_mirror)

# wrangle the lines a bit
carroll <- carroll |>
    mutate(
    text = replace_curly_quote(text),
    text = replace_contraction(text),
    text = gsub("'", "", text),
    text = gsub("[[:punct:]]+", " ", text),
    text = gsub("[[:space:]]+", " ", text),
    text = trimws(text)
)

# tokenize, create token-count list
tkns <- tibble(token = tokenize_words(carroll$text) ) |>
        unnest(token) |>
        count(token, sort = TRUE)
```

Next, we'll feed each unique token to `hunspell_check()` and find the "misspelled" words in Carroll's books.

```
tkns <- tkns |>
    mutate(correct = hunspell_check(token) ) |>
    unnest(correct, keep_empty = TRUE)

tkns |>
    filter(correct == FALSE) |>
    print(n=30)
```

`hunspell` flagged several types as misspelled. Many top "misspelled" words are names or "nonsense" words that Carroll invented (e.g., Jabberwock, Bandersnatch). We'll also find acronyms and company names (or other proper nouns) flagged as misspelled.[18]

`hunspell` also suggests alternative spellings—how? First, it uses a dictionary of common typos (e.g., "alot" for "a lot"). Second, it compares the character sequence to the "closest" correct sequence in the dictionary. Here, "closest" is the nearest neighbor on the keyboard! For example, it would suggest "node" for the token "nide," because "o" is right next to "i" on the standard QWERTY keyboard.

```
tkns |>
    filter(correct == FALSE) |>
    filter(token != "oo") |> # let's skip this token
    mutate(replacement = hunspell_suggest(token)) |>
    unnest(replacement) |>
    print(n=30)
```

This is one algorithm for comparing string similarities based on **edit distance**.[19] There are many slight variations on this including, the Hamming, Levenshtein, and Jaro-Winkler distance. Let's compare our

[18] The Cupertino effect is when a spell checker erroneously replaces words because they are *not* in its dictionary. In the 1990s, Microsoft Word would change the non-hyphenated "cooperation" to "Cupertino" (the corporate headquarters of Apple Inc.).

[19] Edit distance quantifies how many "edits"—editions, deletions, replacements—it would take to turn one string into another. For example, to turn "water" into "wine," would entail one deletion and two replacements.

[20] In addition to reducing dimensionality by merging similarly spelled words, these measures of string similarity can be especially useful when working with archival records that have been OCRed and linking different datasets by text-based variables—see especially `RecordLinkage`.

flagged words to the unflagged words using Levenshtein, the default in `adist()`.[20]

```
correct   <- tkns[tkns$correct==TRUE, ]
incorrect <- tkns[tkns$correct==FALSE,]

leven <- adist(x = correct$token, y = incorrect$token,
               ignore.case = FALSE, counts = FALSE)

rownames(leven) <- unlist(correct$token)
colnames(leven) <- unlist(incorrect$token)
```

Which word is the "max" and "min" distance from Jabberwock?

```
which.max(leven[, "Jabberwock"] )
which.min(leven[, "Jabberwock"] )
```

A popular alternative to "edit distance" comparisons is **soundex**, which converts a string into a phonetic "soundex" code. A pairwise comparison gets a 1 if two tokens have the same soundex code; otherwise, 0. `stringdist` provides several "edit distance" measures including soundex, and `ipa` provides tools to convert to phonetic alphabets for comparison.

THIS SECTION NEEDS:

- quanteda
- tidytext
- tidyverse
- text2map
- gutenbergr

REMOVING WORDS AND STOPLISTS

Why would we remove or "stop" *words* entirely from our corpus? First, many text sources interact with automated content creators—for example, bots or metadata. If we are analyzing emails, there is some automated content in the email, but we typically only care about the human-produced content. Consider, for instance, an analysis of the pager messages sent during the September 11th terrorist attacks in the US. Back and colleagues (2010) placed words in each message into one of three emotion categories: sadness, anxiety, anger. They found *anger* intensified as compared to sadness and anxiety. Unfortunately, they failed to catch one automated technical code that included the word "critical" (Pury 2011; Back et al. 2011). Had they accounted for this, they would have found no evidence that anger increased over the timeline. In some cases, though, our research may center on automated content, such as how bots may spread hate speech on social media (Uyheng and Carley 2020).

Second, if we have fewer types of words—by definition—we have fewer dimensions! Removing words limits the feature space. Third, removing types of words can reduce computational demands—hopefully with minor trade-offs. Fourth, sometimes we'll want to visualize words, but there are just too many (e.g., it looks like a ball of flies). Here too, we hope to keep the most visually "informative" words. Finally, we often remove words that are not *discriminant*, those which distinguish one document from another.[21]

Researchers often compile a list of words to remove or "stop" into a negative dictionary or **stoplist**. This practice started with information retrieval as early automated indexing prioritized efficiency. As computing resources improved, however, the "general trend in [information retrieval] systems ... [is from] standard use of quite large stop lists (200–300 terms) to very small stop lists (7–12 terms) to no stop list whatsoever" (Manning et al. 2010:27).

There are no such things as "stopwords"[22]—that is, there is no explicitly agreed-upon set of words (in any language) we *must* remove in every analysis. Which words are "stopped" is often a matter of convention—treated like the angel's share of whiskey—and reinforced by default settings on functions. This is problematic because it obscures a dimension reduction step. Nevertheless, the misnomer "stopword" is a fixture of text analysis.

Before we dive into constructing stoplists, let's review several ways to remove words from our text data. The method depends on our data structure: we can remove words directly from our **raw text**, from a **token-list** or **token-count list**, and finally, we can remove words from a **DTM**. Let's demonstrate using Carroll's works again.

```
book.ids <- c(11, 12, 13, 620, 651)
my_mirror <- "http://mirrors.xmission.com/gutenberg/"
carroll <- gutenberg_download(book.ids,
                              meta_fields = "title",
                              mirror = my_mirror)
carroll <- carroll |> mutate(text = tolower(text))
```

We'll first use `gsub()` to create a new column of text with stoplist words removed. For this, collapse the stoplist with `paste()` using the vertical bar `|`.[23] In effect, this tells R to substitute a "no-space" whenever it encounters $word_1$ or $word_2$, on up to $word_n$ in our stoplist.

```
# create stoplist
list_stop <- c("bandersnatch", "jabberwock")
stop_pattern <- paste(list_stop, collapse = "|")

carroll$text <- gsub(stop_pattern, "", carroll$text,
                     ignore.case = TRUE)
```

What if we have a token-list or token-count list? If we turn them into dataframes, we can remove any *rows* matching words in our stoplist. Let's work through four methods to remove rows based on a word matched in a negative dictionary.

First, using base `R`, we'll use the `%in%` operator, which means "every X *contained in* Y." This creates a vector of `TRUE` and `FALSE` elements the length of the rows in our dataframe. We can use this to keep every `TRUE` and remove every `FALSE`. Second, we'll use `dplyr`'s `filter()` while negating the `%in%` operator.[24] Third, we'll use `dplyr`'s `anti_join()`.[25] The fourth, and last, method uses `quanteda`'s functions for removing words from a token-list.

[24] When preceded with the negator `!`, it means "every X *NOT* contained in Y."

[25] Most join functions "merge" two dataframes by matching columns. This function removes all the rows that match.

```
# create a token-count dataframe
df_tkns <- carroll |>
        select(title, text) |>
        unnest_tokens(word, text) |>
        count(title, word, sort = TRUE)


# #1 filter with Base R subsetting
idx  <- !df_tkns$word %in% list_stop
df_tkns1 <- df_tkns[idx, ]

# #2 filter with filter()
df_tkns2 <- df_tkns |> filter(!word %in% list_stop)

# #3 filter with anti_join()
df_stop <- data.frame(word = list_stop)
df_tkns3 <- df_tkns |> anti_join(df_stop, by  = "word")

# #4 removing words from quanteda's token-list
ls_tkns <- tokens(carroll$text)
ls_tkns4 <- tokens_remove(ls_tkns, list_stop)
```

Finally, let's look at removing words if we have a DTM. Removing words this way is efficient because we only need to match a term once and delete its corresponding column from our matrix. `quanteda` and `text2map` provide functions to remove columns from DTMs.

```
# create a quanteda dtm
dtm <- tokens(carroll$text) |> dfm()
# #5 remove words from a quanteda dtm
dtm <- dfm_remove(dtm, pattern = list_stop)
# #8 remove words from a text2map dtm
dtm <- dtm_stopper(dtm, stop_list = list_stop)
# #9 removing column names not matching our list
dtm <- dtm[  , !colnames(dtm) %in% list_stop]
```

Now we know how to remove words. How do we decide *which* words? In practice, there are three strategies to identify candidates for "stopping."

The first uses frequency. Most words infrequently occur (i.e., Zipf's law). As proportions, nearly any document of similar length (in the same language) shares a high proportion of words! In many cases, however, our research questions hinge on how documents *differ*. For instance, Nelson (2021a) asks how the writings of US women's movement organizations change between the first and second waves. With such questions, we'll want to increase the centrality of *discriminant* words. We could do this by weighting our DTM to place more emphasis on words unique to a document (i.e., $tf\text{-}idf$). Or, we could remove the most common (i.e., "non-discriminant") words *in all our documents*.[26]

A second strategy for identifying "non-discriminant" words is grammar. The grammatical types likely to be candidates for removal include articles, prepositions, conjunctions, demonstratives, and pronouns. Sometimes researchers remove the most frequent words falling into one of these classes, or remove all the words within a class. Other times, however, these are precisely the words to retain. For example, an investigation (Mosteller and Wallace 1963) of who authored the anonymous *Federalist Papers* compared the frequency of *by*, *from*, and *to* with writing samples by three potential authors, Hamilton, Madison, and Jay. Alternatively, we may only want to retain nouns and verbs (e.g., Mohr et al. 2013). In either case, we'd need to sort words into grammatical classes.[27]

The final strategy is to use *pre-compiled* stoplists. Several stoplists (at least for English) are provided in text analysis packages (see Table 7.5).[28] The most widely used English stoplists are based on the information retrieval research from the 1960s and 1970s (e.g., Van Rijsbergen 1979), and subsequent stoplists extend these earlier lists (Kaur and Buttar 2018). Although, in theory, early stoplists included only *frequent* words, it was Fox's "A Stop List for General Text" (1989) that first incorporated empirical word frequencies into generating a stoplist.[29]

Table 7.5: A Selection of Stoplists

List	Year	N words	Packages	
van Rijsbergen	1979	250	text2map	
Fox	1990	421	text2map	
SMART	1993	571	stopwords ,	text2map
ONIX	2000	198	text2map	
Snowball	2001	127	text2map	
Snowball	2014	175	stopwords ,	text2map
NLTK	2009	179	stopwords ,	text2map
Jockers	2013	5902	lexicon	
Loughran-McDonald	2015	570	lexicon	
Marimo	2020	237	stopwords ,	text2map
Tiny	2020	33	text2map	

[26] It is also common to remove words occurring very *infrequently*. This will reduce our vocabulary considerably, and thus the computational requirements of our analysis. Recall, one-quarter of the vocabulary, or more, appears just once!

[27] See **Tagging Words**.

[28] The **Snowball stoplist** (the original 2001 or 2014 version) used in Martin Porter's Snowball stemmer (1980) is the default English stoplist for most packages. The NLTK package and CoreNLP stoplists build on the Snowball list. The Snowball stoplist is, in turn, based on van Rijsbergen's 250 word **Van stoplist**. The **SMART stoplist** is another common negative dictionary based on the SMART retrieval system (Salton 1981).

[29] Fox used the Brown Corpus (Kučera and Francis 1967).

These pre-compiled lists vary, for example, whether lists include all forms of a word or are built using frequency and grammatical considerations. Documentation is, unfortunately, difficult to find. Even worse, publications often state only that "stop words were removed," without being explicit about *which* words were removed. We should always proceed with caution when choosing to remove words from our data since this can dramatically impact our findings.

We built a minimal stoplist called "tiny" (in `text2map`) with the intent to remove only the most frequent tokens in any genre. We began by selecting the top 20 words in several large corpora: the Brown Corpus, the Google Books 1 Trillion Word Corpus, and Wikipedia (as of 2019). The only verb we include is "to be" which includes 8 different forms ("be", "is", "are", "was", "am", "were", "being", and "been"). We omitted negated forms and contractions. We include singular and plural pronouns, but not gendered or possessive pronouns. The resulting stoplist includes 33 tokens. It is a lightweight and documented alternative.

To recap, words are pruned based on their (1) frequency, (2) grammatical class, or using (3) pre-compiled stoplists. Words are removed to aid visualization, speed up computational processes, and remove redundant information. However, such processes may not help us understand the texts and may even curtail some analytical techniques (Schofield et al. 2017). We must always keep our research aims in mind when deciding to remove words. As a best practice, we should test how removing words shapes our findings and documenting which words are removed when sharing these findings with our communities.

REPLACING WORDS

In the previous sections, we removed or replaced *characters* (e.g., deleting punctuation or extra whitespace), and we removed entire tokens (for example, with stoplists). When might we want to *replace words*?

First, we often don't want to. If using a dictionary, modifying word forms can hamper matches.[30] Or, if we're counting different parts of speech, we'll want to keep our words as is. "Running," "runs," and "ran" are all inflections of the base "run." If researchers need to differentiate between these inflections—say, to identify who *will run* for political office, who *is running* for office, and who *ran for* office—again, words should be left as is.

Are we agnostic to the differences between "run," "running," "runs," and "ran," and only wish to identify references to the act of "going faster

THIS SECTION NEEDS:

- textstem
- tidyverse
- stringi
- tidytext
- text2map
- proustr
- udpipe
- textclean
- text2vec

[30] To identify, say, news media organizations, the entries for CBS references might be "CBS"; then we do not want to remove capitalization since "CBS" would become "cbs."

than a walk" (Merriam-Webster 2020)? Or do we not care that "boat" is a noun, "boated" is a verb, and "boating" can be a noun or a verb, and only care about the general discourse around boating? If the latter is the case, we can drastically reduce the dimensions of our data by either *stemming* or *lemmatizing* our tokens. Let's discuss stemming first.

Stemming

Stemming is the process of reducing words down to their "stems" or "roots"—that is, the "core" character sequence without *affixes*.[31] Automated word-stemming procedures use rule- or dictionary-based functions to return one or more of these word stems per word in a text or corpus.

Consider the following words: "roll," "rolls," "rolling," and "rolled." Let's take each word and separate the base form from the affix—specifically, the suffix:

> **roll** -
> **roll** - *s*
> **roll** - *ing*
> **roll** - *ed*

Roll is the stem; it is the base to which suffixes are attached to indicate plurality (-*s*), continuous tense (-*ing*), and past tense (-*ed*). These are all examples of *inflectional suffixes*: suffixes used to change a word's grammatical features, such as the number or tense, but which do not alter the word's part of speech or meaning.

Now consider the word **roller**: a person who (or thing that) revolves. We can decompose this word down to its stem and suffix as well:

> **roll** - *er*

This is a *derivational suffix*: it creates a noun (if treating "roll" and its inflections as verbs), or a different type of noun (if treating "roll" and its inflections as nouns). All *prefixes* in English are also derivational since they alter the grammatical category and/or meaning of the base word, such as *un*-**roll**.

Stemming algorithms try to reduce terms to common forms: for example, "roll." Two popular stemmers are the "Porter" and "Porter2" stemmers. These stemmers mostly deal with inflectional rather than derivational affixes, and both focus on suffixes. The Porter stemmer uses a rule-based system first outlined in a 1980 paper by Martin Porter (Porter, et al. 1980) to strip (mostly) inflectional suffixes.[32] The Porter2 stemmer—also known as the "English stemmer"—is a revision of the original Porter algorithm, but functions the same way (Porter et al.

[31] While the social scientist may be more interested in the stems, the linguist may find the affixes more useful, for example, for studying morphology.

[32] As an undergraduate, the computational linguist Julie Beth Lovins published the first paper (1968) systematically comparing potential stemming algorithms, discussed key challenges in developing stemmers, and also proposed the Lovins Stemmer.

2002). Both stemmers are implemented in Snowball—a programming language for implementing stemmers across a range of human languages (Porter 2001).

We can use the Porter2 algorithms to stem whole documents. Consider the following corpus of lines from Durkheim's (1895) *The Rules of Sociological Method*.

```
docs <- c(
"society is not the mere sum of individuals",
"the system formed by their association",
"it is from this combination that social life arises",
"individuals give birth to a being"
)
```

We'll use `stem_strings()` . This function tokenizes each string—that is, each document— stems each token, and then pastes the stemmed tokens together. We'll set `language = "english"` which indicates we want to use Porter2.

```
stem_strings(docs, language = "english")
```

This returns the following:

```
[1] "societi is not the mere sum of individu"
[2] "the system form by their associ"
[3] "it is from this combin that social life aris"
[4] "individu give birth to a be"
```

Stemming doesn't always do what we want. Sometimes the stemming is too aggressive. For example, "Universities" would be stemmed as "Univers." A different word—"Universes"—would *also* stem to "Univers." Chances are we don't care that both words derive from the Latin word for "the whole" and we do not want these words to be equivalent in our DTM. We can address issues such as these by turning to a different form of word normalization: **lemmatizing**.

Lemmatizing

Whereas (rule-based) stemming involves affix-stripping, lemmatization is a dictionary-based method that maps inflected forms of a word onto its canonical form, "headword," or "lemma" (Crystal 2011:273): "an abstract representation, subsuming all . . . lexical variations which may apply."

Consider again "roll" and its inflected variants: "rolls," "rolling," and "rolled." Lemmatizing takes each word as inputs and returns "roll" as the output. But the pathway to get there is different. Stemming returns "roll" for each inflection using a series of "if-then" rules—if a word ends in *-ing*, for instance, then drop that suffix. In the simplest case, lemmatizing uses a lemma-token *dictionary* lookup to find the lemma that matches that token.

In the case of words such as "rolls" and "rolling," the returned lemma and stem are the same: "roll." But now consider the words "continue," "continues," and "continuing." The stem for each of these words is "continu." If we lemmatize these words using a lemma-token dictionary, then we'll get "continue" as the lemma for each word. Already we see a potential benefit to lemmatizing over stemming: lemmatizing always returns a conventual word. For example, "universities" is lemmatized as "university," "universes" becomes "universe."

Consider when verb tense necessitates a different word. The verb "be," which, depending on tense, can form "being" (continuous tense), "was"/"were" (past tense), "been" (past participle), or "am"/"are"/"is" (present tense). Other than "being" and "been," none stem to "be." Lemmatization, however, only requires that these conjugations be "linked" (as tokens) with a common lemma. In our case, it returns "be" for all these conjugations.

An advantage of lemmatizing over stemming is that it can normalize irregular verbs (i.e., words that don't conjugate using standard suffix rules). Say we want to lemmatize "break," "breaks," "broke," and "broken." While Porter2 stemming would normalize "break" and "breaks" to "break," it would not normalize "broke" and "broken"—which stem to "broke" and "broken," respectively. Lemmatizing returns the same lemma for each word: "break." Chances are this is what we want.

Let's use `lemmatize_words()` to lemmatize "be" and its other verb forms. This involves eight different words, so we'll first dump the words into a character vector and then pass this vector to the function using pipes.

```
data("hash_lemmas", package = "lexicon")

c("be", "being", "was", "were", "been", "am", "are", "is") |>
                lemmatize_words(dictionary = hash_lemmas)
```

As we can see, this process returns "be" as the lemma for each word. This is what we expected to see.

Notice that we specified a lemma-token dictionary instead of a stemming language. `lexicon` contains many dictionaries for text analysis. The dictionary of interest here is called `hash_lemmas`.[33] `textstem` also provides functionality to create corpus-specific dictionaries derived from the Hunspell and TreeTagger (Schmid 2013) dictionaries.

[33] This uses Michal Měchura's English lemma-token dictionary: github.com/michmech/lemmatization-lists

```
     token lemma
 1:     'm    be
 2:     am    be
 3:    are    be
 4:   arst    be
 5:   been    be
 6: being    be
 7:     is    be
 8:      m    be
 9:    was    be
10:   wass    be
11:   were    be
```

[34] This uses `split_tokens()` to tokenize before applying the lemmatizer. This function first removes all capitalization and disambiguates between words and punctuation flush against the words. Be mindful when using a tokenizer or lemmatizer that does not do these things.

`lemmatize_words()` uses a lookup procedure to match tokens to their lemma and then replace that token with that lemma. Let's find the assorted tokens associated with the "be" lemma in the Měchura dictionary (see the marginal note).

```
filter(hash_lemmas, lemma == "be")
```

All these tokens are lemmatized to the same lemma—that's exactly what we want! Now let's lemmatize a whole document using the excerpt from Durkheim (1895) using `lemmatize_strings()` .[34]

```
lemmatize_strings(docs, dictionary = hash_lemmas)
```

```
[1] "society be not the mere sum of individual"
[2] "the system form by their association"
[3] "it be from this combination that social life arise"
[4] "individual give birth to a be"
```

Let's incorporate lemmatizing into the wrangling workflow we just discussed using the *Star Trek: The Next Generation* corpus.

```
data("corpus_tng_season5", package = "text2map.corpora")
```

```
df_trek <- corpus_tng_season5 |>
  filter(!is.na(line)) |>
  select(number, title, airdate, character, line)
```

```
df_trek <- df_trek |>
mutate(
    lemma = tolower(line),
    lemma = gsub("[[:digit:]]+", " ", lemma),
    lemma = lemmatize_strings(lemma, dictionary = hash_lemmas),
    lemma = gsub("[[:punct:]]+", " ", lemma),
    lemma = gsub("[[:space:]]+", " ", lemma),
    lemma = trimws(lemma)
)
```

Now we see how line #17 looks with lemmatizing:

```
df_trek$lemma[17]
```

```
"captain s log stardate we have arrive at starbase
two thirty four where i have take the opportunity
to make a proposal to fleet admiral shanthi"
```

In addition to lemmatizing, we removed capitalization, numbers, punctuation, and excess whitespace. Lemmatizing, unlike stemming, does not automatically remove -'s (denoting possession)—for example, -'s in "captain's." `gsub()` removed *all* punctuation, replacing it with a space. There are multiple ways we can avoid getting "captain s" here. We could retain all punctuation between word characters, remove all instances of -'s, or remove tokens consisting of only one character.[35]

Using our preprocessed and lemmatized lines, let's create a DTM and remove words from the Snowball stoplist.

[35] Related, lemmatizing does not replace contractions; for this, we can use `replace_contraction()` .

```
dtm <- df_trek |>
    mutate(doc_id = rownames(df_trek)) |>
    dtm_builder(lemma, doc_id) |>
    dtm_stopper(stop_list = get_stoplist("snowball2014"))
```

Look at the first few columns of our DTM.

```
dtm[1:5, 1:7]
```

```
  aft shield buckle transfer auxiliary power go
1   1      1      1        .         .     .  .
2   .      1      .        1         1     1  .
3   1      1      .        .         .     .  1
4   .      .      .        .         .     .  .
5   .      .      .        .         .     .  .
```

The dictionary lookup method has a limitation: How to deal with homonymy? Consider the word "saw." This word could be a past-tense verb ("I saw an airplane fly by."), a verb indicating "to cut" ("I had to saw the plank of wood in half."), or a noun ("I had to buy a saw for the project."). Ideally, lemmatizers can distinguish between homonyms. For this, some lemmatizers "tag" each token with its predicted part of speech.[36] The lemma for the token is assigned *conditional on* that token's part of speech.

The TreeTagger model does this (Schmid 2013). We can also use `udpipe`. We'll talk more about `udpipe` in the next chapter on non-English part-of-speech tagging; for now, though, we'll quickly illustrate lemmatizing with parts of speech using this package. First, we'll download an English language model[37] that allows us to tag the parts of speech and then assign lemmas using those tags.

[36] See **Tagging Words**.

[37] This language model is trained on the GUM corpus.

```
eng <- udpipe_download_model(language = "english-gum")
ud_eng <- udpipe_load_model(eng$file_model)
```

Now let's do some tagging. We'll first create a small corpus using the "saw" homonym issue. We'll then use `udpipe_annotate()` to tag the documents and assign the lemmas.

```
docs <- c(
    "I saw an airplane",
    "I had to saw the wood",
    "I have a saw for work"
)
```

```
udpipe_annotate(x = docs, object = ud_eng) |>
    as.data.frame() |>
    select(doc_id, token, lemma, upos)
```

And we'll get the following output (we're printing only the document ID, token, lemma, and part of speech tag here).

```
  doc_id    token   lemma upos
1   doc1        I       I PRON
2   doc1      saw     see VERB
```

```
3    doc1        an        a DET
4    doc1  airplane airplane NOUN
5    doc2         I        I PRON
6    doc2       had     have VERB
7    doc2        to       to PART
8    doc2       saw      saw VERB
9    doc2       the      the DET
10   doc2      wood     wood NOUN
11   doc3         I        I PRON
12   doc3      have     have VERB
13   doc3         a        a DET
14   doc3       saw      saw NOUN
15   doc3       for      for ADP
16   doc3      work     work NOUN
```

The first instance of "saw" was tagged as a verb and lemmatized to "see." The second instance of "saw" was also tagged as a verb but lemmatized to "saw." The final "saw" was tagged as a noun and left alone. This allows us to distinguish between homonyms, which could be important for some research questions.[38]

We can incorporate the udpipe method for lemmatizing in our workflow with the following. For speed, we'll only use the first 20 lines from our *Star Trek* corpus. Using as_tibble() to tidy the output and count() we'll create a token-count "tripletlist" dataframe. Notice we also filter out any rows with lemmas matching [[:punct:]]+ (output in margin).

```
df_samp <- df_trek |>
    head(n = 20) |>
    mutate(lemma = tolower(line),
           lemma = gsub("[[:digit:]]+", " ", lemma))
```

```
df_trip <- udpipe_annotate(
    x = df_samp$lemma,
    object = ud_eng) |>
    as_tibble() |>
    select(doc_id, lemma) |>
    filter(!grepl("[[:punct:]]+", lemma)) |>
    count(doc_id, lemma)
```

We can then convert this tripletlist to a DTM with tidytext , but substituting in term = lemma in place of term = word (since the word column is called "lemma" instead of "word").

```
dtm <- df_trip |>
    cast_dfm(
        document = doc_id,
        term = lemma,
        value = n
    )
```

```
dtm[1:3, 1:7]
```

```
docs    aft buckl shield command course enter five
  doc1    1     1      1       0      0     0    0
  doc10   0     0      0       1      1     1    2
  doc11   0     0      1       0      0     0    0
```

doc_id	lemma	n
doc1	aft	1
doc1	buckl	1
doc1	shield	1
doc10	command	1
doc10	course	1
doc10	enter	1
doc10	five	2
doc10	mark	1
doc10	my	1
doc10	on	1

We have more assurances with this last DTM that homonyms have been accurately lemmatized.

Lemmatizing in French

udpipe can lemmatize many different languages.[39] Let's lemmatize some paragraphs from Proust's *Du côté de chez Swann* using a corpus from proustr , a package with seven books by the late-19th- and early-20th-century French novelist, Marcel Proust. Let's look at one paragraph.

```
data("ducotedechezswann", package = "proustr")
```

```
ducotedechezswann$text[60]
```

Next, we'll need to download a French-language model.

```
fre <- udpipe_download_model(language = "french-gsd")
ud_fre <- udpipe_load_model(fre$file_model)
```

Now, we can lemmatize the text. Let's go with the 60th paragraph.

```
ducotedechezswann$text[60] |>
    udpipe_annotate(object = ud_fre) |>
    as_tibble() |>
    select(doc_id, token, lemma, upos)
```

	doc_id	token	lemma	upos
1	doc1	—	—	PUNCT
2	doc1	Françoise	Françoise	PROPN
3	doc1	,	,	PUNCT
4	doc1	imaginez	imaginer	VERB
5	doc1	-vous	vous	PRON
.				
.				
.				
40	doc1	elle	il	PRON
41	doc1	arrive	arriver	VERB
42	doc1	après	après	ADP
43	doc1	l'	le	DET
44	doc1	élévation	élévation	NOUN
45	doc1	.	.	PUNCT

WRANGLING WORKFLOW

Table 7.6 lists some common text wrangling decisions. Further, below is an overview of a typical text preparation script we might use. These steps are not what *should* always be taken; rather, we'll use *variations* on these scripts, testing the effects of different decisions on our analyses. Furthermore, whether we take these steps ought to be *reported* in our final analysis—as a bare minimum.

[39] Currently, udpipe has 65 language models. To see what is available, run help(udpipe_download_model)

"—Françoise, imaginez-vous que Mme Goupil est passée plus d'un quart d'heure en retard pour aller chercher sa sœur ; pour peu qu'elle s'attarde sur son chemin cela ne me surprendrait point qu'elle arrive après l'élévation."

Table 7.6: Common Text Wrangling Decisions

Step	Specification
Punctuation	What punctuation is removed and retained?
Transliteration	Are some characters replaced with equivalents?
Numbers	Are all numbers removed? Are they replaced?
Lowercasing	Are all tokens lowercased? Are some retained?
Stopped Words	Were tokens removed (stopped)? Which words?
Stemming	Are tokens stemmed? How are they stemmed?
Lemmatizing	Are tokens lemmatized? How are they lemmatized?

Typically, we do not want our findings to change drastically by any single decision; if it does, we need to theorize why this might be the case.

Using `mutate()`, we can remove a task by "commenting out" a line with the `#`. For example, if we want to remove all numbers, rather than replace them with their written equivalents, we comment out all the five `replace_*` lines, and uncomment `gsub()` that matches the `[[:digit:]]+` regex pattern.

```
df_text <- df_text |> mutate(
    ## transliterate and lowercase
    text = stri_trans_general(
        text,
        id = "Any-Latin;Latin-ASCII"
    ),
    text = tolower(text),
    ## punctuation
    text = replace_curly_quote(text),
    text = gsub("(\\w+[_'-]+\\w+)|[[:punct:]]+", "\\1", text),
    text = replace_contraction(text),
    text = gsub("[[:punct:]]+", " ", text),
    ## numbers
    #    text = replace_number(text),
    #    text = replace_ordinal(text),
    #    text = replace_money(text),
    #    text = replace_date(text),
    #    text = replace_time(text),
    text = gsub("[[:digit:]]+", " ", text),
    ## spaces
    text = gsub("[[:space:]]+", " ", text),
    text = trimws(text)
)
```

What about the more specialized issues we raised, such as hashtags, encoding problems, misspellings, etc.? We only need to run these if we think these issues are present. How do we know they are present? If we gain an intimate knowledge of our documents by reading some, we'll pick up on the peculiarities of the corpus. Another helpful tool is provided by `textclean` called `check_text`, which checks for twenty-three possible issues.

Altering text in ways discussed here is as much about dimension reduction as more advanced techniques we'll discuss later. Each step potentially limits the "feature space" we are using to represent our documents: two tokens that are similarly spelled or associated by a dictionary or rule are merged into one type. This is not a trivial process.

Just as when cartographers decide to omit landscape features, whether words or characters *ought* to be removed or altered is an analytical decision informed by a purpose—a decision that ultimately must be justified as it relates to our research aims. Fortunately, in many cases, we can repeat analyses with systematic adjustments to these decisions, comparing the effect of each on our final interpretations (e.g., Denny and Spirling 2018; Lucchesi et al. 2022).

8

Tagging Words

*...all the familiar landmarks of thought—our thought, the thought that bears
the stamp of our age and our geography—breaking up all the ordered surfaces
and all the planes with which we are accustomed to tame the wild profusion of
existing things...*
                                                                    —M. Foucault

BORGES' infamous (tongue-in-cheek) taxonomy of animals from the
Celestial Emporium of Benevolent Knowledge epitomizes a notion we often
encounter in the social sciences: classifications are shaky. Realizing this
shakiness led to Foucault's "laughter that shattered, as [he] read [Borges']
passage, all the familiar landmarks of [his] thought" (Foucault 2005).

- embalmed ones
- suckling pigs
- stray dogs
- fabled ones
- those included in this classification

While there are regularities to our perception of the world (Lakoff
2008), a discrete and complete classification of anything is unlikely
(Douglas 1966). Many of our tools incorporate classification schemes
that we did not craft for our corpora, but rather impose upon them.
When we classify text, we often rely on someone's interpretation, which
is contextual and open to revision.[1]

Classifiers are automated processes that associate text with labels
based on patterns in the text. These boundaries between labels are often
fuzzy and graded. But this is not unique to text analysis. Ponds and lakes
are "bodies of water surrounded by land," and the difference is that one
is larger, deeper, or colder. How much larger, deeper, or colder? There is
no precise answer.

It is common to use "accuracy" and "performance" to describe a
classifier's *validity*. However, as we'll see throughout this book, classifiers
are compared to someone's interpretation. So, it is more appropriate
to think of the *agreement* between our tools and other benchmarks of
meaning, including with our own judgment.

Document classifiers tell us whether a piece of text—in its entirety—
belongs to a predefined category.[2] Below we introduce *sub-document*
classifiers, or **taggers**. Taggers share much with qualitative content analysis because pieces of relatively short pieces of texts are "coded" as
instantiating a category or theme and each document may contain multiple tags.

Tagging can be a method of analysis in itself—for example, finding the "dependencies" between words or phrases[3] in a sentence to

Mapping Texts: Computational Text Analysis for the Social Sciences. Dustin S. Stoltz
and Marshall A. Taylor, Oxford University Press. © Oxford University Press 2024.
DOI: 10.1093/oso/9780197756874.003.0008

identify semantic motifs (Stuhler 2022b) or subject-action-object gram-
mars (Franzosi 2004). Or, researchers might use a tagger to further
preprocess texts (say, to identify the part of speech for each word) for later
analysis, or use tagging to extract useful variables (e.g., named people or
organizations). The goal, then, is to "label" words (or other sub-document
units) as being of different linguistic types or meaningful categories
using rule- and dictionary-based methods. In the rule-based approach,
semantic and syntactic features inform how a target unit is tagged. In the
dictionary-based approach, units are matched (either literal characters or
regex patterns) to a *key*, and given the associated *value*.

DICTIONARY TAGGING

We begin with a straightforward (computationally, at least) example:
tagging the "gender" of pronouns, titles, and names. This method relies
on dictionaries, a data structure with a **key** (here, a unique given name,
title, or pronoun) and a **value** (here, the gender category associated with
that name, title, or pronoun). Let's create a simple pronoun tagger by
building a dictionary (see output in the margin).

THIS SECTION NEEDS:

- tidytext
- tidyverse
- text2map
- gender
- genderdata
- stringi

```
# basic gender -tagging dictionary
fem_pronouns <- c("she", "her", "hers")
mas_pronouns <- c("he", "him", "his")

gender <- data.frame(
    word = c(fem_pronouns, mas_pronouns),
    gender = c(rep("feminine", 3), rep("masculine", 3))
)
gender
```

Let's test this dictionary on a sample of 100 posts from the CMU
Political Blogs Corpus (Eisenstein and Xing 2010).

```
word    gender
she     feminine
her     feminine
hers    feminine
he      masculine
him     masculine
his     masculine
```

```
data("corpus_cmu_blogs100", package = "text2map.corpora")

# let's unnest by token and join our tagger by "word"
corpus_cmu_blogs100 |>
    unnest_tokens(word, text) |>
    left_join(gender, by = "word") |>
    count(gender)
```

We also have a slightly larger gender-tagger, the `tiny_gender_tagger()`
(in `text2map`), which uses the same dictionary-based method, but
includes more pronouns as well as titles (mother, father, mister, mrs, etc.).
Let's compare.

```
     gender      n
1   feminine    117
2  masculine    532
3      <NA>  46817
```

```
corpus_cmu_blogs100 |>
    unnest_tokens(word, text) |>
    left_join(tiny_gender_tagger(), by = "word") |>
    count(gender)
```

```
     gender      n
1   feminine    184
2  masculine    668
3      <NA>  46614
```

In addition to counting explicitly gendered pronouns and titles in texts, researchers often want to infer the gender of named individuals in texts or the authors of texts. For this, we can treat databases, like those from the US Social Security Administration, as dictionaries.

To see this in action, we'll use a dataset comprising the 2020 *Annual Review of Sociology*, which includes 70 authors. Each row in the dataset is one author; therefore, co-authors are associated with the same titles, abstracts, etc. First, we'll grab only the first name of each author. We'll use gsub() with a regex pattern to extract anything before the first space, and add the first name as a new column using mutate() . The package we'll use also requires lowercase names, so we'll use tolower() .

```
data("corpus_annual_review", package = "text2map.corpora")

df_ars <- corpus_annual_review |>
    mutate(fname = gsub("^(.*?)\\s.*", "\\1", authors),
           fname = tolower(fname))

unique(df_ars$fname)
```

```
 [1] "samuel"      "claude"      "nora"         "jennifer"  "achim"
 [6] "tom"         "danielle"    "christopher"  "fabian"    "paula"
[11] "noura"       "peter"       "michael"      "thomas"    "rachael"
[16] "cameron"     "edward"      "raina"        "matthew"   "adam"
[21] "geneviève"   "anna"        "dorothy"      "oliver"    "lauren"
[26] "nicole"      "shannon"     "nina"         "steven"    "juliet"
[31] "tod"         "cynthia"     "kimberly"     "santiago"  "john"
[36] "brooke"      "leonard"     "arvid"        "leslie"    "neal"
[41] "kenneth"     "todd"        "christine"    "stefanie"  "frédéric"
[46] "sorah"       "damon"       "eric"         "kumiko"    "jacqueline"
[51] "joshua"      "melinda"     "felix"        "stefan"    "rebecca"
[56] "abdoumaliq"  "kathleen"    "erin"         "alyssa"    "liang"
[61] "malcolm"     "liz"         "mariana"      "ethan"     "mary"
[66] "carlos"
```

There are 70 authors, but some share first names, resulting in 66 unique names. Next, let's load a package specifically for associating names with gender. This package also requires downloading additional datasets. But first, important words of caution from the package authors (Mullen 2021:2):

1. Your analysis and the way you report it should take into account the limitations of this method, which include its reliance on data created by the state and its inability to see beyond the state-imposed gender binary. At a minimum, be sure to read our article explaining the limitations of this method, as well as the review article that is critical of this sort of methodology, both cited below.

2. Do not use this package to study individuals: it is at most useful for studying populations in the aggregate.

3. Resort to this method only when the alternative is not a more nuanced and justifiable approach to studying gender, but where the alternative is not studying gender at all. For instance, for many historical sources this approach might be the only way to get a sense of the sex ratios in a population. But ask whether you really need to use this method, whether you are using it responsibly, or whether you could use a better approach instead.

This package relies on historical records to match names to gender (but often sex assigned at birth in state records). As the authors warn, since these databases typically record gender as binary, it overlooks much of the gender spectrum, including non-binary individuals. The authors provide several datasets of historical records to use as dictionaries.[4]

```
data("ssa_national", package = "genderdata")

# let's have a quick look
names <- c("irving", "myrna")
ssa_national |>
  filter(name %in% names) |>
  filter(year == 1915)
```

```
  name  year female male
irving  1915      5 1385
myrna   1915    128    0
```

Blevins and Mullen note that "[t]he algorithm calculates the proportion of male or female uses of a name in a given birth year or range of years. It thus can provide not only a prediction of the gender of a name, but also a measure of that prediction's accuracy" (Blevins and Mullen 2015). Thus "accuracy" is the extent a name is exclusively associated with "male" or "female" in a database.

The `name` column of the gender-tagging dataset is all lowercase, which is why we lowercased our first names (because this is the *key* in our dictionary). Although `gender()` allows us to restrict the datasets used and the years used, we'll skip that here. The function outputs a dataset with each first name and five other columns.

```
df_tagged <- unique(df_ars$fname) |> gender()

nrow(df_tagged)
```

Our new dataset only has 62 rows and therefore only contains 62 gender-tagged names. But, we have 66 unique names for our 70 authors! The discrepancy is because some authors' first names do not match any "key" in our gender tagging dataset. One reason relates to letters that are non-standard in English.[5] Let's transliterate these letters using `stri_trans_general()` and see if it improves.

```
df_tagged <- df_ars |>
    mutate(fname = stri_trans_general(
      fname, "Any-Latin; Latin-ASCII"
      ))

df_tagged <- unique(df_tagged$fname) |> gender()

nrow(df_tagged)
```

We now have 64 of 66. We'll either have to accept that some names have no matches, or hand-label these names. Let's "join" our two datasets by matching first names in both. Now, let's compare female to male authors (and be sure to include the names that were not tagged at all). We'll use a "waffle" plot, but first we'll generate our summary table.

```
df_ars <- left_join(df_ars, df_tagged, by = c("fname" = "name"))

df_ars <- df_ars |>
    count(gender) |>
    mutate(gender = replace_na(gender, "missing"))
```

[6] Code adapted from Parker (2011).

Now, we can create our waffle plot.[6] First, we create a grid of 7 rows by 10 columns, large enough to fit each data point (70 authors). Next, we apply the gender labels proportional to their relative cell counts. We're now ready to make the plot, which is shown in Figure 8.1.

```
waffle_grid <- expand.grid(y = 1:7, x = seq_len(sum(df_ars$n) / 7))
waffle_grid$cell <- rep(df_ars$gender, df_ars$n)

waffle_grid |>
  ggplot(aes(x = x, y = y, fill = cell)) +
  geom_tile(color = "white") +
  theme(axis.ticks = element_blank(), axis.line = element_blank(),
        axis.text = element_blank(), panel.grid = element_blank()) +
  labs(title = "Authors' Predicted Gender", x = NULL, y = NULL)
```

Authors' Predicted Gender

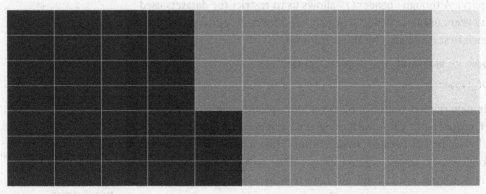

Figure 8.1: Authors in 2020
Annual Review of Sociology.

In the US, the membership of the American Sociological Association (2021) was 53.9% women, 44.2% men, and 1.9% trans or non-binary in 2020. But, there are fewer authors classified as "female" and "male" in this volume of the *Annual Review of Sociology*, indicating that male sociologists may be overrepresented in major publications. Drawing on lessons learned in **Corpus Building**, though, we must also consider that the *Annual Review of Sociology* is not a typical scholarly journal because authors are invited.

Now, imagine we have tens of thousands of articles with tens of thousands of authors. Keeping in mind potential measurement error, automated gender tagging may be the only feasible option. Even so, we'll want to keep Mullen et al.'s words of caution in mind and be sure to discuss these limitations when sharing our findings with our communities.

NAMED-ENTITY RECOGNITION

Sometimes we need to know who, or what, is being discussed across texts in a corpus. If we know a fair bit about our texts—or if we want mentions of specific entities—then perhaps we could build a custom dictionary consisting of entity names and use that to identify how frequently each text "name-drops" these entities. For example, how frequently do Republican presidents mention the Democratic Party in their State of the Union (SOTU) addresses (and vice versa)? We can just count the times the SOTUs mention these exact two-word phrases.

What if we know little about the people or organizations that texts in a corpus might be mentioning? Then we can use **named-entity recognition** (NER). NER taggers input text documents and return the "entities" found in those texts: for example, people's names, organizations, locations, and dates, to name a few. NER is useful for information extraction problems and also for helping construct dictionaries because it can be used to identify the people, places, things, etc., that are referenced most frequently in a corpus.

NER is increasingly used in the social sciences. We (Stoltz and Taylor 2017) used NER to identify protest events in newspaper data and run multilevel models with news stories nested within events. Mohr and colleagues (2013) used NER to locate the major geopolitical actors in US National Security Strategy documents. Van de Rijt and colleagues (2013) used NER in the Lydia text analysis system to model fame turnover in newspapers, and Shor and colleagues (2015) used the same system to study the gender gap in media coverage over time.[7]

THIS SECTION NEEDS:

- tidyverse
- entity
- tidytext

[7] For more examples of NER applications in social science, see Shor and colleagues (2014), and Traag and colleagues (2015). For a discussion of using NER as a preprocessing strategy for further analysis, see D'Orazio and colleagues (2014:230–231).

In what follows, we'll first address—in a general sense—how NER works. We'll then provide a demonstration of NER tagging in R .

How Named-Entity Recognition Works

Consider the following text (adapted from Mack 2019). NER taggers that are optimized correctly should return these "named entities" and the entity tags to which they belong, like so:

> Star Trek: Picard, which debuted in **January 2020** [Date/Time] on **CBS** [Organization] All Access, saw **Patrick Stewart** [Person] reprise his role as the noble leader more than 20 years after Star Trek: Next Generation ended. The trailer for the new show showed Picard retired at a vineyard on **Earth** [Location], but feeling out of place and longing for space travel.

In this example, there are four entity taggers: ones that identify person names, organization names, dates/times, and locations, respectively. These are common entity tags, but this varies by the specific NER tagger used. entity also has taggers for money and percentages. The Stanford NLP Group's CoreNLP library comes with more, including nationality, religion, and even cause of death (Manning et al. 2014).

How NER algorithms "learn" to identify entity tags varies. They all rely on **training data**. These training data are sentences that have already been tagged by a human (or set of humans). For example, training data for a "person name" tagger would look like this:[8]

> The CEO of Apple, <START:person> Tim Cook <END>, unveiled the new iPhone . Mr . <START:person> Cook <END> was joined on the stage by Chief Operating Officer , <START:person> Jeff Williams <END> .

The training file would need to contain at least 15,000 line-separated annotated sentences (Apache 2020).

So, the training documents are parsed by sentence, separated by line breaks, and the names are hand-labeled. A model then iterates through pre-specified context variables—what is called a "feature set" (Apache 2020).[9] Some context variables might include: Is the word capitalized? Does the word follow a prefix such as "Mr.", "Mrs.", or "Dr."?

The algorithm uses co-occurrences between the tagged words and the context variables to develop a weight for each variable indicating the strength of the association between that variable and a class—here, either "is a person" or "is not a person."[10] The output of any NER model are weights—that is, the "importance"—for each of the context variables.

[8] The training data format must match the software being used. For the OpenNLP library, there must be one annotated sentence per line (Apache 2020).

[9] NER models typically have pre-specified context variables, but we can provide custom feature sets.

[10] The OpenNLP NER tool uses generalized iterative scaling for this.

The trained NER model can then be used to predict the entity classes in new, unannotated texts.[11] The NER model we'll use is **pretrained**. So, no annotated training data are necessary. The `OpenNLP` NER model appears to have been[12] trained on 318 *Wall Street Journal* articles forming the training set for a series of NLP evaluation tasks at the Sixth Message Understanding Conference (MUC-6) (Nouvel et al. 2016:61).

Prior work finds that the performance of pretrained NER models will vary by corpus but tends to accurately classify between 75–95% of entities. After tagging, it is always a good idea to look for false positives.

Named Entities in R

The package we'll use for named entity recognition is `entity` .[13] It is an `R` "wrapper" for the Java-based OpenNLP library maintained by the Apache Software Foundation.[14]

Let's use the *Star Trek: Picard* paragraph as a quick illustration (output in the margin):

```
para <- "Star Trek: Picard, which debuted in January 2020 on CBS All
    Access, saw Patrick Stewart reprise his role as the noble leader
    more than  20 years after Star Trek: Next Generation ended. The
    trailer for the new show showed Picard retired at a vineyard on
    Earth, but feeling out of place and longing for space travel."

person_entity(para)
organization_entity(para)
location_entity(para)
date_entity(para)
```

All entities were identified and correctly tagged.

Let's work through a larger example with the CMU Political Blogs Corpus (Eisenstein and Xing 2010). These blog posts from six political blogs were collected in 2008. Three of the sources are liberal-oriented (*Digby, ThinkProgress,* and *Talking Points Memo*) and the other three are conservative-oriented outlets (*American Thinker, Hot Air,* and Michelle Malkin's blog).

We'll use a random sample of 100 blog posts. When we read it into `R` , we'll also assign it to an object with a shorter name to save some space, but this is not necessary. Let's look at a portion of one of the shorter posts, which comes from *Hot Air*:[15]

```
data("corpus_cmu_blogs100", package = "text2map.corpora")
blogs <- corpus_cmu_blogs100 # rename it so it's tidier

blogs$text[[46]]
```

```
[1] "John Edwards got shunned by Democrats at this
convention for his extramarital affair with Rielle
```

[11] This is done with maximum entropy ("maxent") modeling in the case of `OpenNLP` .

[12] The `OpenNLP` training data was difficult to ascertain. We sleuthed the MUC-6 data from a 2010 discussion post by Joern Kottmann on the OpenNLP SourceForge repository.

[13] If `entity` won't download from CRAN, try installing from the maintainer's GitHub: `trinker/entity` .

[14] We also need Java installed on our machine.

```
[1] "Patrick Stewart"
[1] "CBS"
[1] "Earth"
[1] "January 2020"
```

[15] We could not track down the original author of this blog post.

Hunter and the shady financial connections between
himself, Hunter, and Andrew Young...

When we use `person_entity()` on the full blog post, it returns the
following:

```
person_entity(blogs$text[[46]])
```

```
[[1]]
[1] "John Edwards"   "Hunter"
[3] "Andrew Young"   "Fred Baron"
[5] "Hunter"         "Baron"
[7] "John Edwards"   "Chuck Schumer"
```

Let's tag multiple documents at once. We'll first subset the blogs by
political lean—"Liberal" versus "Conservative"—and also only extract the
"text" column.

```
text_lib <- blogs |>
    filter(rating == "Liberal") |>
    select(text)

text_con <- blogs |>
    filter(rating == "Conservative") |>
    select(text)
```

We'll then apply the `person_entity` tagger separately to these two
vectors of texts.

```
ppl_lib <- person_entity(text_lib)
ppl_con <- person_entity(text_con)
```

Below, we'll tally the times we see each unique name using `table()`.
We then limit the dataframe to only names occurring at least twice.
Finally, we'll order the `entity` variable by the number of times it
occurs.

```
ppl_lib <- table(ppl_lib, dnn = "entity") |>
        data.frame() |>
        mutate(lean = "Liberal")

ppl_con <- table(ppl_con, dnn = "entity") |>
        data.frame() |>
        mutate(lean = "Conservative")

df_ppl <- rbind(ppl_lib, ppl_con)

df_ppl <- df_ppl |>
    filter(Freq >= 3) |>
    mutate(entity = reorder_within(entity, by = Freq, within = lean))
```

And, now we can make bar plots showing the people named at least
three times across the liberal and conservative blogs (Figure 8.2).

```
df_ppl |>
    ggplot(aes(x = entity, y = Freq, fill = lean)) +
    geom_col() +
    labs(x = "People", y = "Count") +
    facet_wrap(~lean, scales = "free_y") +
```

```
coord_flip() +
scale_x_reordered()
```

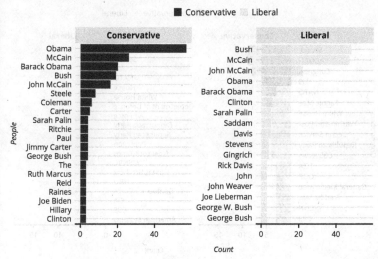

Figure 8.2: People Mentioned in Blogs by Political Lean.

And what about organizations? Re-use the two vectors of texts from conservative and liberal blogs, respectively. Apply the organization tagger to each.

```
org_lib <- organization_entity(text_lib)
org_con <- organization_entity(text_con)
```

We'll also prepare the plotting dataframes like we did before, and only include named organizations that occur at least three times. The plots present the organizations named at least three times across the liberal and conservative blogs (Figure 8.3).

```
org_lib <- table(org_lib, dnn = "entity") |>
        data.frame() |>
        mutate(lean = "Liberal")

org_con <- table(org_con, dnn = "entity") |>
        data.frame() |>
        mutate(lean = "Conservative")

df_org <- rbind(org_lib, org_con)

df_org <- df_org |>
    filter(Freq >= 3) |>
    mutate(entity = reorder_within(entity, by = Freq,
                            within = lean,
    ))

df_org |>
    ggplot(aes(x = entity, y = Freq, fill = lean)) +
    geom_col() +
    labs(x = "Organizations", y = "Count") +
    facet_wrap(~lean, scales = "free_y") +
```

```
coord_flip() +
scale_x_reordered()
```

Figure 8.3: Organizations Mentioned in Blogs by Political Lean.

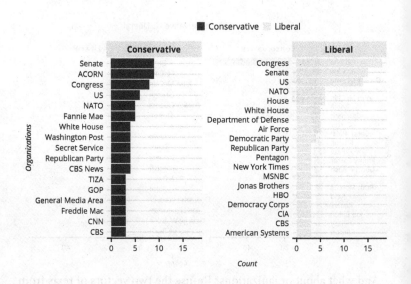

Count

[16] Also, as discussed previously, some tokenizing techniques *require* part-of-speech tagging (Attia 2007; Farghaly and Shaalan 2009).

PART-OF-SPEECH AND DEPENDENCY PARSING

Many methods rely on "bags-of-words" representations of documents (i.e., a DTM). An assumption behind these sorts of models is that outside of some measure of word co-occurrence, the *order* of words within a document does not matter. Similarly, in "bags-of-words" approaches, the *syntactical structure* (i.e., grammar) of the documents does not matter.

Researchers may, however, need to know something about grammar—for instance, the **parts of speech** to which the words in the documents belong.[16] Klebanov and colleagues (2008), for example, coded the verbs, nouns, adjectives, adverbs, and proper names in their analysis of Margaret Thatcher's rhetorical style using her 1977 speech at the Conservative Party Conference. Graesser and colleagues (2006) used parts of speech to identify complex syntax in survey questions. Diemeirer and colleagues (2012:44) used parts of speech in US congressional speeches to disambiguate between word senses and how they predict senators' ideological positioning (where, e.g., *taxing* as a verb was predictive of conservative speech, but not *tax* as a noun). In addition to using parts of speech, these studies share another thing in common: they each used an automated part-of-speech tagger to do so. **Part-of-speech (POS)**

tagging classifies each word in a document by its predicted part of speech: for instance, whether a word is a noun, verb, adverb, preposition, and the like.

Again, this could be accomplished with a dictionary—for example, whenever there is a /the/ we tag it with the POS "article." We could also add a rule involving the context: for example, whatever word follows /the/ is a "noun." Finally, we can train a probabilistic model on already tagged text. Often, POS tagging uses a combination of the above, with researchers using a pretrained model and improving it with rules and dictionaries.

How POS Tagging Works

Models, rules, and dictionaries for POS tagging vary by how fine-grained the grammatical classes are. Stanford NLP Group's POS tagger, for example, identifies nine different classes: adjectives, adverbs, conjunctions, determiners, nouns, numbers, prepositions, pronouns, and verbs. In comparison, models trained on the Penn Treebank[17] annotation scheme comprise 48 tags, detailed in Table 8.1 (adapted from Taylor et al. 2003:8).

Consider the *Star Trek* example paragraph again. Read it to get a quick sense of the different *word senses*: in the first sentence, "*Stark Trek: Picard*" is a noun, "debuted" is a verb, "in" is a preposition, and "2020" is a number.[18]

The package we use in the demonstration below, `tagger` —an R wrapper for the Java-based `OpenNLP` library like `entity` —is trained to tag English parts of speech using the Penn Treebank (Taylor et al. 2003).[19] POS tags are standard annotations in treebanks.

Like its NER counterpart, the `OpenNLP` POS tagger uses a maxent model to predict the appropriate Penn Treebank tag. Researchers may supply their own annotated training data, but we'll rely on the pretrained `OpenNLP` POS model below.

Part-of-Speech Tagging in R

To show how we can get the counts of parts-of-speech, we'll use `tagger` .[20] Consider the *Star Trek: Picard* paragraph again. Let's pass that along to `tag_pos()` :

```
para <- "Star Trek: Picard, which debuted in January 2020 on CBS All
    Access, saw Patrick Stewart reprise his role as the noble leader
    more than  20 years after Star Trek: Next Generation ended. The
    trailer for the new show showed Picard retired at a vineyard on
    Earth, but feeling out of place and longing for space travel."
```

tag_pos(para)

[17] A **treebank** is a corpus where the words have been *annotated* to capture different linguistic elements.

[18] POS tagging is a form of word sense "disambiguation."

[19] The Penn Treebank is a corpus of 7 million POS-annotated words from "IBM computer manuals, nursing notes, *Wall Street Journal* articles, and transcribed telephone conversations, among others" (Taylor et al. 2003:5)

[20] As with `entity` , we may need to install this from GitHub: `trinker/tagger` . We must also install `termco` and `coreNLPsetup` from `trinker/` .

Table 8.1: Penn Treebank Part-of-Speech Tags

Tags	Description	Tags	Description
CC	Coordinating conj.	TO	Infinitival to
CD	Cardinal number	UH	Interjection
DT	Determiner	VB	Verb, base form
EX	Existential there	VBD	Verb, past tense
FW	Foreign word	VBG	Verb, gerund/present pple
IN	Preposition	VBN	Verb, past participle
JJ	Adjective	VBP	Verb, non-3rd ps. sg. present
JJR	Adjective, comparative	VBZ	Verb, 3rd ps. sg. present
JJS	Adjective, superlative	WDT	Wh-determiner
LS	List item marker	WP	Wh-pronoun
MD	Modal	WP$	Possessive wh-pronoun
NN	Noun, singular or mass	WRB	Wh-adverb
NNS	Noun, plural	#	Pound sign
NNP	Proper noun, singular	$	Dollar sign
NNPS	Proper noun, plural	.	Sentence-final punctuation
PDT	Predeterminer	,	Comma
POS	Possessive ending	:	Colon, semi-colon
PRP	Personal pronoun	(	Left bracket character
PP$	Possessive pronoun	)	Right bracket character
RB	Adverb	"	Straight double quote
RBR	Adverb, comparative	'	Left open single quote
RBS	Adverb, superlative	"	Left open double quote
RP	Particle	'	Right close single quote
SYM	Symbol	"	Right close double quote

```
"Star/NNP Trek/NNP :/: Picard/NNP ,/, which/WDT
debuted/VBD in/IN January/NNP 2020/CD on/IN
CBS/NNP All/DT Access/NNP ,/, saw/VBD Patrick/NNP
Stewart/NNP reprise/NN his/PRP$ role/NN as/IN
the/DT noble/JJ leader/NN more/JJR than/IN 20/CD
years/NNS after/IN Star/NNP Trek/NNP..."
```

Look at the first sentence. How well did the tagger do? Referring to the Penn Treebank tag table above, "Star," "Trek," "Picard," "CBS," "Access," "Patrick," "Stewart," "Next," and "Generation" were each labeled proper singular nouns. These all make sense as proper singular nouns—defined as "the name[s] of a particular person, place, or object that . . . [are] spelled with a capital letter" (Mack 2019)—within the grammatical structure of the sentence. *Star Trek: Picard* is the name of the show, January is a month, *CBS All Access* is the name of a streaming platform,[21] Patrick Stewart is the actor who plays Picard, and *Star Trek: Next Generation* is the name of an earlier TV show.

21 Though "All" here was labeled a determiner, since it is being read as indicating the amount of "access" being given rather than as part of a formal name.

Let's return to our random sample of 100 blog posts from the CMU Political Blogs Corpus. We'll tag the whole sample, once again separating the data by political ideology:

```
data("corpus_cmu_blogs100", package = "text2map.corpora")
blogs <- corpus_cmu_blogs100 # rename so it's tidier

text_lib <- blogs |> filter(rating == "Liberal")
text_con <- blogs |> filter(rating == "Conservative")

pos_lib <- tag_pos(text_lib$text)
pos_con <- tag_pos(text_con$text)
```

The output is a nested list. We'll need to wrangle these into dataframes by first counting each unique tag with table() .

```
df_lib <- names(pos_lib[[1]]) |>
    table(dnn = "pos") |>
    data.frame() |>
    mutate(lean = "Liberal")

df_con <- names(pos_con[[1]]) |>
    table(dnn = "pos") |>
    data.frame() |>
    mutate(lean = "Conservative")

df_pos <- rbind(df_lib, df_con)

df_pos <- df_pos |>
  filter(Freq >= 2) |>
  mutate(pos = reorder_within(pos, by = Freq, within = lean))
```

And now we plot (see Figure 8.4).

```
df_pos |>
    ggplot(aes(x = pos, y = Freq, fill = lean)) +
    geom_col() +
    labs(x = "Blog Parts of Speech",
         y = "Proportion of Total Words") +
    facet_wrap(~lean, scales = "free_y") +
    coord_flip() +
    scale_x_reordered()
```

Outside of linguistics, these fine-grained grammatical mappings may not be useful—for example, the difference between a superlative and a comparative adjective. We can simplify the tagset with two functions: as_universal() and as_basic() . as_universal() transforms the tags into the "universal" tagset—that is, more or less universal across many languages (Petrov et al. 2011). This tagset reduces the 48 Penn Treebank tags[22] to 12 tags: nouns, verbs, adjectives, adverbs, pronouns, determiners/articles, prepositions/postpositions, numbers, conjunctions, particles, "." for all punctuation, and "X" for unidentified word senses (Petrov et al. 2011:2). The as_basic returns an even simpler tagset, consisting of nouns, verbs, adjectives, adverbs, prepositions,

[22] tagger appears to use 46 Penn Treebank tags. penn_tags() does not include the pound sign (#), the opening single quotation mark ('), or the closing single quotation mark ('). However, the pound sign is still successfully tagged using the package; the single quotation marks are tagged with their double quotation mark counterparts (" and ").

interjections, articles, conjunctions, and pronouns (with "." and "X" serving the same purpose as in the universal tagset).

Figure 8.4: Penn Part of Speech Tagging.

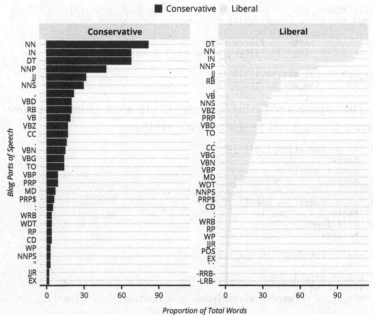

Proportion of Total Words

We'll focus here on the most basic tagset.

```
pos_lib <- pos_lib |> as_basic()
pos_con <- pos_con |> as_basic()
```

Let's look at snippets from conservative blog posts to get an idea of what this new tagset looks like. We can do this by highlighting and running the name of the object, `pos_con`.

```
pos_con
```

1. In/preposition the/article "forgotten/adjective war/noun "/. that/pronoun is/verb ...
2. A/article poll/noun of/preposition 12,000/adjective citizens/noun in/preposition ...

.
.
.

1. Oprah/noun Winfrey/noun and/conjunction her/pronoun TV/noun staff/noun are/verb ...
2. Intrepid/noun bloggers/noun at/preposition Sweetness/noun &/conjunction ...
3. It/pronoun appears/verb Dan/noun Rather/noun was/verb unable/adjective ...
4. The/article Hispanic/noun National/noun Bar/noun Association/noun has/verb ...

As we can see, all nouns are tagged as just that: nouns. For example, there is now no distinction between proper nouns

(Oprah/noun Winfrey/noun and Hispanic/noun National/noun/ Bar/noun Association/noun) and common nouns (citizens/noun and group/noun).[23]

Perhaps researchers want to see if the grammatical structures differed between the three liberal blogs in the sample (we'll select columns for presentation purposes). We'll use `count_tags ()` to tally tags within each group and `CrossTable()` to cross-tabulate blog source and part of speech.

```
df_tag_lib <- count_tags(pos_lib, text_lib$blog) |>
              as.data.frame()
```

We'll subset the output of `count_tags` to include only tags (adjectives, adverbs, nouns, and verbs). We'll also assign the blog's names to the `rownames` of our dataframe (this is necessary because all the cells of a matrix must be, in essence, the *same* variable, and not a mix of characters and counts like a dataframe). Finally, we'll convert our object into a `matrix` so it can be used by `CrossTable()` .

```
df_tag_lib |>
    select(blog, adjective, adverb, noun, verb) |>
    column_to_rownames(var = "blog") |>
    as.matrix() |>
    CrossTable(
        prop.c = FALSE,
        prop.chisq = FALSE,
        prop.t = FALSE
    )
```

```
Cell Contents
|-------------------------|
|                       N |
|             N / Row Total |
|-------------------------|

Total Observations in Table:  16065
```

	adjective	adverb	noun	verb	Row Total
db	2008	885	4486	2749	10128
	0.198	0.087	0.443	0.271	0.630
tpm	279	133	774	386	1572
	0.177	0.085	0.492	0.246	0.098
tp	670	318	2168	1209	4365
	0.153	0.073	0.497	0.277	0.272
Column Total	2957	1336	7428	4344	16065

This cross-tabulation shows the frequency distribution of (predicted) adjectives, adverbs, nouns, and verbs across *Digby*, *ThinkProgress*, and

[23] No tagger—nor any method—is perfect! Look at document #62. The sentence starts with "Intrepid bloggers." Clearly, "intrepid" is an adjective, as it describes the subject of the sentences: bloggers. However, the tagger coded this word as a noun—perhaps, in part, because it was capitalized.

Talking Points Memo. The table also includes the row percentages—that is, the percent of each blog's total words tagged by part of speech. Unsurprisingly, we see each of the blogs' writers appear to follow the same grammatical structure: mostly nouns, followed by verbs, then adjectives, and adverbs.[24]

We can also look at the *specific* nouns, verbs, etc., that are used the most frequently. What are the top nouns used in conservative blogs? Below we'll take posts with the basic "tagset" and turn them into a series of character vectors per blog post. We'll `unlist()` this into a single, long, character vector. Next we'll do a tiny bit of wrangling, by removing "curly quotes" that have somehow made their way into the tagged nouns. Then we'll arrange the nouns by frequency in descending order and retain the top 10.

```
noun_lib <- pos_lib |>
  select_tags("noun") |>
  unlist()

noun_lib <- table(noun_lib, dnn = "noun") |>
  data.frame() |>
  filter(!grepl("[[:punct:]]", noun)) |>
  mutate(lean = "Liberal") |>
  slice_max(Freq, n = 10)


noun_con <- pos_con |>
  select_tags("noun") |>
  unlist()

noun_con <- table(noun_con, dnn = "noun") |>
  data.frame() |>
  filter(!grepl("[[:punct:]]", noun)) |>
  mutate(lean = "Conservative") |>
  slice_max(Freq, n = 10)
```

What were the top nouns for the liberal and conservative blogs?

```
cbind(noun_lib, noun_con)
```

	noun	Freq	lean	noun	Freq	lean
1	McCain	126	Liberal	Obama	157	Conservative
2	Obama	61	Liberal	McCain	85	Conservative
3	Bush	55	Liberal	campaign	57	Conservative
4	people	51	Liberal	people	36	Conservative
5	Iraq	48	Liberal	Barack	35	Conservative
6	John	38	Liberal	government	31	Conservative
7	time	33	Liberal	media	30	Conservative
8	Americans	29	Liberal	time	29	Conservative
9	years	28	Liberal	John	28	Conservative
10	war	27	Liberal	voters	27	Conservative

---

[24] This is a feature of the English language, since each "grammatically correct" sentence has a subject and a predicate. Adjectives and adverbs, however, are not necessary for a "standard" sentence.

As forecasted by the NER tagging of these blog posts in the previous section, the most common noun in the liberal blog posts is the Republican presidential candidate "McCain." In contrast, the most common noun in conservative blog posts is the Democratic presidential candidate "Obama."

Dependency Parsing

We can take tagging further by retaining the *relations* between different words. This is called **dependency parsing**. Let's consider a short example using `spacyr` .[25] Then, as with `udpipe` , we'll need to select an English-specific language model. The `en_core_web_sm` is a lightweight model pretrained on blogs, news articles, and social media comments. As this uses the Python package `spacy` , we'll need to download the language model to our conda environment.[26] We'll also use this environment to "initialize" the model, which makes it available to `R` functions.

[25] `udpipe` also provides dependency parsing functions.

[26] See **Computing Basics**.

```
spacy_download_langmodel("en_core_web_sm", envname = "myenv")

spacy_initialize(model = "en_core_web_sm", condaenv = "myenv")
```

Dependency parsing builds on POS tagging by tracking how the different entities in the text interact. For example, take the sentence "Elmo and Bert scare the pigeons." Here, there are three main entities and an action. Basic co-occurrence methods would note Elmo, Bert, and pigeon *co-occur* with "scare," but not who is scared by whom. Dependency parsing keeps track of the "head token" of each word. For instance, the head token of "the" is "pigeon," but the head token of "pigeon" is "Elmo."

```
text <- "Elmo and Bert scare the pigeons"
spacy_parse(text, dependency = TRUE) |>
    select(token_id, token, pos, head_token_id, dep_rel)
```

```
  token_id   token   pos head_token_id dep_rel
1        1    Elmo   ADJ             4   nsubj
2        2     and CCONJ             1      cc
3        3    Bert PROPN             1    conj
4        4   scare  VERB             4    ROOT
5        5     the   DET             6     det
6        6 pigeons  NOUN             4    dobj
```

We can visualize the dependency between words using a directed graph like Figure 8.5.

Figure 8.5: Dependency Parsing Graph.

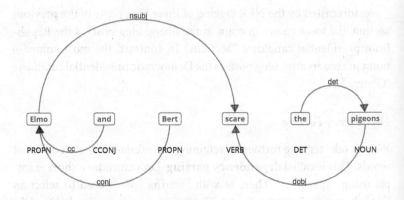

Part-of-Speech Tagging for French

`tagger` uses tools trained entirely on English-language corpora. `udpipe`
offers a suite of tokenizing, parsing, and tagging tools that currently
works with 65 languages, trained on treebanks from the Universal Dependencies project (McDonald 2013).[27]

[27] universaldependencies.org/

As an example, let's return to the Europarl Corpus from a previous
chapter, which, as a refresher, contains 5,000 sentences in French and
the same 5,000 sentences in English from the European Parliament
Proceedings (1996–2011).

First, we need to download language-specific models. Many languages
have several language models to choose from with `udpipe`. For French,
we'll use the treebank based on the UD French GSD corpus (Guillaume
et al. 2019), the original corpus for the French Universal Dependencies
project, with 400,000 tokens from newspaper articles, Wikipedia articles,
blogs and consumer reviews. For English, we'll use the treebank based on
the GUM Corpus (Zeldes 2017), with Web-based texts expanded over the
years to include 113,385 tokens.

```
# download language models, this may take a couple minutes
ud_fr <- udpipe_download_model(language = "french-gsd")
ud_en <- udpipe_download_model(language = "english-gum")
ud_fr <- udpipe_load_model(file = ud_fr$file_model)
ud_en <- udpipe_load_model(file = ud_en$file_model)
```

Next, use these models to annotate the lines of text. Be sure to limit the
text by the `language` column. The output is large because each word in
each line has its own POS tag.

```
data("corpus_europarl_subset", package = "text2map.corpora")
```

Annotate only French lines:

```
text_fr <- corpus_europarl_subset |>
    filter(language == "French")

pos_fr <- udpipe_annotate(
    x = text_fr$text,
    tagger = "default",
    parser = "none",
    object = ud_fr
)
```

Annotate only English lines:

```
text_en <- corpus_europarl_subset |>
    filter(language == "English")

pos_en <- udpipe_annotate(
    x = text_en$text,
    tagger = "default",
    parser = "none",
    object = ud_en
)
```

Let's use `table()` to count each unique POS and then wrangle our variables into a dataframe. Next, use `left_join()` to join the two dataframes side-by-side.

```
df_fr <- as.data.frame(pos_fr)

df_fr <- table(df_fr$upos) |>
    as.data.frame() |>
    rename(pos = Var1, fr_freq = Freq)

df_en <- as.data.frame(pos_en)

df_en <- table(df_en$upos) |>
    as.data.frame() |>
    rename(pos = Var1, en_freq = Freq)

df_pos <- left_join(df_fr, df_en, by = "pos")
```

Finally, let's plot the counts of each POS tag to see if there are any noticeable differences between the two languages (see Figure 8.6). Remember these are based on line-by-line translations, and while we see obvious similarities (e.g., nouns are the most common for both languages), there are clear differences in the distribution of parts-of-speech (e.g., particles are more common in English).

```
df_pos |>
    mutate(pos = reorder(pos, en_freq)) |>
    ggplot() +
    geom_segment(aes(x = pos, xend = pos,
                     y = en_freq, yend = fr_freq)) +
    geom_point(aes(x = pos, y = en_freq, color = "English"), size=3) +
    geom_point(aes(x = pos, y = fr_freq, color = "French"), size=3) +
    coord_flip() +
    labs(x = NULL, y = "POS Frequencies, French and English")
```

Figure 8.6: Comparing French and English POS Tags.

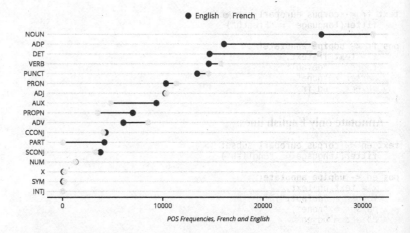

POS Frequencies, French and English

Broadly, we discussed ways of tagging sub-document units using rules, dictionaries, and pretrained language models. We also explored several pretrained language models, such as those provided by Stanford's OpenNLP, udpipe 's annotation models for English and French, and spacy 's language models. Regardless of what is tagged—gender, parts of speech, named-entities—these models rely on hand-annotated corpora to learn features that best predict those tags. As such, we're relying on annotators' interpretations. We can also train our own models by annotating tokens in our own corpora.[28] When doing so, we recommend building on the best practices in corpus linguistics (e.g., McEnery and Hardie 2011, Kennedy 2014).

[28] For technical details, consult the documentation for udpipe_train .

Part V

The Document and Beyond

9
Core Deductive

TELESCOPES amplify the eye, allowing us to examine the entrails of celestial bodies or chart the cosmic neighborhood of the Milky Way. In the previous chapters, we took a microscope to our texts, altering and classifying sub-document units. In the following chapters, we'll take a telescopic view, classifying documents and measuring meaning over our corpora.

Deductive approaches begin with a targeted meaning. For instance, perhaps we are interested in "whether and when the new issue of rising economic inequality was covered by the media" (Nelson et al. 2021:206) or the extent "popular music addresses inequality" (Carbone and Mijs 2022:2). With such research aims, we begin with a concept in mind, here inequality, and then use tools to find this concept.

Targeted meanings rely on classification schemes that emerge from iteratively (and inductively) close-reading a sample of our corpus (Nelson 2020; Small 2009). Schemes may draw on other metadata—for example, how a website or database classifies a document, or author-level variables like social identity or affiliation. We often build on prior work, where schemes are adopted and fine-tuned. Developing a classification scheme is an interpretive process that we won't rehash here.[1] What is important is the *structure* of the classification scheme.

First, we can measure if documents either *are* or *are not* associated with a label **discretely**. We can also measure whether a document is *more or less* associated with each label **gradationally**. This may be probabilistic or rank order.[2]

The second concerns the extent the labels cover the space of possible meanings. Labels are **exhaustive** if each document could be, in theory, placed into one category at a consistent level of generality.[3] Labels are **exclusive** such that a document is only in a *single* category. This matters because we need to know how necessary it is to place *every* document into a category.

Once we have a classification scheme, how do we assign these labels to the appropriate documents? In traditional qualitative content analysis, we'd systematically read the texts, assigning labels as we go. With

[1] There are many excellent guides—for example, Weber (1990:15–40) and Krippendorf (Krippendorff 2018: 132–43).

[2] We sometimes use continuous classifications to assign discrete memberships—for example, using the label with the highest probability.

[3] For example, "sociology" and "economics" are the same level, but not "social science" which encompasses the latter two.

Mapping Texts: Computational Text Analysis for the Social Sciences. Dustin S. Stoltz and Marshall A. Taylor, Oxford University Press. © Oxford University Press 2024. DOI: 10.1093/oso/9780197756874.003.0009

the increasing availability of large amounts of texts, scholars quickly encounter the *problem of excess* (Chakrabarti and Frye 2017). This becomes untenable with tens of thousands or millions of documents. Furthermore, we encounter conceptual *drift* (Chakrabarti and Frye 2017). As we read more documents, we may alter our understanding of a concept. As a result, our labeling of documents read earlier misaligns with our labeling of documents read later. Re-reading and re-labeling are one solution to this problem. Multiple re-readings, however, become impractical with thousands or millions of documents. This is where automated techniques can augment interpretive coding.

There are two automated approaches we'll discuss here: (1) discrete indicators and (2) weighted indicators. Both rely on dictionary and rule-based procedures to tag or weight a given document by its engagement with a concept or entity of interest.[4]

[4] Despite differences, both typically include selecting a vocabulary.

Most researchers use keywords with search engines to collect primary documents and scholarly literature. Once collected, we use the "find" function to search for keywords in texts. Both tasks use vocabulary and rule-based string matching. If we are interested in, say, "political attitudes of working-class youth in Seattle," we'd collect recent scholarly articles discussing "political attitudes and class," or "political attitudes of youth" or "political attitudes and Seattle," etc. We may actively discard articles without such keywords or allow the databases' search engine to omit these. Even if somewhat unsystematic, these are deductive procedures.

Content analysts use several terms to denote a unit of meaning in text. These include themes, thematic units, categories, codes, labels, expressions, and more. Researchers may arrange these into a hierarchical classification scheme with, for example, higher-order categories encompassing lower-order themes. We'll simplify things by using concepts or categories for deductive approaches and topics or themes for inductive approaches.[5] We do not wish to overlook the potential theoretical use of keeping these many terms distinct; however, the strategy used to measure a unit of meaning often remains the same: *Are certain terms, phrases, or relations denoting a given meaning present and, if so, to what extent?*

[5] We reserve "entity" for more concrete referents, like people or organizations as in Named-Entity Recognition.

THIS SECTION NEEDS:

- `tidyverse`
- `quanteda`
- `Matrix`
- `irr`

DISCRETE INDICATORS

A basic discrete indicator is noting the *absence* or *presence* of certain concepts or entities in texts. For example, do articles in sociology journals mention "nuance" or not (Healy 2017:120). We call this "binary" as we can use a zero for absent or a one for present (or Boolean and use

TRUE or FALSE). This is a species of categorical measure. A term may be associated with a label, and by using that term, a document is tagged with that label.[6]

Recall a dictionary is a data structure comprising a key and a value. The key is any unique character string (or regular expression). In the simplest case, the value is a simple tag of presence (and by omission, absence). Therefore, the binary indicator is likely the most pervasive technique in computer-assisted text analysis.

Consider Griswold's "The Fabrication of Meaning." The evidence Griswold uses to support the claim that multivocal cultural objects garner more cultural power is, in part, whether reviews of the Barbadian novelist George Lamming's books were "positive" or not and referred to the book as depicting "ambiguity" or not. In Table 9.1 below (reproduced from Griswold (1987:1109), we compare the proportion of book reviews engaging a unit of meaning by a single covariate: the novel a review is targeting.

Table 9.1: Ambiguity and Evaluation by Novel

Novel	Mention Ambiguity	Favorable
In the Castle of My Skin	50%	67%
The Emigrants	31%	19%
Of Age and Innocence	42%	75%
Season of Adventure	33%	25%
Water with Berries	63%	50%
Natives of My Person	40%	47%

Griswold tagged each review by hand. Correll and colleagues (2020:1031–2), similarly hand-label over two hundred employee performance evaluations using a team of three researchers (see also Hallett et al. 2019:552).

This kind of hand-tagging of documents remains the "gold standard" against which automated indicators are measured.[7]

How might one expand this from tens or hundreds of documents to thousands or more? One strategy is to use automated methods to identify relevant subsets before hand-labeling. For instance, DeSoucey and Waggoner (2022:59) collected over two thousand "documents and comments submitted on Regulations.gov... in response to... 'Enhancing Airline Passenger Protections'" and subset based on "mentions of

[6] Discrete indicators can involve several categories; thus, binary indicators are categorical, but not all categorical indicators are binary.

[7] For varying views on this subject, see Biernacki (Biernacki 2012, 2014, 2015), and the various responses (and responses to the responses) (Lee and Martin 2014, 2015; Spillman 2014, 2015; Reed 2015), and an edited volume on the matter (Reed and Alexander 2015).

[8] The asterisk will match zero or more of the preceding type in regex—for example, returning plurals.

[9] Reliability is a technical term referring to the consistency of a given measure. Imagine asking students of a high school shop class to use a tape measure to cut a foot of lumber. We'd expect some variation in measurements. If that variation is low, we have high reliability. If instead of a tape measure, we gave each student a foot of yarn to use, we'd expect lower reliability.

Krippendorff's alpha

Subjects = 5
  Raters = 3
  alpha = 0.741

[10] For example, if coders are tagging documents for mentions of "bats," they all need to know whether this means baseball gear or the adorable flying mammal.

peanuts and food allergy" by matching the terms 'peanut,' 'peanut allergy,' 'allerg,' 'nut*,' and 'food allergy' (2022:73).[8]

Another strategy is to rely on more people. The corpus is typically divided among the raters into partially overlapping sections. We can then calculate *inter-rater reliability* on any documents coded by two or more people. While there are many inter-rater reliability measures, we'll use Krippendorf's α (alpha): one minus the observed disagreement divided by the expected disagreement.[9] We like this measure because it is not impacted by how many categories documents are sorted into or how many individuals do the sorting.

As an example, assume three researchers are reading the reviews of Lamming's novels and tagging them for the concept of "ambiguity." Say all three read each of five reviews. We'll create a reviewer-by-document matrix for this below.

```
# create a matrix
mat <- matrix(0, nrow = 3, ncol = 5)

# add each reviewers tagging for "ambiguity"
mat[, 1] <- c(1, 0, 1)
mat[, 2] <- c(0, 0, 0)
mat[, 3] <- c(1, 1, 1)
mat[, 4] <- c(0, 0, 0)
mat[, 5] <- c(1, 1, 1)

     [,1] [,2] [,3] [,4] [,5]
[1,]   1    0    1    0    1
[2,]   0    0    1    0    1
[3,]   1    0    1    0    1
```

Let's use `kripp.alpha()`. Our binary variable is a "nominal" variable, so we need to tell the function (output in the margin).

```
kripp.alpha(mat, method = "nominal")
```

The consensus threshold for high reliability is, generally, an α above 0.7. Falling below this threshold means we must align each rater's interpretation of the task—or redefine the task.[10] To help, we can build dictionaries for each concept with terms signaling the concept's presence in the text. In the case of Griswold (1987), we could create a set of terms denoting a positive evaluation and a set indicating ambiguity. Once we build this dictionary, however, we can also use it to automatically tag the documents.

In "Soldiers, Mothers, Tramps and Others," Mohr (1994) coded how relief organizations described their clientele and relief activities. He simplified this task by identifying key terms for each identity: "[T]he program searches each text string for the presence of a single word, in other cases, entire phrases were necessary to trigger a binary variable"

(1994:336). Importantly, dictionaries often must be tailored to the focal corpus.[11]

Table 9.2: Example Dictionary from Mohr (1994)

Value	Key	
blind/deaf	Speech is defective	Blinded
	Defective sight	Deaf
	Defective hearing	Deafness
	Speech disorders	Deaf-mutes
	Blind	Dumb

[11] Note the term "dumb" in Table 9.2 below (Mohr 1994:335–338). As this analysis used the 1907 New York City Charity Directory, "dumb" was used (at the time) as a clinical term for being mute/speechless.

Using this binary indicator, Mohr then constructed a matrix of identities (rows) by relief activities (columns) associated with those identities where the cells were the absence (0) or the presence (1) of co-occurrences of these identities and activities (Mohr 1994:342–3).

In practice, it is common to use automated dictionary methods to tag documents alongside hand-labeling (e.g., Friedman and Reeves 2020). For example, consider Bonikowski and Gidron's (2016) "The Populist Style in American Politics." The authors use over 2,400 public speeches from the Annenberg/Pew Archive of Presidential Campaign Discourse. They build a dictionary to automatically classify speeches, which includes a set of unigrams and up to a five-gram. After using the dictionary to tag a subset of speeches as populist, they manually code each—identifying false positives. This method allowed the authors to save significant time.

Let's replicate part of their analysis. Begin by loading the public campaign speeches from text2map.corpora .

```
data("corpus_presidential", package = "text2map.corpora")

df_pres <- corpus_presidential |>
        select(year, party, text)
```

The dimensions of the dataframe are 2,475 rows and 13 columns. Let's grab the variables we need: year, party, and text. Bonikowski and Gidron provide their final dictionary, which they break down into unigrams on up to one five-gram. Below, we'll create a version of this dictionary. We'll focus on the unigrams and bigrams, starting with building the unigram dictionary.

```
unigrams <- c("bureaucrat", "loophole", "millionaire",
        "baron", "venal", "crooked",
        "unresponsive", "uncaring", "arrogant")
```

Now, we'll create a DTM using dfm() .

```
tkns <- df_pres$text |>
  str_replace_all("[[:punct:]]+", " ") |>
  tokens()

dtm <- dfm(tkns)
```

Now that we've created a DTM with unigrams, let's convert this raw count matrix into a binary matrix. Recall that we are only interested in whether a term occurs in a document, not how many times it does. There are several ways to create a binary matrix. quanteda includes a function that can reweight a DTM using several schemes including "boolean"—another label for either/or classifications.

```
dtm_bin <- dfm_weight(dtm, scheme = "boolean")
```

Next, identify columns matching our dictionary using the %in% operator. The output is an index of TRUE and FALSE . Use it to subset the columns in our DTM by retaining only the columns that align with a TRUE .

```
matched <- colnames(dtm_bin) %in% unigrams
dtm_sub <- dtm_bin[, matched]
df_pres$populist_unigram <- ifelse(rowSums(dtm_sub) > 0, 1, 0)
```

We've created our populist measure using the unigram dictionary. Now, let's find the proportion of speeches per year that are populist. We do so by "grouping" by the year variable and then "summarizing" our other variables: the total number of speeches within a year and the total number of populist speeches in a year. We then take the last number divided by the first to get the percent of speeches in a year that are populist.

```
df_plot <- df_pres |>
  group_by(year) |>
  summarize(total = n(),
            populist = sum(populist_unigram),
            percent = populist / total)
```

Now, let's visualize it. We are mapping the percent variable to the height of the bars (our y-axis); therefore, we'll tell ggplot() that our axis is percentages. The plot is shown in Figure 9.1.

```
df_plot |>
  ggplot(aes(x = year, y = percent)) +
  geom_col() +
  scale_y_continuous() +
  labs(title = "Populist Speeches, 1952-1996",
       y = "% Populist Speeches",
       x = NULL)
```

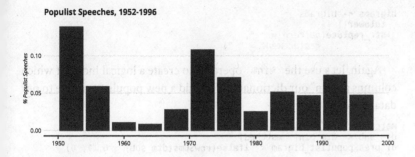

Populist Speeches, 1952-1996

Figure 9.1: Populist Speeches
with Unigram Dictionary.

Our unigram dictionary would lead us to believe the 1952 campaigns were heavily populist—but recall that Bonikowski and Gidiron used the dictionary to identify possible populist speeches which they then verified by reading them. Let's try out our bigram dictionary. First, we'll create a DTM with bigrams instead of unigrams.

```
tkns <- df_pres$text |>
  str_replace_all("[[:punct:]]+", " ") |>
  tokens()

tkns <- tkns |> tokens_ngrams(n = 2L)
dtm <- dfm(tkns)
```

Recall, underneath the `quanteda` DFM is an augmented sparse matrix from `Matrix`. So, we can also quickly convert our DTM into a "logical" sparse matrix (lMatrix) where `TRUE` indicates the presence of the term.

```
is(dtm, "Matrix")

dtm_bin <- as(dtm, "lMatrix")
```

```
bigrams <- c(
    "Special interest", "big government",
    "Wall Street", "Main Street", "big corporations",
    "ordinary taxpayer", "your money", "wealthy few",
    "professional politician", "big interest",
    "old guard", "big money", "Washington elite",
    "rich friend", "power monger", "power grabbing",
    "power hungry", "easy street", "privileged few",
    "forgotten Americans", "too big", "long nose"
)
```

We built the above dictionary based on terms presented in their appendix (Bonikowski and Gidron 2016:1619). The default practice in text analysis for representing n-grams greater than one is to use the underscore as a replacement for spaces or dashes. Furthermore, if we check the columns of our DTM—where the terms are—they have been lower-cased. So, let's make sure our dictionary matches this bit of preprocessing.

```
bigrams <- bigrams |>
  tolower() |>
  str_replace(pattern = " ",
              replacement = "_")
```

Again, let's use the `%in%` operator to create a logical index of which columns are "in" our dictionary. We'll add a new populist variable to our dataframe.

```
matched <- colnames(dtm_bin) %in% bigrams
dtm_sub <- dtm_bin[, matched]
df_pres$populist_bigram <- ifelse(rowSums(dtm_sub) > 0, 1, 0)
```

Find the proportion per year *by political party*. To do so, we tell `R` to group by both variables year and party, and then summarize our variables in the same way we did with the unigram dictionary.

```
df_plot <- df_pres |>
  group_by(year, party) |>
  summarize(total = n(),
            populist = sum(populist_bigram),
            percent = populist / total)
```

Like before, we are mapping the percentage of populist speeches to the height of the bars, but we also map the color of the bars (`fill`) to the political party of the speakers (Figure 9.2).

```
df_plot |>
  ggplot(aes(x = year, y = percent, fill = party)) +
  geom_col(position = "dodge") +
  scale_y_continuous() +
  labs(title = "Populist Speeches by Party",
       y = "% Populist Speeches",
       x = NULL)
```

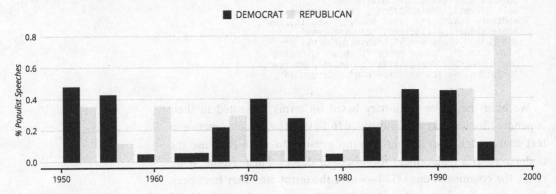

Figure 9.2: Populist Speeches with Bigram Dictionary.

Just as we compare two hand-labeling or automated classifiers to hand-labelings, we can assess the agreement between two automated classifiers. Here, Cohen's κ (kappa) is common; however, we can also use Krippendorf's α - the underlying logic is similar. Both of these measures would tell us the extent each dictionary identifies the same documents.

```
mat <- df_pres |> select(populist_unigram, populist_bigram)
# documents must be columns, so transpose with t()
mat <- t(as.matrix(mat))

kripp.alpha(mat, method = "nominal")
```

Krippendorff's alpha
    Subjects = 2475
    Raters = 2
    alpha = 0.043

This low α indicates that they are picking different speeches (output in margin). Here, it indicates that they are not redundant measures and Bonikowski and Gidron were right in incorporating more than the unigram dictionary. Here too, we see that *iteration* is central to robust text analysis.

WEIGHTED INDICATORS

Frequency-Weighted

The previous section used dictionaries to classify documents as engaging a concept or composing a category in an either/or (a.k.a. binary, or Boolean) fashion. Often researchers also use keyword occurrences to indicate *magnitude*: higher counts mean an increase in engagement with an idea or more attention toward an entity. This is an example of a weighted indicator.

For example, Mohr and colleagues (2013) used Named-Entity Recognition[12] to inductively build a dictionary of the "actors" in a set of political texts—the US National Security Strategy reports. An obvious set of actors identified were various nation-states. Using a heat map, which associates darker shades with higher frequencies, they plotted references to nation-states each year. This, they state:

> ...shows which nations were given **more attention** across the years. We can see there is a **focus** in the early NSS documents on the Soviet Union and Ukraine. Afghanistan and Pakistan are **more salient** in later years. Bosnia is a **hot spot** between 1995 and 2000. Iraq takes on **importance** with the first Gulf War.... (Mohr and colleagues, 2013, 679, emphasis added)

Here, the authors link a term's count to the "attention," "importance," or "salience" of what it denotes. This presumes a relation between the

THIS SECTION NEEDS:

- text2map
- sentimentr
- tidymodels
- rsample
- text2vec
- glmnet
- stringr

[12] See **Tagging Words**.

[13] One way to check the validity of such measures is by reading documents falling at different parts of our distribution—high, medium, and low.

frequencies of keywords and the author's intentions, and perhaps the reader's perceptions (Carley & Palmquist, 1992; Popping, 2000, 39).[13]

Let's build a dictionary of thirteen nation-states needed to reproduce the heatmap presented by Mohr and colleagues. Note that, for simplicity, assume that "Soviet" is only the Soviet Union. This way we can stick with unigrams, but a more robust analysis would include bigram and even trigram dictionaries.

```
dict <- c(
  "Ukraine", "Soviet", "Pakistan", "Kosovo",
  "Japan", "Israel", "Iraq", "Iran", "India",
  "Germany", "China", "Bosnia", "Afghanistan"
)

data("corpus_usnss", package = "text2map.corpora")

dtm <- corpus_usnss |>
  mutate(text = tolower(text),
         text = gsub("[[:punct:]]+", " ", text)) |>
  dtm_builder(text, year)

dtm <- dtm[, colnames(dtm) %in% tolower(dict)]
```

We'll use `dtm_melter()` to "melt" our DTM into a triplet dataframe, which includes the year of the report, the subset of terms (here, nation-states) matching our dictionary, and how many times each term occurs in each report (Figure 9.3).

```
dtm |>
  dtm_melter() |>
  ggplot(aes(x = doc_id, y = term, fill = freq)) +
  geom_tile() +
  labs(x = "Year", y = "Nation") +
  theme(legend.position = "right",
        legend.direction = "vertical")
```

We can see that the NSS reports reference "soviet" many more times in the earliest reports, 1987 through 1991—so much that it overshadows the rest of the counts.

Counting concrete named entities within clearly bounded domains—like nation-states in national security reports—is where term frequency measures encounter their limits. Researchers are often interested in the extent texts engage with abstract concepts—for example, populism or masculinity. This is still a magnitude: researchers move beyond absence/presence to indicate prevalence of, or engagement with, more generic meanings within documents. Here, however, the words themselves are not assumed to be independent.

Term-Weghted Dictionaries

One drawback with mapping keyword counts directly to the magnitude of engagement with a concept or category is that some words may be

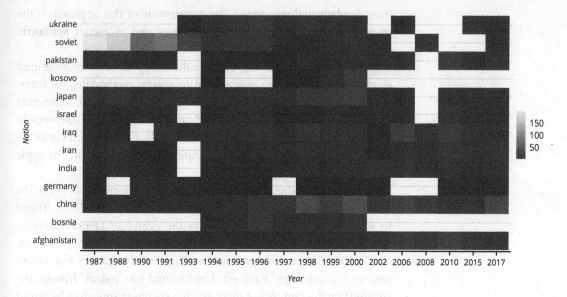

Figure 9.3: Nation-States Referenced in US NSS.

more central to that concept or category than others—regardless of their frequency. This is perhaps most obvious in the case of emotion: "love" is more intense than "like," for instance. To overcome this, we could *weight* each term in our dictionary along a spectrum.

In sociology, perhaps the most common term-weighted dictionaries are occupational prestige or status rankings. Duncan's Socioeconomic Index (SEI) (Duncan 1961) offered one of the first attempts to arrange discrete occupational titles into a gradational scale of status.[14] Each key in this dictionary is a unique occupation, and the value is the associated prestige.

Another body of term-weighted dictionaries, commonly used in social psychology, comes from affect control theory (ACT).[15] Beginning in the 1970s and continuing to the most recent 2015 dictionary, ACT researchers built dictionaries of terms categorized as *actors*, *behaviors*, and *objects*. Each actor, behavior, and object is assigned a ranking along the dimensions of *evaluation* (goodness, badness), *potency* (powerfulness, weakness), and *activity* (liveliness, calmness). From here, more scenarios can be built algebraically and predict, for instance, whether people will experience a situation as strange (Kelly 2022).

A key mechanism in this theory is *deflection*: the discrepancies between *fundamental* meanings which reflect social consensus about a situation and *transient* meanings of the situation itself. When interacting, people act to minimize these discrepancies. But from where do researchers get

[14] Duncan used a combination of income and education data from the 1950 US Census to assign prestige scores from the 1947–8 NORC occupational prestige survey.

[15] The basic premise of affect control theory is that "people characterize themselves and others by social identities... evoking sentiments that serve as guidelines for interpreting and [behaving] in the given situation" (Heise 1977:163).

these fundamental meanings? The cornerstone of this approach is the study of word *norms* in general, and Osgood and colleagues' **semantic differential** method in particular.

In the early 20th century, the idea that attitudes could be measured along a single spectrum was central to several methodological innovations. Here, respondents are presented with a series of statements about a topic or object. They then indicate how favorable or unfavorable they find the statement along a numerical scale. A respondent's answers are then aggregated to arrive at a summary attitude about the topic or object.

For example, using 256 words drawn from Thorndike's (1921) *The Teacher's Word Book*, Charles Mosier (1941:125–7) "presented [them] to subjects for their judgments as to the degree of favorableness or unfavorableness" with 11 being the most favorable and 1 being the least. The "subjects" were undergraduate "students in introductory and second courses in psychology." Each word had around 140 "judges." Mosier discovered that the rankings of most words were linear enough to be placed on a single-dimensional scale, defining "completely unsatisfactory" as zero (see Table 9.3).[16]

[16] What Mosier is presenting is one of the first examples of a weighted *sentiment* dictionary and possibly the first weighted dictionary.

Table 9.3: Terms in Mosier's Favorableness Scale

Term	Scale Value
completely unsatisfactory	0.00
repulsive	0.50
disgraceful	1.00
wrong	1.50
unnecessary	2.00
disputable	2.36
excusable	2.85
average	3.08
pardonable	3.48
comfortable	4.04
desirable	4.50
highly agreeable	5.02
diving	5.50
very, very desirable	5.66

Mosier selected words explicitly about judgment. Osgood's insight was to generalize this: unlike some theoretical constructs which may be "distributed along a single continuum ... we accept at the outset that meanings vary in some unknown number of dimensions" (1952:222). In one study, for example, Osgood found that nearly all subjects associated "large" with "loud," "near" with "fast," and "bright" with "happy." The semantic differential method involved asking a respondent to place a word along several continua "definable by a pair of polar terms" (1952:227), for example, kind-cruel, sad-happy, fast-slow, big-small, fair-unfair, etc. Osgood goes further to suggest that different "ways in which meanings vary" may be "essentially equivalent" and thus reducible to a single, shared dimension.[17]

Through a series of studies, they found that something like Mosier's favorableness, alongside two other dimensions, can explain a large proportion of variation in these continua which label evaluation, potency, and activity (elsewhere called valence, dominance, and arousal, respectively).

Broadly, it is this discovery—diverse judgments can be "explained" by a few linear spectra—that provides the theoretical justification for weighted dictionaries. In each dictionary, a token (typically, a unigram or lemma) is rated along one or a few meaningful dimensions. For example, Bail and colleagues (2017) use the LIWC dictionaries (Tausczik and Pennebaker 2010) designed to measure psychological content to capture the public discussion surrounding advocacy organizations from Facebook comments.

In addition to being the (probable) first weighted dictionaries (with Mosier's work), sentiment dictionaries are also the most commonly used dictionary of any kind. Flores (2017), using a sentiment dictionary (like Mosier's), found an increase in negative sentiment toward Mexican and Hispanic immigrants in a corpus of tweets resulting from an uptick in anti-immigrant users. Using Google's autocomplete search data, Dorius and Swindle (2019) show a positive relationship between the sentiment of the autocomplete text associated with a country and its position on global development indices. The first study used the Liu and colleagues (2005) dictionary, while the second used the SenticNet dictionary, and dozens more such dictionaries exist. lexicon , for example, contains fourteen.[18]

To measure the sentiment of a text, each token is matched to a term in the dictionary and the token is then assigned the weight of that term. Let's work through a toy example. First, load the Jockers-Rinker sentiment dictionary.

```
data("hash_sentiment_jockers_rinker", package = "lexicon")
df_jr <- hash_sentiment_jockers_rinker # rename so it's tidier
head(df_jr)
```

```
            x     y
1:     a plus  1.00
2:    abandon -0.75
3:  abandoned -0.50
4:  abandoner -0.25
5: abandonment -0.25
6:   abandons -1.00
```

Given the expectation that sentiment varies through longer texts (e.g., in a political speech, the orator may move from anger or fear to end on joy and hope), it is generally understood that scores should be assigned to chunks smaller than a paragraph—such as a sentence or a tweet.[19] For instance, consider a quote from a real positive guy, Mr. Rogers: "Taking care is one way to show your love" (output in the margin).

[17] This is the same notion that motivates "fitting" a regression model, see **Math Basics**.

[18] For a comparison, see Gonçalves et al. (2013) and Ribeiro and colleagues (2016).

[19] Weighted dictionaries, in general, are probably ill-suited for long documents (Aslanidis 2018:1245–50; Hanna 2013:376–9; Stoltz and Taylor 2021).

```
text <- "taking care is one way to show your love"
tkns <- strsplit(text, " ") |> unlist()
```

```
df_jr |> filter(x %in% tkns)
```

	x	y
1:	care	1.00
2:	love	0.75

Most of the words are not in the dictionary—even with eleven thousand words. This is the **out-of-vocabulary (OOV)** problem. The typical strategy is to average the weights of the matched words, in this case giving us a sentiment score of 0.875. However, what about the text "I *don't* care and I do *not* love you"? Our match-and-average system would score this as positive when it is the opposite. Therefore, we need to use another dictionary of valence or polarity "shifters" (output in the margin).

```
data("hash_valence_shifters", package = "lexicon")
```

```
hash_valence_shifters |>
    group_by(y) |>
    slice_head(n = 1)
```

	x	y
1	ain't	1
2	absolutely	2
3	almost	3
4	although	4

Instead of weights, though, each word is assigned to one of four categories: (1) negator, (2) amplifier, (3) de-amplifier, or (4) neutral context word. sentimentr combines polarity scores and valence shifters to calculate an aggregate sentiment score.

Using the Jinkers-Rocker polarity dictionary with the valence shifters dictionary, we'll test the emotional polarity of "real" and "fake" news. The original dataset contained roughly 20,000 articles from Reuters, a real news service, and roughly 20,000 articles from a variety of sources deemed fake or unreliable (Ahmed et al. 2017, 2018). We provide a random sample of 1,000 "real" and 1,000 "fake" articles (to speed things up).

```
data("corpus_isot_fake_news2k", package = "text2map.corpora")
```

Our "rating" variable is a character vector, so let's also convert it to a numeric 1 (for real) or 0 (for fake).

```
df_isot <- corpus_isot_fake_news2k |>
    mutate(rating = ifelse(rating == "real", 1, 0)) |>
    rowid_to_column(var = "element_id")
```

Use get_sentences() to break each document down into sentences (this primarily uses punctuation marks). Next, using sentiment , we'll calculate the sentence-level sentiment score with our two dictionaries. Finally, we'll join the output with the original dataframe containing the categorical veracity of the article.

```
df_polar <- df_isot$text |> get_sentences() |> sentiment()
```

```
df_mod <- left_join(df_polar, df_isot, by = "element_id")
```

[20] See **Math Basics**.

Since we are predicting a binary outcome (fake or real), we'll use logistic regression (by setting family to "binomial" within glm()).[20] We'll use the sentiment scores for each sentence to predict whether it is in an article from a "real" or "fake" news source.

```
mod <- glm(rating ~ sentiment, family = binomial, data = df_mod)
tidy(mod)
```

```
term          estimate std.error statistic   p.value
(Intercept)     -0.210    0.0104     -20.1   2.80e-90
sentiment        0.139    0.0385      3.61   3.10e- 4
```

Recall that a "1" means the sentence is from "real" news sources. As our estimate (i.e., coefficient) is a positive number, this means articles from "real" news sources are more likely to have positive sentences than those in "fake" news sources.[21] Broadly, this replicates what other scholars have found on different (and much larger) corpora (e.g., Zaeem et al. 2020).

[21] Following standard assumptions, it is statistically significant at the conventional level.

We can also test whether fake or real news is more or less "emotional" by taking the absolute value of the sentiment scores.

```
df_mod <- df_mod |> mutate(emotionality = abs(sentiment))
```

```
mod <- glm(rating ~ emotionality, family = binomial, data = df_mod)
tidy(mod)
```

```
term          estimate std.error statistic    p.value
(Intercept)     -0.158    0.0151     -10.5    1.27e-25
emotionality    -0.267    0.0561      -4.76   1.96e- 6
```

The negative estimate for emotionality suggests real news is *less emotional* overall.[22]

[22] Again, following standard assumptions, it is statistically significant at the conventional level. See **Extended Deductive**.

SELECTING AND BUILDING DICTIONARIES

The methods discussed here all rely on dictionaries in various ways, which are the pairing of a key and value: a *vocabulary*, on the one hand, and some *rule* about what is to be done when a word is matched to this vocabulary, on the other. Here, we focus a bit more on selecting and building these dictionaries.

When we are first exploring our data, we may decide to build a dictionary by hand. This process begins with deciding what kind of dictionary we need—binary or weighted—and then selecting our vocabulary. Binary dictionaries are the least resource-intensive as the presence of keywords is enough to justify classifying a given piece of text as engaging our concept (or not). This is an *iterative* process (e.g., DeSoucey and Waggoner 2022; Bonikowski and Gidron 2016).

When building a weighted dictionary—where all (or at least most) of the words in our corpus would receive an associated value—researchers often recruit several raters and take the average of their ratings. Today, researchers often use crowd-sourcing platforms like Amazon MTurk. The downside of this procedure is that it may be cost-prohibitive. Another option is to hand-modify already existing dictionaries.

Pre-Built Dictionaries

Why rebuild the wheel? Pre-constructed dictionaries are a great place to start when exploring our corpus. We already discussed several (often included with packages), and we can also request dictionaries from researchers. And, like Mosier's sentiment dictionary, many are buried in appendices, waiting to be rediscovered.

These dictionaries fall into several groups. The simplest are the various "stoplists" discussed earlier.[23] A second group, and closely related, are word frequency lists. Frequency lists were useful for teaching, and one of the earliest was Thorndike's *Teacher's Word Book of 30,000 Words* (Bontrager 1991; Fries 1941). With the onset of digitized corpora, Kucera and Francis's (1967) list became the gold standard, with frequencies calculated on the Brown Corpus. More recent frequency dictionaries for English are based on the Common Crawl of webpages, Wikipedia data dumps, the Google Web Trillion Word Corpus, Google Books N-Gram Corpus, or collections of film and television subtitles (Brysbaert and New 2009).

A third group relates to Osgood's tripartite *evaluation*, *potency*, and *activity* (i.e., valence, dominance, and arousal) which include sentiment dictionaries (the evaluation or valence dimensions). In addition to psychological research using Osgood's semantic differential method (Warriner et al. 2013), affect control theory researchers in sociology continue to build and validate dictionaries in this tradition (Smith-Lovin 2019).

A fourth set emerges from studies of word "concreteness"—also called "abstractness," "construal," or "imageability."[24] For example, "pray" is more concrete, while "religion" is less so. This work began with language instruction as more concrete words are, typically, easier to remember (De Groot and Keijzer 2000). As early work on concreteness focused on the visual modality, this spurred expanding word norms to all sensorimotor modalities (Lynott et al. 2020).

A final group relates to the Linguistic Inquiry and Word Count project, or LIWC. This project encompasses a variety of "psychological" dictionaries building upon the General Inquirer (Stone et al. 1966) and MRC (Wilson 1988)—caged in proprietary software. So, LIWC lacks the transparency and flexibility of the dictionaries discussed previously.[25] We mention it mainly because researchers build dictionaries formatted to work with LIWC's user interface—for example, the Moral Foundations dictionary (Hopp et al. 2021). quanteda 's dictionary() can work with LIWC-formatted dictionaries.

Building Dictionaries with Supervised Learning

The last dictionary construction method we'll discuss falls under the label "supervised learning." This procedure requires we already know how a set of texts ought to be classified—this is what is meant by "supervised." We then "learn" what best predicts those labels. We call the output a "model," but in the examples below, it is a weighted dictionary like any other.

To begin, we need a hand-labeled corpus. This is often called "ground truth" or "gold standard" because validity is established by human raters. For example, a human coder might label a review of the 1999 science-fiction film *The Matrix* as "positive" if the reviewer discusses "enjoying the movie" or they might label a campaign speech as addressing "refugees" if it discusses "sanctuary cities."

[23] See **Wrangling Words**.

[24] See Yeomans (2021) for a comparison.

[25] These other dictionaries are often stored as easily shared and edited plain-text files or spreadsheets.

Let's walk through a toy example first. Let's use lines from Mary Shelley's *Frankenstein* and Octavia Butler's *Parable of the Sower*. We'll *weight* words by how they "predict" the author of the line.

```
shelley <- data.frame(
    text = c(
      "destroy your own creature oh praise the eternal justice",
      "of man yet i ask you not to spare me listen to me and",
      "then if you can and if you will destroy"
    )
)

butler <- data.frame(
    text = c(
      "we are earthlife maturing",
      "earthlife preparing to fall away from the parent world",
      "we are earthlife"
    )
)

shelley$butler <- 0
butler$butler <- 1

corpus <- rbind(butler, shelley)
```

Now we turn our mini-corpus into a DTM. We treat the terms as predictors in our regression and the author as the outcome. For this illustration, we also convert our DTM to a `data.frame` so we can append our outcome variable.

```
dtm <- corpus |>
  rowid_to_column(var = "doc_id") |>
  dtm_builder(text, doc_id = doc_id)

dtm <- as.data.frame(as.matrix(dtm))
dtm$butler <- corpus$butler
```

We're ready to predict the author using terms in each line. Note that using the period means use all columns in the dataframe except our outcome variable (here, "butler").

```
mod <- glm(butler ~ ., family = binomial, data = dtm)
```

Instead of inspecting the model (as we did previously), let's just extract an estimate (coefficient). Ignoring the numbers, the estimate for "earthlife" is positive (like we expect). This means, if we were to apply this small dictionary to new texts, the presence of "earthlife" would make it more likely we would label a text as authored by "Butler."[26]

```
round(coef(mod)["earthlife"], 6)

earthlife
49.13214
```

Let's scale this up. To begin, we'll use a corpus of four thousand posts across five social media sites. Each comment has been hand-labeled as containing a positive or negative sentiment by three human labelers.

```
data("corpus_senti_bench4k", package = "text2map.corpora")
```

[26] We're being a little loose for illustration. In practice, we need many more examples and many more terms to build this dictionary because, as we learned in **Text to Numbers**, language is sparse.

```
df <- corpus_senti_bench4k |>
  mutate(text = tolower(text),
         text = gsub("[[:punct:]]+", " ", text),
         text = gsub("[[:digit:]]+", " ", text),
         text = str_squish(text)) |>
  mutate(positive = ifelse(polarity > 0, TRUE, FALSE))
```

Now, not only do we want to predict these labeled data, but also we want to use our model to, eventually, predict *unlabeled* data. If our model exactly fits our training data, but doesn't work on new data, we call this **overfitting**. The standard way to address overfitting is by dividing our labeled corpus into a training set and then one or more "hold out" or "unseen" datasets (James et al. 2021:176).[27] We then later compare results using the two separate sets. Typically, we hold out about 25 to 30 percent of our data (cf. Afendras and Markatou 2019; Joseph 2022). We'll use helper functions from `rsample`. Since the function we'll use to divide our sample— `initial_split()` —makes the splits randomly (in our case, stratifying by news source), we'll set a seed to make the results reproducible.

```
set.seed(5439)
init <- initial_split(df, prop = 3 / 4, strata = "source")
df_trn <- training(init)
df_tst <- testing(init)
```

Next, we'll represent our documents as DTMs, weighted by relative term frequencies (using `normalize()`). Note we are creating two DTMs, but the vocabulary must be the same. `dtm_builder()` has the `vocab` option for this. Again, for illustration, let's restrict terms to only those that show up in at least 15 documents in our training set and less than 2,700 documents.

```
dtm_trn <- df_trn |>
    dtm_builder(text, doc_id = doc_id) |>
    dtm_stopper(stop_docfreq = c(15, 2700))
dtm_trn <- dtm_trn[, sort(colnames(dtm_trn))]

dtm_tst <- df_tst |>
    dtm_builder(text, doc_id = doc_id,
                vocab = colnames(dtm_trn))

dtm_trn <- normalize(dtm_trn)
dtm_tst <- normalize(dtm_tst)
```

As the outcome is binary, we'll again use logistic regression. This time, however, our data is quite large: we'll predict the labels of several thousand documents with potentially thousands of terms. So, we'll use `glmnet` to fit our model.[28]

```
fit <- cv.glmnet(
    x = dtm_trn,
    y = df_trn$positive,
    family = "binomial",
    intercept = FALSE
)
```

Next, we'll use the model to "predict" the labels of our test set. As we also know the intended labels, we can calculate the accuracy of our prediction (or, the *agreement* between our tool and human annotators).

[27] This is a form of **cross validation**—which cut its teeth debunking Rorschach tests as a predictor of job success (Kurtz 1948). The final sample used is typically called the "test" set and the one or more intermediary samples are called "validation" sets used to fine-tune a model (Ripley 1996:354).

[28] glmnet performs penalized regression. These models are preferred when there is a large number of predictors relative to observations. cv.glmnet performs the regression by separating the observations into k subsets—or "folds." Using all observations outside of that fold, it predicts the labels in the heldout subset to find the weight (lambda) for how much the penalty term should factor into the model's cost function.

```
confusion.glmnet(fit,
    newx = dtm_tst,
    newy = df_tst$positive,
    s = "lambda.min")
```

```
            True
Predicted FALSE TRUE Total
   FALSE    595  242   837
   TRUE      36  139   175
   Total    631  381  1012
```

```
 Percent Correct:  0.7253
```

Using a "confusion matrix," a table that tallies which guesses we got right and which we got wrong, we can see it did okay.[29] The articles not labeled with positive sentiment (the FALSE column) were only misclassified a little. We didn't do as well guessing which articles were labeled with positive sentiment (the TRUE column). We may need to incorporate valence shifters or other fine-tuning—dictionary building is, after all, an iterative process.

Another way we can see how well our dictionary "learned" sentiment is by comparing it to one of the pre-constructed sentiment dictionaries. We'll use inner_join to only keep the words present in both, and then use cor() to calculate correlations between them.

```
data("hash_sentiment_jockers_rinker", package = "lexicon")

dict <- data.frame(term = rownames(coef(fit)),
                   weight = coef(fit)[, 1])
dict <- inner_join(dict, hash_sentiment_jockers_rinker,
                   by = c("term" = "x"))

cor(dict$weight, dict$y)
```

```
[1] 0.4218874
```

Our learned dictionary is positively correlated with one of the best pre-built sentiment dictionaries available—albeit moderately. As a first run, though, that's not bad!

When classifying documents, precompiled dictionaries are a great place to start. Like all methods in this book, results from such dictionaries should be checked against our intuitions, prior research, and our research questions.[30] If we do end with a custom dictionary, however constructed, we must share this dictionary with our community. Otherwise, researchers will struggle to reproduce or build upon our findings—or correct our errors.

[29] Setting s to "lambda.min" means we use the lambda weights giving the smallest average mean-squared error when predicting the heldout subsets.

[30] We direct readers to the very useful literature on **construct validity** and its various cousins. However, if we continue to fail to find what we are looking for, our corpus may simply be talking about something else!

10
Core Inductive

INDUCTIVE approaches find patterns in text, just like deductive approaches. However, we now allow the patterns to show themselves. Imagine creating a map for a community. If we assume they require a road map, we'd proceed deductively, from a set of "road-like" features (highways, interstates, streets) to our representation of those features. If instead, we track where people tend to wander using wearable GPS devices and then create a representation of paths that emerge, we've engaged in inductive reasoning. In inductive research, generally, we identify patterns as they emerge from our research.

This chapter reviews some core inductive approaches in computational text analysis. We start with finding **document similarities**. We then move to **clustering documents** and then discuss a popular family of inductive approaches called **topic modeling**.

THIS SECTION NEEDS:

- tidyverse
- text2map
- text2vec

DOCUMENT SIMILARITY

Quantifying *similarities* is foundational to computational text analysis—especially finding *document similarities*. In fact, many text analysis applications that we encounter when writing and teaching revolve around document similarities—for instance, plagiarism detection software (Bail 2012). While we can use similarity metrics deductively—if, say, we have a hypothesis about which authors write more similarly—we can also use them inductively, allowing patterns of similarity to emerge from a corpus.

One-Mode Projections

DTMs are bimodal matrices: the documents are in the rows, the words are in the columns, and each cell indicates the extent to which a word is present in a document. Thinking of DTMs like this opens a world of analytical possibilities from network science.

Recall the *one-mode projection*, which turns a two-mode matrix into one-mode matrices.[1] We'll focus on the document-level projection here.

[1] See **Math Basics** and **Text to Numbers**.

Mapping Texts: Computational Text Analysis for the Social Sciences. Dustin S. Stoltz and Marshall A. Taylor, Oxford University Press. © Oxford University Press 2024. DOI: 10.1093/oso/9780197756874.003.0010

This is the dot product between each pair of documents. Bigger dot products indicate two documents with more vocabulary overlap.

Consider the small example below. Create a corpus of three documents, each one sentence long, taken from Hughes' poem, *Dreams*. Then use `dtm_builder()` to turn this corpus into a DTM.

```
toy_corpus <- data.frame(
    id = 1:3,
    docs = c(c("hold fast to dreams"),
             c("for when dreams go"),
             c("life is a barren field"))
    )

toy_dtm <- toy_corpus |> dtm_builder(docs, id, dense = TRUE)
```

```
# Document-Term Matrix

  hold fast to dreams for when go life is a barren field
1    1    1  1      1   0    0  0    0  0 0      0     0
2    0    0  0      1   1    1  1    0  0 0      0     0
3    0    0  0      0   0    0  0    1  1 1      1     1
```

We'll need to multiply this DTM by the *TDM*—the *transpose* of the DTM (compare above with output in the margin).

```
toy_tdm <- t(toy_dtm)
```

Remember, matrix multiplication is different from regular multiplication. We find the dot product between the *row* vectors of the DTM and the *column* vectors of the TDM. Below, we take the first row of the DTM and the second column of the TDM.

```
row1 <- toy_dtm[1, ] # row vector
col1 <- toy_tdm[, 2] # column vector

proj <- sum(row1 * col1) # dot product of the two vectors
```

This gives us a "1." In the document-level projection, we expect "1" where the first document and second document intersect (and vice versa since the projection is symmetric). This "1" is easy to interpret: documents 1 and 2 share a single word in common, *dreams*.

Let's find the document-level projection using `tcrossprod()` .[2]

```
tcrossprod(toy_dtm)
```

```
  1 2 3
1 4 1 0
2 1 4 0
3 0 0 5
```

Sure enough, the doc_1, doc_2 and doc_2, doc_1 cells have a 1. We also see documents 2 and 3 are the least similar (no words in common). The diagonal is the total words in each document.

```
# Term-Document Matrix

       1 2 3
hold   1 0 0
fast   1 0 0
to     1 0 0
dreams 1 1 0
for    0 1 0
when   0 1 0
go     0 1 0
life   0 0 1
is     0 0 1
a      0 0 1
barren 0 0 1
field  0 0 1
```

[2] Recall, this is an efficient version of DTM %*% t(DTM) .

Let's consider some abstracts from the *Annual Review of Sociology*. Which abstracts are the most similar to, for example, the abstract for "Employer Decision Making" (Rivera 2020)? We'll load the corpus and remove capitalization and punctuation, and then create a DTM. We also remove duplicate abstracts (because of multi-authored papers) by "grouping by" titles and "summarizing" the abstracts.

```
data("corpus_annual_review", package = "text2map.corpora")

df_sim <- corpus_annual_review |>
    select(title, authors, abstract) |>
    group_by(title) |>
    summarize(abstract = first(abstract)) |>
    mutate(abstract = gsub("[[:punct:]]+", " ", abstract),
           abstract = tolower(abstract))

dtm_sim <- df_sim |> dtm_builder(abstract, title)
```

And, now we find the article-level projection.

```
doc_proj <- tcrossprod(dtm_sim)
```

So, which abstracts were the most similar to Rivera's abstract?

```
doc_proj[, "Employer Decision Making"] |>
    sort(decreasing = TRUE) |>
    head(5) |>
    names()
```

```
[1] "Employer Decision Making"
[2] "Relational Work in the Economy"
[3] "Black Immigrants and the Changing Portrait..."
[4] "Climate Change and Society"
[5] "Computational Social Science and Sociology
```

These article abstracts have the most vocabulary overlap—and are therefore the most similar to—Rivera's abstract. Obviously, the article with the most vocabulary overlap is the article itself! While this is a simple example, researchers could use a version of this technique to identify the diversity of research trends across fields.

Euclidean Distances and Cosine Similarities

In addition to comparing exact vocabulary overlap, many document similarity methods involve thinking of our vocabulary as a *vector space*.[3] In this space, each document's position is that document's word vector: its frequency distribution across the terms in the DTM. Imagine a two-dimensional vector space and two two-word documents. We have document **i** with terms x and y occurring x_i and y_i times, and document **j** with terms x and y but occurring x_j and x_j times.

[3] See **Math Basics**.

How do we measure the distance between these points? We could find the (1) *length of the straight line* between the documents, or the (2) *angle from the origin* between the documents. For both, the words (*x* and *y*) and their frequencies ($[x_i, y_i]$ and $[x_j, y_j]$) are the "coordinates" of each document in the shared space. The straight line or angle establishes the *distance* between them. The smaller the distance, the greater the similarity.

The length of the straight line is the **Euclidean distance**. Let's use `dist()` in base R to get the Euclidean distances between the articles in our *ARS* corpus. We pass our DTM to the function and specify `method = "euclidean"`.

Then, sort the articles in *ascending* order so the top texts are those with small distances to some target text.[4] Here, our target is Rivera's article. How do the top five most similar articles compare to the ones we got with the one-mode projections above?

```
mat_dist <- dist(dtm_sim, method = "euclidean") |> as.matrix()

mat_dist[, "Employer Decision Making"] |>
    sort(decreasing = FALSE) |>
    head(5) |>
    names()
```

```
[1] "Employer Decision Making"
[2] "The Comparative Politics of Collective Memory"
[3] "Class Position and Political Opinion in Rich..."
[4] "Multiracial Categorization, Identity..."
[5] "The Sociology of Creativity..."
```

The two lists do not share a single article in common! Why might this be?

Both projections and Euclidean distances are sensitive to *document length*—the total words per document. For projections, each word where two documents share non-zero entries contributes to the dot product of those two documents. If two documents repeat the same word repeatedly, this inflates the similarity score. Similarly, since calculating Euclidean distance involves summing the squared differences between overlapping words in two documents, a document with lots of the same word can enlarge the distance between the two documents.

What about measuring the *angle* between two documents? It turns out **cosine similarity** is not as sensitive to word counts. This means we can more accurately compare documents of different lengths. Consider our toy example again. Let's preserve the "direction" of the documents but still increase the document length (i.e., repeating each word in one document).

```
toy_corpus_2 <- data.frame(
    id = 1:3,
    docs = c(c("hold fast to dreams hold fast to dreams"),
            c("for when dreams go"),
            c("life is a barren field"))
    )

toy_dtm_2 <- toy_corpus_2 |> dtm_builder(docs, id, dense = TRUE)
```

How do the Euclidean distances and cosine similarities compare?

```
# Euclidean distance for the original DTM
dist(toy_dtm, method = "euclidean") |> as.matrix()
# Euclidean distance for the new DTM
dist(toy_dtm_2, method = "euclidean") |> as.matrix()
```

```
Original DTM                 New DTM
        1       2 3                1 2        3
0.00000 2.44949 3          0.000000 4 4.582576
2.44949 0.00000 3          4.000000 0 3.000000
3.00000 3.00000 0          4.582576 3 0.000000
```

```
# Cosine similarity for the original DTM
sim2(toy_dtm, method = "cosine")
# Cosine similarity for the original DTM
sim2(toy_dtm_2, method = "cosine")
```

```
Original DTM       New DTM
   1    2 3          1    2 3
1.00 0.25 0        1.00 0.25 0
0.25 1.00 0        0.25 1.00 0
0.00 0.00 1        0.00 0.00 1
```

The Euclidean distances between the first document and the other two increase. But, not for the cosine similarities, which remain the same.

Note that cosine similarity ranges between [0,1].[5] Euclidean distances have minimum values of 0, but the maximum Euclidean distance varies: it is the maximum possible square root of the sum of squared differences.

Let's make the two metrics more comparable by dividing each Euclidean distance by the maximum *possible* (not necessarily the maximum *observed*) Euclidean distance. This is tricky when the columns are word counts with no known possible maximum. We'll assume the longest observed document in the corpus has the highest "possible" word count. We then find the Euclidean distance between two *simulated documents* which are this maximum length but sharing no words. Let's create a function that finds this.

```
get_maxeuc <- function(dtm) {
    mx <- max(rowSums(dtm))
    d1 <- c(mx, 0)
    d2 <- c(0, mx)
    re <- dist(rbind(d1, d2), method = "euclidean")[1]
    return(re)
}
```

[5] At least, if the DTM contains only positive values, for example, when the DTM weighting is term frequencies, relative frequencies, or *tf-idf* scores.

Now, divide each Euclidean distance by this simulated maximum to get our distances inside a [0,1] range. We'll call these **normalized Euclidean distances**.

```
toy_max_euc <- get_maxeuc(toy_dtm)
(dist(toy_dtm, method = "euclidean") / toy_max_euc) |> as.matrix()

          1         2         3
0.0000000 0.3464102 0.4242641
0.3464102 0.0000000 0.4242641
0.4242641 0.4242641 0.0000000
```

That makes Euclidean distances more interpretable! As we'll see, this normalization does not overcome the effect of word count differences. Let's repeat our previous test. This time we'll substract each normalized Euclidean distance from 1 so we have **normalized Euclidean similarities**. The two metrics now run in the same direction (larger scores indicate more similarity for both).

```
# Normalized Euclidean similarity for the original DTM
max1 <- get_maxeuc(toy_dtm)
1 - as.matrix(dist(toy_dtm, method = "euclidean") / max1)
# Normalized Euclidean similarity for the new DTM
max2 <- get_maxeuc(toy_dtm_2)
1 - as.matrix(dist(toy_dtm_2, method = "euclidean") / max2)

Original DTM
          1         2         3
1.0000000 0.6535898 0.5757359
0.6535898 1.0000000 0.5757359
0.5757359 0.5757359 1.0000000

New DTM
          1         2         3
1.0000000 0.6464466 0.5949537
0.6464466 1.0000000 0.7348350
0.5949537 0.7348350 1.0000000
```

The cosine and Euclidean similarities are more comparable now. While the Euclidean similarities don't seem to move *that* much, recall the cosines didn't change *at all*.

Let's return to our *Annual Review of Sociology* example. Using cosine, which article abstracts are the most similar to the one for Rivera's article?

```
dtm_cos <- sim2(dtm_sim, method = "cosine")

dtm_cos[, "Employer Decision Making"] |>
    sort(decreasing = TRUE) |>
    head(5) |>
    names()

[1] "Employer Decision Making"
[2] "Relational Work in the Economy"
[3] "Violence in Latin America..."
[4] "Multiracial Categorization, Identity..."
[5] "The Social Consequences of Disasters..."
```

These three lists—from the projections, Euclidean distances/ similarities, and cosine similarities—all look somewhat different. While many factors could cause discrepancies between metrics, that document length changes our Euclidean measures is why cosine similarity is far more popular. There are many other similarity metrics to explore that could cross-validate discrepancies. Each metric, though, should be compared with a close reading of a sample of documents.

DOCUMENT CLUSTERING

Cluster analysis is a ubiquitous technique and one of the first forms of "unsupervised learning" discussed in data science texts. **Document clustering** is a suite of methods for inductively grouping texts based on similar distributions. These distributions could be word counts across a vocabulary, topics, emotion classification scores—anything.

Clustering methods find the partition of documents minimizing the differences between documents *within* a cluster and maximizing the differences between documents *across* clusters (Evans and Aceves 2016:32). This is done with an *objective function* (we'll flesh this out shortly) used to successively determine whether any two documents should be clustered together.[6]

Miller (1997), for example, used hierarchical clustering to identify "frames" in a corpus of Associated Press news articles on wetlands issues; around the same time, Kabanoff, Waldersee, and Cohen (1995) used a type of k-means clustering to identify the value structures across a sample of Australian organizations using their organizational literature. Document clustering is still in rotation in contemporary computational text analysis—clustering is integrated with topic modeling (more on that later) to, for example, cluster authors (Tierney et al. 2021). We focus on two popular forms: hierarchical clustering and k-means clustering (Grimmer et al. 2022:123–37). One of these requires a distance matrix and one does not.

Hierarchical Clustering

Hierarchical clustering creates not one cluster solution,[7] but many. This forms a hierarchy, where lower-level clusters are nested within higher-level clusters. Just as each document is in only one cluster, so too must each cluster be nested within a single cluster at the higher level. This means the maximum number of clusters is the total documents in the

---

THIS SECTION NEEDS:

- stringr
- text2map
- text2vec
- factoextra
- tidyverse
- tidytext

[6] Documents need not be the units to be clustered. For example, instead of clustering documents based on similar word count distributions, we could instead cluster the words in the vocabulary based on their similar distributions across documents.

[7] This is any partition into k number of clusters.

corpus ($k = N$, where N is the total document count), while the minimum number is one ($k = 1$).

There are two forms of hierarchical clustering: *agglomerative* and *divisive* (Jain et al. 1999:274).[8] We'll focus on agglomerative clustering because it is more popular than divisive clustering (Roux 2018:345).

So, we start with each document in its own cluster and then successively merge clusters until all documents are in one. We merge clusters based on similarity. But how do we decide which two clusters are the most similar? This is where the **distance matrix** comes in. Two clusters are merged if they are the closest to one another relative to all other possible pairwise cluster comparisons, based on the distance between them.

Implicit here is our **objective function**: minimizing distances between all documents within a cluster. We'll need to select a **merging criterion**: a means of deciding whether the distance between two clusters is the smallest possible given all other possible cluster mergers, and then joining those two clusters based on that minimization. There are many merging criteria but the most popular are the complete-linkage, single-linkage, and Ward's method (Jain et al. 1999:275).

No one merging criterion is consistently favored. Justification for selecting one criterion is rarely provided, outside of picking the one passing the "eye-test"—that is, providing clusters matching expectations given researchers' substantive knowledge or theory.

Regardless of criterion, clustering provides inductively derived groups of semantically similar documents. Let's see. We'll work with the State of the Union speeches—specifically Bill Clinton's first SOTU in 1993 to Donald J. Trump's speech in 2020.[9]

Load the data, take care of some wrangling, and create the DTM. We'll remove all punctuation except for any underscores, commas, or dashes internal to a word, and also remove capitalization, numbers, and excess spaces. We eventually want to see the top words per cluster, so we'll remove words in the 2014 Snowball stoplist as part of our DTM construction. The functions we'll use for clustering only work with base R dense matrices.[10]

```
data("data_corpus_sotu", package = "quanteda.corpora")

sotu <- tidy(data_corpus_sotu) |>
  filter(Date >= "1993-02-17") |>
  mutate(
    year = gsub("(\\d+)-.*", "\\1", Date),
    doc_id = paste0(President, "_", year),
    text = tolower(text),
```

[8] They differ in their starting point in the hierarchical clustering structure. With agglomerative clustering, each document starts as its own cluster. Then, the most similar documents—that is, those closest—are grouped. This process is repeated until, theoretically, all documents occupy a single cluster. Divisive clustering works in the other direction: all documents occupy the same cluster and then documents are successively separated until each document occupies its own cluster.

[9] Tree-based clustering can quickly become computationally demanding with even modestly sized corpora.

[10] Recall, this is less memory efficient. See **Text to Numbers**.

```
    text = gsub("\\w+[_'-]+\\w+", "", text),
    text = gsub("[[:punct:]]+", " ", text),
    text = gsub("[[:digit:]]+", " ", text),
    text = str_squish(text)
  )
```

```
dtm_sotu <- sotu |>
  dtm_builder(text, doc_id) |>
  dtm_stopper(stop_list = get_stoplist("snowball2014"), dense = TRUE)
```

Now we need to get our document-by-document distance matrix. Let's go with cosine. We'll use `dist2()` .[11]

```
cos_sotu <- dist2(dtm_sotu, method = "cosine")
```

Next, we'll create our cluster tree.[12] We'll let `hcut()` know this is a distance matrix with `as.dist()` . For our merging criterion, we'll use Ward's method, which we specify with `hc_method = "ward.D2"` .

```
hier_sotu <- hcut(as.dist(cos_sotu), hc_method = "ward.D2")
```

Let's inspect the tree structure of the hierarchical clustering—visualized in the form of a **dendrogram**. We'll use `fviz_dend()` for this, starting with $k = 2$.[13]

```
fviz_dend(hier_sotu, cex = .5, k = 2, horiz = TRUE,
  k_colors = c("#440154FF", "#3A5E8CFF")
)
```

[11] Similarities are the inverse of distances, so we could use `sim2()` again and then subtract the resulting similarities by 1 to get the cosine distances.

[12] We'll use factoextra , although there are many packages for hierarchical clustering.

[13] The cex parameter controls the size of the document labels, and horiz turns the plot left to right.

Figure 10.1: Dendrogram for Hierarchical Clustering.

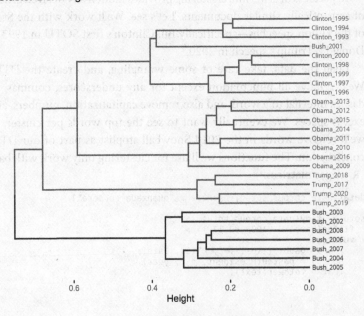

Cluster Dendrogram

Starting from the right of Figure 10.1, each speech starts in its own cluster—as expected with agglomerative clustering. The first cluster (i.e., the first time two documents are grouped) consisted of Clinton's 1998 and 2000 speeches. We know this because, if we "read" right to left, those are the first two speeches merging under one line. This clustering process continues until all speeches are in one cluster.

As this illustrates, where we "cut" the dendrogram leads to different cluster solutions. For instance, cutting the dendrogram at 0.1 (following the x-axis) creates 28 clusters—one for each document. Cutting at 0.6, though, creates three clusters (since we would cross three horizontal lines if we sliced at $x = 0.6$). The inevitable question is: *Where to cut?*

There are two broad ways to decide on k: interpretive and statistical. First, we can compare the cluster solution against domain knowledge and theory. For instance, does it make sense for Bush's '01 speech to be in the same cluster as Clinton's '94 and '95 speeches? What were they talking about? Did they take place during similar social, political, cultural, and/or economic contexts that would account for semantic similarity?

There are also many "fit statistics" to guide the decision for k: the silhouette width statistic, gap statistic, and gamma index, to name a few.[14] We'll focus on one of our favorites: the **silhouette width** statistic.

For each document at a given solution, we calculate its silhouette width by finding the average cosine distance between that document and the other documents in its cluster. Call this c_i. We then calculate the average cosine distance between that document and all other documents cluster by cluster. The smallest average distance between the document and the other clusters is c'_i. The silhouette width for that document is then found by subtracting c_i from c'_i and then dividing that difference by the larger of those two values.

We can then find the average of all documents' silhouette widths. Values range from -1 to 1, where values closer to 1 indicate excellent average cluster placement and values closer to -1 indicate very poor average cluster placement. If we made our decision for k purely on the silhouette width (which we probably wouldn't want to do in practice), we would want the k with the largest average value.

How many clusters does the (average) silhouette statistic recommend? We can determine this using `fviz_nbclust()`. To make this work, we first want to define a function that specifies that we want to perform hierarchical clustering with Ward's method iteratively at different ks.

[14] `NbClust` provides 30 different fit statistics (Charrad et al. 2014).

Then we pass that function to `fviz_nbclust()`, where we also indicate that we want "silhouette," we want to get the average silhouette width from one cluster to `k.max`, and that we have a distance matrix, which we indicate with `diss`. We set `k.max` to 20, and must also supply the original DTM.[15]

[15] Code adapted from Lopez (2017).

```
ward_link <- function(diss, k) {
    hcut(diss, k, hc_method = "ward.D2")
}

fviz_nbclust(dtm_sotu,
    FUNcluster = ward_link,
    method = "silhouette",
    diss = cos_sotu,
    k.max = 20
)
```

Figure 10.2: Silhouette Width for Hierarchical Clustering.

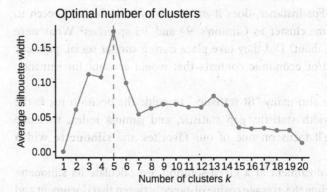

The best statistical fit is five clusters (see Figure 10.2). If we want to group documents into the fewest groups but which are as spread apart as possible, five groups is our best choice. Let's create that now.

```
hier_sotu <- cos_sotu |>
    as.dist() |> hcut(k = 5, hc_method = "ward.D2")
```

Let's assume that, at face value, these clusters make substantive and/or theoretical sense. If they don't, then maybe statistical fit is not the best option for deciding on the number of clusters. In fact, in most social science applications, interpretive validity is the best measure of cluster fit.[16]

[16] Remember: text analysis is about *mapping*, not *mining*, so different cluster solutions can come with different interpretations! Perhaps some more relevant to our research questions than others.

We can dive into mapping what these clusters *mean*. We've borrowed code from Jones (2021) and turned it into a function. First, calculate the proportion of the corpus' total word count that is accounted for by each unique word (that's `prop`). For each cluster (`k`), we subset the DTM to only the documents in that cluster. Then we calculate the proportion of *that cluster's* total words accounted for by each unique word in the cluster and then subtract each word's proportion in the corpus from it.[17] The larger that difference, the more unique that word is to that cluster. We then make a table that sorts each cluster's unique words in descending order and reports the top 5 (see Table 10.1). These words facilitate interpretation.

[17] This is the difference between each word's probability of occurring in a cluster and its probability of occurring at all in the corpus.

```
get_clust_words <- function(dtm, clusters, n_words) {
  prop <- colSums(dtm) / sum(dtm)
  k <- unique(clusters)
  words <- lapply(k, function(x) {
      sub <- dtm[clusters == x, ]
      res <- colSums(sub) / sum(sub) - prop
      res <- names(sort(res, decreasing = TRUE))
      res <- paste(res[seq.int(n_words)], collapse = ", ")
      return(res)
  })
  return(data.frame(
        cluster = k,
        size = tabulate(clusters),
        top_words = unlist(words)))
}

get_clust_words(dtm_sotu, hier_sotu$cluster, n_words = 5)
```

Table 10.1: Five Clusters and Top Words (Hierarchical Clustering)

Cluster	N Documents	Top Words
1	4	people, care, health, government, work
2	5	must, children, century, ask, challenge
3	7	iraq, terrorists, america, terror, freedom
4	8	jobs, energy, get, like, businesses
5	4	american, thank, great, administration, united

A quick inspection of the top words seems to suggest five general themes that differentiate the SOTUs: healthcare policy, community and its challenges, terrorism and national security, economy and jobs, and "make American great again" (MAGA) discourse.

k-Means Clustering

An alternative to hierarchical clustering is **k-means clustering**. Both are "hard" partitions: each document belongs to one and only one cluster. k-means clusters, though, are formed by recursively moving documents to find the most "compact" clusters. With this algorithm, documents *within* groups will be very similar. Unlike hierarchical clustering, though, we are not trying to maximize the difference *between* groups.

First, we must pick k number of clusters. Then, each document is randomly[18] allocated to one of the k clusters. We then calculate the vector means or "centroids" of all documents in a cluster. With our typical DTM, these vectors are term counts. The result is k number of means. The algorithm minimizes the errors for all documents in a cluster to find the most "compact" solution.[19]

The error is the squared difference between each document's vector and the cluster's centroid. We then sum these errors to get the "sum of squared errors" (SSE). Each document is moved to a new cluster to see if this reduces the SSE, and remains in the cluster leading to the largest reduction in SSE. Once all documents are assessed (and moved, if applicable), the k vector means and SSE are recalculated. The algorithm continues until the SSE can be minimized no further—that is, the clusters are as compact as possible.

Let's continue with our SOTU example. We'll use kmeans() from base R . In addition to our DTM, we'll need to provide k. Let's start with $k = 5$ since the silhouette width statistics favored that number.[20] As we randomly sort the documents into initial clusters, we'll use set.seed() to reproduce the cluster solution.[21]

```
set.seed(58901)
kmeans_sotu <- kmeans(dtm_sotu, 5)
```

We can now look at which speeches are in each cluster.

```
kmeans_sotu$cluster
```

The clusters seem to differentiate on the president giving the speech. Let's look at the words unique to each cluster relative to the corpus as a whole. We'll use the same function as before, only this time providing the clusters from k-means (see Table 10.2).

```
get_clust_words(dtm_sotu, kmeans_sotu$cluster, n_words = 5)
```

Table 10.2: Five Clusters and Top Words (k-Means Clustering)

Cluster	N Documents	Top Words
4	4	people, work, say, welfare, cut
5	8	must, century, ask, st, children
2	8	iraq, terrorists, must, america, security
3	4	jobs, energy, get, like, businesses
1	4	american, thank, great, administration, united

[18] There are non-random ways to start clustering (e.g., Hartigan 1975:88; Pena et al. 1999).

[19] There are different versions of k-means clustering. The base R function kmeans() —which we use—defaults to the Hartigan-Wong algorithm (1975; 1979).

[20] We'll also use the default algorithm, Hartigan-Wong, but we could specify another with the algorithm = parameter.

[21] We can set nstart = which reruns the initial clustering nstart times and uses the initial clusters with the minimum SSE.

Compare the top words from the hierarchical clusters (HC) and the *k*-means clusters (KC). We see 1-to-1 correspondences:

- HC #1 is KC #4
- HC #2 is KC #5
- HC #3 is KC #2
- HC #4 is KC #3
- HC #5 is KC #1

We can also see this correspondence with the document placements: only two speeches vary. This suggests our corpus has speeches that are quite distinct, creating groups that are internally close and externally distant.

```
data.frame(hierarchical_clusters = hier_sotu$cluster,
           kmeans_clusters = kmeans_sotu$cluster) |>
        table()
```

```
                     kmeans_clusters
hierarchical_clusters 1 2 3 4 5
                    1 0 1 0 3 0
                    2 0 0 0 1 4
                    3 0 7 0 0 0
                    4 0 0 8 0 0
                    5 4 0 0 0 0
```

Clusters are like any categorical variable. We can stratify our corpus by cluster to explore patterns within the groups or throw the cluster variable into our favorite regression model—whatever we want.

Topic Modeling

The beauty of hierarchical and *k*-means clustering is their simplicity. But there are shortcomings. One being that these clustering methods allocate each document to a single cluster. Reconsider Figure 10.1. Cutting the dendrogram at five clusters makes the Trump speeches the "MAGA" speeches. But, what if we cut it at two clusters? We'd still get the "terrorism and national security" cluster—essentially, all Bush's speeches after 9/11—but we'd have an amorphous second cluster mixing themes on healthcare policy, community, MAGA, and economy and jobs. This would be a cluster that is too general for most empirical applications. But also, are each of these speeches just *about one thing*? Clearly not.

There are forms of **fuzzy clustering** where, given *k* clusters, we measure *how much* each document relates to each cluster. For instance, if we clustered science fiction novels by their topics, we want to classify

THIS SECTION NEEDS:

- tidyverse
- tidytext
- text2map
- lsa
- topicmodels
- topicdoc

Butler's *Parable of the Sower* partially with "climate change" and partially with "inequality."

The most popular form of fuzzy clustering is **topic modeling**. There are several topic modeling methods. They all share a focus on uncovering the *latent themes* of a corpus. These are all dimension reduction methods, where the goal is to find the major axes of variation, or dimensions, along which word co-occurrences are organized. We could call these dimensions a variety of things—categories, themes, labels—but we'll stick with topics.

Most of what goes by "topic modeling" are probabilistic models. We'll start, though, with a non-probabilistic form of topic modeling, but one which nonetheless allows topics to be present in documents to varying degrees.

Topic Modeling with LSA

The most basic form of topic modeling is using *singular value decomposition* (SVD) on the DTM.[22] This method has been around for quite some time, though by a different name: *latent semantic analysis* (LSA) (Deerwester et al. 1990), also known as *latent semantic indexing*.

[22] See **Math Basics**.

Assuming the DTM has d documents and t terms in it (i.e., d rows and t columns), the square document-topic matrix[23] will have $d \times d$ topics and the square topic-term matrix will have $t \times t$ topics. The diagonal of the diagonal matrix will have as many non-zero entries as there are documents or terms, whichever is smallest (usually documents); the rest of the diagonal—including the non-diagonal entries—are zero.

[23] Our "dimensions" or "singular vectors" from SVD are "topics" in LSA nomenclature.

We haven't reduced the dimensionality of the DTM yet—if anything, we've increased it! First, we can ignore the topics (singular vectors) from the topic-term matrix that extend beyond the dimensionality of the document-topic matrix (or vice versa, if we have more documents than we do terms). These topics will have singular values of zero. So, now we are left with $d \times d$ and a $t \times d$ matrices.[24]

[24] The number of non-zero singular values is the **rank** of the original DTM.

Recall that singular vectors and singular values are rank-ordered: this means that the kth topic of the document-topic matrix and the kth topic of the transpose of the topic-term matrix correspond to the kth singular value, and these are arranged by *variance explained*. Still, we don't know how many topics we want to retain. This is, just like clustering, an open question. We want topics that make sense (we'll get to interpretation soon). We also want to discard topics with tiny singular values because they explain little variance in the semantic structure of the DTM.

If we take each singular value, square it, and then divide by the sum of the squared singular values, then we can express the singular values in the form of *proportion of the total variance in the DTM that is explained by that topic*. We then retain the number of topics where even the "smallest" topic explains a reasonable amount of variance.

After deciding on k, we'll need to get the top terms for that k. First, we'll transpose the topic-term matrix. Then we'll sort the terms' loadings (i.e., their "weights" on the topic) in descending order for each column. We'll retain enough terms to interpret the topic. We then repeat this process with the document-topic matrix[25] to find the documents loading the highest on each topic. These documents are candidates for close reading. Let's work through an example with our SOTU corpus.[26]

```
data("data_corpus_sotu", package = "quanteda.corpora")
```

```
df_sotu <- tidy(data_corpus_sotu) |>
  filter(Date >= "1993-02-17") |>
  mutate(
    year = gsub("(\\d+)-.*", "\\1", Date),
    doc_id = paste0(President, "_", year),
    text = tolower(text),
    text = gsub("\\w+[_'-]+\\w+", "", text),
    text = gsub("[[:punct:]]+", " ", text),
    text = gsub("[[:digit:]]+", " ", text),
    text = str_squish(text)
  )
```

```
dtm_sotu <- df_sotu |>
  dtm_builder(text, doc_id) |>
  dtm_stopper(stop_list = get_stoplist("snowball2014"))
```

Base `R` has `svd()` . There are also dedicated packages for LSA like `lsa` —with convenience functions for applying SVD to DTMs. We'll use both to show their equivalence. Let's pass our DTM to `svd()` . We'll use the raw term frequencies as our weighting scheme.[27]

```
svd_sotu <- svd(dtm_sotu)
lengths(svd_sotu)
```

```
d     u     v
28   784 243768
```

Look at the resulting object, `svd_sotu` . We'll see three matrices: our diagonal matrix of singular values (`$d`), the document-topic matrix (`$u`), and the topic-term matrix (`$v`). We'll also see that we have 28 topics – as expected, since an SVD on a 28×9477 DTM produces 28 non-negative singular values (the length of the rows or columns, whichever is the smallest). Let's look at the distribution of variance explained. Recall we do this by squaring our singular values and dividing them by the sum of the squared singular values.

[25] There is no need to transpose this matrix, since the dimensions are already in the columns.

[26] Note that the preprocessing retains inter-word punctuation and removes words in the Snowball stoplist.

[27] The DTM is often weighted by *tf-idf* scores when using LSA in information retrieval research.

```
prop.table(svd_sotu$d^2) |> head()
```

```
[1] 0.70084810 0.03687220 0.03266792
    0.02435380 0.02101393 0.01654950
```

Dimension #1 accounts for over 70% of the variance in our DTM. The explanatory power of the remaining dimensions drops off considerably: the next three explain only 10% combined.

It might be tempting to retain only this first dimension. However, lsa recommends a slightly different strategy. Let's first generate our SVD using lsa . The function expects a TDM instead of DTM, so we'll first take the transpose of our SOTU DTM.[28]

```
lsa_sotu <- lsa(t(dtm_sotu))
# quick look
lengths(lsa_sotu)
```

```
   tk    dk    sk
69648   224     8
```

[28] lsa() gives the same output whether the input is a DTM or a TDM, but mislabels the output for a DTM. So, we'll supply a TDM to avoid that confusion.

Comparing lsa_sotu to svd_sotu , we'll see they are almost identical.

- $d in svd_sotu (the vector of singular values) is $sk in lsa_sotu .
- $u in svd_sotu (the document-topic matrix) is $dk in lsa_sotu .
- $v in svd_sotu (the term-topic matrix) is $tk in lsa_sotu .

Notice one significant difference: only eight dimensions in lsa_sotu . This is because lsa() keeps the dimensions accounting for at least 50% of the variance in the original DTM.

Following the strategy above, though, this should result in only one topic—not eight. The difference is that lsa() doesn't square the singular values; instead, each singular value is divided by the sum of the singular values. So, if we take svd_sotu$d and apply prop.table() as before but with no squaring, we should see that the first eight topics account for at least 50% of the variance and that the first seven do not.

```
prop.table(svd_sotu$d)[1:8] |> sum() # first 8 dimensions
prop.table(svd_sotu$d)[1:7] |> sum() # first 7 dimensions
```

Sure enough, using this strategy, the first eight topics account for 52% of the variance, while the first seven accounts for 49%. Eight topics it is.

Each term and each document have a loading on these topics. While these loadings are not probabilities, they do mean documents engage more than one topic.

Let's move on to interpreting our topics. For each topic in the term-topic matrix, we'll sort the terms (rows) in descending order and focus on the 10 highest-loading terms. Before that, though, we confront a shortcoming of LSA: nothing prevents negative values in the document-topic and term-topic matrices. Do negatives indicate dissimilarity, or is it the absolute value that matters?

These are not settled debates: some recommend focusing on the terms and documents with the largest absolute loadings on the dimensions; others recommend focusing only on those with the highest positive loadings. The question is: Is a topic one "pole" of a dimension? Or is a topic *the dimension*, and the two poles are the different extremes of that topic? For example, are discussions of poverty on a spectrum from wealth to deprivation, or just deprivation? This is a case where our research aims will guide our selection.

We'll focus on terms with the largest absolute values to define the topics. We'll also use scatterplots of the dimensions to see if the poles can help interpret the contrasts internal to a topic. We'll get the top 4 terms for all topics with a for-loop.

```
top_names <- paste0("V", seq.int(8))

for (i in top_names) {
  abs(lsa_sotu$tk) |>
    as.data.frame() |>
    arrange(desc(get(i))) |>
    rownames() |>
    head(4) |>
    print()
}

[1] "people" "new" "can" "america"
[1] "must" "jobs" "children" "ask"
[1] "america" "people" "work" "iraq"
[1] "people" "now" "health" "government"
[1] "thank" "people" "american" "america"
[1] "plan" "us" "must" "care"
[1] "must" "ask" "help" "challenge"
[1] "government" "health" "care" "new"
```

There are words consistent across topics—for example, "american" and "people."[29] SOTUs are quite formalized and formulaic. Other words are not semantically rich: for example, modal verbs such as "must." So let's remove some words from our DTM and redo the analysis. This will prioritize differences between the speeches.

[29] Even after removing words from the Snowball stoplist, there will be words common to our corpus.

```
to_remove <- c(
    "will", "must", "can", "american", "america",
    "year", "people", "country", "also", "now", "have",
    "thank", "good", "new", "come", "get", "know", "would",
    "just", "let", "make", "congress", "like", "every",
```

```
      "take", "americans", "st", "us", "government", "these"
)

dtm_sotu_sub <- dtm_sotu |> dtm_stopper(stop_list = to_remove)

# redo the LSA
lsa_sotu_sub <- lsa(t(dtm_sotu_sub))
```

And now we can look at the top terms (notice that LSA now recommends nine topics).

```
top_names <- colnames(as.data.frame(lsa_sotu_sub$tk))

for (i in top_names) {
  abs(lsa_sotu_sub$tk) |>
    as.data.frame() |>
    arrange(desc(get(i))) |>
    rownames() |>
    head(5) |>
    print()
}
```

```
[1] "years" "work" "one"  "world" "tonight"
[1] "children" "say" "ask" "work"  "united"
[1] "jobs" "ask" "children" "security" "iraq"
[1] "health" "care"  "first" "tonight" "security"
[1] "health" "century" "welfare" "help" "care"
[1] "plan" "care" "work" "tax" "health"
[1] "challenge" "want" "ask" "help" "gun"
[1] "tax" "health" "care" "last" "world"
[1] "security" "social" "century" "challenge" "children"
```

[30] Note that we could use any size *n*-grams here, not just unigrams.

These topics look better.[30] They probably are not as differentiated from one another as they could be—for example, some topics seem to be about the economy and tax cuts with no distinction between them. This could mean some topics should be combined, or perhaps that some topics are too general and must be decomposed further. This is an example of where a statistical criterion does not always agree with the eye test.

Usually, we'd iterate between different model specifications: using different preprocessing, thresholds, and *k* topics. We want to avoid reading tea leaves, though. We should *never* just rely on the list of top terms for assigning meanings to the topics. *We need to read the texts.*

Let's pick a topic as an example. Three topics list "children" as a top word. Topic #9 seems to be centrally about children, education, and the challenges they face. Let's tentatively call this a "future of education" topic. But let's not base our interpretation on just a list of 5 words. We'll do two things: compare this topic to other topics, and find the speeches that load the highest on this topic.

First, is there another topic about the "future of education"? Possibly, as two others share a keyword, "children": topics #2 and #3. Since LSA builds upon SVD, we can conceptualize our topics as forming a *latent* space. To visualize this space, we'll create a scatterplot of words by their loadings in each topic. This "spreads" out our terms in *two dimensions* and thus can differentiate topics with similar top words.

For space, we'll compare topic #9 (our tentative "future of education" topic) to topic #2. We'll plot each term's raw loading on the topics as opposed to their absolute values. We'll also color words that load high on the topics (arbitrarily using an absolute value greater than 0.1) in different colors. Words that load high on both topics are in their own color. Words that do not load highly on either topics are printed in transparent gray. The plot is shown in Figure 10.3.

```
df_sotu_lsa <- data.frame(
    term = rownames(lsa_sotu_sub$tk),
    topic9 = lsa_sotu_sub$tk[, 9],
    topic2 = lsa_sotu_sub$tk[, 2]) |>
  mutate(abs9 = abs(topic9),
         abs2 = abs(topic2),
      color = case_when(
          abs9 >  .1 & abs2 <= .1 ~ "high9",
          abs9 <= .1 & abs2 >  .1 ~ "high2",
          abs9 >  .1 & abs2 >  .1 ~ "both",
          TRUE ~ NA_character_),
      alpha = case_when(
          abs9 <= .1 & abs2 <= .1 ~ .6,
          TRUE ~ 1)
    )
```

```
df_sotu_lsa |>
  ggplot(aes(topic9, topic2, label = term)) +
  geom_text(aes(color = color, alpha = alpha)) +
  geom_hline(yintercept = 0, linetype = "dashed") +
  geom_vline(xintercept = 0, linetype = "dashed") +
  labs(x = "Topic #9", y = "Topic #2") +
  guides(alpha = "none", color = guide_legend(nrow = 2)) +
  scale_colour_discrete(
      breaks = c("high9", "high2", "both", NA),
      labels = c("Loads High on #9", "Loads High on #2",
                 "Loads High on Both", "Loads High on Neither"),
      na.value = "gray50"
  )
```

Only one pole of topic #2 addresses something similar to topic #9. The other pole of topic #2 seems more concerned with terrorism, national security, and, perhaps, American exceptionalism. It seems that this topic differentiates between foreign issues and domestic issues. While topic #9 focuses on the future of education, topic #2 might be conceptualized as a "foreign versus domestic issues" topic.

Let's assume our comparison with topic #3 leaves us little reason to question the "future of education" interpretation of topic #9. Now we can read the top-loading documents (by absolute value) for the topic and see if that leads to something different (output in the margin).

Figure 10.3: Comparing topic #9 to topic #2.

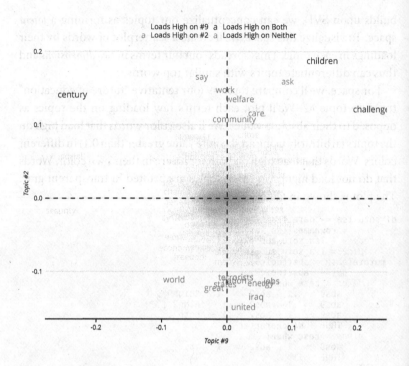

"Clinton_1999"
"Clinton_1996"
"Clinton_2000"
"Obama_2015"

```
abs(lsa_sotu_sub$dk) |>
  as.data.frame() |>
  arrange(desc(V9)) |>
  rownames() |>
  head(4)
```

```
"Clinton_1999"
"Clinton_1996"
"Clinton_2000"
"Obama_2015"
```

Clinton's 1999 speech loads the highest on this topic. Now is a good time to read this speech. How exactly are children, education, and the future discussed? Does it mesh with our initial interpretation of the topic? Let's find out.

```
df_sotu |> filter(doc_id == "Clinton_1999") |> select(text)
```

The speech is lengthy so we won't print it here. Bur portions of the speech revolve around what to do with the then $70 billion surplus—the government's revenues above and beyond debts. He recommended setting aside portions for Social Security and Medicare to strengthen safety nets and welfare for future generations.

In the excerpt below, we see a focus on education as well.

Now, there are more children from more diverse backgrounds in our public schools than at any time in our history. Their education must provide the knowledge and nurture the creativity that will allow our entire Nation to thrive in the new economy.

In all, this topic does have a "future of education" element to it—but it seems more general than that. Given the focus on investing in childrens' futures, perhaps "securing our children's future" is a better interpretation of the topic.

Let's look at one more document to see if we overspecified our interpretation.[31] We'll use the speech with another high loading: Bush's 2005 speech.

```
df_sotu |> filter(doc_id == "Bush_2005") |> select(text)
```

> Our generation has been blessed - by the expansion of opportunity, by advances in medicine, and by the security purchased by our parents' sacrifice...
>
> ...Over the next several months, on issue after issue, let us do what Americans have always done, and build a better world for our children and grandchildren.

It does seem like this is a "securing our children's future" topic. Recall that LSA attempts to explain the variation in our DTM using the fewest possible dimensions. This is a spatial interpretation of "variation," built on the vector space approach to meaning.

LSA has a long history as a form of topic modeling. For most researchers, though, LSA is probably not what they have in mind with topic modeling. The reason for this is that in the early 2000s, a new form of topic modeling—one that explicitly defined itself as such—emerged, known as **latent Dirichlet allocation**, or LDA for short (Blei et al. 2003). Let's explore that now.

Topic Modeling with LDA

LDA emerged, in part, because of shortcomings in LSA. For instance, with LSA, nothing is preventing negative values in the singular vectors (for either the terms or documents). Interpreting the singular vectors in an absolute sense is a little tricky.[32] They define a single point for the term/document in the latent space. Larger values indicate that the term/document loads higher on it and is therefore consequential for determining the topic's meaning—but any coordinate on its own is uninterpretable.[33]

Many alternatives to LSA have been proposed to deal with these issues, including *non-negative matrix factorization* (Lee and Seung 1999) and *probabilistic LSA* (Hofmann 2001), but LDA is the one that stuck—at least in the social sciences.[34] We'll therefore focus our attention here.

[31] In practice, we'll want to read more documents per topic to have a robust interpretation of what themes the dimension is picking up on.

[32] For instance, the topic loading for the term "security" on topic #9 (our "securing our children's future" topic) is −0.254 and the loading for the term "challenge" on that same topic is 0.221. So, −0.254 and 0.221 are *what*, exactly?

[33] Some suggest that SVD doesn't perform well for certain tasks, such as finding word similarities (Gamallo and Bordag 2011).

[34] See, for example, the 2013 special issue of the journal *Poetics* (Mohr and Bogdanov 2013).

LDA, and most topic model algorithms stemming from it, follow a generative Bayesian model. This means the algorithm (1) assumes a document-generating process, and (2) given that process, uses an iterative procedure to maximize the likelihood that we'd observe the data that we do in our DTM.

First, there is the document-generating process. With LDA we assume that, for any given document, we: (1) randomly choose a probability distribution over a set of k topics (where the size of k is selected by researchers). Then, (2) we randomly choose one of the topics from the distribution, and then (3) randomly choose a word from that topic (Blei 2012:78). We continue this process for each word in a document as if this is how one goes about writing anything.

Let's walk through that idea. Imagine we're writing a story about zombies. The generative assumption is that we first establish the range of topics we might cover in the story. This might include "eating brains," "zombie apocalypse," "contagious virus," and "consumerism." We're also more likely to discuss some topics over others. For example, if we quantify it, we might say that we have a 40% chance of writing about eating brains, a 10% chance of writing about a zombie apocalypse, a 26% chance of writing about a contagious zombie virus, and a 24% chance of writing about consumerism (using zombies as a critique of American mass consumption). This forms the documents' probability distribution over k (and here, $k = 4$) topics from step (1) above.

From here, we then choose one of the topics to write about. In our example, the most probable candidate is "eating brains," since it has the highest probability of being chosen (40%). Within that topic, we are more likely to use some words over others. For example, in this topic, we're more likely to use words like "brains," "skull," and "gore" than words like "virus," "contagious," or "lab." So, within that topic, we have another probability distribution—but instead of a distribution of our document over a set of k topics, now we have a distribution of the "eating brains" topic over v words, where v is our vocabulary. Within this topic-word distribution, then, we pick a word. In our case, we'll favor words that communicate something about eating brains. This is the word that gets put down on the page.

Writing is a sequential process, so all we have to do is iterate for each word in the document. Keeping the document-topic distribution from step (1), we repeat steps (2) and (3) above to create our zombie story. Then, for any other zombie story in the corpus (produced by us or someone else), we again pick a probability distribution over those k topics (i.e., repeat step [1]), and then go back to steps (2) and (3). And on and on we go until each story is finished.

Notice we assume two types of distributions: each document's probability over topics and each topic's probability over the vocabulary. These are parameters that we do not *initially* derive from the data.[35] The trick, then, is to randomly pick these distributions and then continuously simulate this document-generating process—each time updating these parameters until, eventually, we get the maximum log-likelihood of getting the observed DTM.[36]

If we row-bind our document-topic distributions and row-bind our topic-word distributions, then we get two inductively derived matrices: a *document-topic probability matrix* and a *topic-term probability matrix*. The first is often called the *gamma* (or *theta*) matrix, while the second is called the *beta* (or *phi*) matrix.

These matrices are the core output from LDA. We'll use the topic-term probability matrix to determine what each topic is about, and we use the document-topic probability matrix to determine which topics (or combinations of topics)[37] are more prevalent in the document.

Let's use the same SOTU subset from the LSA example. Recall, we have two versions of our SOTU DTM: one with non-distinguishing terms removed (dtm_sotu_sub) and one without those terms removed (dtm_sotu). We'll start with the latter and see if those terms (or new terms) must be removed to give better topics.

We'll use topicmodels and the LDA() function. We need to supply our DTM and our *k*. Our last LSA model gave us 9 topics, so let's roll with that. We can also specify our estimation method—either variational inference ("VEM") or collapsed Gibbs sampling ("Gibbs"). The original LDA paper uses variational inference (Blei et al. 2003), which is also the default.[38] Since there is randomness to this procedure (unlike LSA), we'll also set a "seed" so our results can be reproducible.

```
opts <- list(seed = 61761)

lda_sotu <- LDA(dtm_sotu, k = 9, control = opts)
```

Let's look at the terms with the highest probability of being associated with each topic. topicmodels has a convenience function for this: terms() .

```
terms(lda_sotu, 5)
```

```
     Topic 1  Topic 2  Topic 3  Topic 4  Topic 5
[1,] "people" "must"   "must"   "people" "america"
[2,] "us"     "people" "america" "can"    "world"
```

[35] These distributions are random draws from *Dirichlet* distributions—thus, the model's name.

[36] There are various strategies for doing this with iteration, namely, collapsed Gibbs sampling and variational inference.

[37] LDA is, therefore, like LSA in that it is fuzzy clustering. LDA models are "mixed membership" (Blei et al. 2003). Each word gets a vector of probabilities across all topics, and each document is assigned a probability for each topic.

[38] It's a good idea to compare outputs using both estimation types (Grimmer et al. 2022:149).

```
[3,] "can"     "now"      "can"       "new"    "people"
[4,] "new"     "work"     "security"  "us"     "must"
[5,] "now"     "can"      "people"    "year"   "us"

     Topic 6    Topic 7      Topic 8      Topic 9
[1,] "must"     "american"   "american"   "new"
[2,] "new"      "thank"      "america"    "can"
[3,] "can"      "people"     "new"        "america"
[4,] "people"   "one"        "one"        "jobs"
[5,] "america"  "americans"  "country"    "work"
```

If we pluck a word at random from topic #1, the word with the highest probability of being chosen is "people."

Before moving on any further, though, it seems that we again have some non-distinguishing words that seem to crop up across many topics. Let's remove that vector of words from the LSA example and see what we get.

```
lda_sotu_sub <- LDA(dtm_sotu_sub, k = 9, control = opts)
terms(lda_sotu_sub, 5)
```

```
     Topic 1   Topic 2    Topic 3   Topic 4   Topic 5
[1,] "world"   "work"     "work"    "jobs"    "tonight"
[2,] "one"     "years"    "health"  "years"   "one"
[3,] "states"  "world"    "care"    "work"    "help"
[4,] "united"  "jobs"     "years"   "one"     "great"
[5,] "years"   "care"     "time"    "need"    "iraq"

     Topic 6      Topic 7    Topic 8      Topic 9
[1,] "years"      "years"    "security"   "jobs"
[2,] "children"   "one"      "world"      "one"
[3,] "work"       "first"    "help"       "years"
[4,] "ask"        "care"     "one"        "energy"
[5,] "help"       "tonight"  "health"     "time"
```

These topics are somewhat distinguishable from one another, but they still appear quite general. If we want more specific, fine-grained topics, then we should consider upping k. Let's try it again, this time looking for 20 topics.

```
lda_sotu_sub_20 <- LDA(dtm_sotu_sub, k = 20, control = opts)
```

The printout of top terms for each of these 20 topics would be quite large. Let's visualize it instead. We can also use this as an opportunity to see the probabilities associated with these terms (per topic).

We want the topic a.k.a. "beta matrix."[39] In addition to wrangling this matrix into a dataframe, the probabilities have been logged, so they must be exponentiated. We'll keep only the terms with top 10 probabilities per topic by using group_by() with slice_max() .

```
df_terms <- tidy(lda_sotu_sub_20, "beta")

df_top <- df_terms |>
```

[39] It is located in @beta in the model object. The use of @ instead of $ is because the output of LDA() is an S4 class object, a more restricted kind of R object. tidytext 's tidy() is a general "tidier," which wrangles common text analysis objects for us, including S4 class objects.

```
  group_by(topic) |>
  slice_max(n = 10, beta) |>
  ungroup() |>
  arrange(topic, beta) |>
  mutate(order = row_number())
```

Now, we're ready to create a bar chart for each topic using `facet_wrap()` with `geom_col()`, but for space we'll only show the first 4 topics. The bar plots are shown in Figure 10.4.

```
df_top |>
  filter(topic <= 4) |>
  ggplot(aes(order, beta)) +
  geom_col(show.legend = FALSE) +
  coord_flip() +
  ylim(0, .013) +
  labs(x = NULL, y = "Probability of Term in Topic") +
  facet_wrap(~topic, scale = "free", ncol = 4) +
  theme(axis.text.x = element_blank()) +
  scale_x_continuous(breaks = df_top$order, labels = df_top$term)
```

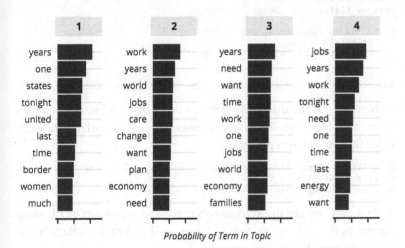

Figure 10.4: Top Terms for 20-Topic Solution (first 4 topics).

These look a little better. There are still terms that are prevalent across many topics. This makes it hard to discriminate between topics.

Before removing more words, however, let's see if the issue is our k. While the topics should always pass the eye test with a deep reading of the documents with high probabilities per topic, we can also use some diagnostic statistics to help us locate the right k. We follow Roberts and colleagues (Roberts et al. 2014) and recommend two complementary statistics: *semantic coherence* and *exclusivity*.

Semantic coherence quantifies the extent high-probability terms in a topic occur in the same documents (Mimno et al. 2011).[40] Topics with high-probability terms rarely co-occurring might signal a noisy topic.

[40] A smoothing number —usually, 1—is added to avoid the logarithm of zero. While coherence typically ranges from 0 and below, this smoothing number allows for positive coherence in the limiting case where co-occurrence equals occurrence.

If this holds across topics for a given k, the coherence value will be smaller and that k may not be the best.

Exclusivity, by contrast, measures the extent to which a topic tends to monopolize the presence of particular words (Bischof and Airoldi 2012). A larger exclusivity score means that the topic's most probable terms are more isolated to that topic (they have low probabilities across the other topics).[41]

Coherence and exclusivity are topic-level statistics. If we take the averages across all topics for a particular k, we'll see which number of topics best balances internal consistency and topic separation. Let's see what k this workflow recommends. First, we need to estimate several topic models with different k. We'll get models ranging from $k = 4$ to $k = 16$, going up in increments of 2. We'll also create a new function to use with `lapply()` .[42]

```
k_topic <- seq(4, 16, by = 2)
opts <- list(seed = 10001)

multi_lda <- function(k, dtm, opts) {
    print(k)
    return(LDA(dtm, k, control = opts))
}

lda_mods <- lapply(k_topic, multi_lda, dtm_sotu_sub, opts)
```

Now, we get the diagnostic statistics for each model using functions from `topicdoc` . We'll derive our coherence and exclusivity statistics using the top 10 terms per topic.

```
diag_list <- lapply(lda_mods, topic_diagnostics, dtm_sotu_sub, 10)
names(diag_list) <- k_topic
df_diag <- bind_rows(diag_list, .id = "K")
```

And, now we get the average coherence and exclusivity per k using `group_by()` and `summarize()` . Then, we'll plot each k's statistics to see which topic best balances them.

```
df_diag |>
  group_by(K) |>
  summarize(coherence = mean(topic_coherence),
            exclusivity = mean(topic_exclusivity)) |>
  ggplot(aes(coherence, exclusivity)) +
  geom_text(aes(label = K)) +
  labs(x = "Coherence", y = "Exclusivity")
```

In Figure 10.5, the best candidates are those toward the top right. Although $k = 16$ has the highest exclusivity, it has a lower coherence. So, let's go with $k = 10$, which has a better balance. We can use the 10-topic solution we already estimated; we only need to extract it from the `lda_models` list. In our case, it is the 4th element of the list.

```
lda_sotu_10 <- lda_mods[[4]]
```

[41] Proposed measurement of exclusivity includes the frequency-exclusivity harmonic mean (Bischof and Airoldi 2012:3) and the FREX score (Roberts et al. 2014:1068).

[42] Note that this chunk of code may take about 20 minutes, so feel free to reduce the upper bound on our k.

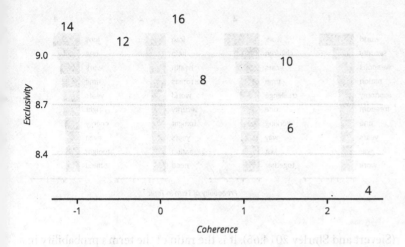

Figure 10.5: Coherence and Exclusivity.

Now, let's tidy() the beta matrix, then grab the top 10 terms within each topic, and then sort the resulting dataframe by those probabilities.

```
df_terms <- tidy(lda_sotu_10, "beta")

df_top <- df_terms |>
    group_by(topic) |>
    slice_max(n = 10, beta) |>
    ungroup() |>
    arrange(topic, beta) |>
    mutate(order = row_number())
```

Now, we can create a bar chart—like with the 20-topic solution—and only select the first 4 topics (Figure 10.6).

```
df_top |>
    filter(topic <= 4) |>
    ggplot(aes(order, beta)) +
    geom_col(show.legend = FALSE) +
    coord_flip() +
    ylim(0, .015) +
    labs(x = NULL, y = "Probability of Term in Topic") +
    facet_wrap(~topic, scale = "free", ncol = 4) +
    theme(axis.text.x = element_blank()) +
    scale_x_continuous(breaks = df_top$order, labels = df_top$term)
```

There are still some non-distinguishing terms making it difficult to interpret the topics. Instead of removing these terms, let's take another interpretation strategy.

Term relevance is the sum of two term-specific measures: probability and lift. We've already discussed probability: each term has a probability of being allocated to each topic. Terms with a high probability of being used in a topic help determine what that topic is about. **Lift**, on the other hand, is a measure of how *distinctive* the term is to each topic

Figure 10.6: 10-Topic Solution (first 4 topics).

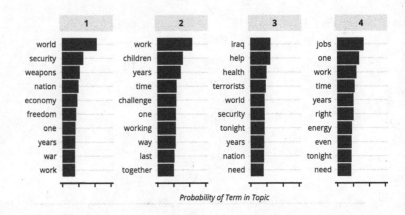

Probability of Term in Topic

(Sievert and Shirley 2014:65). It is the ratio of the term's probability in a topic to the term's probability across all the documents.

Lift can give terms that are idiosyncratic to specific documents. Luckily, term relevance means that we do not have to think about high probability and high lift separately from one another. With term relevance, Sievert and Shirley (Sievert and Shirley 2014:66) provide a way to blend the two metrics.[43]

Of course, we should also read the documents with high probabilities on these topics to ensure they engage the topics in ways we expect. If they do not, then we need to adjust our interpretations. Our document-topic probability matrix is stored in `@gamma`, which we can extract and then relabel the columns (topics) and rows (speeches).

```
df_doc_topics <- tidy(
    lda_sotu_10,
    matrix = "gamma",
    document_names = rownames(dtm_sotu_sub)
)
```

And now we can quickly visualize which speeches are engaging with which topics using a heatmap.

```
df_doc_topics |>
  mutate(topic = as.factor(topic)) |>
  ggplot(aes(topic, document, fill = gamma,
         label = round(gamma, 2))) +
  geom_tile(show.legend = FALSE, color = "white", alpha = 0.55) +
  geom_text() +
  labs(x = "Topics", y = "Speeches")
```

In contrast to clustering, here LDA is a fuzzy clustering method, which allows documents to be categorized gradationally. For instance, in Figure 10.7, Obama's 2012 speech mostly engages topic #7 and has some engagement with topic #4. We can also see that a speaker may

[43] Specifically, weighting a term's topic-specific probability by some scalar (call it λ) and weight the topic-specific lift for that same term by the one minus that weight $(1 - \lambda)$. We then add these two weighted values to get our term's relevance score.

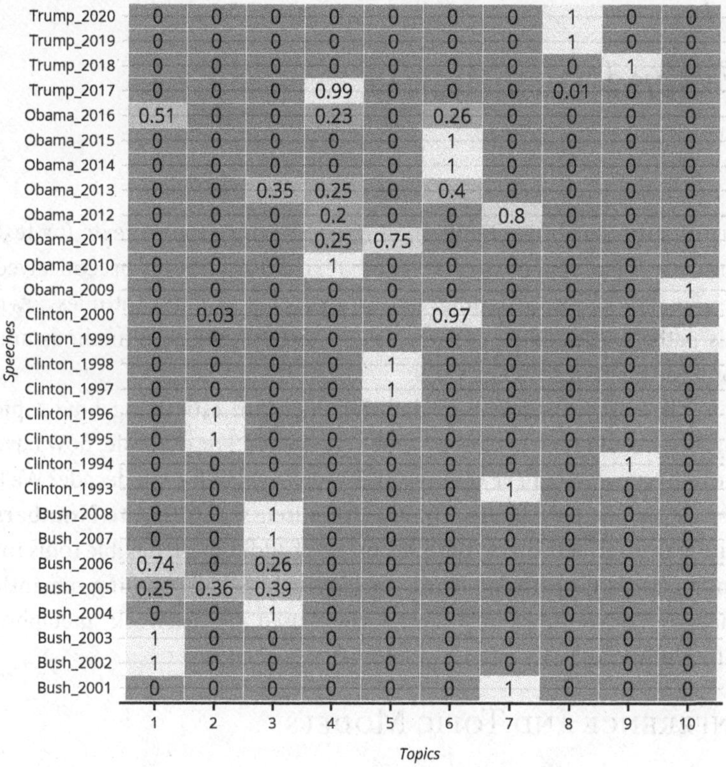

Figure 10.7: Probability of a Speech Engaging a Topic.

Speeches	1	2	3	4	5	6	7	8	9	10
Trump_2020	0	0	0	0	0	0	0	1	0	0
Trump_2019	0	0	0	0	0	0	0	1	0	0
Trump_2018	0	0	0	0	0	0	0	0	1	0
Trump_2017	0	0	0	0.99	0	0	0	0.01	0	0
Obama_2016	0.51	0	0	0.23	0	0.26	0	0	0	0
Obama_2015	0	0	0	0	0	1	0	0	0	0
Obama_2014	0	0	0	0	0	1	0	0	0	0
Obama_2013	0	0	0.35	0.25	0	0.4	0	0	0	0
Obama_2012	0	0	0	0.2	0	0	0.8	0	0	0
Obama_2011	0	0	0	0.25	0.75	0	0	0	0	0
Obama_2010	0	0	0	1	0	0	0	0	0	0
Obama_2009	0	0	0	0	0	0	0	0	0	1
Clinton_2000	0	0.03	0	0	0	0.97	0	0	0	0
Clinton_1999	0	0	0	0	0	0	0	0	0	1
Clinton_1998	0	0	0	0	1	0	0	0	0	0
Clinton_1997	0	0	0	0	1	0	0	0	0	0
Clinton_1996	0	1	0	0	0	0	0	0	0	0
Clinton_1995	0	1	0	0	0	0	0	0	0	0
Clinton_1994	0	0	0	0	0	0	0	0	1	0
Clinton_1993	0	0	0	0	0	0	1	0	0	0
Bush_2008	0	0	1	0	0	0	0	0	0	0
Bush_2007	0	0	1	0	0	0	0	0	0	0
Bush_2006	0.74	0	0.26	0	0	0	0	0	0	0
Bush_2005	0.25	0.36	0.39	0	0	0	0	0	0	0
Bush_2004	0	0	1	0	0	0	0	0	0	0
Bush_2003	1	0	0	0	0	0	0	0	0	0
Bush_2002	1	0	0	0	0	0	0	0	0	0
Bush_2001	0	0	0	0	0	0	1	0	0	0

Topics

monopolize some topics. Topics #1 through #3 are dominated by Bush's speeches, while Obama's speeches dominate topics #4 and #5.

One limitation of LDA is that topics are (more or less) independent of one another. Assuming that the document-generation process begins with drawing document-topic probabilities from a Dirichlet distribution comes with the constraint that no high or low probabilities for one topic are predictive of high or low probabilities for another topic. This is a tough constraint, as it is easy to imagine that topics will co-occur in a document. We'll return to this issue in the next chapter when we discuss *structural topic modeling*.

11

Extended Inductive

INDUCTIVE analysis entails finding *latent* groupings of texts (or text units) or relations between texts (or text units) without preconceived notions about those groupings or relations. This chapter continues down this path. In the following chapters, we extend our core methods and combine them in complex ways.

We'll return to topic modeling but focus on estimating how topic *engagement* and *content* vary by other covariates. For example, how have the topics covered in *The Washington Post* changed in the last decade? We'll also extend the term similarity measures discussed in **Text to Numbers** with **word embeddings**. We'll see that embeddings are flexible tools for finding relations between words and documents and mapping semantic changes. For example, how have authors used the "network" metaphor differently over two centuries (Yung 2021)?

INFERENCE AND TOPIC MODELS

THIS SECTION NEEDS:

- tidyverse
- broom
- marginaleffects

Predicting Topics with Covariates

In this section, we'll cover a few ways researchers might include covariates (or "predictors," or "independent variables") into their topic model analysis.

We've done all the work to get our topics. We've chosen an algorithm—LDA, or perhaps something like CTM (Blei and Lafferty 2007), or maybe the biterm topic model for short texts (Yan et al. 2013) or one that allows us to supply keywords (Eshima et al. 2020). We've run the model with different k, comparing fit statistics across solutions. We've interpreted the topics. Now what? We can treat these topics like any other variable.

We can see how topics may shape other factors. For instance, we might test the effects of positive tax news from US presidential communications on private consumption and investment (Dybowski and Adämmer 2018). We can also see how other factors may shape topics. For example, we can use transcripts from Federal Open Market Committee meetings to assess if speakers with private banking experience were more likely to discuss finance (Fligstein et al. 2017).

Mapping Texts: Computational Text Analysis for the Social Sciences. Dustin S. Stoltz and Marshall A. Taylor, Oxford University Press. © Oxford University Press 2024.
DOI: 10.1093/oso/9780197756874.003.0011

Remember topic modeling results in two probability matrices: a document-topic matrix that shows the probability of documents across topics and a topic-word matrix that shows the probability of topics across the vocabulary. We assume most covariates are at the document or author level, so we'll focus on the document-topic probabilities.

Let's explore a topic model on English-language fiction between 1880 to 1999,[1] estimated by Underwood and colleagues (2022). This study considers the extent changes in culture are explained by "period"—for example, the culture of the 1980s—versus "cohort"—for example, those born in the 1980s. Their model includes 200 topics,[2] and each work has covariates such as first publication date and whether that author is/was American.

The topics were estimated for chunks of each work: each volume spans multiple rows, with each row corresponding to a (roughly) 10,000-word chunk. For the sake of space, we only include a subset. Instead of a random sample of rows, we randomly sample 1,000 unique works.

The supplementary file for the study contains the labels and keywords for each of the 200 topics. We'll focus on one topic—topic #3, labeled "late-20th-century US political thrillers." Higher probabilities for this topic indicate a work is more likely to be in the US political thriller genre.

Say we want to assess time trends for this topic. Are newer or older works in the corpus more likely to be a (or *written like*) late-20th-century US political thrillers? Or, maybe we want to know whether author demographics are associated with this topic? Perhaps American authors are more likely to write on this topic than authors from elsewhere. Lastly, since some works exist in the "gray area" between fiction and nonfiction (Underwood et al. 2020:7), are works in this gray area more likely to be in this topic than in others? Let's investigate these questions now.

Let's run an OLS regression with this topic as the outcome.[3] The predictors are the (1) date of first publication, a (2) dichotomous variable for whether the author is/was American ("False" or "True"), and the (3) probability the work was nonfiction. The topic of interest is "V6." For the date, we'll allow the magnitude and/or direction to be nonlinear by adding a quadratic term (poly(firstpub, 2)).

[1] Works are collected from the HathiTrust Digital Library.

[2] The authors used MALLET (Mimno 2013), a Java program, to estimate topics.

[3] See **Math Basics**.

```
data("stm_fiction_cohort", package= "text2map.pretrained")
stm_fic <- stm_fiction_cohort |>
         mutate(us_national = factor(us_national))

lm(V6 ~ poly(firstpub, 2) + nonficprob + us_national,
   data = stm_fic) |> tidy()
```

term	estimate	std.error	statistic	p.value
1 (Intercept)	0.00174	0.000590	2.95	3.26e- 3

```
2 poly(firstpub, 2)1         0.111     0.0117      9.51 1.44e-20
3 poly(firstpub, 2)2         0.0490    0.0116      4.21 2.79e- 5
4 nonficprob                 0.00409   0.00173     2.36 1.84e- 2
5 factor(us_national)True    0.000758  0.000898    0.844 3.99e- 1
```

Note all our estimates are positive. Focusing on publication date (second and third terms), we see newer works are more likely to be late-20th-century US political thrillers—and this association grows larger over time.[4] The probability of being nonfiction (fourth term) is positively associated with this topic. This is intuitive since political thrillers might include nonfiction details such as depictions of real political events and places. Being an American author (fifth term) seems to have a small effect, but still positive.

Now let's generate predicted probabilities. We'll get probabilities for each publication year three times: once when the nonfiction probability equals the 25th percentile, then the 50th percentile (the median), and then the 75th percentile. Let's prepare that outcome variable below.

```
# get the IQR value for the nonficprob variable
iqr_nonfic <- c(
    quantile(stm_fic$nonficprob, .25, na.rm = TRUE),
    quantile(stm_fic$nonficprob, .5,  na.rm = TRUE),
    quantile(stm_fic$nonficprob, .75, na.rm = TRUE)
)
```

```
# create labels for the plot
lab_nfic <- c(
    "Nonfiction Probability at\n25th Percentile",
    "Nonfiction Probability at\n50th Percentile",
    "Nonfiction Probability at\n75th Percentile"
)
names(lab_nfic) <- iqr_nonfic
```

Let's add an interaction effect between the publication date and the nonfiction probability (and remove the quadratic publication term for simplicity). We'll calculate these probabilities controlling for American nationality by assuming the author is American and focus on the latter portion of the 20th century.

```
df_md <- lm(V6 ~ firstpub * nonficprob + us_national, data = stm_fic)

df_prd <- predictions(model = df_md,
        newdata = datagrid(
        firstpub = seq(1975, 1999, by = 1),
        nonficprob = iqr_nonfic,
        us_national = "True")
        )
```

Now, we can plot the probabilities. They are visualized in Figure 11.1.

```
df_prd |>
    ggplot(aes(x = firstpub, y = estimate)) +
    geom_ribbon(aes(ymin = conf.low, ymax = conf.high), alpha = .2) +
    geom_line() +
```

[4] This should be the case. We'd have a puzzle if works in the 1800s engaged this topic.

```
facet_wrap(~nonficprob,
  labeller = labeller(nonficprob = lab_nfic)) +
labs(x = "Date of First Publication",
     y = "Engaging 'Late 20c US Political Thriller'") +
scale_x_continuous(breaks = seq(1975, 1995, by = 5))
```

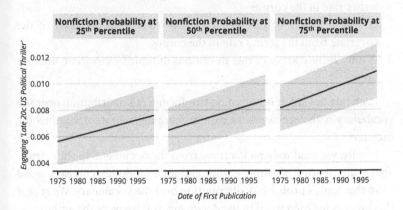

Figure 11.1: Predicted Probabilities.

A work of fiction is more likely to be in (or at least *read like*) a late-20th-century US political thriller in later years.

Topic Prevalence, Conditional on Covariates

Above we used covariates to predict topics. The topic identification *itself*, though, isn't conditional on these covariates. **Structural topic modeling**, or STM (Roberts et al. 2019), incorporates document-level covariates in topic estimation and estimates the effects of these covariates on *topic prevalence* and *topic content*.

Let's briefly discuss the basics of STM so we can see where the prevalence and content covariates come into play in the data-generation process assumed by STM.[5]

STM is a probabilistic model.[6] It attempts to reverse-engineer the data-generating process by finding the model that maximizes the likelihood of observing the documents' word counts that we do. Following Roberts and colleagues (Roberts et al. 2016:991; Roberts et al. 2019:2–3), we randomly draw a probability distribution for each document in the corpus from a logistic normal distribution that has been *conditioned on that document's "prevalence" covariates*.

Then, if there is a *content covariate* (which we discuss next), STM decomposes the document's topic distributions over the corpus vocabulary into two matrices and an array (Roberts et al. 2016:991). The

THIS SECTION NEEDS:

- tidyverse
- textclean
- textstem
- stringi
- tidytext
- text2map
- stm
- stminsights
- marginaleffects
- ggtern

[5] STM builds on CTM, and reduces to it when there are no covariates. There are excellent statistical overviews (e.g., Roberts et al. 2016, 2019).

[6] Like the LDA model we discussed in the previous chapter, see **Core Inductive**.

matrices and array are the following, where k is the number of topics and v is the length of the vocabulary, and c is how many levels are in the content covariate:

1. A k-by-v matrix of rate deviations for each term per topic from the term's rate in the corpus.
2. A c-by-v matrix of rate deviations for each term per level of the covariate from the term's rate in the corpus.
3. A c-by-k-by-v array of rate deviations of topic by covariate interactions.[7]

Each rate deviation is logged, so the document's distribution over the vocabulary is the *exponentiated* sum of these logged rate deviations for each term.

Finally, we randomly pick a topic from the document-specific probability distribution we drew earlier and then randomly choose a word from that topic's probability distribution over the vocabulary. We repeat this process for each word in the document as if we were the author.

STM uses an iterative algorithm[8] to find the best-fitting parameters. The parameters of interest are (1) the document-topic and (2) topic-word probability distributions,[9] and also the (3) topic-prevalence coefficients and the (4) topic-content rate deviations.

Now that we've got the basics of the model out of the way, we can ask: What's the significance of prevalence and content covariates for my topic model analysis? Let's start with prevalence.

Topic **prevalence** is the effect of a covariate on the extent a document engages a topic. We saw, for instance, that newer works of fiction that were also more in the gray area between fiction and nonfiction tended to devote more words in the "late-20th-century US political thrillers" topic. Here, however, STM incorporates those covariates *when estimating* topics.

To demonstrate topic prevalence, let's use an example from Bohr and Dunlap (2018). The researchers use STM on abstracts from environmental sociology articles to map the main topics in the field and how the prevalence of those topics varied over time (among other things). They used Web of Science's Social Science Citation Index (SSCI) to scrape English-language abstracts from articles published between 1990 and 2014 and containing key terms relevant to environmental sociology. The researchers retained only those journals listed by SSCI under the "sociology" category.[10] The corpus also comes with three covariates for each article: publication year, citations per year, and journal ranking.[11]

Let's load the data and take care of wrangling. We'll replace curly quotes with ASCII double-quotes, transliterate the text to "Basic Latin"

[7] An *array* is a data structure with any number of dimensions. A matrix is a two-dimensional array. This array is three-dimensional.

[8] Namely, partially collapsed variational expectation-maximization.

[9] Typically, the first matrix is called *beta*, but stm calls the second matrix *theta*, while most others call it *gamma*. We call it gamma.

[10] Our version of the corpus contains 817 articles, though the published article only includes 815 articles.

[11] Journal ranking is the h5-index score for that journal at the time the authors downloaded the article (Bohr and Dunlap 2018:3).

ASCII characters, replace contractions with their full word variants, remove capitalization, remove punctuation, remove numbers, remove excess whitespace, and then lemmatize with a dictionary look-up procedure (i.e., no POS-tagging) with Měchura's English lemma-token dictionary (the default dictionary in `lexicon` which `lemmatize_strings()` uses).[12]

[12] See **Wrangling Words.**

```
data("corpus_envsociology", package = "text2map.corpora")

df_env <- corpus_envsociology |>
  mutate(text = replace_curly_quote(abstract),
         text = stri_trans_general(text,
                 id = "Any-Latin; Latin-ASCII"),
         text = replace_contraction(text),
         text = gsub("\\Ws\\W", "", text),
         text = tolower(text),
         text = gsub("[[:punct:]]+", " ", text),
         text = gsub("[[:digit:]]+", " ", text),
         text = gsub("\\s+", " ", text)) |>
  mutate(lemma = lemmatize_strings(text))
```

After constructing our DTM, we'll remove words occurring once in the corpus and those from the Snowball 2014 stoplist. We'll also remove "environment" and "environmental"—since all the articles are about environmental sociology.

```
our_sl <- c(get_stoplist("snowball2014"),
            "environment", "environmental")

dtm <- df_env |> dtm_builder(lemma, title) |>
    dtm_stopper(stop_list = our_sl, stop_hapax = TRUE)
```

Now we can estimate our model. This process can take some time, even with a corpus as small as this one. So be prepared.[13] We estimate our topics by conditioning topic prevalence on publication year and topic content on journal ranking. The authors determined that a 25-topic solution was best, so we'll do the same.[14] We'll set `verbose` to `FALSE` so that we don't see every expectation step ("E-step") and maximization step ("M-step").

[13] The algorithm could be sped up by removing more words.

[14] The STM developers offer a few statistical procedures for helping find the optimal *k*, including the coherence-exclusivity tradeoff we covered in the previous chapter. See their paper in the *Journal of Statistical Software* (Roberts et al. 2019) for more information.

```
set.seed(60601)

# this might take a while!
stm_env <- stm(
    documents = dtm,
    K = 25,
    data = df_env,
    prevalence = ~year,
    verbose = FALSE
)
```

Now let's grab the top terms for each topic to begin interpreting. We'll use `tidy()` from `tidytext` to reshape the term-topic probability matrix (beta) into a dataframe. We'll also group by topic, get just the top five words, and then paste them together.

```
stm_beta <- tidy(stm_env, matrix = "beta") |>
    group_by(topic) |>
    slice_max(beta, n = 5, with_ties = FALSE) |>
    summarize(terms = paste0(term, collapse = ", "))

print(stm_beta, n = 15)

    topic terms

       1  scale, study, people, use, new
       2  people, global, change, indigenous, much
       3  research, policy, science, political, knowledge
       4  change, climate, global, adaptation, community
       .
       .
       .
      14  social, movement, examine, organization, global
      15  much, use, gender, policy, fish
```

These look like coherent topics. Let's look at the prevalence of two topics over time: topic #4—which we call "Climate Change"—and topic #14—which we call "Social Movements." How did engagement in the "Climate Change" and "Social Movements" topics vary over time? We can use `estimateEffect()` to get our estimates and confidence intervals and `get_effects()` to tidy the output for easy visualization.

```
df_effs <- estimateEffect(c(4, 14) ~ year, stm_env,
                          metadata = df_env)

df_effs <- get_effects(df_effs, variable = "year",
                       type = "continuous") |>
  mutate(Topics = case_when(
    topic == 14 ~ "Social Movements",
    topic == 4 ~ "Climate Change")
  )

df_effs |>
  ggplot(aes(x = value, y = proportion, fill = Topics)) +
  geom_ribbon(aes(ymin = lower, ymax = upper), alpha = 0.5) +
  geom_line(aes(linetype = Topics)) +
  labs(x = "year")
```

Environmental sociology papers are increasingly discussing climate change and decreasing discussing social movements (see Figure 11.2). This illustration shows how incorporating prevalence into topic modeling can trace the attention of a field over time.

Topic Content, Conditional on Covariates

In addition to seeing how documents' engagement with a topic changes by a covariate, we can also model how topics' contents change by a covariate. More technically, topic **content** is the extent a covariate affects the vocabulary used to articulate a topic. Perhaps, for example, American

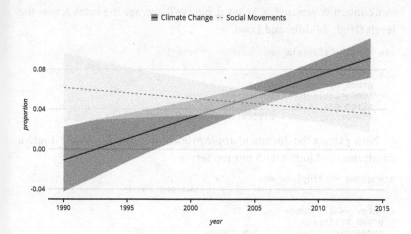

Figure 11.2: Topic Prevalence over time.

authors write US political thrillers in distinct ways compared to non-American authors writing about the same topic. Or, perhaps, environmental sociology articles use "disaster" or "crisis" in their articulation of climate change more if they're published in high-ranking journals.

For our demonstration, we'll use journal rank. This variable has 31 levels for 31 possible ranks. Content covariates, especially those with several levels, slow convergence considerably. So, let's first recode journal ranks into three levels.

```
df_env <- df_env |>
  mutate(rank = case_when(
          journal_rank <= 18 ~ "High",
          journal_rank >= 19 &
          journal_rank <= 23 ~ "Middle",
          journal_rank >= 24 ~ "Low")
  )
```

We're ready to estimate our model. Other than supplying our content covariate, let's keep everything the same as our last estimate, including our prevalence variable (year). Models with content covariates can take a while to converge.[15]

```
stm_env <- stm(
    documents = dtm,
    K = 25,
    data = df_env,
    prevalence = ~year,
    content = ~rank,
    verbose = FALSE
)
```

Now we can extract the top terms from the term-topic probability matrix (beta) and reshape it into a dataframe. Note there is a column for

[15] A pretrained version is in text2map.pretrained .

our content covariate (y.level), but we'll average the betas across the levels (High, Middle, and Low).

```
stm_beta <- tidy(stm_env, matrix = "beta")

stm_beta <- stm_beta |>
    group_by(topic, term) |>
    summarize(beta = mean(beta)) |>
    slice_max(beta, n = 5, with_ties = FALSE) |>
    summarize(terms = paste0(term, collapse = ", "))
```

Now extract the document-topic probability matrix, reshape it into a dataframe, and join it with our top terms.

```
stm_gamma <- tidy(stm_env, matrix = "gamma",
                  document_names = rownames(dtm))

df_prev <- stm_gamma |>
    group_by(topic) |>
    summarise(prevalence = sum(gamma, na.rm = TRUE)) |>
    arrange(desc(prevalence)) |>
    left_join(stm_beta, by = "topic") |>
    mutate(topic = paste0("Topic ", str_pad(topic, 2, pad = "0")),
           topic = reorder(topic, prevalence))
```

And now we can make a plot showing the most prevalent topics and the top five words per topic.

```
df_prev |>
    ggplot(aes(topic, prevalence,
        label = terms, fill = topic)) +
    geom_col(show.legend = FALSE) +
    geom_text(hjust = 0, nudge_y = 0.5, size = 3) +
    coord_flip() +
    ylim(0, 110)
```

In Figure 11.3, Climate Change (topic #4) is dominating environmental sociology. We can also see the Social Movements topic (#14) is in the top 5 most prevalent. Now, let's get the effect of our content covariate for these two topics. This time we want to compare across discrete levels, so we'll select "pointestimate." We'll also do a little tidying of the variables with mutate() .

```
df_effs <- estimateEffect(c(4, 14) ~ rank,
                          stm_env,
                          metadata = df_env)

df_effs <- get_effects(
    estimates = df_effs,
    variable = "rank",
    type = "pointestimate") |>
    mutate(
    Topics = case_when(
             topic == 14 ~ "Social Movements",
             topic == 4 ~ "Climate Change"),
    rank = factor(value, levels = c("Low", "Middle", "High"))
    )
```

Now we can plot the effects in Figure 11.4.

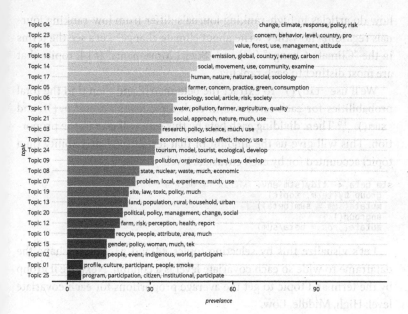

Figure 11.3: Topic Prevalence with Content Covariate.

```
df_effs |>
  ggplot(aes(x = rank, y = proportion)) +
  geom_errorbar(aes(ymin = lower, ymax = upper),
      width = 0.1, size = 1) +
  geom_point(size = 3) +
  facet_grid(~Topics) +
  coord_flip() +
  labs(x = "Rank", y = "Topic Proportion")
```

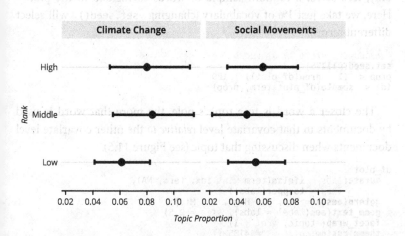

Figure 11.4: Topic Proportions by Content Covariate.

Of course, a benefit of conditioning on a content covariate is seeing how the topic vocabulary differs by levels of that covariate. For example, how do articles in high-ranking journals differ from low-ranking journals regarding how they write about climate change? Let's see the terms in the "Climate Change" (#4) and "Social Movements" (#14) topics that are most distinct to each ranking.

We'll use `tidy()` to extract the beta matrix and then find the total probabilities for each term within each topic using `group_by()` and `sum()` .[16] Then, dividing each beta by this sum will give us the proportion. This will give us the amount of that term's total probability (in a topic) accounted for by each covariate level.

[16] Remember, each word will have a topic-specific probability for each covariate level.

```
stm_beta <- tidy(stm_env, matrix = "beta") |>
  group_by(term, topic) |>
  mutate(sum = sum(beta)) |>
  ungroup() |>
  mutate(prop = beta/sum)
```

Let's visualize this by selecting topics #4 and #14 and reshape the dataframe to wide so each covariate level is a column. Next, we'll group by the term and topic to get the average proportions for each covariate level: High, Middle, Low.

```
df_plot <- stm_beta |>
  filter(topic == 4 | topic == 14) |>
  pivot_wider(names_from = y.level, values_from = prop) |>
  group_by(term, topic) |>
  summarize(High = mean(High, na.rm = TRUE),
            Mid = mean(Middle, na.rm = TRUE),
            Low = mean(Low, na.rm = TRUE))
```

[17] We'll have to tweak some of the plotting parameters to get our same theme colors and fonts—thus, `theme_custom()` .

Let's create ternary plots with `ggtern` . For visualization purposes only, let's select a random sample of words to include in the plot.[17] Here, we take just 1% of vocabulary (changing `set.seed()` will select different terms).

```
# randomly select 1% of vocab
set.seed(011235)
prop <- (1 * nrow(df_plot)) / 100
idx <- sample(df_plot$term, prop)
```

The closer a word is to a topic's pole, the more that word is used by documents in that covariate level *relative to* the other covariate level documents when discussing that topic (see Figure 11.5).

```
df_plot |>
  mutate(labs = ifelse(term %in% idx, term, NA),
         labs = toupper(labs)) |>
  ggtern(aes(x = Low, y = High, z = Mid)) +
  geom_text(aes(label = labs), size = 2.5) +
  facet_wrap(~topic, ncol = 1) +
  theme_custom(col.L = "#541352ff",
               col.T = "#ffcf20ff",
               col.R = "#2f9aa0ff",
               tern.plot.background = "white",
               tern.panel.background = "white")
```

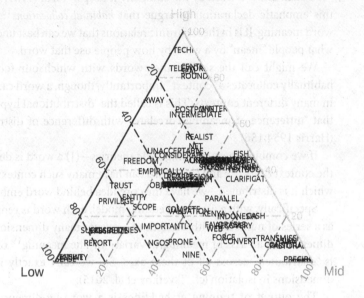

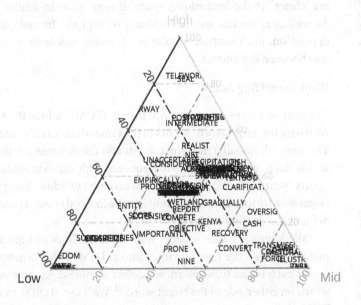

Figure 11.5: Topic Vocabulary by Content Covariate.

WORD EMBEDDINGS: THE FIRST GENERATION

"You shall know a word by the company it keeps!" Firth (1957:11) made this emphatic declaration to argue that *habitual collocations*[18] capture word meaning. It is in these chronic relations that we can best understand what people "mean" by a word by how people use that word.

We might call the set of other words with which our focal word habitually collocates a "context." Importantly, though, a word can pop up in many different contexts. This is called the "distributional hypothesis": that "difference of meaning correlates with difference of distribution" (Harris 1954:156).

If we combine these two linguistic theories—(1) a word is defined by the context of its use and (2) a word can have many such contexts across which it is distributed—we have the core idea behind word embeddings.

Specifically, with a word embedding model, each word is represented as a series of numbers with a length of however many dimensions. Each dimension is an axis of meaningful variation. The meaning[19] of a word is "distributed" across all of these axes. So, we can't exactly interpret dimensions in isolation (cf. Tsvetkov et al. 2015).

The output of training embeddings is a word-by-dimension *word vector matrix*. Each row is a word in the corpus vocabulary and each column is one of the dimensions.[20] Within this matrix, two words' vectors are "closer" in the "embedding space" if they occur in similar contexts. As we'll see, we can use embeddings to explore "formal" relations— opposition, juxtaposition, similarity—between words in a corpus and also between documents.

Word Embedding Basics

The cells of a term-co-occurrence matrix (TCM) include the frequency with which a "target word" occurs in the same context as a "context word." The rows are (usually) the target words and the columns are the context words. Each cell is the (weighted) frequency with which the column word occurs "next to" the target word in a set context window. Every word is a target word distributed across contexts. Each word is also a context word defined as a distinct context.

Take Kennedy's Rice speech. We'll treat the lines as separate documents and turn the first few lines into a TCM with a window of size 5—for each target (row) word, we define a context window as the five words on either side of the target word.[21] We'll use `fcm()` to make our TCM.[22]

---

[18] The consistent co-occurrences of words.

THIS SECTION NEEDS:

- text2map
- text2vec
- stringi
- tidyverse
- textclean
- quanteda
- rtrek
- ggrepel

[19] Here, understood as how authors use a word.

[20] Each unique word might have more than one vector depending on the type of word embedding model. We'll return to this when we discuss token embeddings.

[21] This could be an asymmetric window, for example, five words *on just one side* of the target word.

[22] quanteda calls TCMs "feature co-occurrence matrices"; thus, FCM.

```
df_jfk <- data.frame(text = c(
    "We choose to go to the moon",
    "We choose to go to the moon",
    "We choose to go to the moon in
     this decade and do other things"
))

df_jfk$text |>
    tokens() |>
    fcm(context = "window", window = 5)
```

```
Feature co-occurrence matrix of: 13 by 13 features.
         features
features We choose to go the moon in this decade and
    We    0      3  6  3   3    0  0    0      0   0
 choose   0      0  6  3   3    3  0    0      0   0
    to    0      0  0  6   6    6  2    1      1   0
    go    0      0  0  0   3    3  1    1      0   0
   the    0      0  0  0   0    3  1    1      1   1
  moon    0      0  0  0   0    0  1    1      1   1
    in    0      0  0  0   0    0  0    1      1   1
  this    0      0  0  0   0    0  0    0      1   1
decade    0      0  0  0   0    0  0    0      0   1
   and    0      0  0  0   0    0  0    0      0   0
```

According to this TCM, the word "We" occurs in the same context (of size 5) as "choose" 3 times. We can verify that by looking back at the raw documents: "choose" is fewer than 5 words removed from "We" in each of the three documents, so $1 + 1 + 1 = 3$. We also see "to" occurs in the same context as "moon" 6 times: two instances of "to" occur within 5 words of "moon" in each document, so $(1 + 1) + (1 + 1) + (1 + 1) = 6$. We could also weight each target-context instance by the distance of the context word from the target word in the window so words farther out in the window "count less" in the TCM than words occurring right next to the target word.

Weighting the TCM

This raw frequency matrix is not the best measure of word relatedness for two reasons. First, the matrix is very sparse (lots of zeros). Second, some words are commonplace but not very discriminative, such as "the" and "of." We'll learn *statistically* whether a given context word is *particularly informative* about the target word.

We can address this by weighting the TCM by pointwise mutual information (PMI).[23] PMI measures whether events x and y co-occur more than they occur independently. PMI ranges from negative to positive infinity, but negative values are typically not relevant for our cases.[24] Therefore, it is standard practice to replace all negative values with zero to get *positive* pointwise mutual information, PPMI (Jurafsky and Martin 2000:109).[25]

[23] See **Text to Numbers**.

[24] We'd need enormous corpora, and "unrelatedness" is not intuitive.

[25] PPMI is biased toward infrequent words. See section 6.6 of Jurafsky and Martin (2000).

Let's move to our corpus of season 5 of *Star Trek: The Next Generation*. Load the corpus and do some preprocessing.

```
data("corpus_tng_season5", package = "text2map.corpora")

df_st <- corpus_tng_season5 |>
  mutate(text = stri_trans_general(line, "Any-Latin; Latin-ASCII"),
         text = replace_contraction(text),
         text = tolower(text),
         text = gsub("[[:punct:]]+", " ", text),
         text = gsub("\\s+", " ", text)
  )
```

Now we can make our TCM, which we'll convert to a sparse matrix.

```
tcm <- df_st$text |> tokens() |>
  fcm(context = "window", window = 10) |>
  as("dgCMatrix")
```

Just to speed up the process, let's only keep words with at least 30 co-occurrences.

```
tcm <- tcm[colSums(tcm) > 30, colSums(tcm) > 30]
```

[26] Adapted from text2vec 's coherence() .

Now we can define a function for PPMI weighting.[26] Then we'll apply the weighting scheme to the TCM.

```
weight_ppmi <- function(tcm) {

  ## fix zero self-occurrences
  diag(tcm) <- diag(tcm) + 1
  ## weight by PMI
  tcm <- tcm %*% diag(1 / diag(tcm))
  tcm <- log(tcm)
  ## positive PMI
  tcm[tcm < 0] <- 0
  return(Matrix(tcm, sparse = TRUE))
}
```

```
tcm_ppmi <- weight_ppmi(tcm)
```

Once we have a PPMI-weighted TCM, we can measure the similarities between two rows (i.e., target words) using the cosine similarity statistic we discussed in the previous chapter.

```
vec1 <- tcm_ppmi["captain", , drop = FALSE]
vec2 <- tcm_ppmi["picard", , drop = FALSE]
vec3 <- tcm_ppmi["crusher", , drop = FALSE]

sim2(vec1, vec2, method = "cosine")
sim2(vec1, vec3, method = "cosine")
```

We see "captain" and "picard" occurring in more similar contexts than "captain" and "crusher"—which we expect given that while Picard and Crusher are both characters on the show, Picard is a captain and Crusher is not.

Dimension Reduction with Singular Value Decomposition

PPMI vectors don't solve the sparsity problem! The length of the vector is still the size of the vocabulary, and likely to be tens of thousands elements long. When we start reducing these long vectors to "lower-dimensional" vectors, we take a step toward **word embeddings**. The easiest way to reduce the dimensions of either our raw count or PPMI-weighted TCM is to apply singular value decomposition (SVD).[27]

```
svd_tng <- svd(tcm_ppmi)
```

Somewhere between 100 and 300 dimensions is optimal for representing words (see Yin and Shen 2018). Since we limited our vocabulary, it is best to limit the number of dimensions of our embeddings to the lower end.

```
wv_tng <- svd_tng$v[, 1:100]
rownames(wv_tng) <- rownames(tcm_ppmi)
```

Now, instead of a term-by-term term-context matrix with over 3,000 terms and 3,000 contexts, we have a term-by-dimension context matrix with over 3,000 terms and exactly 100 dimensions. Though both TCMs are technically word vector matrices, the latter is what most mean by word vectors. These new word vectors form a *simpler* representation of the corpus' meanings while still retaining most of the covariances.

Since our word vectors form a geometric space, we can use basic arithmetic to add and subtract word vectors. The classical example goes: If we subtract the vector for "man" from the vector for "king" and then add the vector for "woman," we get a synthetic vector very close to the vector for "queen."

Let's try it. If we subtract the vector for "jean" from the vector for "picard" and then add the vector for "william," we should find that one of the closest words is "riker":[28]

[28] Jean-Luc Picard and William Riker are two main characters on the show.

```
vec1 <- wv_tng["picard", , drop = FALSE]
vec2 <- wv_tng["jean", , drop = FALSE]
vec3 <- wv_tng["william", , drop = FALSE]

vec_syn <- vec1 - vec2 + vec3

sim <- sim2(wv_tng, vec_syn, method = "cosine")
sim[, 1] |> sort(decreasing = TRUE) |> head(n = 5)
```

```
   picard     riker    william   welcome    macduff
0.7496190 0.4816914 0.4608522 0.4011149 0.3690412
```

Sure enough, "riker" is one of the closest words to our synthetic vector.

We can use these geometric properties of the word vector space to consider more social scientific analyses. For example, if we get the cosine of each word from the vector for "boy" and then the vector for "girl" and then take the difference in these cosines, we should see which words in the series were used in more "masculine" contexts and which were used in more "feminine" contexts. Differences in cosine similarities above zero indicate a word more associated with masculinity. Those below zero are more associated with femininity.

Let's try this with the *Star Trek* data. First, get each corpus word's cosine similarity from the "boy" and "girl" vectors and put the results into a new dataframe.

```
focal <- c("boy", "girl")

vecs <- wv_tng[focal, ]
sims <- sim2(vecs, wv_tng, method = "cosine")

df_sims <- data.frame(
    word1 = sims[1, ],
    word2 = sims[2, ],
    term = colnames(sims)
)
```

Now we'll define a new column, "gender_bias," which is each word's difference in cosine similarities. We'll also create a column called "gender" which indicates whether the word is used in more masculine contexts or more feminine contexts. Then we'll plot the top masculine and top feminine words in Figure 11.6.

```
df_plot <- df_sims |>
  mutate(gender_bias = word1 - word2,
         gender = ifelse(gender_bias > 0, "boy", "girl"),
         gender_bias = abs(gender_bias)
  )

df_plot |>
    group_by(gender) |>
    slice_max(gender_bias, n = 30) |>
    mutate(term = fct_reorder(term, gender_bias)) |>
    ggplot(aes(term, gender_bias, fill = gender, label = term)) +
    geom_col() +
    coord_flip() +
    facet_wrap(~gender, scale = "free")
```

Among other things, *leadership* words (leader, certain, integrity) are more associated with "boy," and *vulnerability* words (prisoner, confined, asylum) are more associated with "girl." We'll return to this idea of exploring how contexts vary along sociologically interesting dimensions later in the chapter when we discuss how we might carry out inductive analyses with word embeddings.

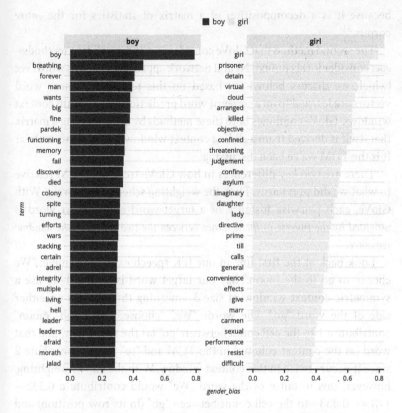

Figure 11.6: Gender Bias in *Star Trek: TNG*, Season 5.

Word Embeddings: The Next Generation

Applying SVD to a (PPMI weighted) TCM is one way of creating word vectors. But it's not the most popular.[29] Broadly, there are three popular embedding methods: the global approach, the neural network approach, and newer "contextualized" approaches. We'll discuss each in the following.

The Global Approach: GloVe

One of the most popular algorithms for training word vectors is the GloVe model (Pennington et al. 2014)—a.k.a., the "Global Vectors" model. GloVe is a combination of two training methods: "global" matrix factorization (thus, the *global* part of the name) and "local" window-sliding methods (Pennington et al. 2014:1532). The matrix of right singular vectors that we get from a latent semantic analysis (LSA) on a DTM[30] are word vectors—only the context is the entire document. This is "global"

[29] For one, SVD may not perform well on large corpora (Pennington et al. 2014:1539).

[30] See **Core Inductive**.

because it is a decomposition of a matrix of statistics for the *entire* corpus.[31]

[31] For example, the frequency of "picard" in the first episode of season 5 of *Star Trek: The Next Generation* is a summary statistic independent of any "local" context in which any one instance of "picard" occurs in that episode.

The second method that GloVe considers—window-sliding methods—*does* consider local context. Neural network approaches such as word2vec (which we discuss below) are based on this technique, where word vectors are learned from a series of word prediction tasks within context windows. GloVe combines both these methods by decomposing a matrix that itself is derived from a sliding context window. What is this matrix? It is the TCM we've been discussing!

There are two key differences in how GloVe treats the TCM relative to what we did previously. First, the weighting scheme is different. With GloVe, each pairwise instance of a target word and context word is *weighted by the inverse of the distance between the two words in the window sequence.*

Look back at the first line in our JFK speech excerpt example: "We choose to go to the moon." Say our target word is "go" and we use a symmetric context window of size 3—meaning three words on either side of the word "go." The words "We," "choose," "the," and "moon" contribute a 1 to the cell count between "go" (as the target row) and that word (as the context column) in the TCM and "to" would contribute 2 since it occurs twice in this context window. With the GloVe weighting, however, this instance of the word "We" would contribute a 0.333— $1/3 \approx 0.333$—to the cell count between "go" (in its row position) and "We" (in its column position). Why? Because "We" is three words removed from "go" in this window. If there is a later context window where "We" is right next to "go" in the word sequence—for example, "We go to the moon"—then that instance of "We" would contribute a 1 to the cell count.

Context words occurring further from the target word in the windows contribute less to the target-context cell in the TCM. This rewards "better" context words, which we assume are those words consistently appearing pretty close to the target word in sequence.

Let's create this with our JFK TCM. Let's move over to text2vec since we'll use it to train GloVe vectors later. We'll use a context window of size 3.

[32] Adapted from the developer's tutorial.

In the code below,[32] we first tokenize each document, and create an iterator to loop over the tokens. create_vocabulary() uses that iterator to identify our unique vocabulary and the term frequencies and document frequencies for those terms. We then use that output to vectorize our vocabulary (i.e., associate each term with an index to speed up the process).

Finally, we create our TCM.[33] The output is a sparse matrix. Since the TCM is symmetric (as the context window is symmetric), only the top triangle of the matrix is returned. (We'll print the output as a regular matrix to get column names printed, and only print the first 10 columns.)

```
words <- space_tokenizer(df_jfk$text)
iterate <- itoken(words)
voc <- create_vocabulary(iterate)
vocab_vec <- vocab_vectorizer(voc)

tcm <- create_tcm(iterate, vocab_vec, skip_grams_window = 3L)
```

	and	decade	do	in	other	things	this	We	choose	go
and	0	1	1.0	0.33	0.50	0.33	0.50	0	0	0.0
decade	0	0	0.5	0.50	0.33	0.00	1.00	0	0	0.0
do	0	0	0.0	0.00	1.00	0.50	0.33	0	0	0.0
in	0	0	0.0	0.00	0.00	0.00	1.00	0	0	0.0
other	0	0	0.0	0.00	0.00	1.00	1.00	0	0	0.0
things	0	0	0.0	0.00	0.00	0.00	0.00	0	0	0.0
this	0	0	0.0	0.00	0.00	0.00	0.00	0	0	0.0
We	0	0	0.0	0.00	0.00	0.00	0.00	0	3	1.0
choose	0	0	0.0	0.00	0.00	0.00	0.00	0	0	1.5
go	0	0	0.0	0.00	0.00	0.00	0.00	0	0	0.0
moon	0	0	0.0	0.00	0.00	0.00	0.00	0	0	0.0
the	0	0	0.0	0.00	0.00	0.00	0.00	0	0	0.0
to	0	0	0.0	0.00	0.00	0.00	0.00	0	0	0.0

The "go"-"We" cell is a 1, which we expect since "We" occurs in "go"'s context window one time in each document and at the very end of the window each time, so $1/3 + 1/3 + 1/3 = 1$.

Weighting is the first difference from our SVD example. The second difference is how this TCM is factorized. As noted previously, the performance of SVD diminishes as corpora grow larger (Pennington et al. 2014:1539). GloVe borrows from context-sliding approaches by turning the factorization into a prediction task using a model[34] to find the word vectors where each pair of word vectors have a dot product[35] that best minimizes the error in predicting the log of that word pair's cell entry in the TCM. Of course, each word pair's prediction error cannot be minimized in isolation, so GloVe finds the total set of word vectors that minimizes a global cost function.[36] This cost function is itself weighted so very frequent word pairs and very infrequent terms do not contribute too much when learning the vectors.

Let's walk through an example using the *Star Trek* data.[37] We already preprocessed our data; it is the dataframe called df_st . In what follows, we first define a GloVe model specifying that we want 100 dimensions. The x_max parameter is part of the weighting scheme for the cost function: it is the "ceiling" on word-pair co-occurrences (preventing very frequent word pairs from getting too big) and the number by which we

[33] We can specify symmetric or asymmetric windows with skip_grams_window_context .

[34] Specifically, a global log-bilinear regression model.

[35] See **Math Basics**.

[36] This is the same logic behind minimizing the sum of squared errors in OLS regression.

[37] This is adapted from Selivanov's tutorial.

divide other word-pairs (assuring very infrequent word-pairs get smaller weights). We set this to 20.[38]

```
g_model <- GlobalVectors$new(rank = 100, x_max = 20)
```

Then we pass our TCM to this model for training. We need to make a TCM for the *Star Trek* data (now using a symmetric context window of size 5).

```
# Create our TCM
words <- space_tokenizer(df_st$text)
iterate <- itoken(words)
voc <- create_vocabulary(iterate)
vocab_vec <- vocab_vectorizer(voc)
st_tcm <- create_tcm(iterate, vocab_vec, skip_grams_window = 5L)

st_vectors <- g_model$fit_transform(st_tcm, n_iter = 50)
```

We'll see progress updates. The "epoch" is the number of iterations that GloVe takes to minimize the cost function. We set that to 50 with `n_iter`. The number labeled as "loss" is the numerical value of the cost function. The smaller that number, the better the predictions—that is, the word vectors should closely reproduce the TCM.

GloVe produces target word (row) vectors and context word (column) vectors. These are roughly equivalent when the TCM is symmetric (like ours). The `st_vectors` are the target word vectors; the context word vectors are in an object called `$components`. There are benefits to combining these two vectors (Pennington et al. 2014:1538–9), which we'll do.[39]

```
st_vectors <- st_vectors + t(g_model$components)
```

We have GloVe vectors! One way to get a snapshot of the embedding space is with a scatterplot. Of course, this is tricky with high-dimensional spaces. We can reduce this to two dimensions with SVD.[40] We'll remove words from the Snowball 2014 stoplist before passing the vectors to the `svd()`.

```
st_2d <- st_vectors |>
    as.data.frame() |>
    mutate(name = rownames(st_vectors)) |>
    filter(!name %in% get_stoplist("snowball2014")) |>
    select(!name)

wv_coords <- svd(st_2d)$u

wv_coords <- wv_coords |>
    as.data.frame() |>
    select(V1, V2) |>
    mutate(name = rownames(st_2d))
```

Then visualize the first two reduced dimensions, only plotting the word labels for those loading high on at least one of the dimensions. In Figure 11.7, we can see various clusters of related terms, like "bajoran,"

[38] Your results should be very close, but not identical to ours. text2vec automatically *parallelizes*. This makes setting seeds and reproducing exact results tricky—for example, see this comment by Selivanov: github.com/dselivanov/text2vec/issues/251

[39] GloVe can also create "positional vectors," tracking the position of each word in the window, and later concatenated (Ibrahim et al. 2021).

[40] There are other proposed methods for visualizing 2D or 3D reductions of embedding spaces, such as tSNE.

"cardassian," and "romulan"—all names for alien civilizations in the *Star Trek* universe.

```
wv_coords |>
  mutate(col = case_when(
         abs(V1) >= 0.03 ~ TRUE,
         abs(V2) >= 0.03 ~ TRUE,
         TRUE ~ FALSE),
       lab = case_when(
         abs(V1) >= 0.03 ~ name,
         abs(V2) >= 0.03 ~ name,
         TRUE ~ NA_character_)) |>
  ggplot(aes(V1, V2)) +
    geom_point(aes(color = col), alpha = 0.1, show.legend = FALSE) +
    geom_text_repel(aes(label = lab), max.overlaps = Inf,
        show.legend = FALSE) +
    labs(x = "Dimension 1", y = "Dimension 2")
```

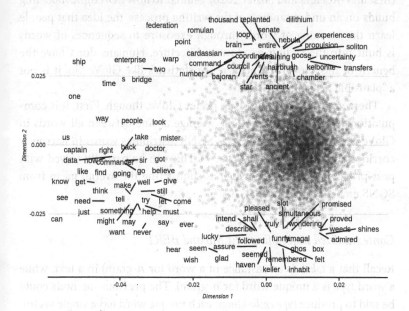

Figure 11.7: SVD of the *Star Trek* GloVe Embeddings.

The Neural Network Approach: CBOW, SNGS, and fastText

While word2vec did not introduce using *neural networks*[41] to create embeddings, it is one of the most popular methods. Like GloVe, word2vec learns reduced representations of term-co-occurrences to predict one of two objectives.

[41] See **Extended Deductive**.

With *Continuous Bag-of-Words (CBOW)*, the model predicts the target word given a context word. With the *Continuous Skip-Gram*, the model tries to predict a context word given a target word. The developers note CBOW is faster, while Skip-Gram is better for infrequent words. More technically, both maximize the average log-probability of a target and context word co-occurring. This "maximization" is measured using either *hierarchical softmax* or *negative sampling*. While both have strengths, by far the most common setup is *Skip-Gram with Negative Sampling (SGNS)*.[42]

An important extension of SGNS is **fastText**, which incorporates "subword" character n-grams—for example, "fluffy" is the co-occurrence of "fl", "lu", "uf", "ff", "fy". The model averages these n-gram vectors to get word vectors, and can even create vectors for out-of-vocabulary words.[43]

While SGNS has comparable performance to GloVe—depending on the task and tuning parameters, such as window size—one reason SGNS is preferred is that it builds on an intuitive model of language learning (Arseniev-Koehler and Foster 2020). Similar to how LDA topic modeling builds on an understanding of the writing process, the idea that people learn the meaning of words through exposure to sequences of words is built into the sliding window architecture. Humans don't have the benefit of the "global" co-occurrence statistics like GloVe. So, it is not a "plausible" learning process.

There are technical reasons to prefer GloVe, though. First, it is computationally simpler. Second, the average cosine between all words in GloVe is much larger than SGNS; SGNS distributes words in narrower corridors of the embedding space.[44] This can be partially solved with post-processing techniques, such as subtracting the overall mean from SGNS embeddings (Mu et al. 2017).

Contextualized Embeddings: ELMo and BERT

Recall that a *token* is an instance of a word (or n-gram) in a text, while a word *type* is a unique word (or n-gram). The previous methods could be said to produce *type embeddings*: each unique word has a single vector. The obvious benefit of this is efficiency. These are also sometimes called "static" embeddings because they do not change with a word's specific context. However, we know that the same words can evoke various *senses* in different contexts, which may be semantically related or unrelated (i.e., homonyms). A common example is a *financial* bank versus a *river* bank.

The tricky question is: How many senses does a word have and how do we define the boundary between senses? Type embeddings overcome this question by trying to summarize all possible senses. So-called contextual models solve this by going in the opposite direction: creating *token embeddings*, which assign a vector to a word in a single context. This

[42] See word2vec (Wijffels 2021).

[43] See fastText (Mouselimis 2022) and fastTextR (Schwendinger and Hvitfeldt 2020).

[44] "Spreading out" words in the space (isotropy) generally improves embeddings on various tasks (Arora et al. 2016; Mu et al. 2017).

is useful if, instead of summarizing a word's meaning across multiple contexts, we wish to know precisely what *this* word means in *this* context.

ELMo (Embeddings from Language Models) builds on neural network embedding methods, with two important differences. Instead of fixed context windows, ELMo uses an (1) arbitrary length window—given the size of sentences or other text sequences vary—and also (2) separately trains the context to the right side of a token and the left side, before concatenating the two vectors. The result is a single vector where some dimensions entirely represent left-side meanings and some represent right-side meanings.

The most popular token embedding model is *BERT (Bidirectional Encoder Representations from Transformers)* and variations on it (Devlin et al. 2018). Like GloVe and word2vec, it is trained on a prediction task: predicting target words from context words, and predicting the probability of a randomly chosen next sequence given a preceding sequence. This sequence-to-sequence prediction is central to the *transformer* model. Instead of focusing on the most recent token, transformers pay attention to the entire sequence (or key parts of the sequence). This initial training is computationally costly. The pretrained model can then be fine-tuned with a local corpus. Furthermore, unlike ELMo, the left and right contexts are kept separate in the base model (i.e., *bidirectional*), and only concatenated during the fine-tuning process.

The BERT "base" model was trained on BookCorpus (Zhu et al. 2015) and English Wikipedia, and restricted to a vocabulary of 30,000 tokens. The final pretrained model has 12 layers.[45] Here is an example output using an excerpt from Kennedy's Rice speech. These vectors are from the final layer.[46]

```
tokens token_id  Dim1    Dim2   ...  Dim768
[CLS]       1    0.590  -0.251        -0.306
we          2    1.44    0.286        -0.825
choose      3    1.31    0.728         0.0677
to          4    1.93   -0.322        -0.641
go          5    0.911  -0.588         0.467
to          6    0.976  -0.349        -0.286
the         7    0.634   0.141        -0.0992
moon        8    1.91    0.830         0.0365
in          9   -0.681  -0.662        -0.422
this       10   -0.135  -0.226         0.213
decade     11    0.958  -0.0750       -0.0239
and        12    1.10    0.0651       -0.565
do         13    1.24    1.00         -0.0328
other      14    0.848   0.419         0.237
things     15    0.847   0.978        -0.889
[SEP]      16    0.0440  0.0162  ...  -0.0312
```

Note that "to" occurs twice and each has its own vector. [CLS] is a special token representing the "pooled" vector for all tokens in the

[45] Each layer is an encoder that outputs token embeddings. There are 12 attention heads in each layer, and each token is represented by a 768-dimension vector.

[46] We obtain these with text (Kjell et al. 2021), which interfaces with models hosted on Hugging Face. Researchers often combine multiple layers, and may select different layers.

sequence. The [SEP] represents the separation between sequences (but we only have one sequence here). Both are necessary for the next sequence prediction task. After tuning, the resulting embeddings are used for several downstream tasks.[47]

One critique of BERT (and similar models) is that it is "overparameterized": layers or dimensions may be redundant. As a response, new models attempt to "distill" BERT into a smaller base model. These include DistilBERT and tinyBERT (Sanh et al. 2019; Jiao et al. 2019). These are significantly smaller, have faster tuning, and achieve near-identical performance to BERT on various benchmarks.

It is, perhaps, too early to know when more involved (and computationally intensive) token embeddings are more appropriate for social scientific analyses (c.f., Li et al. 2021; van Loon and Freese 2022; McLevey et al. 2022). Furthermore, these token embeddings are often averaged together to achieve, presumably, more context-aware "static" type embeddings. However, it is not obvious that token embeddings outperform type embeddings, especially when these type embeddings are themselves tuned or post-processed. The next section includes several tuning methods to "contextualize" otherwise "static" word-type vectors for inductive analysis.

INDUCTIVE ANALYSIS WITH WORD EMBEDDINGS

THIS SECTION NEEDS:

- text2map
- text2map.pretrained
- text2vec
- stringi
- tidyverse
- textclean
- rtrek

As we can see, there are many ways to train word embeddings—each with benefits and limitations. What can we do in our research with an embedding space? We'll explore some methods here and in the next chapter.

Semantic Change

Word embeddings are uniquely suited to analyze semantic change, or the extent of a word's discursive context shifts from one time to another. Hamilton and colleagues (Hamilton et al. 2016:2), for instance, use embeddings to find that the "word *gay* shifted from meaning 'cheerful' or 'frolicsome' to referring to homosexuality" over two centuries based on the relative distance between those terms.

For this, we first need a corpus that varies across periods of time. We then subset the corpus by period, and train word vectors separately for each subset.[48] Next, we "align" the vectors across the periods to position them in the same "coordinate system."

We'll continue with the *Star Trek* scripts. Previously, though, we've used a single season from *The Next Generation* series. Let's use rtrek to get the transcripts for all series and seasons. We'll treat each spoken line as a document and then merge the episode data with those lines.

```
df_trek <- st_transcripts()

df_trek$episode <- rownames(df_trek)

df_lines <- bind_rows(df_trek$text, .id = "episode") |>
            left_join(df_trek[-10], by = "episode")
```

Before we train a unique set of word vectors per series, we'll preprocess the texts.

```
dia_df <- df_lines |>
    mutate(
        text = stri_trans_general(line,
                "Any-Latin; Latin-ASCII"),
        text = replace_contraction(text),
        text = tolower(text),
        text = gsub("[[:punct:]]+", " ", text),
        text = gsub("\\s+", " ", text)
    )
```

Now we'll subset our corpora[49] to separate documents by series. (Some of the *Star Trek* series overlapped a bit—but there is still a chronology to them that we'll follow.) The series variable is called "series," and includes six series (in order of introduction): *The Original Series, The Animated Series, The Next Generation, Deep Space 9, Voyager,* and *Enterprise.* We'll make a unique dataframe of transcript lines for each series, and then put all those dataframes into a single list.

We could also collapse the lines to make each document a unique script.

```
dia_df_list <- list()

for (i in unique(df_trek$series)) {
    dia_df_list[[i]] <- dia_df[dia_df$series == i, ]
}
```

Next, we'll make the TCMs—again, one for each series. We'll follow the same procedure for creating the *TNG* season 5 TCM above, but now we'll dump it all into a function. We'll use lapply() to apply the function to each dataframe in our list of dataframes.

```
make_tcm <- function(df) {
    words <- space_tokenizer(df$text)
    iterate <- itoken(words)
    voc <- create_vocabulary(iterate)
    vocab_vec <- vocab_vectorizer(voc)
    tcm <- create_tcm(iterate, vocab_vec, skip_grams_window = 5L)
    return(tcm)
}

dia_tcm <- lapply(dia_df_list, make_tcm)
```

Now we need to train the vectors. We'll go with 300 dimensions, a co-occurrence maximum of 10 for establishing the weighting function on the cost function, a learning rate[50] of 0.05, and just 10 training iterations to speed things up (this takes ~10 minutes). We'll also dump this into a function and use `lapply()` . We'll put our vectors in a list object called "dia_vecs."

```
make_vectors <- function(tcm) {
    g_model <- GlobalVectors$new(
        rank = 300, x_max = 10,
        learning_rate = 0.05
    )
    vectors <- g_model$fit_transform(tcm, n_iter = 10)
    vectors <- vectors + t(g_model$components)
    return(vectors)
}

dia_vecs <- lapply(dia_tcm , make_vectors)
```

There is one more step needed to compare *across* embeddings—which we're doing with longitudinal analysis of semantic change. We need to *align* our matrices. More specifically, we will align one matrix to a "reference" matrix. This ensures word vectors in different embedding matrices are projected onto the same "coordinate system" (Hamilton et al. 2016:4).

A popular method for doing this is the Procrustes method (Schönemann 1966). This preserves the within-matrix cosines while minimizing between-matrix differences by rotating, flipping, etc.[51]

For our analysis, our reference matrix is the *The Original Series* matrix. To keep things simple, we'll limit the vocabulary in each matrix to the words shared across all matrices.

```
shared_words <- Reduce(
    intersect,
    lapply(dia_vecs, rownames)
)
dia_vecs <- lapply(
    dia_vecs,
    function(i) i[shared_words, ]
)

aligned_vecs <- list()

for (i in seq_len(length(dia_vecs))) {
    if (i != 1) {
        aligned_vecs[[i]] <- find_transformation(
            dia_vecs[[i]],
            ref = dia_vecs[[1]],
            method = "align")
    } else {
        aligned_vecs[[i]] <- dia_vecs[[i]]
    }
}

names(aligned_vecs) <- names(dia_vecs)
```

[50] The learning rate is a limit on how quickly we can improve during each iteration. For reasons we won't get into, we want to limit improvement because otherwise our model may get "stuck" in non-optimal solutions (McLevey 2021:400-4).

[51] Understanding the math isn't necessary, so we won't discuss it here. But, it uses SVD (see **Math Basics**).

We're ready. Say we're interested in how discourse around "humans" might have shifted across the series. We can get a sense of this by examining the cosine similarities between the "human" vector across the series. Let's look specifically at how each series' "human" vector compares to the one for *The Original Series* (output in the margin).

```
for (i in c("TAS", "TNG", "DS9", "VOY", "ENT")) {
    out <- sim2(
      aligned_vecs[["TOS"]]["human", , drop = FALSE],
      aligned_vecs[[i]]["human", , drop = FALSE],
      method = "cosine"
    )
    print(paste0(i, ": ", round(out, 4)))
}
```

```
[1] "TAS: 0.2918"
[1] "TNG: 0.3051"
[1] "DS9: 0.2854"
[1] "VOY: 0.3633"
[1] "ENT: 0.3733"
```

The largest similarity to humanness in *The Original Series* is *Enterprise*. The context in which humanness was articulated in *The Original Series* was most similar to the *Enterprise* series. That said, in absolute terms, we don't see high similarities to *The Original Series* with any other series.[52] If we looked at the pairwise cosines between the "human" vector for the series, we would see they are all similarly low—indicating that, perhaps, humanness is framed differently in each series.

[52] Remember, cosine similarity has a maximum value of 1.

Let's explore that now. In the code below, we loop through each series-specific matrices, get the cosine similarities *within each matrix* to the "human" vector, filter out Snowball 2014 stoplist words,[53] arrange those cosines in descending order for each matrix, and then print the top 5 (we set n = 6 in head() to get five words *other than* "human"). We'll print the output in a table (see Table 11.1).

[53] We'll also remove rogue "s", likely a remnant from apostrophe removal.

Table 11.1: Evolution of "human" across *Star Trek* Series

Series	Context of "human" (in descending order)
TOS	life, us, captain, federation, form
TAS	instant, piece, prevent, perhaps, range
TNG	life, way, like, taking, part
DS9	known, theory, loss, disappeared, probably
VOY	klingon, look, life, correct, need
ENT	one, vulcan, beings, ship, earth

```
for (i in names(aligned_vecs)) {
  sim2(
      aligned_vecs[[i]],
      aligned_vecs[[i]]["human", , drop = FALSE]
  ) |>
      as.data.frame() |>
      filter(!rownames(aligned_vecs[[i]]) %in%
```

```
        c(get_stoplist("snowball2014"), "s")) |>
    arrange(desc(human)) |>
    head(n = 6) |>
    print()
}
```

We could then probe the embedding spaces further and/or do close reading of each series' transcripts to see how these terms contextualize the subject of humanness.

Semantic Directions and Semantic Centroids

Let's discuss two ways of conceptualizing meaningful dimensions in embedding spaces: **semantic directions** and **semantic centroids**.

A direction is a path on which something moves or sits. This is analogous to discursive bias: given two semantic "poles," we can place a document along the line between those poles—and the closer it is to one pole, the more that document is "biased toward" that pole relative to the other one. Our earlier gender bias walk-through involved a *semantic direction*: the closer a word was (using cosine similarity) to the "boy" end of a gender direction, the more that word is used in semantic contexts where "boy" and/or other "boy-related" words tend to be used as opposed to "girl" and/or other "girl-related" words.[54] Semantic directions are, essentially, one-dimensional "subspaces" within the higher-dimensional embedding space.

Semantic directions—analyzing them and how documents and document producers engage with them—is a popular social-scientific use of word embeddings. Kozlowski, Taddy, and Evans (2019) used directions to analyze how meanings of social class shifted over the 20th century. Similarly, Arseniev-Koehler and Foster (2020) used directions to examine the gendered, moral, health-centered, and socioeconomic biases in how *The New York Times* discusses obesity. We (Stoltz and Taylor 2021) analyzed how the racial, moral, and affluence dimensions of immigration vs. citizenship discourse evolved from 1880 to 2000 in American English.

Let's get some directions. We'll switch up the data, though, and now move over to a small random sample of 3,800 articles from the All the News (ATN) corpus (Thompson 2020) that mention either "immigrant" or "immigration" at least once. As of this writing,[55] this is a corpus of 2.7 million news articles from 27 different US-based news organizations. We sampled from an earlier, smaller version of this corpus that we used in Stoltz and Taylor (2021), which consists of 204,135 articles across 18 news organizations.

[54] The "and/or" language here is intentional. As long as domain-specific words reside in the same portions of the embedding space, their coordinates will be similar. This also means that words need not *literally* co-occur to be close. Even if "pie" and "cake" never co-occur, they do share context words like "sweet," and "fruit."

[55] This corpus grows every so often.

We first filtered the 204,135 articles to only those mentioning "immigrant" or "immigration" at least once (irrespective of capitalization or punctuation).[56] We load data below and take care of some preprocessing.

```
data("corpus_atn_immigr", package = "text2map.corpora")
data("contractions", package = "qdapDictionaries")

df_atn <- corpus_atn_immigr |>
  mutate(text = replace_non_ascii(text),
         text = replace_url(text, replacement = " "),
         text = replace_html(text, replacement = " "),
         text = replace_contraction(text,
             contraction.key = contractions,
             ignore.case = TRUE),
         text = str_replace_all(text, "[[:punct:]]", " "),
         text = replace_ordinal(text),
         text = str_replace_all(text, "[\\s]+", " "),
         text = tolower(text)
  )
```

Now we can create a DTM. Since we'll be visualizing these, let's remove words in the Snowball stoplist and very infrequent words.

```
dtm_atn <- df_atn |>
    dtm_builder(text, doc_id) |>
    dtm_stopper(stop_list = get_stoplist("snowball2014"),
                stop_docprop = c(.01, Inf))
```

This time, we won't create word vectors. Instead, we'll use a *pretrained model*—a set of readymade word vectors. The pretrained models we'll use are typically good at picking up on nuanced semantic relationships because they are trained on enormous corpora. Using pretrained models might be ideal when researchers are interested in prevalent "public" meanings. In contrast, *locally trained* (vectors the researcher trains themselves on their own corpus) might be better for picking up on idiosyncratic relationships—especially when the document producers behind the documents in the corpus use argotic language (Rodriguez and Spirling 2022).[57] The articles in the ATN corpus are (more or less) from mainstream news outlets, so this is a good candidate for relying on a pretrained model.

There are many well-known pretrained embedding models—for example, the Stanford GloVe, the HistWords, and Facebook's fastText embeddings. We'll use the fastText embeddings trained on the Common Crawl.[58] This matrix comprises roughly 2 million word vectors (trained on 600 billion tokens), across 300 dimensions. Let's load them.[59] It might take a while for the model to load into the session; it is big.

```
# download the model once
download_pretrained("vecs_fasttext300_commoncrawl")
# load the model each session
```

[56] There are only 17 organizations in the random sample after filtering. This sample of articles is in `text2map.corpora`.

[57] Pretrained models might also be better when the local corpus is tiny or when the researcher believes the semantic relationships within a corpus are not overly idiosyncratic (Rodriguez and Spirling 2022:114).

[58] We can also download the vectors directly from the fastText website: fasttext.cc/docs/en/english-vectors.html.

[59] We only need to download them once.

```
data("vecs_fasttext300_commoncrawl", package ="text2map.pretrained")
wv <- vecs_fasttext300_commoncrawl # rename so it's tidier
```

Now let's create a word vector representation of our DTM by taking the vocabulary *intersection* of the DTM and the embedding matrix. Remember, words are in the DTM's columns and embedding matrix's rows.

```
atn_vectors <- wv[rownames(wv) %in% colnames(dtm_atn), ]
```

We have vectors for only the words used in our ATN corpus—and we didn't have to train ourselves! Now, we'll analyze some semantic directions. We did this earlier by creating a gender direction anchored by "boy" and "girl." Let's turn our attention to a citizenship-immigration direction,[60] but now let's add *more* terms to each pole. This hones in on the area of the embedding space with this precise meaning. Let's go with a list of 12 terms for each pole,[61] though some terms repeat.

Let's first construct our dataframe with each anchor list as a separate column.

```
anchors <- data.frame(
  add = c("immigrants", "immigration", "immigrant", "foreign",
          "foreigner", "outsider", "stranger", "alien", "foreigner",
          "alien", "immigrant", "foreign"),
  sub = c("citizens", "citizenship", "citizen", "domestic", "native",
          "insider", "local", "resident", "resident", "native",
          "local", "familiar")
)
```

We get semantic directions using *vector offset* methods. First, is the *paired method*: each pair of words across the two anchor lists (e.g., "conservative" to "liberal" and "traditional" to "progressive") is an antonym pair, we subtract one of the vectors in the pair from the other, and then the sum of those vector differences is divided by the total number of pairs. This method requires the same number of words in each anchor list—since they have to be pairs—though words can repeat.

Second, is the *pooled method*, which involves finding the average vector for each anchor list (i.e., the average vector for the pole #1 words and the average vector of the pole #2 words) and then taking the difference.[62]

Third, is the *PCA method*. We take the vector differences for each antonym pair (as with the paired method), passing that d-by-v matrix[63] to a *principal components analysis (PCA)*, and then retaining the first principal component (Bolukbasi et al. 2016a, b).

Using `get_direction()` and the paired method (the default), we'll find the semantic direction for "ideological bias."

[60] Immigrants can, of course, be citizens. This direction is instead "understood as measuring a persistent symbolic structure rather than a legal distinction" (Stoltz and Taylor 2021:10). See also Beaman (2016) and Jaworsky (2013).

[61] These are the same terms we used in Stoltz and Taylor (2021).

[62] Note that with either the paired or pooled method, we get the offsets *before* calculating cosines. We did the opposite with the gender bias illustration.

[63] d is the number of dimensions and v the number of vector differences.

```
cit_imm <- get_direction(anchors = anchors, wv = atn_vectors)
```

The row is the direction, labeled with the first word in the anchor list for the "positive" pole (i.e., the side *from which* we subtract) followed by "_pole." Let's see what words tend to occur more when citizenship is discussed versus when immigration is.

```
sim_dir <- sim2(cit_imm, atn_vectors, method = "cosine")

df_dir <- data.frame(immigrants_pole = sim_dir["immigrants_pole", ],
                     terms = colnames(sim_dir)) |>
  mutate(cit_imm_label = ifelse(
           immigrants_pole >= 0,
           "Immigration", "Citizenship"),
       cit_imm = abs(immigrants_pole)
  )
```

```
df_dir |>
  group_by(cit_imm_label) |>
  slice_max(cit_imm, n = 30) |>
  mutate(term = fct_reorder(terms, cit_imm)) |>
  ggplot(aes(term, cit_imm, fill = cit_imm_label, label = terms)) +
  geom_col() +
  guides(fill = "none") +
  labs(x = NULL, y = "Cosine Similarity to Pole") +
  coord_flip() +
  facet_wrap(~cit_imm_label, scale = "free")
```

Figure 11.8 shows, to the extent US-based news media articles tend to adopt the public meanings of citizenship and immigration (as defined by the massive Common Crawl archive), citizenship is "local," synonymous with "community" and "providing." In contrast, immigration is "non-white," colonization," and associated with "blackness." News media tends to present citizenship in favorable terms while perpetuating racialized stereotypes about immigrants.[64]

Related to the semantic direction is the *semantic centroid*. A centroid is an averaged vector.[65] Semantic centroids are useful on their own if we want to know what the discursive context of some domain of interest is, rather than the context of that domain *relative* to another (which is what we get with directions). For example, we may want to know the general context in which "immigration" is discussed — not *relative to* how "citizenship" is discussed. Nelson (2021b), for instance, uses semantic centroids in her analysis of the *intersection* of social categories of people across institutional spheres in first-person narratives in the 19th-century US South, and Lix and colleagues (2022) also used centroids to study how discursive diversity impacts the work performance of remote software development teams.

Let's use `get_centroid()` to see the terms most similar to an "immigration" centroid.[66]

[64] For research on the association between Blackness and immigration in US discourse, see Mora and Paschel (2020).

[65] This is what we'd get with the pooled method for vector offsetting but before taking the difference between our two average vectors. This is also one strategy for creating **sentence embeddings**.

[66] The centroid is labeled with the first word in the anchor list followed by "_centroid."

Figure 11.8: Citizenship-Immigration in ATN Corpus.

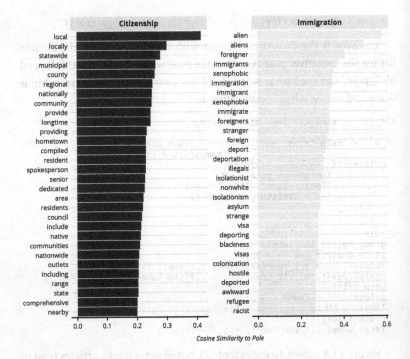

Cosine Similarity to Pole

```
imm_cen <- get_centroid(anchors = anchors$add, wv = atn_vectors)

sims <- sim2(atn_vectors, imm_cen, method = "cosine")
names(head(sort(sims[,1], decreasing = TRUE)))
```

```
alien immigrant foreigner foreign immigrants aliens
```

As we can see, the context terms for this centroid are not that different from those we get when considering immigration *relative* to citizenship. A good way to think about the difference between directions and centroids is that directions are better for picking up on relational *biases* (i.e., terms that favor one pole at the exclusion of the other), while centroids are better for identifying general contexts or the *intersection* of contexts.

Ultimately, though, this depends on what *meanings* we are attempting to measure. Some meanings *are* tightly organized into binary spectra; others are not. A more theoretical way to consider the contrast between centroids and directions is using the linguist Gremais "semiotic square" (Greimas 1983). Gremais organized meanings in terms of *four* poles. In our example, these would be "immigration" and "citizenship," as well as "not-immigration" and "not-citizenship." While semantic directions get at immigration/citizenship juxtaposition, centroids get closer to immigration/not-immigration or citizenship/not-citizenship oppositions. Here, theoretical motivation and subject expertise will drive which strategy is most appropriate for our research aims.

Word Mover's Distance

Word embeddings most readily lend themselves to word- and meaning-level analyses. Often we want to learn something about documents or authors. For instance, can we measure the extent any document writes about the same things and in the same way as the other documents in the corpus?

We use **Word Mover's Distances** (WMDs) for this (Kusner et al. 2015).[67] WMD is a measure of the minimum cost it would take to move all words in one document to the locations of the words in another document.[68]

More specifically, the WMD between document i and document j is the minimum sum of the products of two numbers for each pair of words across the two documents: the cosine distance and the cell entry for that word pair in what is known as a "flow matrix."[69] WMD finds the cell entries under the constraints that (1) the sum of the row word is the relative frequency of that word in i and (2) the sum of the column word is the relative frequency of that word in j. Finding the minimum cost is computationally demanding so Kusner and colleagues (2015:4) propose *relaxed* Word Mover's Distance (RWMD). However calculated, the result is a distance score where larger values indicate less context similarity between the two documents and smaller values indicate more context similarity. We'll stick with RWMD given the computational complexity of WMD (cf. Brunila and LaViolette 2021).

Say we want the contextual similarities between our news articles—all mentioning "immigrant" and "immigration" at least once—and a collection of press releases by a group of civil society organizations devoted to immigration-related issues.[70] Following our earlier work (Stoltz and Taylor 2021), let's examine the extent left-wing and right-wing news sources use language similar to these immigration-focused civil society organizations.

We've already wrangled articles and pretrained vectors; now we need to wrangle the press releases. Let's load and wrangle them using the same preprocessing workflow we used for the All the News (ATN) articles.

[67] There are other strategies. See Lix and colleagues (2022) for one approach.

[68] It is an offshoot of Earth Mover's Distance (EMD), which compares how similar two probability distributions are.

[69] Finding this matrix is called a *transportation problem*.

[70] The press releases are provided with `text2map.corpora` and scraped from the website from two right-wing organizations (the Center for Immigration Studies and the Federation of American Immigration Reform) and two left-wing organizations (The National Network for Immigrant and Refugee Rights and the Women's Refugee Commission).

```
data("corpus_ittpr", package = "text2map.corpora")
data("contractions", package = "qdapDictionaries")

df_ittpr <- corpus_ittpr |>
    mutate(text = replace_non_ascii(text),
           text = replace_url(text, replacement = " "),
           text = replace_html(text, replacement = " "),
           text = replace_contraction(text,
               contraction.key = contractions,
               ignore.case = TRUE),
           text = str_replace_all(text, "[[:punct:]]", " "),
           text = replace_ordinal(text),
           text = str_replace_all(text, "[\\s]+", " "),
           text = tolower(text)
    )

dtm_ittpr <- df_ittpr |>
    dtm_builder(text, doc_id) |>
    dtm_stopper(stop_list = get_stoplist("snowball2014"),
                stop_docprop = c(.01, Inf))
```

Now we want to subset our ATN DTM to only include articles by our left-wing and right-wing sources. We'll go with *Talking Points Memo*, *New York Times*, and *Buzzfeed News* as our left-wing sources and *Breitbard*, *Fox News*, and *National Review* as our right-wing sources.

```
df_atn_sub <- df_atn |>
    select(doc_id, lean, date, publication, text) |>
    filter(publication == "Talking Points Memo" |
           publication == "New York Times" |
           publication == "Buzzfeed News" |
           publication == "Breitbart" |
           publication == "Fox News" |
           publication == "National Review")

dtm_atn_sub <- df_atn_sub |> dtm_builder(text, doc_id)
```

The vocabulary across all three items—ATN DTM, press release DTM, and embedding space—must be identical. Let's ensure that now.

```
vocab <- intersect(rownames(atn_vectors), colnames(dtm_atn_sub))
vocab <- intersect(vocab, colnames(dtm_ittpr))

atn_vecs_sub <- atn_vectors[vocab, ]
dtm_atn_sub  <- dtm_atn_sub[, vocab]
dtm_ittpr    <- dtm_ittpr[, vocab]
```

And, now we can find WMD scores using `text2vec`.[71]

```
wmd_mod <- RWMD$new(x = dtm_ittpr, embeddings = atn_vecs_sub)
wmd_dis <- wmd_mod$sim2(x = dtm_atn_sub)
```

This leaves us with a a-by-p matrix, where a is the number of articles and p is the number of press releases. Each a, p cell tells us the similarity of a to p, where higher values indicate greater similarity.[72]

There's a host of things we could do with this matrix. If the press releases were all published before the news articles (they weren't), we

[71] Even with RWMD, this might take a while. This is despite text2vec implementing "linear-complexity RWMD" (Atasu 2017), which speeds up the process even more! Previously, this could take days.

[72] Yes, it's Word Mover's *Distance*, but using this with `sim2()` outputs a *similarity*.

could use diffusion modeling. Nonetheless, we can get a sense of which articles are more likely to write about the same things—and in the same way—as these immigration civil society groups. Let's see, for instance, if left-wing or right-wing news organizations have higher similarities to left- or right-wing immigration groups. We'll use a simple visualization for this—though we could employ statistical tests.

We'll first convert our a-by-p distance matrix into a dataframe, add some row names, and then use those row names to merge some ATN metadata to the similarities. This allows us to see how similarities differ by article characteristics.

```
df_sim <- wmd_dis |>
    as.data.frame() |>
    rownames_to_column(var = "doc_id")

df_sim <- left_join(df_sim, df_atn_sub, by = "doc_id")
```

Next, we'll get the mean similarity for each article to the right-leaning and left-leaning press releases. The distance matrix columns are in the order of the press releases. We'll create an index of TRUE and FALSE to subset it correctly.

```
r_idx <- df_ittpr$lean == "Right"
l_idx <- df_ittpr$lean == "Left"

df_atn_sub$wmd_r <- rowMeans(wmd_dis[, r_idx])
df_atn_sub$wmd_l <- rowMeans(wmd_dis[, l_idx])
```

Then reshape the dataframe into "long form," and then make the plot.

```
df_plot <- df_atn_sub |>
    select(doc_id, lean, date, wmd_r, wmd_l) |>
    pivot_longer(cols = c("wmd_r", "wmd_l")) |>
    mutate(name = case_when(
            grepl("wmd_r", name) ~ "Right-Wing Press Releases",
            grepl("wmd_l", name) ~ "Left-Wing Press Releases")
    )
```

```
df_plot |>
    ggplot(aes(x = as.Date(date), y = value, color = name)) +
    geom_smooth(aes(linetype = name)) +
    scale_linetype_manual(values=c("twodash", "solid"))+
    labs(x = NULL, y = "Average Similarity to Press Releases") +
    guides(linetype = guide_legend(nrow = 2)) +
    theme(legend.position = c(.65, .1)) +
    facet_wrap(~lean)
```

Figure 11.9 suggests that, among other things, left-wing news sources use similar language to both left-wing and right-wing immigration organizations in equal quantities when discussing immigration, while right-wing news is a bit more right-leaning overall when it comes to immigration discourse.

Figure 11.9: Context Similarity between News Articles and Press Releases.

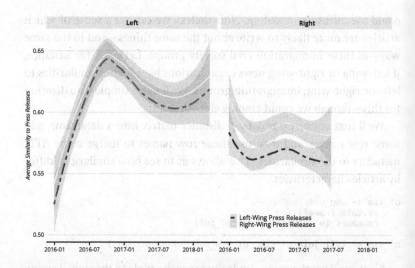

Looking back, we've covered much ground: from extending topic modeling by incorporating covariates, to building high-quality representations of word meanings by summarizing co-occurrences, then using those word representations to explore the meanings in focal corpora. While these patterns emerge inductively from our texts, it is always important to remember that how we process our texts will shape these patterns, and our interpretations of them.

12
Extended Deductive

DEDUCTIVE analysis entails searching for a meaning in our corpora. We'll already have a sense for the pattern we seek. Is this tweet about a celebrity wedding? Does this speech bring up welfare reform? Is this news article discussing conspicuous consumption?

To answer questions like these, researchers commonly hand-label a manageable random sample of documents. The key question is whether these *labels* are used to build classifiers, validate classifications, or both. Here, we'll discuss using labels to build classifiers (i.e. supervision) and use these labels to validate classifications. We'll also explore using pre-trained models to classify documents.

These methods build on both supervised and unsupervised methods discussed previously and, specifically, extend dictionary-based approaches discussed in **Core Deductive**. The techniques we discuss here are helpful when our classifications are not discrete, we have two or more categories, or when a unique lexicon does not clearly distinguish categories.

SUPERVISION AND VALIDATION

Let's assume we already have a classification scheme. Let's also assume we have unread, unlabeled documents that are too numerous to read and label. Say we label 5% of our corpus. We could then try to *predict* those labels. This is called **supervision** because we know the intended labels and our model predicts those labels. As a result, any supervised classifier is only as good as those labels—and ultimately *learns* the labeler's interpretation.

Once trained, we can reuse our model on *unlabeled* data. We've already used many of these *pretrained* models. Optical character recognition (OCR) research, for instance, played a significant role in advancing such classifiers. We don't need to retrain OCR models each time because characters do not usually change much.[1]

In contrast, we may jump right to automatically classifying without first labeling. We covered a version of this in **Core Deductive** with

[1] Although, recall Tesseract allows fine-tuning a model to recognize a specific person's handwriting.

Mapping Texts: Computational Text Analysis for the Social Sciences. Dustin S. Stoltz and Marshall A. Taylor, Oxford University Press. © Oxford University Press 2024.
DOI: 10.1093/oso/9780197756874.003.0012

[2] The weights in, for example, a precompiled sentiment dictionary form a simple "model," but we don't call it "learning" because the weights were assigned by people, and not "statistically learned" from the data.

dictionary methods. By matching terms in our dictionary to terms in our documents, we can assign labels to documents.[2] Here, we'll also discuss using pretrained models to augment these basic dictionary methods.

Whether labels are used explicitly in the model training process, labels are often still used in the **validation** step. Our process *will* associate labels to documents even if the results are nonsense. Regardless of the specifics, our goal is to ensure that pairing a document with a label would make sense to a human rater. There will always be some "error." And, we wouldn't even expect agreement across all human raters all the time. Accepting that, we still hope there is *face validity* to how our classifier assigns labels to documents and does so better than chance.

Representing Objects as Features

We'll discuss a range of *document classifiers* falling under the label "machine learning" or "statistical learning" (Vapnik 1998). These methods begin by representing the objects to be classified by a set of "features." Consider a simple image classification task. Let's use the Fashion-MNIST Dataset, several thousand greyscale images labeled as one of ten clothing items.

Figure 12.1: Images as Feature Matrices.

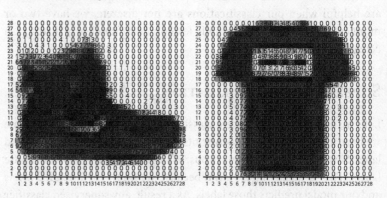

Each fashion item is a greyscale image loaded as a matrix (see Figure 12.1). Each cell identifies a "pixel" in our image. The number in the cell is the color along the greyscale spectrum, with higher numbers being closer to black. Next, we "unroll" that matrix into a long string, where each column is now a unique row-column from the original matrix. Our basic greyscale image becomes a *feature vector*. Each image is a 28 by 28 matrix and becomes a vector with 784 numbers. If we stacked those vectors, we'd have an image-feature matrix.

Therefore, another way to think about text wrangling and building a DTM is as a kind of **feature selection**, that is, isolating some attributes of texts among all the possible ones.[3] This reinforces the notion that when we engage in "preprocessing," the analysis has already started and may directly impact how well our classifier works. This basic affinity also allows document and image classification research to cross-fertilize.

[3] This is why quanteda uses **DFM** instead of **DTM**.

Splitting Corpora

If our model fits our training data precisely but doesn't work on new data, it is "overfitted." Why are we concerned with overfitting? Our training documents are a possible manifestation of an otherwise "latent" meaning.[4] The documents in our corpora are an exposed instance of this hidden range. Furthermore, each document is never *just* about a single meaning. When training then, our model may identify a pattern that accurately predicts the labels, but this pattern may not exist in another sample of texts.

[4] For example, there are many ways one could discuss opulence, and Veblen's *Leisure Class* is but one. These unseen but theoretically plausible manifestations may exist outside our sample, waiting to be collected, or simply be hypothetical possibilities.

Say we collect tweets in July of 2021 using the word "wedding." We're interested in which discuss "celebrity" weddings. We hire a dozen raters to hand-label tweets as whether they are about a "celebrity wedding" or not. We fit a model to this corpus and find it achieves over 90% accuracy. Great! We then collect more tweets a few months later and use our model to predict the "celebrity wedding" category. But, when we manually inspect these new results, they do not seem valid. We return to the training data and notice most of our "celebrity wedding" tweets share a hashtag: #thedishulwedding. Our classifer isn't good at identifying "celebrity wedding," but rather really good at identifying the tweets discussing the wedding of the singer Rahul Vaidya and actress Disha Parmar on July 16, 2021.

We may have a training data issue, but before we collect more data, the standard strategy is to divide our labeled corpus into a training set and one or more "hold-out" or "unseen" datasets (James et al. 2021:176). Recall we often hold out about 25 to 30% of our data.[5]

[5] Specifically, revisit building a weighted sentiment dictionary using logistic regression in **Core Deductive**.

After hand-labeling documents, representing them as features, and splitting our corpus into training and test sets, we enter the meat-and-potatoes of machine learning: selecting how to **weight** the features to predict the associated labels. The output of any training algorithm—many we've already encountered—are (1) weights associated with features, and then the (2) method for representing a new input as these compatible "features." By now, we're experts on representing texts as

[6] Recall that LDA and STM are generative models—see **Core Inductive** and **Extended Inductive**.

"features"—typically, a preprocessed selection of terms. So, we'll dive into the task of associating weights with those features.

CLASSIC TRAINING WITH SUPERVISION

Training methods are commonly divided into two main types. *Logistic regression* is a classic example of a family called **discriminative** classifiers. The alternative is a family called **generative** classifiers, and the classic example here is *naive Bayes*. Generative classifiers, as the name implies, try to model how the observed data are generated.[6] This model is then used to find a boundary within our data. Discriminative classifiers are just trying to find this boundary directly.

As Vapnik states (Vapnik 1998:12), we should "try to solve the problem directly and never solve a more general problem as an intermediate step," and so discriminative classifiers are (at least) a good place to start. On the other hand, generative models are considered less susceptible to overfitting.

The generative/discriminative distinction, however, is less clear than it appears. There are "hybrid" generative-discriminative models, and we can use some models like logistic regression for both. A more pressing distinction is between models which assign labels **discretely** and models which assign them **gradationally**.

In the following, we'll walk through popular supervised learning methods based on (1) logistic regression, (2) naive Bayes, and finally, (3) neural networks. We'll get a sense of the differences between each method, but also their similarities. Namely, each entails several iterations, checking its accuracy at the task,[7] and updating the weights as it does (i.e., optimizing). The model stops when the improvements are minimal (i.e., the model *converges*), or after a set number of iterations (McLevey 2021:400–4).

[7] That is, the "agreement" between model predictions and actual labels.

Logistic Regression

Like regular linear regression, *logistic* regression tries to predict an outcome using some other variables. Here, we'll keep it simple and assume our outcome is a variable with two values: yes or no? Is the document in a category or not? Researchers encounter questions like this when, for example, attempting to subset an otherwise enormous corpus for close reading. Logistic regression is especially suited for this scenario.

Our outcome is whether a document is a "1" or a "0"—a "yes" or a "no"—but we model the *probability* of getting a "1" or "0."[8] Then, we typically assign labels discretely using a probability threshold (e.g., above and below 0.5).

[8] See **Math Basics**.

Let's begin by preparing our text. We'll use the 2,000 articles from the ISOT Fake News dataset, which includes several news articles labeled real or fake news by reference to their sources.

```
data("corpus_isot_fake_news2k", package = "text2map.corpora")

df_isot <- corpus_isot_fake_news2k |>
  mutate(text = tolower(text),
         text = gsub("[[:punct:]]+", " ", text),
         text = gsub("[[:digit:]]+", " ", text),
         text = str_squish(text)
  )
```

We'll also split our corpus into a training and test set.

```
set.seed(19063)
init <- initial_split(df_isot, prop = 3 / 4, strata = "rating")

df_trn <- training(init)
df_tst <- testing(init)
```

The "features" (i.e., terms) in our DTM must be identical across all training and test sets: same words in the exact order. So, we'll create a DTM for the training set, and remove rare words. Then, we'll use the vocabulary from that DTM as the input to `vocab` when building the second DTM. This assures both matrices have identical features.

```
dtm_trn <- df_trn |>
  dtm_builder(text, doc_id = doc_id) |>
  dtm_stopper(stop_docfreq = c(3L, Inf))

dtm_tst <- df_tst |>
  dtm_builder(text, doc_id = doc_id, vocab = colnames(dtm_trn))
```

Here, we'll use `quanteda`'s text regression functions so we can stay with the same terminology across training methods.[9] To fit a logistic regression, then, we just use:

[9] In **Core Deductive**, we used generic functions to fit a logistic regression, `cv.glmnet()` and `glm()`.

```
lr_fit <- textmodel_lr(
    x = as.dfm(dtm_trn),
    y = as.factor(df_trn$rating)
)
```

Here, x is our features (or, in our case, the term frequencies), and y is the document labels to predict (in our case, whether a news article is "fake news" or "real news"). The function also turns our DTM from a raw count matrix into a relative frequency DTM, by dividing by each cell by the sum of its respective row.

The output or "model" is a list of features (again, here they are terms) and the associated weights. We can then use our test documents by associating the features in those hold-out documents with weights, then using those weights to predict a label (here, type being "class" means we want a *discrete* labeling). We then compare our predicted labels to the actual labels.

```
lr_pred <- predict(lr_fit, newdata = as.dfm(dtm_tst),type = "class")
```

Since we have a binary classification, real or fake, we can show how well we predicted the labels in our test set with a confusion matrix (output in the margin).

```
confusionMatrix(lr_pred, as.factor(df_tst$rating))
```

```
          Reference
Prediction fake real
      fake  248    0
      real    2  250

Accuracy : 0.996
```

We correctly predicted nearly *every label* in our test corpus: we only missed two. That is a high-performing classifier! Indeed, it looks *too* good. Let's investigate.

Instead of predicting the category, let's crack open the model. Recall, pretrained models are primarily *weights associated with features*. Using coef() we can extract those weights. Let's create a function to see which words have the highest weight toward a "real news" rating.

```
feat_weights <- function(model, n) {
  return(
    coef(model) |> as.matrix() |>
      as.data.frame() |> rename(value = 1) |>
      rownames_to_column("term") |>
      select(term, value) |>
      slice_max(value, n = n, with_ties = FALSE)
  )
}

feat_weights(lr_fit, n = 5)
```

```
     term    value
  reuters 4.448754
     mark 0.000000
      has 0.000000
     been 0.000000
   accused 0.000000
```

As suspected, there's a problem. All our "real" news articles are from Reuters. So, almost all "real" news articles contain the word "reuters." As this single word is nearly perfectly correlated with our labels, it alone is driving most of the accuracy! Let's remake our DTMs, but this time remove "reuters."

```
dtm_trn_wo <- df_trn |>
  dtm_builder(text, doc_id = doc_id) |>
  dtm_stopper(stop_list = "reuters", stop_docfreq = c(3L, Inf))

dtm_tst_wo <- df_tst |>
  dtm_builder(text, doc_id = doc_id, vocab = colnames(dtm_trn_wo))
```

One thing to note: it takes significantly longer to fit this new model. It needs more iterations to converge now that the task is more complicated (output in the margin).

```
lr_fit_wo <- textmodel_lr(
    x = as.dfm(dtm_trn_wo),
    y = as.factor(df_trn$rating)
)


lr_pred_wo <- predict(lr_fit_wo,
    newdata = as.dfm(dtm_tst_wo),
    type = "class"
)

confusionMatrix(lr_pred_wo, as.factor(df_tst$rating))
```

```
            Reference
Prediction fake real
      fake  232    5
      real   18  245

Accuracy : 0.954
```

Still accurate! We could, of course, extract feature weights to see which words are most predictive of real words, but let's move on.

Instead of treating our classification as a discrete (either/or) category, let's measure *gradationally*. Perhaps there are real articles that read like prototypically fake articles (and vice versa). Instead of predicting the "class," we'll predict "probabilities." Let's compare the probability distributions with and without "reuters" (see Figure 12.2).

```
lr_pred <- predict(lr_fit,
  newdata = as.dfm(dtm_tst),
  type = "probability") |>
  as.data.frame()


lr_pred_wo <- predict(lr_fit_wo,
  newdata = as.dfm(dtm_tst_wo),
  type = "probability") |>
  as.data.frame() |>
  rename_all(paste0, " (w/o reuters)")


df_plot <- cbind(lr_pred, lr_pred_wo)
df_plot$rating <- df_tst$rating


df_plot |>
  select(rating, real, fake,
         `real (w/o reuters)`,
         `fake (w/o reuters)`) |>
  pivot_longer(!rating) |>
  ggplot(aes(value, fill = rating)) +
  geom_density() +
  labs(fill="Predicted Probability of Label") +
  theme(legend.title = element_text()) +
  facet_wrap(~name)
```

The probability distributions of "real" and "fake" news do not overlap much in either model. After removing the word "reuters," though, there are many more articles in the middle of the distribution. This indicates slightly more of a graded relationship between a document and a given

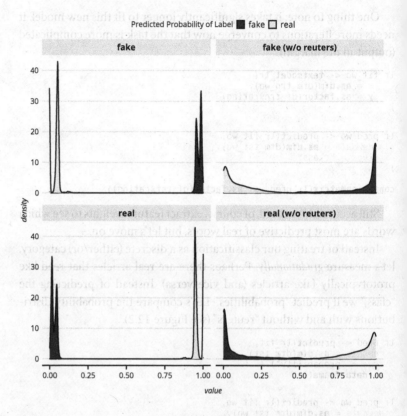

Figure 12.2: Classifier Density Plot.

label. Nevertheless, our logistic regression classifier is still pretty good at predicting the discrete labels.

Now what? We want to use this model on new data. For example, we could measure the spread of fake news on an online forum by automatically classifying the links people post. But, all "real" news articles are from Reuters. If we had links to, for example, the *Chicago Tribune*, would our model erroneously classify them as fake because they are too different from Reuters? Our model is likely overfitted and may not generalize to other "real" new sources. Below we will cover another method generally considered more robust to overfitting.

Naive Bayes

We'll stick with the DTMs without "reuters" to show another popular classifier: naive Bayes. This classifier is related to logistic regression in that we are looking for the probability of a label *conditional* upon the presence of a term. This is called the *posterior* probability. Finding this involves Bayes theorem: the posterior is equal to the product of the probability that the word occurs in a document assigned to the label times the probability of the label in the corpus, divided by the probability of the word in the corpus.

One problem with classic Bayes theorem is that we'd need to calculate the probability of a term conditional upon a label *and all other terms*. As our predictor variables are term frequencies, and we typically have tens of thousands of terms, this is computationally unfeasible. This is where the "naive" part comes in. We assume that each term is independent, and this cuts the complexity considerably. What we end up doing in the naive Bayes case, then, is finding, for each document, the probability of a label given the words in that document, which is proportional to the probability of the label in the corpus times the product of each word's probability given that it occurs in a document assigned to that label. Let's fit a naive Bayes classier (output in the margin):

```
nb_fit <- textmodel_nb(
    x = as.dfm(dtm_trn_wo),
    y = as.factor(df_trn$rating)
)

nb_pred <- predict(nb_fit, newdata = as.dfm(dtm_tst_wo))

confusionMatrix(nb_pred, as.factor(df_tst$rating))
```

```
          Reference
Prediction fake real
      fake 5409  282
      real  298 5072

Accuracy : 0.9476
```

The methods discussed thus far can easily be generalized beyond binary labels to predicting several labels a.k.a. multinomial classifiers.

Training with Neural Networks

Imagine taking the output of logistic regression and fitting *another* logistic regression on that output. The second logistic regression is predicting the labels like usual. The first one, though, is predicting membership in some arbitrary number of categories. This first step is applying "dimension reduction" to our DTM. We then use this lower-dimensional matrix to predict the labels in the next step.

A **neural network**[10] is roughly equivalent. However, instead of only logistic functions, we can use any number of **activation functions**, and instead of just two steps or **layers**, we can add as many as we want. The minimal neural network has three layers: input, hidden, and output. The hidden layer makes this different from the classic methods already discussed.

THIS SECTION NEEDS:

- tidyverse
- text2map
- rsample
- caret
- keras
- reticulate

[10] More technically, "a multilayer setup that models the output (Y) as a concatenation of simple nonlinear functions of the linear combinations of inputs (X)" (Molina and Garip 2019:31). For an overview see McLevey (2021:394–410) and for a theoretical grounding see Roberts and colleagues (Roberts et al. 2022).

This last point is important. Neural networks are not always the right tool. Simpler procedures often outperform (or perform on par with) more advanced techniques (Salganik 2020). It is on the researcher to justify the need for more complex techniques. Calling it "state-of-the-art" doesn't cut the mustard! As a general rule, begin with simpler methods and try to end with simpler methods.

Now, let's get acquainted with neural networks as document classifiers. We'll be using Python packages, so we'll need to set our conda environment before loading the required packages.[11]

```
use_condaenv(condaenv = "myenv")
```

Load a new corpus of food ratings and reviews from Amazon, for example, "I love this flavor of ramen! Five stars!" This time we'll use three outcome labels: a score of four or higher is 0, exactly three is a 1, and two or less a 2.

```
data("corpus_finefoods10k", package = "text2map.corpora")

df_food <- corpus_finefoods10k |>
  mutate(text = tolower(text),
         text = gsub("[[:punct:]]+", " ", text),
         text = gsub("[[:digit:]]+", " ", text),
         text = str_squish(text),
         label = case_when(
           score >= 4 ~ 0,
           score == 3 ~ 1,
           score <= 2 ~ 2)
  )

set.seed(19063)
init <- initial_split(df_food, prop = 3 / 4, strata = "label")

df_trn <- training(init)
df_tst <- testing(init)


dtm_trn <- df_trn |>
  dtm_builder(text, doc_id = review_id) |>
  dtm_stopper(stop_docfreq = c(3L, Inf))

dtm_tst <- df_tst |>
  dtm_builder(text, doc_id = review_id, vocab = colnames(dtm_trn))
```

Neural networks work with matrices in specific shapes. We'll use array_reshape() and to_categorical() from keras to handle reshaping our predictors (here, term frequencies) and outcomes (the food was reviewed as good, neutral, or bad).

```
ke_dtm_trn <- array_reshape(as.matrix(dtm_trn), dim = dim(dtm_trn))
ke_dtm_tst <- array_reshape(as.matrix(dtm_tst), dim = dim(dtm_tst))

y_trn <- to_categorical(df_trn$label, num_classes = 3)
y_tst <- to_categorical(df_tst$label, num_classes = 3)
```

Next, we'll decide on our **model architecture**, which includes the (1) number and types of "layers," how we'll (2) measure accuracy and (3) update our weights as we go. First, we initialize a "sequential" network. We then decide to use two layers (in addition to our "input" layer).

The first `layer_dense()` is our "hidden" layer between the input and output steps.[12] Here, we reduce our input matrix, which has 15,758 columns, to just 1,200. This is arbitrary, though, and changing it may improve our final results. The informal rule is to select a number somewhere between the size of the input (here, 15,758) and the size of the output (here, 3).

Our one hidden layer uses the popular activation function RELU, in which negative inputs return a zero, while positive inputs return the input value.

The final layer is just logistic regression. "Logistic" is a family of similar functions. When we only have two classes, we use the "sigmoid" function; when we have more than two, we use "softmax." The number of units of this output layer is the number of labels to predict.

```
ke_mod <- keras_model_sequential()

ke_mod |>
  layer_dense(units = 1200,
              activation = "relu",
              input_shape = ncol(ke_dtm_trn)) |>
  layer_dense(units = 3,
              activation = "softmax")
```

To recap, our neural network has three layers: (1) the input DTM with 15,758 "dimensions," (2) the "hidden" layer reduces our 15,758 to 1,200 using the RELU activation function, and (3) the output layer reduces 1,200 down to just 3 using logistic regression. Without the hidden layer, we'd just be doing logistic regression!

Next, we'll configure how to measure performance and use that information to update our weights during each iteration. There are many **loss functions** that measure how well a model predicts our labels. The "categorical cross-entropy" is suited for more than two labels.[13] To update, we'll use "stochastic gradient descent" (SGD), which compares the predicted values to a random sample of the input. This reduces the complexity for each pass, but does require more iterations to converge than if we used the entire input every time. Finally, when the model converges, we'll want to see some metrics on the final predictions. **Accuracy** tells us the percent of the documents that were labeled correctly.

Configure our loss, optimizer, and accuracy measures:

[12] It's "hidden" because we won't inspect or use it outside of this task. We do see the input data, of course, and we'll be inspecting and using our output (i.e., weights on features and predicted labels).

[13] Cross-entropy compares the "entropy" (the negative log of a probability) for the predicted labels and the actual labels.

```
ke_mod |>
  compile(loss = "categorical_crossentropy",
          optimizer = "sgd",
          metrics = "accuracy")
```

We have our model architecture; now we can "fit" or train the model. Also, instead of waiting for the model to converge on its own, let's just go through ten rounds for this example.

```
history <- ke_mod |>
  fit(ke_dtm_trn, y_trn, epochs = 10)
```

Recall the loss function is a *continuous* measure of error, while accuracy is a *discrete* measure. Therefore, we can find ourselves in four situations: (1) low accuracy, but big errors on most predictions; (2) low accuracy, but small errors on most predictions; (3) high accuracy, but big errors on a few data; and finally (4) high accuracy and small errors overall.

Now that we trained the model, let's see how well it predicts the labels of our test set.

```
ke_mod |> evaluate(ke_dtm_tst, y_tst, verbose = 0)
```

```
    loss accuracy
0.480646 0.818000
```

Our model is pretty good at predicting the test set labels. Let's complicate our neural network, and see if we can improve this. Let's add a word embedding layer. Instead of using a DTM, we are also going to use a document-sequence matrix. To do so, we first associate each word in the vocabulary with a unique integer, for the v most frequent words. The matrix includes the first N words. The columns are the position of a word, while the cell is the integer associated with the word. Let's set n_words to the first 100 words in each document.[14]

```
n_words <- 100

seq_trn <- df_trn |>
  seq_builder(text, maxlen = n_words)

seq_tst <- df_tst |>
  seq_builder(text, maxlen = n_words)

# add 1 for "zero"
v_vocab <- length(attr(seq_trn, "dic")) + 1
```

Below we added a new first layer: an embedding layer.[15] This creates word embeddings with 128 dimensions, and only uses co-occurrences within a 100-word limit. After we've created these embeddings, the input to the next hidden layer won't be the right "shape." So, we've added another layer that averages all the vectors in each document,

[14] If we don't want to truncate any documents, we'd set n_words to whatever the longest document is.

[15] This uses the SGNS word2vec algorithm. See **Extended Inductive**.

respectively.[16] Then, this vector representation of the document is passed to the same layers as in our first model.

```
ke_mod <- keras_model_sequential()

ke_mod <- ke_mod |>
  layer_embedding(input_dim = v_vocab, output_dim = 128,
                  input_length = n_words) |>
  layer_global_average_pooling_1d() |>
  layer_dense(units = 1200, activation = "relu") |>
  layer_dense(units = 3, activation = "softmax")
```

Our loss, optimizer, and accuracy metric are the same as before. The only thing to note is that we need to use our *document-sequence matrix* to predict our outcome labels.

```
ke_mod <- ke_mod |>
  compile(loss = "categorical_crossentropy",
          optimizer = "sgd",
          metrics = "accuracy")

history <- ke_mod |>
  fit(seq_trn, y_trn, epochs = 10)

ke_mod |> evaluate(seq_tst, y_tst, verbose = 0)


    loss  accuracy
0.7066723 0.7628990
```

Interestingly, our loss increased and our accuracy decreased. Perhaps using pretrained word embeddings might help? We turn to this in the next section.

DEDUCTIVE ANALYSIS WITH PRETRAINED MODELS

In the preceding example, we trained our own models. Eventually, we'd use these models on data not used in the training process—not just "testing" data, but also unlabeled data. This is what is meant by using a *pretrained* model. As open science gains ground, pretrained models will proliferate. How do we go about using them to augment deductive methods?

Here, we'll focus on pretrained *word embeddings*. Recall pretrained models are typically made up of weights on features, and sometimes they include methods for matching inputs to the necessary features. Embeddings are typically matrices, where the rownames are the terms, and the columns are the d dimensions of the embedding space. Each unique word is represented by a vector of length d. To use these embeddings, we'll match all the words in our documents to those in the embeddings.[17]

[17] For example, if the terms in the embeddings are stemmed or uppercased, then we need to stem or uppercase the terms in our corpus.

There are four reasons to use pretrained embeddings. First, we save time and resources. Second, it increases replicability across studies. Third, our focal corpus may be too small for training purposes. Finally, embeddings trained on only our focal corpus may be overfit.

THIS SECTION NEEDS:

- tidyverse
- stringi
- textclean
- keras
- reticulate

Neural Networks with Pretrained Embeddings

We'll use posts on a popular discussion board from Reddit (i.e., a subreddit) called "Am I the Asshole" (AITA). The guidelines are simple: "Tell us about any non-violent conflict you have experienced; give us both sides of the story, and find out if you're right, or you're the asshole." Forum members decide which party is in the wrong: the author, the other party, everyone, no one—or in some cases, not enough information to determine. Predicting "who is the asshole" using text is a complicated classification task.

```
data(corpus_reddit_aita10k, package = "text2map.corpora")

df_aita <- corpus_reddit_aita10k |>
  mutate(text = stri_trans_general(text,
          id = "Any-Latin; Latin-ASCII"),
      text = tolower(text),
      text = replace_curly_quote(text),
      text = replace_contraction(text),
      text = gsub("[[:punct:]]+", " ", text),
      text = gsub("[[:digit:]]+", " ", text),
      text = str_squish(text)
  )
```

[18] See **Computing Basics**.

We will use Python packages again, so set the conda environment.[18]

```
use_condaenv(condaenv = "myenv")
```

Let's use the embeddings we used previously, the fastText embeddings trained on the Common Crawl, found in `text2map.pretrained`. We'll assume the model is already downloaded.

```
# load the model each session
data("vecs_fasttext300_commoncrawl", package ="text2map.pretrained")
ft_wv <- vecs_fasttext300_commoncrawl # rename so it's tidier
```

[19] Recall, in this matrix, columns are positions in a document (first word, second word, etc), and the cells are integers corresponding to terms occurring in that position.

Let's turn our corpus into a document-sequence matrix using only the first 2,000 words in each post.[19]

```
n_words <- 2000

seq_trn <- df_aita |>
  seq_builder(text, maxlen = n_words) |>
  as.matrix()
```

We also need to prepare the outcome variable, which has five categories indicating who is in the wrong according to the majority: Other,

Nobody, Author, Everbody, and Info (more information is needed). Let's first convert these five categories to integers from 0 to 4,[20] then create a keras -friendly matrix.

[20] Python starts counting from 0, and keras uses Python.

```
df_aita <- df_aita |>
  mutate(labeln = case_when(
          label == "AUTHOR" ~ 0,
          label == "OTHER" ~ 1,
          label == "NOBODY" ~ 2,
          label == "EVERYBODY" ~ 3,
          label == "INFO" ~ 4,
        )
    )

y_trn <- to_categorical(df_aita$labeln, num_classes = 5)
```

Put our "weights" (i.e., our pretrained embeddings) into a list, and add it to the weights argument in layer_embedding() and do not allow training (trainable = FALSE).

```
ke_mod <- keras_model_sequential()

ke_mod <- ke_mod |>
  layer_embedding(
      input_dim = nrow(ft_wv),
      output_dim = 300L,
      input_length = n_words,
      weights = list(ft_wv),
      trainable = FALSE) |>
  layer_global_average_pooling_1d() |>
  layer_dense(units = 50, activation = "relu") |>
  layer_dense(units = 5, activation = "sigmoid")

ke_mod <- ke_mod |>
  compile(loss = "categorical_crossentropy",
          optimizer = "sgd",
          metrics = "accuracy"
    )

history <- ke_mod |>
  fit(seq_trn, y_trn, epochs = 10)
```

We didn't use a test set this time. We'll just use the model to get the labels for our training data. Note that each post has a probability of being classified as one of the five labels.

```
preds <- ke_mod |> predict(seq_trn)

colnames(preds) <- c("AUTHOR", "OTHER", "NOBODY",
                     "EVERYBODY", "INFO")

df_aita <- cbind(df_aita, preds)
```

Let's see how well our model predicts the community judgment for one post: "AITA for feeding my vegan nephew meat?" The gist of this post is the author taking their 7-year-old nephew out to eat while their parents went on a date. The parents and the child are vegan. When the author asked the kid where he would like to eat, he says "Five Guys" —a popular hamburger restaurant. The author's sister stated they were "out of line to change his diet without their permission." The scores were:

- 631: the sister is in the wrong.
- 276: the author is.
- 229: nobody is.
- 26: everyone is.
- 7: more information is needed.

So, the majority sided with the author that the "other" party is in the wrong. Let's see how our model did.

```
df_aita |>
  filter(title == "AITA for feeding my vegan nephew meat?") |>
  select(AUTHOR:INFO)


AUTHOR      OTHER    NOBODY EVERYBODY         INFO
0.7772692 0.9145786 0.5613233 0.3398936 0.07852602
```

That tracks the vote tally pretty closely!

Suppose our research calls for sorting documents into multiple categories, and the methods discussed in **Core Deductive** are not producing desired results; then using pretrained embeddings with neural networks is a good choice. However, at least some documents must be labeled. What if we don't have labeled data? We'll discuss one classification strategy for unlabeled documents next.

THIS SECTION NEEDS:

- tidyverse
- textclean
- text2map
- text2map.pretrained
- stringi
- gutenbergr

Concept Mover's Distance with Pretrained Embeddings

Recall that *supervision* means we're using labels *to train* the classifier. They are not optional. A strength of dictionary methods is that they do not *require* labeling.

Could we augment dictionary methods with pretrained models? Specifically, could we use word embeddings to account for the semantic similarities between terms? Good news everybody! We can with **Concept Mover's Distance** (CMD) (Stoltz and Taylor 2019a; Taylor and Stoltz 2021). This method extends dictionary methods as we'll need one or more "anchor" terms. We'll then use pretrained word embeddings to augment this process by weighting each word in our documents by its cosine to these anchors.[21]

Our anchor list defines a location in the embedding space. In the simplest scenario, this is a single word—say "death." We then associate each word in our DTM with a location in the embedding space. Documents,

[21] To do this, CMD relies on *Word Mover's Distance*; see **Extended Inductive**.

then, are clouds of locations. We want to measure the *minimum cost* of moving all the words in our documents to this single point. Cost is a function of distance and weight: for us, cosine and relative frequency, respectively.

We'll try to predict the "deaths" in 37 plays from Shakespeare's First Folio using metadata we created about the plays. This includes the unique ID of the work hosted on Project Gutenberg. We'll then use `gutenbergr` to download each play, creating a dataframe where each row is a line in the play. Let's also collapse these lines so there is one row per play.

```
data("meta_shakespeare", package = "text2map")

my_mirror <- "mirrors.xmission.com/gutenberg/"

df_text <- meta_shakespeare |>
    select(gutenberg_id) |>
    gutenberg_download(mirror = my_mirror) |>
    group_by(gutenberg_id) |>
    summarize(text = paste(text, collapse = " ")) |>
    mutate(gutenberg_id = as.character(gutenberg_id))
```

These are OCRed documents, so let's transliterate, and take care of these pesky curly quotes, expand any contractions we can, and then remove punctuation and numbers. Then, build a DTM.

```
df_text <- df_text |>
  mutate(text = replace_non_ascii(text),
         text = tolower(text),
         text = replace_curly_quote(text),
         text = replace_contraction(text),
         text = gsub("[[:punct:]]+", " ", text),
         text = gsub("[[:digit:]]+", " ", text),
         text = str_squish(text)
  )

dtm <- df_text |> dtm_builder(text, doc_id = gutenberg_id)
```

Load the fastText embeddings.

```
data("vecs_fasttext300_commoncrawl", package ="text2map.pretrained")
ft_wv <- vecs_fasttext300_commoncrawl # rename so it's tidier
```

Since "death" is similar to "life," let's also calculate each play's engagement with the semantic direction life-death, rather than just the single word "death."[22]

```
terms <- cbind(c("death", "demise", "dying"),
               c("life", "birth", "living"))
dir_death <- get_direction(terms, ft_wv)
```

In a DTM, each document is represented as a distribution of word counts. How "sensitive" is each estimate to a given distribution of words? We can test this sensitivity by resampling (with replacement) from each document's word distribution. We do this by setting the `sens_interval` to `TRUE` . Underneath, we're using `dtm_resampler()` to estimate 100 new DTMs and re-running CMD on each, before reporting a given interval (default is c(0.025, 0.975)). We'll use the default settings. The results are visualized in Figure 12.3.

```
cmd_play <- CMDist(
    dtm = dtm,
    cv = dir_death,
    wv = ft_wv,
    sens_interval = TRUE,
    n_iters = 100L
)

df_cmd <- meta_shakespeare |>
    mutate(doc_id = as.character(gutenberg_id)) |>
    left_join(cmd_play, by = "doc_id")


df_cmd |>
    ggplot(aes(x = body_count, y = death_pole)) +
    geom_errorbar(aes(
        x = body_count, y = death_pole,
        ymin = death_pole_lower,
        ymax = death_pole_upper
    ), alpha = 0.5) +
    geom_point(aes(color = genre), size = 2) +
    labs(x = "Number of Deaths in the Play",
         y = "Closeness to 'Death'")
```

Figure 12.3: Plays' Engagement with 'Death'.

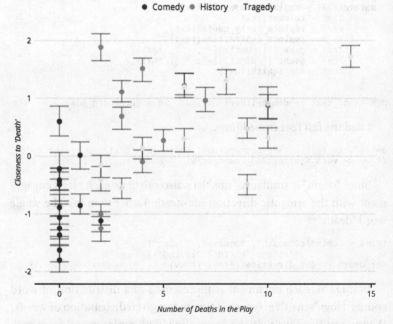

We can see that Shakespeare's comedies tend to engage less with death, while histories and tragedies tend to engage more with death. Overall, this is a useful method for deductively mapping a particular concept in our texts without labeling them first.

Retrofitting Pretrained Embeddings for Deductive Analysis

A criticism of the previous process might be that fastText embeddings are trained on the 2015 Wikipedia Data Dump, but Shakespeare was writing over 400 years ago. Recall many embedding methods (implicitly or explicitly) assign words vectors such that their cosine approximates their probability of co-occurring in the corpus. In other words, we can use pairwise cosine to re-create a TCM.

We can also go the other way: use a focal TCM to "retrofit" pretrained embeddings. We'll start with all the plays in the First Folio, but won't collapse lines. Then we'll do the same preprocessing as before and remove any blank lines.

```
data("meta_shakespeare", package = "text2map")

my_mirror <- "mirrors.xmission.com/gutenberg/"

df_shake <- meta_shakespeare |>
  select(gutenberg_id) |>
  gutenberg_download(mirror = my_mirror) |>
  left_join(meta_shakespeare)
```

```
df_shake <- df_shake |>
  mutate(gutenberg_id = as.character(gutenberg_id)) |>
  rename(line = text) |>
  mutate(text = replace_non_ascii(line),
         text = replace_curly_quote(text),
         text = replace_contraction(text),
         text = gsub("[[:punct:]]+", " ", text),
         text = gsub("[[:digit:]]+", " ", text),
         text = tolower(text),
         text = str_squish(text)) |>
  filter(text != "")
```

Let's create a TCM with a context window of 5 using text2vec . Remember, by default, create_tcm() weights each word by the inverse of its distance from the target word.

```
tkns <- unlist(df_shake$text) |> str_split(" ")

vectorizer <- itoken(tkns) |>
             create_vocabulary() |>
             vocab_vectorizer()

tcm_sh <- itoken(tkns) |>
             create_tcm(vectorizer, skip_grams_window = 5L)
```

Load in the fastText embeddings trained on the Common Crawl.

```
# load the model each session
data("vecs_fasttext300_commoncrawl", package ="text2map.pretrained")
ft_wv <- vecs_fasttext300_commoncrawl # rename so it's tidier
```

THIS SECTION NEEDS:

- tidyverse
- stringi
- gutenbergr
- text2map
- text2map.pretrained
- text2vec
- rsvd
- tidytext
- spacyr
- semgram

The vocabulary of the embeddings and the TCM must match. To ensure this, we'll subset both with the *intersection* of their vocabularies.

```
vocab <- intersect(rownames(ft_wv), rownames(tcm_sh))
tcm_sh <- tcm_sh[vocab, vocab]
pre_wv <- ft_wv[vocab, ]
```

Next, we'll "tug" our pretrained embeddings to better fit our local TCM. This is "retrofitting" (also "fine-tuning" and "enriching") and there are several useful methods that incorporate information from the TCM built on a local corpus (Dingwall and Potts 2018), information from semantic databases like WordNet (Faruqui et al. 2014), or even the demographics of the authors of texts (Hovy and Fornaciari 2018).[23] We can incorporate this information by retrofitting.

We'll use a "retrofitter" function building on the previous chapters.[24] Remember creating word embeddings using just the TCM and SVD? Let's follow similar procedures to create cheap word vectors fitting the local corpus. We then "align" the SVD embeddings with our pretrained embeddings—as we did with diachronic analysis. Finally, recall training the GloVe embeddings, we added embeddings together—this function does the same. Adding SVD embeddings should "pull" the pretrained embeddings slightly, creating an embedding space fitting our local corpus a bit more.[25]

```
retrofitter <- function(x, ref) {
    x <- find_transformation(x, method = "norm")
    ref <- find_transformation(ref, method = "norm")
    ref <- rsvd(ref, k = ncol(x))$v
    ref <- find_transformation(ref, x, method = "align")
    ref <- x + ref
    ref <- find_transformation(ref, method = "norm")
    return(ref)
}
```

Let's get our retrofit word embeddings by using our Shakespeare TCM as reference. This decreases the most extreme differences between our word embeddings and the co-occurrences of the local corpus.[26]

```
ret_wv <- retrofitter(pre_wv, tcm_sh)
```

Let's use them on a single play, *Two Gentlemen of Verona*—believed to be Shakespeare's first play. We'll remove a bit of the front matter (e.g., table of contents) with `sub()` .

```
df_tgov <- df_shake |>
    filter(short_title == "Two Gentlemen of Verona") |>
    group_by(gutenberg_id) |>
    summarise(text = paste(line, collapse = " ")) |>
    mutate(text = sub("^.*(ACT 1.*)", "\\1", text))
```

Next, we'll group the lines by their respective speakers. We do this with a regex pattern that matches *right before* any word with all capital letters followed immediately by a period and space: \\W(?=[A-Z]+\\.) Then, we'll preprocess these speaker lines (grabbing the speaker's name).

```
df_tgov <- df_tgov |> filter(text != "") |>
    unnest_tokens(line, text,
        token = "regex",
        pattern = "\\W(?=[A-Z]+\\. )",
        to_lower = FALSE) |>
    mutate(speaker = sub("^([A-Z]+).*", "\\1", line),
        position = row_number(),
        doc_id = paste0("doc_", position))

df_tgov <- df_tgov |>
  mutate(text = replace_non_ascii(line),
        text = replace_curly_quote(text),
        text = replace_contraction(text),
        text = gsub("[[:punct:]]+", " ", text),
        text = gsub("[[:digit:]]+", " ", text),
        text = tolower(text),
        text = str_squish(text)
)
```

We'll use our retrofit embeddings to estimate new engagement scores for each line in *Two Gentlemen of Verona*. This time we'll measure engagement with the semantic direction of love to hate (we'll also estimate death-life for use later).

```
terms <- cbind(c("love", "affection"), c("hate", "disdain"))
dir_love <- get_direction(terms, ret_wv)

dtm_tgov <- df_tgov |> dtm_builder(text, doc_id)
cmd_play <- CMDist(dtm = dtm_tgov, cv = dir_love, wv = ret_wv)
df_cmd <- left_join(df_tgov, cmd_play)
```

Let's see how the main characters engage with love and hate over the narrative. We'll select the 6 characters with the most lines.

```
characters <- table(df_tgov$speaker) |>
            sort() |> tail() |> names()


"SILVIA"    "LAUNCE"    "JULIA"
"SPEED"     "PROTEUS"   "VALENTINE"

df_cmd |>
  filter(speaker %in% characters) |>
  mutate(fill = case_when(
      love_pole > 0 ~ "To Love",
      love_pole < 0 ~ "From Love")) |>
  ggplot(aes(position, love_pole)) +
  geom_col(aes(fill = fill), width = 8) +
  geom_smooth(se = FALSE, alpha = 0.5) +
  facet_wrap(~speaker) +
  scale_fill_manual(values = c("black", "darkgrey"))
```

Looking at Figure 12.4., Valentine—the protagonist—falls for the Duke's daughter Silvia, and his lines tip heavily toward love throughout

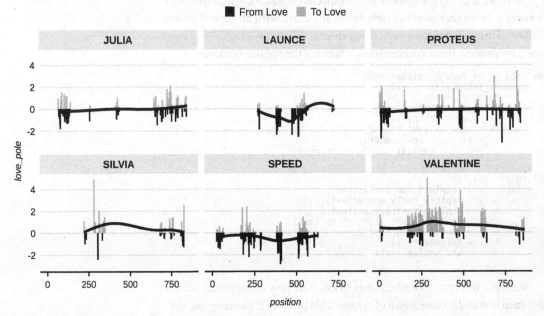

Figure 12.4: Characters' Engagement with 'Love'.

the play. Launce's parts, by contrast, lean heavily toward contempt and away from affection. Let's select this character's first line to see it on the page:

> I think Crab my dog be the sourest-natured dog that lives: my mother weeping, my father wailing, my sister crying, our maid howling, our cat wringing her hands, and all our house in a great perplexity; yet did not this cruel-hearted cur shed one tear. He is a stone, a very pebble stone, and has no more pity in him than a dog....

This passage aligns quite well with our intuitions about "contempt." Now, let's explore the character's relationships in the play as their speaking parts relate to the engagement with love and hate. We will rely on pretrained models for dependency parsing from spacyr and the en_core_web_sm language model.[27] Remember, we need to specify our Python environment.[28]

[27] See **Tagging Words**.

[28] See **Computing Basics**.

```
## Download the language model if necessary
# spacy_download_langmodel("en_core_web_sm", envname = "myenv")
spacy_initialize(model = "en_core_web_sm", condaenv = "myenv")
```

```
df_parse <- df_tgov |>
  select(doc_id, line) |>
  rename(text = line) |>
  spacy_parse(entity = FALSE, dependency = TRUE)
```

We can summarize these dependency relations with **narrative motifs** (Franzosi 2004; Stuhler 2022b). Specifically, let's extract when "I" is the entity vs. "you." Next, we'll compare two *motifs*: (1) the *action* of an entity vs. (2) the *treatment* of an entity (Stuhler 2022b:3).

```
motifs <- extract_motifs(df_parse, entities = c("*"))
motifs <- motifs[c("actions", "treatments")]

df_motifs <- bind_rows(motifs) |>
    pivot_longer(action:treatment) |>
    filter(Entity %in% c("I", "you")) |>
    left_join(df_cmd) |>
    na.omit()
```

Finally, let's see how the relative proportion of love-to-hate engagement shifts for each entity and motif (Figure 12.5). We can further disaggregate by speaker. For instance, Valentine's line "O! flatter me; for love delights in praises" has among the highest engagement with love, and Valentine is acted upon ("flatter me").

```
df_motifs |>
    filter(speaker %in% characters) |>
    mutate(love = love_pole - min(love_pole)) |>
  ggplot(aes(x = love_pole, fill = Entity)) +
    geom_density(position = "fill", alpha = 0.7) +
    facet_grid(name ~ speaker) +
    labs(x = "Toward Love (From Hate)")
```

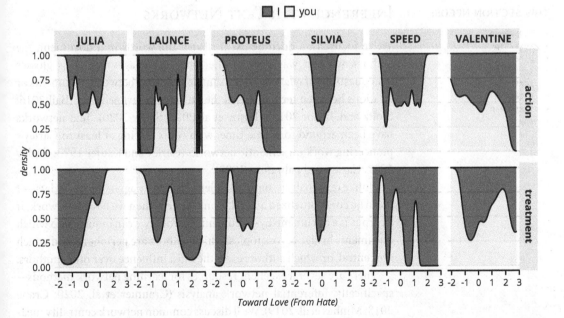

Figure 12.5: Entities, Motifs, and Engagement with 'Love'.

Take a moment to explore the plot—a lot is going on. Look at Julia—the object of Proteus's affection. When she is talking about love, the entity involved—whether acting (action) or being acted upon (treatment)—is "you." For example, after discovering Proteus also loves Silvia, Julia says:

> Because methinks that she lov'd you as well As you do love your lady Silvia.
> She dreams on him that has forgot her love:

Here, Julia (dressed in disguise) discusses Proteus in the second person and he is being "treated": *she lov'd you*.

Here, we incorporated text preprocessing and pretrained models to provide a cursory "distant" reading of a single play. Unlike hand-labeling and dictionary methods, for instance, little time is needed to alter concepts, that is, select different anchors for semantic centroids and directions. We could quickly expand this basic infrastructure to include not only Shakepeare's First Folio, but also hundreds of playwrights, thousands of plays, perhaps over centuries.

Labeling is not necessary to obtain these classifications. However, to test the validity of these methods, we could hand-label a random sample of the texts, and see how well our classifier agrees with these labels (e.g., Carbone and Mijs 2022).

THIS SECTION NEEDS:

- tidyverse
- text2map
- ggraph
- igraph
- text2vec
- backbone
- textclean
- sna

INFERENCE WITH TEXT NETWORKS

We've focused on documents' *attributes*: the words in a document, the authors, when it was written, the topics it engages, etc. This glosses over questions of *relations*—for example, relations between documents or relations between terms. This is the purpose of *text networks* (Bail 2016; Stoltz and Taylor 2019b; Basov et al. 2020; Segev 2020). Text networks have been around for some time, with roots tracing at least to Carley's pioneering work on semantic networks (Carley and Kaufer 1993; Carley 1997; Carley and Palmquist 1992).

Unlike text analysis, network science is largely agnostic about data—if it can be conceptualized as a relational matrix, then we have a network. If a corpus is a document-by-document network, we can inquire into which documents bridge across topics, which authors are peripheral and which are central, or which authors exert the most influence over other authors.

There are several excellent resources for learning network methods—specifically, inferential network analysis (Cranmer et al. 2020; Crane 2018; Minhas et al. 2019). We'll discuss common network centrality measures and then introduce tools for making inferences with text networks:

finding network backbones, using univariate inference with CUG tests, and multivariate inference with dyadic regression with QAP. Each uses the document-level networks (as opposed to word networks).[29]

Until now, we've mostly avoided *inferential statistics* — the territory of classic quantitative methods, especially survey research. The following assumes some familiarity with significance testing (which we did not cover in **Math Basics**). So, let's walk through the basic intuition. Imagine a network of some size and shape. We want to know the *mechanism* that could generate such a network. We don't know the mechanism, but we may have theories. The mechanism, though, might just be *randomness*. If randomness can plausibly account for what we see in our network, then probably none of our theories hold water. So, when we assess statistical significance, we're seeing if we can rule out randomness as an explanation.

Building Text Networks

Let's go back to our *Annual Review of Sociology* corpus from earlier and recreate it using the same wrangling steps as before, including dropping words from the Snowball stoplist and dropping words occurring just once (i.e., hapax).

```
data("corpus_annual_review", package = "text2map.corpora")

df_ars <- corpus_annual_review |>
  select(title, authors, abstract) |>
  group_by(title) |>
  summarize(abstract = first(abstract)) |>
  mutate(abstract = gsub("[[:punct:]]+", " ", abstract),
         abstract = tolower(abstract))

dtm_ars <- df_ars |>
    dtm_builder(abstract, title) |>
    dtm_stopper(stop_hapax = TRUE,
                stop_list = get_stoplist("snowball2014"))
```

Let's convert it to a base R dense matrix and look at the first five rows and a random sample of three columns.

```
set.seed(234)
dtm_ars <- as.matrix(dtm_ars)
dtm_ars[1:3, sample(ncol(dtm_ars), 3)]
```

```
                                  affinity settlement shifts
My Life in Words and Numbers             1          0      0
Of Modernity and Public...               0          0      0
Advances in the Science of Asking...     0          0      0
```

Recall the network matrix for the Florentine family data.[30] Our DTM is also a network matrix with two differences. First, the cells are now

[29] If you are unfamiliar with network analysis or need a refresher, see **Math Basics**.

[30] See **Math Basics**.

weighted. The entry tells us more than just the presence or absence of a tie. It tells us *how many times* a term appears in a document. Second, the row and column entities are different—we have documents *and* terms, not just family names in both rows and columns. In network terms, a matrix with different row and column entities is called a *two-mode matrix*. The graph equivalent is called a *bipartite graph*.[31] If we put these two things together, then we can call our DTM a *weighted bipartite graph*. The graph is visualized in Figure 12.6.

[31] One-mode networks—such as the Florentine family network—are called *unipartite* graphs. *Bipartite* graphs are also called *affiliation networks*, usually when the entities are people and organizations.

```
set.seed(37201)

dtm_ars |>
  ggraph(layout = "fr") +
  geom_edge_link(color = "gray50", alpha = .2) +
  geom_node_point(aes(fill = type), size = 3,
                  shape = 21, color = "black") +
  scale_fill_discrete(labels = c("Article Abstract", "Term"))
```

Figure 12.6: ARS Corpus as a Bipartite Graph.

● Article Abstract ○ Term

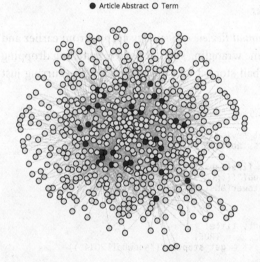

The dark nodes in the graph are the article abstracts and the light nodes are the terms. The network has a hub-and-spoke structure. All term nodes seem to radiate out from the article nodes. None of those term nodes connect to—that is, are "adjacent to"—other term nodes.

How do we go about finding patterns in bipartite graph like this? Generally, we proceed in three ways. First, we could ignore the bipartite structure and use standard unipartite network analysis.[32] Second, we could use newer tools and methods designed to work specifically on two-mode relational data. Third, we could convert the weighted bipartite

[32] This is probably not a good idea for reasons beyond our scope.

graph into two separate weighted unipartite graphs—one for each mode—and carry out analyses on those. We'll take this third strategy.

We already know how to get a weighted document-by-document matrix where the cell entries tell us how much vocabulary overlap there is between two documents using `tcrossprod()`. We can get the term-by-term matrix with `crossprod()`.

```
doc_proj <- tcrossprod(dtm_ars)
term_proj <- crossprod(dtm_ars)
```

When visualizing, the document graph would render quickly but not the term graph. We won't even try to visualize the term graph here because it takes considerable computational power and the figure would not be insightful. The term graph would be what network researchers call a "hairball" (Dianati 2016)—the ties in the middle would make a gray blob.

The one-mode projections from a DTM are usually very *dense*. Unless we have concise texts, it is unlikely that two documents share *no* vocabulary or two terms share *no* documents. Second, even a tiny vocabulary still means potentially thousands of nodes. Even though the document-level graph is typically *denser* than the term-level one, there will be fewer nodes.

In our case, the *ARS* corpus has only 33 documents. The term graph has 510 nodes and 59,616 ties. These documents are already short (just article abstracts). The document graph has a network density of 0.97—that is, 97% of the possible ties in the document network are actually present!

When visualizing, setting ties with small weights to zero might help, but this may not help us *interpret* the patterns. To aid interpretation, then, we can turn to standard network metrics. We focus on the most common: centrality.

Centrality

Node centrality is a way to measure each node's importance in a graph.[33] Definition of "importance" can vary, but there are two in particular (we focus on document-level analyses here, though the same applies to the term network):

[33] There are also measures of tie centrality.

1. The strength of a document's similarity to other documents.
2. The extent a document is a broker between other documents that otherwise do not have much in common.

We'll quickly cover two measures, one corresponding to one of these definitions of importance: degree centrality and betweenness centrality.[34]

Degree Centrality

Weighted degree centrality is the sum of the tie weights of a particular node. For our document network, this means, for each document, summing its dot products (excluding the dot product with itself, if we ignore the diagonal of the matrix). The higher the value, the more similar that document is to other documents in that corpus.

The simplest way to get this is by summing the rows of the document-level projection with the self-references (i.e., diagonal) zeroed.[35] Let's do that below and then find the five documents with the highest degree centralities (Table 12.1).

```
doc_proj <- tcrossprod(dtm_ars)
diag(doc_proj) <- 0

data.frame(degree = rowSums(doc_proj)) |>
  slice_max(degree, n = 4, with_ties = FALSE)
```

Table 12.1: Documents with Highest Degree Centrality

	centrality
Computational Social Science and Sociology	854
Urban Mobility and Activity Space	663
Tracking US Social Change Over a Half-Century	587
Relational Work in the Economy	551

"Computational Social Science and Sociology" is the most central, suggesting that this abstract has the most vocabulary overlap with the other abstracts in the corpus.

Betweenness Centrality

Next up is *betweenness centrality*, which measures the extent to which a node is a bridge in a network. Higher values indicate a node is adjacent to nodes that otherwise are not adjacent to one another. If we think about the "flow" of a network, the idea is that nodes with high betweenness monopolize that flow.

If unweighted, betweenness centrality is the sum of ratios of shortest paths (also known as *geodesics*) between any two documents that *include* the focal document to the total number of shortest paths between those two documents at all. If weighted, the shortest path between two documents is the inverse of the "path of least resistance" (Opsahl et al. 2010:248; Newman 2001). This is the weighted path between two documents with the largest sum.[36]

Let's get some weighted betweenness scores for our documents. We'll use `igraph`, which treats the weights in a network as costs rather than strengths. So, we must invert the weights before passing to `betweenness()`.

[36] Just as with degree, high weighted betweenness can be driven by two things: the (1) document being on a large number of longer paths with higher weights, or the (2) document being on a large number of shortest paths. See Opsahl and colleagues (2010) for a correction.

```
get_betweenness <- function(x) {
  gr <- graph.adjacency(x, mode = "undirected",
                   weighted = TRUE, diag = FALSE)
  E(gr)$weight <- 1 / E(gr)$weight
  df <- data.frame(centrality = betweenness(gr))
  return(df)
}

get_betweenness(doc_proj) |>
  slice_max(centrality, n = 4, with_ties = FALSE)
```

Our article with the highest degree is also the biggest broker in the text network (see Table 12.2). Perhaps this is because computational social science is an interdisciplinary field that bridges across other (sometimes disparately connected) specializations.

Table 12.2: Documents with Highest Betweenness Centrality

	centrality
Computational Social Science and Sociology	235
Urban Mobility and Activity Space	59
Relational Work in the Economy	32
Organizations and the Governance of Urban Poverty	28

Network Backbones

Text networks are usually undirected, weighted, and very dense. For the document network, a tie is absent if two documents share no words. Absent heavy-handed vocabulary pruning and short texts, this is unlikely. In other words, our document networks are *fully connected graphs*, where every possible tie is present.

This complicates visualization—the "hairball" problem—but also the statistical analysis of the network. We can address this with two non-exclusive procedures: removing ties and removing weights. We can do this manually—recoding weights to "0" if the weight is below the 75th

percentile, for instance, and a "1" otherwise. We can also take a statistical approach by finding the *network backbone*.

The backbone is a subset of the network created by the "significant" ties. For a weighted network, it is an unweighted network "preserv[ing] only those [ties] whose weights are sufficiently large" (Neal 2014:84). Finding the backbone for a weighted network that is the one-mode projection of a bipartite graph (such as a DTM) is tricky. The backbone algorithms tailored to "native" one-mode weighted networks do not account for the bipartite nature when deciding to retain a tie (Neal 2014:84). Though backbone algorithms for weighted bipartite graphs exist (e.g., Neal 2017), DTMs tend to make convergence difficult (if not impossible, in some cases). So, we'll use a document-similarity matrix (DSM) created as the document-level projection of a DTM.

We'll do so with the *disparity filter* (Serrano et al. 2009). This filtering mechanism draws on a "statistical significance" test. So, we must choose a significance level, or "alpha" (α).[37] For us, the null hypothesis is that any tie weight between two documents is as good as random.

Let i and j be any two documents in the corpus and D be a document in the DSM. For each document i, we normalize its tie weights so the sum of its tie weights equals 1. We then create a simulation of D_i (call it D_i') where (1) i's degree and neighborhood (i.e., set of alters) are the same as in D_i, and (2) the tie weights are pulled from a uniform distribution and normalized so that each tie weight has the same probability. The distribution of these tie weights for D_i' reflects a null hypothesis that any given weight attached to one of i's ties is random.[38]

We then find the probability of getting a tie weight *at least as large* as the one we observe between i and j if the null hypothesis were true. This is known as a right-tailed p-value. If the p-value is smaller than our significance level,[39] then it is unlikely we would observe the ij tie weight if it was just as likely as any other tie weight in i's neighborhood. This also means the tie gets a "1" in the unweighted backbone network, and otherwise a "0." We repeat this process for every tie in the network.

We'll use a sample from news articles mentioning "immigration" in the All the News (ATN) corpus. For expediency, let's also limit ourselves to 400 articles.[40]

```
data("corpus_atn_immigr", package = "text2map.corpora")
set.seed(2063)
df_atn <- corpus_atn_immigr |> sample_n(size = 400)
```

[37] Alpha is the probability below which we are willing to reject a null hypothesis when, in fact, it is true.

[38] Specificaly, the probability of the weight for the ij tie is no different from the probability of the weight attached to any of i's other ties.

[39] That is, "statistically significant."

[40] We'll preprocess our text by transliterating to Basic Latin, removing URLs, HTML, punctuation, and excess whitespace, and then replacing contractions and ordinal numbers.

```
df_atn <- df_atn |>
  mutate(text = replace_non_ascii(text),
         text = replace_url(text, replacement = " "),
         text = replace_html(text, replacement = " "),
         text = replace_contraction(text),
         text = str_replace_all(text, "[[:punct:]]", " "),
         text = replace_ordinal(text),
         text = str_replace_all(text, "[\\s]+", " "),
         text = tolower(text)
  )
```

Then we'll get the document-level projection using `tcrossprod()`. Remember, this measures the vocabulary overlap between two documents. We'll pass this to `disparity()` in backbone . The significance level is set to 0.01, meaning that we give any tie weight whose p-value under the null hypothesis is smaller than 0.01 a "1" and a "0" if it is equal to or greater than 0.01.

```
dtm_atn <- df_atn |> dtm_builder(text, doc_id, dense = TRUE)
dsm_atn <- tcrossprod(dtm_atn)
dsm_backbone <- disparity(dsm_atn, alpha = 0.01)
```

The output is a sparse, unweighted representation of our (very dense) weighted network. Indeed, we can see below (output in the margin) that we retained only 3% of the total ties! This network is much easier to handle with statistical tests.

```
# check sparsity
total    <- nrow(dsm_backbone) * ncol(dsm_backbone)
nonzero <- sum(dsm_backbone)
nonzero / total
```

[1] 0.0318

Univariate Network Inference

The *conditional uniform graph (CUG) test* is the network analog to the one-sample z- and t-test for a mean.[41] The idea is: We measure something about our observed network, call it q.[42] We then randomly draw simulated networks. These simulated networks are the same size as the observed network and drawn from a uniform probability distribution (i.e., where each random network of that size is equally likely to be selected). We then calculate q for each simulated network. Like before, we also need a significance level, say 0.05. With that, we can find two proportions:

1. The proportion of simulated q larger than or equal to our observed q (the empirically derived *right*-tailed p-value).
2. The proportion of simulated q smaller than or equal to our observed q (the empirically derived *left*-tailed p-value).

[41] For a much more detailed overview of CUG tests and the dyadic regression we cover in the next section, see Cranmer, Desmarais, and Morgan (2020).

[42] This can be anything, say, the graph-level transitivity or mean degree centrality.

If our observed q is larger than 95% of the simulated q, randomness is unlikely to generate an observed q *at least that large*. If our observed q is smaller than 95% of the simulated q, randomness is unlikely to generate an observed q *at least that small*. In either case, we conclude that random chance does not account for what we see in our network.

Let's walk through an example using the backbone network we created with the ATN DTM. Our quantity of interest, q, is the mean degree centrality. We'll use a CUG test to see if q reflects randomness or some unique quality of this network.

We first define a function to calculate the mean degree centrality, which we'll pass to `cug.test()` . We want all simulated networks to be the same size as our observed network, which we specify with the `cmode` parameter. We'll also specify an undirected graph with `mode` . Let's generate 100 simulated networks (output in the margin).[43]

```
mean_degree <- function(x) {
  mean(rowSums(x))
}
set.seed(2063)
cug.test(dsm_backbone, FUN = mean_degree, mode = "graph",
         cmode = "size", reps = 100)
```

Observed Value: 371.035
    Pr(X>=Obs): 1
    Pr(X<=Obs): 0

All simulated q are larger than or equal to the observed q: Pr(X>=Obs): 1 or 100%. No simulated q is smaller than or equal to the observed q: Pr(X<=Obs): 0 or 0%. So, on average, these news articles share less significant vocabulary overlap than we expect by random chance.

Multivariate Network Inference

CUG tests are limited to hypothesis testing on one variable. What about multivariate modeling? We can handle this with the *quadratic assignment procedure* (QAP) (Cranmer et al. 2020). QAP is a method for adjusting *p*-values in *dyadic regression models*, where observational independence (an assumption of regular regression models) is not justifiable.

The unit of analysis in dyadic regression is the dyad—as opposed to individuals in regular regression models. For a document network, this is the presence (or absence) of significant vocabulary overlap between documents—not the documents themselves. Once the coefficients are estimated,[44] QAP then computes the proportion of coefficients from simulated networks at least as extreme as the coefficient we get from the observed network.

Let's assess the "political homophily" effect in our backbone network. In network theory, *homophily* is when two nodes have a higher probability of being connected when they share an attribute. For us, we want to know if news articles are more likely have significant vocabulary overlap if they share political lean.[45]

We'll use `netlm()` . Before we run the regression, though, we need to create our homophily network: a document-by-document network where a cell gets a "1" if the organizations publishing the two articles have the same political lean, and a "0" if otherwise.

[45] This is a bivariate analysis, so we could report the *assortativity coefficient* to help assess this (Newman 2003).

```
df_hmph  <- model.matrix(~ lean - 1, df_atn)
mat_hmph <- tcrossprod(df_hmph)
```

The `netlm()` function will "vectorize" both of our networks: both our vocabulary overlap network, y, and our homophily network, x, are "unrolled" into vectors, one for each dyad. We then regress the y on the x. We'll specify that we want QAP-adjusted p-values and that we want to base these p-values off of 120 repetitions.

```
set.seed(2063)
netlm(y = dsm_backbone, x = list(mat_hmph),
     nullhyp = "qap", reps = 120, mode = "graph")


Coefficients:
            Estimate    Pr(<=b)    Pr(>=b)     Pr(>=|b|)
(intercept) 0.02697203  0.9750000  0.025000000 0.025
x1          0.02105918  0.9916667  0.008333333 0.075
```

The estimates (i.e., coefficients) come from a *dyadic regression* model. While the units are dyads, we interpret the coefficients the same as any regression model. We only have one predictor: homophily. The coefficient for this variable is 0.02. When two articles are published by organizations sharing political lean, the probability of significant vocabulary overlap increases, on average, by 2%. The right-tailed p-value is statistically significant,[46] meaning that we can reject the null hypothesis that randomness plausibly explains our coefficient since fewer than 1% of the coefficients from the simulated networks are larger than or equal to the observed coefficient.

[46] The *p*-value is below the conventional 0.01.

The political lean is attached to the organization publishing the articles. Perhaps, what explains vocabulary overlap is being from the same news organization, and the effect of political lean is spurious. We can model this by creating another homophily matrix, but this time using the publication. Then, we'll include both homophily matrices as predictors.

```
df_orgs <- model.matrix(~ publication - 1, df_atn)

mat_orgs <- as.matrix(df_orgs) |> tcrossprod()
```

```
set.seed(2063)
netlm(y = dsm_backbone, x = list(mat_orgs, mat_hmph),
    nullhyp = "qap", reps = 120, mode = "graph")
```

```
Coefficients:
              Estimate       Pr(<=b)      Pr(>=b)      Pr(>=|b|)
(intercept)   0.0269720329   0.97500000   0.025000000  0.02500000
x1           -0.0004690426   0.01666667   0.983333333  0.01666667
x2            0.0231017133   0.99166667   0.008333333  0.03333333
```

The first estimate (x1) is the effect of being published by the same organization. The right-tailed p-value is not statistically significant, but the left-tailed and two-tailed are. The second estimate (x2) is the effect of being published by organizations with the same political lean. It remains statistically significant. So, political ideology increases vocabulary overlap in our corpus, which is unlikely to result from random chance.

Broadly, converting our text matrices into graphs, brings both a useful theoretical metaphor and a swathe of techniques to chart the relations between elements in our texts. Social scientists use text networks to study, for example, public debate instigated by advocacy organizations (Bail 2016; see also Puetz et al. 2021); the influence of climate change contrarians on American news media and politicians (Farrell 2016); the relationship between a screenplay's network size and the box office success of the film (Hunter III et al. 2016); and charting the connections between our texts and the social networks of authors (e.g., Basov et al. 2020).

13
Project Workflow and Iteration

*"That's another thing we've learned from your Nation," said Mein Herr, "map-making. But we've carried it much further than you.... **We actually made a map of the country, on the scale of a mile to the mile!"***

"Have you used it much?" I enquired.

"It has never been spread out, yet," said Mein Herr: "the farmers objected: they said it would cover the whole country, and shut out the sunlight! So we now use the country itself, as its own map, and I assure you it does nearly as well."

—L. Carroll

THE PARADOX OF THE COMPLETE MAP

COMPUTATIONAL methods are often lauded for their ability to **scale**. Indeed, we even discuss how corpora may be so large as to render traditional qualitative content analysis impracticable. Computational methods step in to augment the human reader, directing our attention, sharing the workload, providing insight, etc.

Scale is not an endless virtue, however. A one-to-one map of Okinawa, the exact size of this Ryukyuan island, would be a 1,200 square kilometer hindrance to Okinawan life. In mapping texts too, size can be a hindrance to understanding. Large Language Models (LLMs) epitomize this paradox. In one sense, they are "overfitted" for social scientific purposes—the computational equivalent of adding theoretical nuance for the sake of nuance.[1] Social scientists should be skeptical of scale-hype. Not only because of the potential environmental and social costs of ever-larger models.[2] But also what does our community learn when we (humans) project meaning onto a language model parroting probabilistic prose (Bender et al. 2021)?[3] We could learn much more from better documentation on corpus construction and model architecture than from greater complexity.

When mapping texts, we simplify their information for particular uses. Mapping, then, is *reduction to aid interpretation* (Lee and Martin 2014). For example, we learned several methods for sorting documents

[1] "It blocks the process of abstraction on which theory depends, and it inhibits the creative process that makes theorizing a useful activity" (Healy 2017:119).

[2] Training GPT-3 produced the carbon equivalent of driving a car 435,000 miles—nearly to the moon and back (Quach 2020), and CEO of OpenAI described the "compute costs" of ChatGPT as "eye-watering."

[3] This isn't a rhetorical question.

Mapping Texts: Computational Text Analysis for the Social Sciences. Dustin S. Stoltz and Marshall A. Taylor, Oxford University Press. © Oxford University Press 2024. DOI: 10.1093/oso/9780197756874.003.0013

into a few categories. We also learned how to identify the topics or themes a collection of documents' authors are discussing. For instance, Fligstein and colleagues (2017) were interested in how participants of Federal Open Market Committee meetings understood the "economy" leading up to the 2008 Financial Crisis. Using methods discussed in this book, they divided this discursive space into fifteen frames—a manageable number. In all these cases, we are reducing complexity and summarizing semantic patterns.

Mapping texts is an iterative process. A project vacillates between the familiar and the strange and novel—the hallmark of an abductive approach. We begin in mid-conversation with prior studies, social scientific theories, and—importantly—the actual texts under analysis. In their study of militant groups, Karell and Freedman (2019) used computational methods to "defamiliarize" radicalism: "[W]e used the computational measurement of the corpus to identify puzzling aspects of radical expression" (2019:730).

Computational methods are uniquely equipped to **iterate**. We are not only building an organizational scheme but an architecture for repetition. Crucially, though, **we need to know what we did and why we did it**. As we log our journey through a project, we should always annotate code and write analytic memos *as if* for someone else because, in a few months, *we will be someone else*.[4] We will, for example, forget small steps or change our understanding of a concept. We should not burden ourselves with remembering every detail when we can simply write it down. Only then can we understand our patterns, be prepared for the novel, simulate the null, and share our findings with our communities. Therefore, in keeping with the spirit of this book, science, language, and *Finnegans Wake*, we end by returning to the beginning.

CONTAINERIZE OUR PROJECTS

We *aspire* to create projects that are entirely contained. The main pieces of any project include: (1) prose, (2) scripts, (3) data, (4) outputs, and (5) administrative documents.

Programming languages are written in plain text. We can also write **prose** (reports, articles, memos, etc.) in plain text—no need for clunky word processors.[5] A benefit of writing in plain text is that we can embed code alongside prose. Plain text is also relatively future-proof. It has been around as long as personal computing and can be used on any platform—no proprietary software required!

[4] We annexed this quote from Alessandra Lembo. Thanks, Ale!

[5] See Healy (2018b). This doesn't work for everyone all the time, but IDEs include spell-checkers and other add-ons to aid writing. We wrote this entire book in RMarkdown!

Each plain-text file with only code (no prose) is a **script**. There are three primary steps for computational methods involving pattern detection, pattern refinement, and pattern confirmation (Nelson 2020). As we argue, however, there is never just one pattern waiting to be unearthed. Every instance of pruning, stopping, tagging, and transforming our texts involves an analytic decision. If we can automate the reproduction of these decisions with scripts, we should.[6] The best practice is to focus our scripts around one or very few outputs—this helps identify the sources of errors (i.e., debugging). For example, we can have one script for wrangling our raw text into a dataframe or matrix, or one script for creating word embeddings. The goal is to run the script from top-to-bottom without error, reproducing a given output. We must also annotate our code so that other researchers (and our future selves!) know what the code is doing and why we need it.

Outputs include figures (PNGs, PDFs, etc.), models, or datasets processed in some way. With each output, we should know precisely how to re-create it. We also want to maintain a version of our **data** in its raw form—how we found or collected it originally. Not only will we be able to fix mistakes, but this practice also forces us to keep track of *how* we got from the raw form to the final form. Lastly, we will need to keep track of **administrative documents** such as IRB approval forms, consent forms, funding documents, and labeling protocols. In the margin, see the example folders for a well-organized project directory (Navarro 2022).

Every time we open `R` to work on a project, the top-level folder—here, `new_project` —is our designated *working directory*. This should also be self-contained: we can move `new_project` to, say, a new hard drive and the code would still work.

Note the **archive** folders. A best practice is to **never delete** anything we've written—or, at least, the bar for deleting is very high. Instead, we archive. A piece of software that aids this is *git*.[7] This is a *version control system* that tracks changes in project directories and changes *within* any plain-text files. Git is also how repository websites like GitLab, Codeberg, and GitHub operate.[8] While the benefits of git are legion, there is a steep learning curve. A low-tech alternative is to copy files into archive folders periodically. Again, though, we should avoid the burden of remembering:

> *"You need regular, redundant, automatic, offsite backups of your work.* Because you are lazy and prone to magical thinking, you will not do this responsibly by yourself. This is why the most useful backup systems are the ones that require a minimum amount of work to set up and, once organized, *back up everything automatically without you having to remember to do anything."*
> (Healy 2018b:11–2)

[6] This way, we're more likely to catch our errors, but also other people may catch our errors when they attempt to replicate using our scripts.

```
Documents
|-- new_project
    |-- admin
    |   |-- IRB
    |   |-- funding
    |-- data
    |   |-- archive
    |-- figures
    |-- memos
    |-- paper
    |-- scripts
        |-- archive
```

"Everything not saved will be lost." — Nintendo "Quit Screen" Message

[7] Mercurial and Subversion are common alternatives.

[8] We used git and GitLab as our version control system for this book.

[9] Such as Dropbox or Google Drive.

[10] Some examples of total system backups would be SpiderOak, Carbonite, Backblaze, or Crashplan.

[11] In particular, avoid special regular expression symbols as we often match filenames with regex to read them into R . See **Wrangling Words**.

[12] Note the file extensions. Some operating systems hide this by default, but this can and should be changed by the user.

Backup systems are slightly different from "cloud sync" platforms[9] as they typically back up an entire system and only in one direction. This allows us to reinstate an older version of our system should our current system be damaged beyond repair.[10]

Folders are intuitive organizational tools. So are file names. Names should be unique and informative. They should avoid capitalization and spaces, because different operating systems and programs may treat these inconsistently. We should also avoid "special characters," such as & or ().[11] and sort similar files together. Below are a few examples (see also Bryan and Hester 2019).[12]

```
01_script_load_packages.R
02_script_wrangle_text.R
data_survey_attitudes_movies.csv
data_survey_attitudes_books.csv
data_demographics_nmsu.txt
2020-05-01_scrape_reddit_maliciouscompliance.rds
```

MEMOING AND DATASHEETS

In qualitative research, especially ethnography, it is common practice to write "analytic memos." This is different from "field-notes" in that the focus is *self*-reflection and *self*-observation. What did we do today? What did we learn? How has our thinking changed today? What will we do differently tomorrow? This is also where we explicitly bring together theory and analysis. This is the narrative counterpart to our coding. Certainly, researchers will have different strategies, but at minimum, we should approach a day of coding as a day *in the field* and set aside time for memoing, and periodically review these memos as a project progresses.

Despite some tendencies to use the largest available corpora, we cannot ignore the ways every analysis of text is drawn from a subset. We need to know, as best we can, what subset we're studying. If we do not consider this, we can mistake patterns in the assembly of the corpus for patterns within the texts. Essential to this process, then, is *documenting*—in meticulous detail—the steps we take to collect and select our texts.

Our analytic memos, with our scripts, can be used later to create **datasheets**. To keep in step with open science, our corpus and/or derivatives will need to be shared with our community. Without accompanying documentation, researchers may use our corpus but misunderstand their findings. Therefore, following Gebru and colleagues (2021:86), we argue that "every dataset be accompanied with a datasheet that documents its motivation, composition, collection process, recommended uses, and so on."[13] To know whether we have a fair sample of texts, and communicate this to others, we must document how a corpus was created (as best as we can). This entails retelling the journey we take in acquiring and selecting documents.

[13] For sample datasheets, see Gebru et al. (2021); Bandy and Vincent (2021).

REPEATING, REPLICATING, AND SIMULATING THE NULL

When sharing datasheets, data, scripts, and methodological appendices, our primary goal is **repetition**: Can we or anyone else repeat all the steps necessary to exactly re-create analyses presented in publications? This is the bare minimum for open science. Could different researchers start with the raw text, and follow our instructions such that they end with the same findings? By sharing this information other researchers may, for example, discover coding errors that change findings—advancing our collective knowledge.[14]

Datasheets and scripts can also help with **replication**: Can we replicate the finding *using different data*? Given the many steps involved in wrangling messy text into neat dataframes, we must describe what was done and why it was done so other researchers can use those same steps on new texts. Even if our code were to "break," researchers could re-implement the detailed procedure in our methodological appendices. We should also present detailed corpus statistics in any publication— just as we usually report summary statistics for our datasets in survey research.

[14] Precise repetition is not always possible given dependencies and "floating-point errors."

While there is a recent push for replication, computational methods are perhaps uniquely suited for *anti-replication*. By this we mean testing the limits of theories by simulating the circumstances that—if the theories' tenets are valid—should not produce a finding. Or, approaching it from the opposite direction, what if we have a 1 in 10,000 finding that only holds under a random initialization with a specific seed? Easy: we loop through our analysis 10,000 times using different seeds.

Questions on randomization-based inference are not new in statistics circles (Darlington and Hayes 2016; Edgington and Onghena 2007; Ernst 2004; Taylor 2020). In this sense, if computational methods involve iteration, then many of us have been using computational methods under the guise of things like Monte Carlo permutation tests for quite some time. What *is* a relatively new idea is simulating "new worlds" by redoing our analyses but slightly altering the steps in our computational infrastructure. This is similar to *computational multimodel analysis* (Young and Holsteen 2017; Muñoz and Young 2018), which aims to

15 As well as the reporting of false positives, that is, publication bias.

16 "A map does not just chart, it unlocks and formulates meaning; it forms bridges between here and there, between disparate ideas that we did not know were previously connected" (Larsen 2009:138).

minimize model uncertainty[15] by creating distributions of model estimates derived from models under many different conditions. The question is: Does our "preferred" model estimate "stand out" as unique when compared to other ways of simulating and modeling the world? If it does, is this a good or bad thing?

KNOWLEDGE TAKES A VILLAGE

Three millennia after Babylonian astronomers carved the habits of Venus into the tablet of Ammisaduqa, Venera 1 grazed the Venusian atmosphere; two millennia after Anaximander flattened the earth to paper, Tenzing Norgay and Edmund Hillary used this tool to summit Earth's highest point. Maps offload cognitively demanding tasks, create snapshots of ever-changing conditions, and allow us to visualize obscured attributes in startling relief.[16] Mapping, too, seeks to make representations of complex domains in ways that facilitate ongoing conversations.

We hope this book is an invitation to join these conversations. Like all scholarly research, computational text analysis is a community activity. Our work stands on the shoulders of many, and we hope this has been clear throughout. We believe more researchers and more collaborations—not more data and larger models—are the paths to more robust insights into social and cultural experience. Repeating our analyses, documenting our analytic procedures, sharing our data and code, and participating in ongoing discussions—are all necessary to push human understanding forward.

Appendix

Table 13.1: All R Packages Used

Package	Version	Citation	Package	Version	Citation
backbone	2.1.1	Neal (2022)	reshape2	1.4.4	Wickham (2007)
caret	6.0.93	Kuhn (2022)	reticulate	1.27	Ushey et al. (2023)
coreNLPsetup	0.0.1	Rinker (2017)	rsample	1.1.1	Frick et al. (2022)
entity	0.1.0	Rinker (2015)	rsvd	1.0.5	Erichson et al. (2019)
factoextra	1.0.7	Kassambara and Mundt (2020)	rtrek	0.3.3	Leonawicz (2021)
gender	0.6.0	Mullen (2021)	semgram	0.1.0	Stuhler (2022a)
genderdata	0.6.0	Mullen (2023)	sentimentr	2.9.0	Rinker (2021)
ggpubr	0.5.0	Kassambara (2022)	sna	2.7	Butts (2022)
ggraph	2.1.0	Pedersen (2022a)	spacyr	1.2.1	Benoit and Matsuo (2020)
ggrepel	0.9.2	Slowikowski (2022)	stm	1.3.6	Roberts et al. (2019)
ggtern	3.4.1	Hamilton and Ferry (2018)	stminsights	0.4.1	Schwemmer (2021)
glmnet	4.1.6	Friedman et al. (2010); Simon et al. (2011)	stringi	1.7.12	Gagolewski (2022)
gmodels	2.18.1.1	Warnes (2022)	tagger	0.0.2	Rinker (2016)
googleLanguageR	0.3.0	Edmondson (2020)	termco	0.5.11	Rinker (2018b)
guardianapi	0.1.1	Odell (2019)	tesseract	5.1.0	Ooms (2022b)
gutenbergr	0.2.3	Johnston and Robinson (2022)	text2map	0.1.6	Stoltz and Taylor (2022a)
hunspell	3.0.2	Ooms (2022a)	text2map.corpora	0.1.4	Stoltz and Taylor (2022b)
igraph	1.3.5	Csardi and Nepusz (2006)	text2map.pretrained	0.1.0	Stoltz and Taylor (2022c)
irr	0.84.1	Gamer et al. (2019)	text2vec	0.6.3	Selivanov et al. (2022)
keras	2.11.0	Allaire and Chollet (2022)	textclean	0.9.3	Rinker (2018c)
lexicon	1.2.1	Rinker (2018a)	textstem	0.1.4	Rinker (2018d)
lsa	0.73.3	Wild (2022)	tidygraph	1.2.2	Pedersen (2022b)
marginaleffects	0.8.1	Arel-Bundock (2022)	tidymodels	1.0.0	Kuhn and Wickham (2020)
Matrix	1.5.3	Bates et al. (2022)	tidyquant	1.0.6	Dancho and Vaughan (2022)
network	1.18.0	Butts (2015)	tidytext	0.4.1	Silge and Robinson (2016)
proustr	0.4.0	Fay (2019)	tidyverse	1.3.2	Wickham (2019)
qdapDictionaries	1.0.7	Rinker (2013)	tokenizers	0.3.0	Mullen et al. (2018)
quanteda	3.2.4	Benoit et al. (2018)	topicdoc	0.1.1	Friedman (2022)
quanteda.corpora	0.9.2	Benoit (2020)	topicmodels	0.2.13	Grün and Hornik (2022)
quanteda.textmodels	0.9.5.1	Benoit et al. (2022)	udpipe	0.8.11	Wijffels (2023)
remotes	2.4.2	Csárdi et al. (2021)			

Table 13.2: Functions by Package(s) and Chapter(s)

Function	Package(s)	Chapter(s)
activate	tidygraph	6
aes	ggplot2, ggtern	3, 4, 5, 6, 8, 9, 10, 11, 12
annotate	ggplot2, ggtern	4
anti_join	tidygraph, dplyr	7
arrange	tidygraph, dplyr	6, 10, 11

Function	Package(s)	Chapter(s)
array_reshape	reticulate, keras	12
arrow	ggplot2	4, 8
as_basic	tagger	8
as_factor	forcats	6
as_tbl_graph	tidygraph	6
as_tibble	tidygraph, dplyr, tidyr, tibble	7
as.dfm	quanteda	12
betweenness	sna, igraph	12
bind_rows	dplyr	10, 11, 12
case_when	dplyr	10, 11, 12
cast_dfm	tidytext	6, 7
cast_sparse	tidytext	6
chunk_text	tokenizers	6
column_to_rownames	tibble	8
compile	keras	12
confusion.glmnet	glmnet	9
coord_flip	ggplot2	6, 8, 10, 11
count	tidyquant, dplyr	6, 7, 8
count_tags	tagger	8
create_tcm	text2vec	11, 12
create_vocabulary	text2vec	11, 12
cug.test	sna	12
cv.glmnet	glmnet	9
datagrid	marginaleffects	11
dataset_fashion_mnist	keras	12
date_entity	entity	8
desc	dplyr	6, 10, 11
dfm	quanteda	6, 7, 9
dfm_remove	quanteda	7
dfm_tfidf	quanteda	6
dfm_weight	quanteda	6, 9
disparity	backbone	12
dist2	text2vec	10
download_pretrained	text2map.pretrained	11
dtm_builder	text2map	6, 7, 9, 10, 11, 12
dtm_melter	text2map	9
dtm_stats	text2map	6
dtm_stopper	text2map	7, 9, 10, 11, 12
element_blank	ggplot2	4, 6, 8, 10
element_line	ggplot2	4
element_text	ggplot2	12
evaluate	keras, termco	12
extract_motifs	semgram	12
facet_grid	ggplot2	6, 11, 12
facet_wrap	ggplot2	5, 6, 8, 10, 11, 12
fcm	quanteda	6, 11
fct_reorder	forcats	6, 11
filter	tidygraph, dplyr	5, 6, 7, 8, 9, 10, 11, 12
find_transformation	text2map	11, 12
first	tidyquant, dplyr	6, 10, 12
fit	text2vec, keras	12
fit_transform	text2vec	11
fviz_dend	factoextra	10
fviz_nbclust	factoextra	10
gender	gender	8
geom_abline	ggplot2	6
geom_bar	ggplot2	5
geom_boxplot	ggplot2	3
geom_col	ggplot2	6, 8, 9, 10, 11, 12
geom_curve	ggplot2	4
geom_density	ggplot2	12
geom_edge_arc	ggraph	6, 8
geom_edge_link	ggraph	4, 12
geom_errorbar	ggplot2	11, 12
geom_hline	ggplot2	10
geom_label	ggplot2	6
geom_label_repel	ggrepel	4
geom_line	ggplot2	5, 11

Function	Package(s)	Chapter(s)
geom_node_label	ggraph	4, 6, 8
geom_node_point	ggraph	12
geom_node_text	ggraph	8
geom_path	ggplot2	5
geom_point	ggplot2	3, 4, 6, 8, 11, 12
geom_ribbon	ggplot2	11
geom_segment	ggplot2	4, 6, 8
geom_smooth	ggplot2	5, 6, 11, 12
geom_text	ggplot2	10, 11, 12
geom_text_repel	ggrepel	11
geom_tile	ggplot2	8, 9, 10, 12
geom_vline	ggplot2	4, 10
get_centroid	text2map	11
get_direction	text2map	11, 12
get_effects	stminsights	11
get_sentences	sentimentr	9
get_stoplist	text2map	7, 10, 11, 12
ggarrange	ggpubr	3, 4, 6, 12
ggplot	ggplot2, ggtern	3, 4, 5, 6, 8, 9, 10, 11, 12
ggraph	ggraph	4, 6, 8, 12
ggtern	ggtern	11
graph_from_data_frame	igraph	8
graph.adjacency	igraph	12
group_by	ggpubr, tidygraph, dplyr	5, 6, 9, 10, 11, 12
gu_content	guardianapi	5
guide_legend	ggplot2	10, 11
guides	ggplot2	10, 11
gutenberg_download	gutenbergr	7, 12
hcut	factoextra	10
html_elements	rvest	5
html_text	rvest	5
hunspell_check	hunspell	7
hunspell_suggest	hunspell	7
initial_split	rsample	9, 12
inner_join	tidygraph, dplyr	9
install_github	remotes	3
install_gitlab	remotes	3
itoken	text2vec	11, 12
keras_model_sequential	keras	12
kripp.alpha	irr	9
label_rect	ggraph	8
labeller	ggplot2	11
labs	ggplot2	4, 5, 6, 8, 9, 10, 11, 12
layer_dense	keras	12
layer_embedding	keras	12
layer_global_average_pooling_1d	keras	12
left_join	tidygraph, dplyr	8, 9, 11, 12
lemmatize_strings	textstem	7, 11
lemmatize_words	textstem	7
lims	ggplot2	4
load_pretrained	text2map.pretrained	11, 12
location_entity	entity	8
lsa	text2vec, lsa	10
melt	reshape2	6
mutate	ggpubr, tidygraph, dplyr	3, 5, 6, 7, 8, 9, 10, 11, 12
n	tidygraph, network, dplyr	5, 6, 9
netlm	sna	12
normalize	text2vec, igraph, keras	9
ocr	tesseract	5
organization_entity	entity	8
parse_date_time	lubridate	5
person_entity	entity	8
pivot_longer	tidyr	5, 6, 11, 12
pivot_wider	tidyr	11
predictions	marginaleffects	11
recode	dplyr	5
rename	tidygraph, dplyr	6, 8, 12
rename_all	dplyr	12

Function	Package(s)	Chapter(s)
reorder_within	tidytext	8
replace_contraction	textclean	7, 11, 12
replace_curly_quote	textclean	7, 11, 12
replace_date	textclean	7
replace_html	textclean	11, 12
replace_kern	textclean	7
replace_money	textclean	7
replace_na	tidyr	8
replace_non_ascii	textclean	11, 12
replace_number	textclean	7
replace_ordinal	textclean	7, 11, 12
replace_time	textclean	7
replace_url	textclean	11, 12
replace_word_elongation	textclean, sentimentr	7
row_number	dplyr	10, 12
rowid_to_column	tibble	6, 9
rownames	quanteda	6, 7, 9, 10, 11, 12
rownames_to_column	tibble	6, 11, 12
rsvd	rsvd	12
sample_n	tidygraph, dplyr	9, 12
scale_colour_discrete	ggplot2	10
scale_fill_discrete	ggplot2	12
scale_fill_gradient	ggplot2	12
scale_linetype_manual	ggplot2	11
scale_x_continuous	ggplot2	10, 11
scale_x_log10	ggplot2	6
scale_x_reordered	tidytext	8
scale_y_continuous	ggplot2	4, 9
scale_y_log10	ggplot2	6
select	tidygraph, dplyr	5, 7, 8, 9, 10, 11, 12
select_tags	tagger	8
sentiment	sentimentr	9
separate	tidyr	5
seq_builder	text2map	12
session	rvest	5
session_jump_to	rvest	5
sim2	text2vec	6, 10, 11
slice_head	dplyr	9
slice_max	dplyr	6, 8, 10, 11, 12
space_tokenizer	text2vec	11
spacy_initialize	spacyr	8, 12
spacy_parse	spacyr	8, 12
st_transcripts	rtrek	11
stat_function	ggplot2	4
stem_strings	textstem	7
stm	stm	11
str_count	stringr	5
str_pad	stringr	11
str_replace	stringr	9
str_replace_all	stringr	9, 11, 12
str_split	stringr	12
str_squish	stringr	5, 9, 10, 12
stri_extract_all_words	stringi	7
stri_trans_general	stringi	7, 8, 11, 12
summarise	dplyr	11, 12
summarize	dplyr	5, 6, 9, 10, 11, 12
tag_pos	tagger	8
terms	topicmodels	10
testing	rsample	9, 12
textmodel_lr	quanteda.textmodels	12
textmodel_nb	quanteda.textmodels	12
textmodel_svm	quanteda.textmodels	12
theme	ggplot2	4, 6, 8, 9, 10, 11, 12
theme_custom	ggtern	11
theme_minimal	ggplot2, ggtern	4
theme_void	ggplot2, ggtern	6
tibble	dplyr, tidyr, tibble	7
tidy	tidytext, rsample, marginaleffects	5, 6, 9, 10, 11

Function	Package(s)	Chapter(s)
tiny_gender_tagger	text2map	8
to_categorical	keras	12
tokenize_character_shingles	tokenizers	6
tokenize_characters	tokenizers	6
tokenize_ngrams	tokenizers	6
tokenize_word	quanteda	7
tokenize_words	tokenizers	6, 7
tokens	quanteda	6, 7, 9, 11
tokens_ngrams	quanteda	9
tokens_remove	quanteda	7
top_n	tidygraph, dplyr	6
tq_get	tidyquant	5
training	rsample	9, 12
udpipe_annotate	udpipe	7, 8
udpipe_download_model	udpipe	7, 8
udpipe_load_model	udpipe	7, 8
ungroup	tidygraph, dplyr	10, 11
unit	ggplot2	4, 8
unnest	tidyr	7
unnest_tokens	tidytext	6, 7, 8, 12
use_condaenv	reticulate, keras	12
user_agent	httr	5
vocab_vectorizer	text2vec	11, 12
xlab	ggplot2	4
xlim	ggplot2	4
ylab	ggplot2	4
ylim	ggplot2	4, 10, 11

References

Adams, Julia and Hannah Brückner. 2015. "Wikipedia, sociology, and the promise and pitfalls of Big Data." *Big Data & Society* 2:205395171561433.

Afendras, Georgios and Marianthi Markatou. 2019. "Optimality of training/test size and resampling effectiveness in cross-validation." *Journal of Statistical Planning and Inference* 199:286–301.

Ahmed, Hadeer, Issa Traore, and Sherif Saad. 2017. "Detection of online fake news using *N*-gram analysis and machine learning techniques." In *Intelligent, Secure, and Dependable Systems in Distributed and Cloud Environments*, pp. 127–38. Springer International Publishing.

Ahmed, Hadeer, Issa Traore, and Sherif Saad. 2018. "Detecting opinion spams and fake news using text classification." *Security and Privacy* 1:e9.

Allaire, J. J. and François Chollet. 2022. *keras*. R package version 2.11.0.

American Sociological Association. 2021. "ASA Membership by Gender." https://www.asanet.org/research_trend/asa-membership-gender/. Accessed: 2023-3-15.

Apache. 2020. "Apache OpenNLP Developer Documentation."

Arel-Bundock, Vincent. 2022. *marginaleffects*: R package version 0.8.1.

Aristotle. 1907. *The Poetics of Aristotle*. Macmillan.

Aronoff, Mark. 1992. "Segmentalism in linguistics." *The Linguistics of Literacy* 21:71.

Arora, Sanjeev, Yuanzhi Li, Yingyu Liang, Tengyu Ma, and Andrej Risteski. 2016. "A latent variable model approach to PMI-based word embeddings." *Transactions of the Association for Computational Linguistics* 4:385–99.

Arseniev-Koehler, Alina and Jacob Foster. 2020. "Machine learning as a model for cultural learning." *Sociological Methods & Research* 51:1484–1539.

Aslanidis, Paris. 2018. "Measuring populist discourse with semantic text analysis." *Quality & Quantity* 52:1241–63.

Atasu, Kubilay, et al. 2017. "Linear-complexity relaxed word Mover's distance with GPU acceleration." In *2017 IEEE International Conference on Big Data (Big Data)*, pp. 889–96. IEEE.

Attia, Mohammed. 2007. "Arabic tokenization system." In *Proceedings of the 2007 Workshop on Computational Approaches to Semitic Languages*, pp. 65–72. aclweb.org.

Back, Mitja D., Albrecht C. P. Küfner, and Boris Egloff. 2010. "The emotional timeline of September 11, 2001." *Psychological Science* 21:1417–19.

Back, Mitja D., Albrecht C. P. Küfner, and Boris Egloff. 2011. "Automatic or the people?". *Psychological Science* 22:837.

Bail, Christopher. 2012. "The fringe effect." *American Sociological Review* 77: 855–79.

Bail, Christopher. 2016. "Combining natural language processing and network analysis to examine how advocacy organizations stimulate conversation on social media." *PNAS* 113:11823–8.

Bail, Christopher, Taylor Brown, and Marcus Mann. 2017. "Channeling hearts and minds." *American Sociological Review* 82:1188–213.

Bail, Christopher, Brian Guay, Emily Maloney, Aidan Combs, D. Sunshine Hillygus, Friedolin Merhout, et al. 2020. "Assessing the Russian Internet Research Agencys impact on the political attitudes and behaviors of American Twitter users in late 2017." *PNAS* 117:243–50.

Ball, C. N. 1994. "Automated text analysis." *Literary and Linguistic Computing* 9:295–302.

Bandy, Jack and Nicholas Vincent. 2021. "Addressing 'documentation debt' in machine learning research." arXiv preprint. arXiv:2105.05241.

Barbaro, Michael and Tom Zeller, Jr. 2006. "A face is exposed for AOL searcher no. 4417749." *The New York Times.*

Barthes, Roland and Lionel Duisit. 1975. "An introduction to the structural analysis of narrative." *New Literary History* 6:237–72.

Basov, Nikita, Ronald Breiger, and Iina Hellsten. 2020. "Socio-semantic and other dualities." *Poetics* 78: 101433.

Bates, Douglas, Martin Maechler, and Mikael Jagan. 2022. *Matrix: Sparse and Dense Matrix Classes and Methods.* R package version 1.5-3.

Bauer, Laurie. 1998. *Language Myths.* Penguin UK.

Bauer, Martin W. and George Gaskell. 2000. *Qualitative Researching with Text, Image and Sound.* SAGE.

Beaman, Jean. 2016. "Citizenship as cultural." *Sociology Compass* 10:849–57.

Bearman, Peter S. and Katherine Stovel. 2000. "Becoming a Nazi." *Poetics* 27: 69–90.

Becker, Howard. 2017. *Evidence.* University of Chicago Press.

Bender, Emily, Timnit Gebru, Angelina McMillan-Major, and Shmargaret Shmitchell. 2021. "On the dangers of stochastic parrots." In *Proceedings of the 2021 ACM Conference on Fairness, Accountability, and Transparency*, pp. 610–23.

Benoit, Kenneth. 2020. *quanteda.corpora.* R package version 0.9.2.

Benoit, Kenneth and Akitaka Matsuo. 2020. *spacyr.* R package version 1.2.1.

Benoit, Kenneth, Kohei Watanabe, Haiyan Wang, Paul Nulty, Adam Obeng, Stefan Müller, et al. 2018. "quanteda." *Journal of Open Source Software* 3:774.

Benoit, Kenneth, Kohei Watanabe, Haiyan Wang, Patrick O. Perry, Benjamin Lauderdale, Johannes Gruber, et al. 2022. *quanteda.textmodels.* R package version 0.9.5-1.

Bently, Lionel and Tanya Aplin. 2019. "Whatever became of global, mandatory, fair use? A case study in dysfunctional pluralism." In *Is Intellectual Property Pluralism Functional?* Edward Elgar Publishing, pp. 8–36.

Berlind, David. 2015. "What is an API, Exactly?"

Bernstein, Basil. 2003. *Class, Codes and Control.* Psychology Press.

Biber, Douglas. 1993. "Representativeness in corpus design." *Literary and Linguistic Computing* 8:243–57.

Biernacki, Richard. 2012. *Reinventing Evidence in Social Inquiry.* Springer.

Biernacki, Richard. 2014. "Humanist interpretation versus coding text samples." *Qualitative Sociology* 37:173–88.

Biernacki, Richard. 2015. "Erratum: How to do things with historical texts." *American Journal of Cultural Sociology* 3:311–52.

Bischof, Jonathan and Edoardo M Airoldi. 2012. "Summarizing topical content with word frequency and exclusivity." In *Proceedings of the 29th International Conference on Machine Learning*, pp. 201–8.

Blei, David. 2012. "Probabilistic topic models." *Communications of the ACM* 55:77–84.

Blei, David and John D. Lafferty. 2007. "A correlated topic model of science." *The Annals of Applied Statistics* 1:17–35.

Blei, David, Andrew Y. Ng, and Michael I. Jordan. 2003. "Latent dirichlet allocation." *Journal of Machine Learning Research* 3:993–1022.

Blevins, Cameron and Lincoln Mullen. 2015. "Jane, John... Leslie? A historical method for algorithmic gender prediction." *Digital Humanities Quarterly* 9.

Bloomfield, Leonard. 1933. *Language*. Holt.

Bohr, Jeremiah and Riley E. Dunlap. 2018. "Key topics in environmental sociology, 1990–2014." *Environmental Sociology* 4:181–95.

Bollen, Johan, Marijn Ten Thij, Fritz Breithaupt, Alexander T. J. Barron, Lauren A. Rutter, Lorenzo Lorenzo-Luaces, et al. 2021. "Historical language records reveal a surge of cognitive distortions in recent decades." *PNAS of the United States of America* 118.

Bolukbasi, Tolga, Kai-Wei Chang, James Zou, Venkatesh Saligrama, and Adam Kalai. 2016a. "Quantifying and reducing stereotypes in word embeddings." *arXiv preprint arXiv:1606.06121* .

Bolukbasi, Tolga, Kai-Wei Chang, James Y. Zou, Venkatesh Saligrama, and Adam T. Kalai. 2016b. "Man is to computer programmer as woman is to homemaker? debiasing word embeddings." *Advances in Neural Information Processing Systems* 29.

Bonikowski, Bart and Noam Gidron. 2016. "The populist style in American politics." *Social Forces* 94:1593–621.

Bontrager, Terry. 1991. "The development of word frequency lists prior to the 1944 Thorndike-Lorge list." *Reading Psychology* 12:91–116.

Bourdieu, Pierre. 1991. *Language and Symbolic Power*. Harvard University Press.

Boutyline, Andrei, Alina Arseniev-Koehler, and Devin J. Cornell. 2023. "School, studying, and smarts: Gender stereotypes and education across 80 years of American print media, 1930–2009". *Social Forces* 102: 263–286.

Brandt, Philipp and Stefan Timmermans. 2021. "Abductive logic of inquiry for quantitative research in the digital age." *Sociological Science* 8:191–210.

Breiger, Ronald L. 1974. "The duality of persons and groups." *Social Forces* 53:181–90.

Brown, Nicole M., Ruby Mendenhall, Michael L. Black, Mark Van Moer, Assata Zerai, and Karen Flynn. 2016. "Mechanized margin to digitized center: Black feminism's contributions to combatting erasure within the digital humanities." *International Journal of Humanities and Arts Computing* 10:110–25.

Brown, Nicole M., Ruby Mendenhall, Michael Black, Mark Van Moer, Karen Flynn, Malaika McKee, et al. 2019. "In search of Zora/when metadata isn't enough: Rescuing the experiences of black women through statistical modeling." *Journal of Library Metadata* 19:141–62.

Brunila, Mikael and Jack LaViolette. 2021. "WMDecompose: A Framework for Leveraging the Interpretable Properties of Word Mover's Distance in Sociocultural Analysis." *arXiv preprint arXiv:2110.07330.*

Bryan, Jennifer and Jim Hester. 2019. "What they forgot to teach you about R." https://rstats.wtf/.

Brysbaert, Marc and Boris New. 2009. "Moving beyond Kucera and Francis." *Behavior Research Methods* 41:977–90.

Bush, Vannevar. 1945. "As we may think." *The Atlantic.*

Butts, Carter. 2015. *network*. The Statnet Project (http://www.statnet.org). R package version 1.13.0.1.

Butts, Carter T. 2022. *sna*. R package version 2.7.

Bybee, Joan, Revere Perkins, and William Pagliuca. 1994. *The Evolution of Grammar*. University of Chicago Press.

Cambridge University Press. 2020. "Proper Noun: Definition."

Carbone, Luca and Jonathan Mijs. 2022. "Sounds like meritocracy to my ears: Exploring the link between inequality in popular music and personal culture." *Information, Communication and Society* 25: 707–725.

Carley, Kathleen. 1993. "Coding choices for textual Analysis." *Sociological Methodology* 23:75–126.

Carley, Kathleen. 1994. "Extracting culture through textual analysis." *Poetics* 22:291–312.

Carley, Kathleen. 1997. "Extracting team mental models through textual analysis." *Journal of Organizational Behavior* 18:533–58.

Carley, Kathleen and David Kaufer. 1993. "Semantic connectivity." *Communication Theory* 3:183–213.

Carley, Kathleen and Michael Palmquist. 1992. "Extracting, representing, and analyzing mental models." *Social Forces* 70:601–36.

Carpena, P., P. Bernaola-Galván, M. Hackenberg, A. V. Coronado, and J. L. Oliver. 2009. "Level statistics of words." *Physical Review E* 79:03510.

Carroll, Lewis. 1925. *Through the Looking Glass and What Alice Found There*. John C. Winston.

Chakrabarti, Parijat and Margaret Frye. 2017. "A mixed-methods framework for analyzing text data." *Demographic Research* 37:1351–82.

Charrad, Malika, Nadia Ghazzali, Véronique Boiteau, and Azam Niknafs. 2014. "NbClust." *Journal of Statistical Software* 61:1–36.

Childress, Clayton. 2017. *Under the Cover*. Princeton University Press.

Clarke, David. 1973. "Archaeology: The loss of innocence." *Antiquity* 47:6–18.

Clausner, Christian, Apostolos Antonacopoulos, and Stefan Pletschacher. 2020. "Efficient and effective OCR engine training." *International Journal on Document Analysis and Recognition* 23:73–88.

Correll, Shelley J., Katherine R. Weisshaar, Alison T. Wynn, and Joanne Delfino Wehner. 2020. "Inside the black box of organizational life." *American Sociological Review* 85:1022–50.

Coulmas, Florian. 2003. *Writing Systems*. Cambridge University Press.

Crane, Harry. 2018. *Probabilistic Foundations of Statistical Network Analysis*. Chapman and Hall/CRC.

Cranmer, Skyler J., Bruce A. Desmarais, and Jason W. Morgan. 2020. *Inferential Network Analysis*. Cambridge University Press.

Croft, William and D. Alan Cruse. 2004. *Cognitive Linguistics*. Cambridge University Press.

Crystal, David. 2011. *A Dictionary of Linguistics and Phonetics*, volume 30. John Wiley & Sons.

Csárdi, Gábor, Jim Hester, Hadley Wickham, Winston Chang, Martin Morgan, and Dan Tenenbaum. 2021. *remotes*. R package version 2.4.2.

Csardi, Gabor and Tamas Nepusz. 2006. "The igraph software package for complex network research." *InterJournal Complex Systems*: 1695.

Dancho, Matt and Davis Vaughan. 2022. *tidyquant*. R package version 1.0.6.

Daniels, Peter T. and William Bright. 1996. *The World's Writing Systems*. Oxford University Press.

Darlington, Richard B. and Andrew F. Hayes. 2016. *Regression Analysis and Linear Models*. Guilford Press.

Davidson, Donald. 2005. *Truth, Language, and History*. Clarendon Press.

Davis, A., B. B. Gardner, and M. R. Gardner. 1941. *Deep South*. University of Chicago Press.

De Groot, Annette M. B. and Rineke Keijzer. 2000. "What is hard to learn is easy to forget." *Language Learning* 50:1–56.

de Mesquita, Ethan Bueno and Anthony Fowler. 2021. *Thinking Clearly with Data*. Princeton University Press.

Deerwester, Scott, Susan T. Dumais, George W. Furnas, Thomas K. Landauer, and Richard Harshman. 1990. "Indexing by latent semantic analysis." *Journal of the American Society for Information Science* 41:391–407.

Dennett, Daniel C. 2017. *Consciousness Explained*. Little, Brown.

Denny, Matthew J. and Arthur Spirling. 2018. "Text preprocessing for unsupervised learning." *Political Analysis* 26:168–89.

Deo, Meera, Jenny Lee, Christina Chin, Noriko Milman, and Nancy Wang Yuen. 2008. "Missing in action." *Social Justice* 35:145–62.

Derrida, Jacques and Avital Ronell. 1980. "The law of genre." *Critical Inquiry* 7: 55–81.

DeSoucey, Michaela and Miranda R. Waggoner. 2022. "Another person's peril." *American Sociological Review* 87:50–79.

Devlin, Jacob, Ming-Wei Chang, Kenton Lee, and Kristina Toutanova. 2018. "BERT: Pre-training of deep bidirectional transformers for language understanding." *arXiv preprint arXiv:1810.04805*.

Di Paolo, Ezequiel A., Elena Clare Cuffari, and Hanne De Jaegher. 2018. *Linguistic Bodies*. MIT Press.

Dianati, Navid. 2016. "Unwinding the hairball graph." *Physical Review E* 93:012304.

Diermeier, Daniel, Jean-François Godbout, Bei Yu, and Stefan Kaufmann. 2012. "Language and ideology in Congress." *British Journal of Political Science* 42: 31–55.

D'ignazio, Catherine and Lauren F Klein. 2020. *Data Feminism*. MIT Press.

Dingwall, Nicholas and Christopher Potts. 2018. "Mittens: An extension of glove for learning domain-specialized representations." *arXiv preprint arXiv:1803.09901*.

Dixon, R M W. 1997. *The Rise and Fall of Languages*. Cambridge University Press.

D'Orazio, Vito, Steven T. Landis, Glenn Palmer, and Philip Schrodt. 2014. "Separating the wheat from the chaff." *Political Analysis* 22:224–42.

Dorius, Shawn F. and Jeffrey Swindle. 2019. "Developmental idealism in internet search data." *Sociology of Development* 5:286–313.

Douglas, Mary. 1966. *Purity and Danger*. Routledge.

Duncan, Otis Dudley. 1961. "A socioeconomic index for all occupations." In *Occupations and Social Status*, edited by A. J. Reiss, pp. 109–61. Free Press.

Durkheim, Emile. 1895. *The Rules of The Sociological Method*. Free Press.

Dybowski, T. P. and Philipp Adämmer. 2018. "The economic effects of US presidential tax communication." *European Journal of Political Economy* 55: 511–25.

Edgington, Eugene and Patrick Onghena. 2007. *Randomization Tests*. Chapman and Hall/CRC.

Edmondson, Mark. 2020. *googleLanguageR*. R package version 0.3.0.

Eisenstein, Jacob and Eric Xing. 2010. *The CMU 2008 Political Blog Corpus*. Carnegie Mellon University, School of Computer Science.

Emirbayer, Mustafa. 1997. "Manifesto for a relational sociology." *American Journal of Sociology* 103:281–317.

Erichson, N. Benjamin, Sergey Voronin, Steven L. Brunton, and J. Nathan Kutz. 2019. "Randomized matrix decompositions using R." *Journal of Statistical Software* 89:1–48.

Ernst, Michael. 2004. "Permutation methods." *Statistical Science* 19: 676–85.

Eshima, Shusei, Kosuke Imai, and Tomoya Sasaki. 2020. "Keyword assisted topic models." *arXiv preprint arXiv:2004.05964* .

Evans, James A. and Pedro Aceves. 2016. "Machine translation." *Annual Review of Sociology* 42:21–50.

Everett, M. G. and S. P. Borgatti. 2013. "The dual-projection approach for two-mode networks." *Social Networks* 35:204–10.

Farghaly, Ali and Khaled Shaalan. 2009. "Arabic natural language processing." *ACM Transactions on Asian Language Information Processing* 8:1–22.

Farrell, Justin. 2016. "Network structure and influence of the climate change counter-movement." *Nature Climate Change* 6:370–4.

Faruqui, Manaal, Jesse Dodge, Sujay K. Jauhar, Chris Dyer, Eduard Hovy, and Noah A. Smith. 2014. "Retrofitting word vectors to semantic lexicons." arXiv preprint arXiv:1411.4166.

Fauconnier, Gilles. 1997. *Mappings in Thought and Language*. Cambridge University Press.

Fay, Colin. 2019. *proustr*. R package version 0.4.0.

Fenton, Frances. 1910. "The influence of newspaper presentations upon the growth of crime and other anti-social activity." *American Journal of Sociology* 16: 342–371.

Fillmore, Charles J. 1979. "Innocence: A second idealization for linguistics." *Annual Meeting of the Berkeley Linguistics Society* 5:63–76.

Firth, John R. 1935. "The technique of semantics." *Transactions of the Philological Society. Philological Society* 34:36–73.

Firth, John R. 1957. "A synopsis of linguistic theory, 1930–1955." In *Studies in Linguistic Analysis*, ed. J.R. Firth, pp. 1–32. Oxford, UK: Blackwell.

Fishman, Joshua A. 2011. *Advances in Language Planning*. Walter de Gruyter.

Fligstein, Neil, Jonah Stuart Brundage, and Michael Schultz. 2017. "Seeing like the Fed." *American Sociological Review* 82:879–909.

Flood, Barbara J. 1999. "Historical note: The start of a stop list at Biological Abstracts." *Journal of the Association for Information Science and Technology* 50:1066.

Flores, René D. 2017. "Do anti-immigrant laws shape public sentiment? A study of Arizona's SB 1070 using twitter data." *American Journal of Sociology* 123: 333–84.

Foucault, Michel. 2005. *The Order of Things*. Routledge.

Fowler, Alastair. 1982. *Kinds of Literature*. Harvard University Press.

Fox, Christopher. 1989. "A stop list for general text." *SIGIR Forum* 24:19–21.

Franzosi, Roberto. 2004. *From Words to Numbers*. Cambridge University Press.

Freelon, Deen. 2018. "Computational research in the post-API age." *Political Communication* 35:665–68.

Frick, Hannah, Fanny Chow, Max Kuhn, Michael Mahoney, Julia Silge, and Hadley Wickham. 2022. *rsample*. R package version 1.1.1.

Friedman, Doug. 2022. *topicdoc*. R package version 0.1.1.

Friedman, Jerome, Trevor Hastie, and Robert Tibshirani. 2010. "Regularization paths for generalized linear models via coordinate descent." *Journal of Statistical Software* 33:1–22.

Friedman, Sam and Aaron Reeves. 2020. "From aristocratic to ordinary." *American Sociological Review* 85:323–50.

Fries, Charles C. 1941. *English Word Lists, a Study of Their Adaptability for Instruction*. American Council on Education.

Fruchterman, Thomas M. J. and Edward M. Reingold. 1991. "Graph drawing by force-directed placement." *Software* 21:1129–64.

Gagolewski, Marek. 2022. "stringi." *Journal of Statistical Software* 103:1–59.

Gamallo, Pablo and Stefan Bordag. 2011. "Is singular value decomposition useful for word similarity extraction?" *Language Resources and Evaluation* 45:95–119.

Gamer, Matthias, Jim Lemon, and Ian Fellows Puspendra Singh <puspendra.pusp22 gmail.com>. 2019. *irr*. R package version 0.84.1.

Gazarov, Petr. 2016. "What is an API? In English, please." *freeCodeCamp.org* .

Gebru, Timnit, Jamie Morgenstern, Briana Vecchione, Jennifer Wortman Vaughan, Hanna Wallach, Hal Daumé Iii, et al. 2021. "Datasheets for datasets." *Communications of the ACM* 64:86–92.

Geertz, Clifford. 1973. *The Interpretation of Cultures*. Basic Books.

Gellner, Ernest. 1998. *Language and Solitude*. Cambridge University Press.

Goldberg, Adele E. 1995. *Constructions*. University of Chicago Press.

Gonçalves, Pollyanna, Matheus Araújo, Fabrício Benevenuto, and Meeyoung Cha. 2013. "Comparing and combining sentiment analysis methods." In *Proceedings of the First ACM Conference on Online Social Networks*, COSN '13, pp. 27–38.

González-Bailón, Sandra. 2017. *Decoding the Social World*. MIT Press.

Graesser, Arthur C., Zhiqiang Cai, Max M. Louwerse, and Frances Daniel. 2006. "Question Understanding Aid (QUAID) a web facility that tests question comprehensibility." *Public Opinion Quarterly* 70:3–22.

Greimas, Algirdas. 1983. *Structural Semantics*. University of Nebraska Press.

Grimmer, Justin, Margaret Roberts, and Brandon Stewart. 2022. *Text as Data*. Princeton University Press.

Griswold, Wendy. 1987. "The fabrication of meaning." *The American Journal of Sociology* 92:1077–1117.

Grün, Bettina and Kurt Hornik. 2022. *topicmodels*. R package version 0.2-13.

Guillaume, Bruno, Marie-Catherine de Marneffe, and Guy Perrier. 2019. "Conversion et améliorations de corpus du français annotés en Universal Dependencies." *Traitement Automatique des Langues* 60:71–95.

Hallett, Tim, Orla Stapleton, and Michael Sauder. 2019. "Public Ideas." *American Sociological Review* 84:545–76.

Hamilton, Nicholas E. and Michael Ferry. 2018. "ggtern." *Journal of Statistical Software, Code Snippets* 87:1–17.

Hamilton, William L., Jure Leskovec, and Dan Jurafsky. 2016. "Diachronic word embeddings reveal statistical laws of semantic change." *arXiv preprint arXiv:1605.09096*.

Hanna, Alexander. 2013. "Computer-aided content analysis of digitally enabled movements." *Mobilization* 18:367–88.

Haralambous, Yannis and Martin Dürst. 2018. "Unicode from a linguistic point of view." *Proceedings of Graphemics in the 21st Century, Brest*, pp. 167–83.

Harris, Zellig S. 1954. "Distributional structure." *Word & World* 10:146–62.

Hartigan, John A. 1975. *Clustering Algorithms*. John Wiley & Sons.

Hartigan, John A. and Manchek A. Wong. 1979. "Algorithm AS 136: A k-means clustering algorithm." *Journal of the Royal Statistical Society* 28:100–8.

Healy, Kieran. 2017. "Fuck nuance." *Sociological Theory* 35:118–27.

Healy, Kieran. 2018a. *Data Visualization*. Princeton University Press.

Healy, Kieran. 2018b. "The plain person's guide to plain text social science."

Heise, David R. 1977. "Social action as the control of affect." *Systems Research* 22:163–77.

Hinton, Leanne, Johanna Nichols, and John J. Ohala. 2006. *Sound Symbolism*. Cambridge University Press.

Hofmann, Thomas. 2001. "Unsupervised learning by probabilistic latent semantic analysis." *Machine Learning* 42:177–96.

Hopp, Frederic R., Jacob T. Fisher, Devin Cornell, Richard Huskey, and René Weber. 2021. "The extended Moral Foundations Dictionary (eMFD)." *Behavior Research Methods* 53:232–46.

Hota, Argamon, Koppel, and Zigdon. 2006. "Performing gender: Automatic stylistic analysis of Shakespeare's characters." In *Proceedings of Digital Humanities 2006*, pp. 100–104.

Hovy and Fornaciari. 2018. "Increasing in-class similarity by retrofitting embeddings with demographic information." In *Proceedings of the 2018 Conference on Empirical Methods in Natural Language Processing*, pp. 671–677.

Hunter III, Starling David, Susan Smith, and Saba Singh. 2016. "Predicting box office from the screenplay." *Journal of Screenwriting* 7:135–54.

Ibrahim, Mohammed, Susan Gauch, Tyler Gerth, and Brandon Cox. 2021. "WOVe: Incorporating word order in GloVe word embeddings." arXiv preprint arXiv:2105.08597.

Ignatow, Gabe and Rada Mihalcea. 2016. *Text Mining*. SAGE.

Ignatow, Gabe and Rada Mihalcea. 2017. *An Introduction to Text Mining*. SAGE.

Jain, Anil K., M. Narasimha Murty, and Patrick J. Flynn. 1999. "Data clustering." *ACM Computing Surveys (CSUR)* 31:264–323.

James, Gareth, Daniela Witten, Trevor Hastie, and Robert Tibshirani. 2021. *An Introduction to Statistical Learning*. Springer.

Jaworsky, Bernadette Nadya. 2013. "Immigrants, aliens and Americans." *American Journal of Cultural Sociology* 1:221–53.

Jefferson, Gail, et al. 2004. "Glossary of transcript symbols with an introduction." *Pragmatics and Beyond New Series* 125:13–34.

Jeong, Sarah and Michael Hoven. 2012. "People v. Harris." *Jolt Digest*. https://jolt.law.harvard.edu/digest/people-v-harris.

Jiao, Xiaoqi, Yichun Yin, Lifeng Shang, Xin Jiang, Xiao Chen, Linlin Li, et al. 2019. "TinyBERT: Distilling BERT for natural language understanding." arXiv preprint arXiv:1909.10351.

Johnson, Mark. [1987] 2015. *The Body in the Mind*. University of Chicago Press.

Johnston, Myfanwy and David Robinson. 2022. *gutenbergr*. R package version 0.2.3.

Jones, Karen Sparck. 1972. "A statistical interpretation of term specificity and its application in retrieval." *Journal of Documentation* 39:88.

Jones, Thomas W. 2021. "Document clustering." https://cran.r-project.org/web/packages/textmineR/vignettes/b_document_clustering.html.

Joseph, V. Roshan. 2022. "Optimal ratio for data splitting." *Stat. Anal. Data Min.* 15:531–38.

Jurafsky, Daniel and James Martin. 2000. *Speech and Language Processing*. Pearson.

Kabanoff, Boris, Robert Waldersee, and Marcus Cohen. 1995. "Espoused values and organizational change themes." *Academy of Management Journal* 38:1075–1104.

Kahn, David. 1996. *The Codebreakers*. Simon and Schuster.

Karell, Daniel and Michael Freedman. 2019. "Rhetorics of radicalism." *American Sociological Review* 84:726–53.

Kassambara, Alboukadel. 2022. *ggpubr*. R package version 0.5.0.

Kassambara, Alboukadel and Fabian Mundt. 2020. *factoextra*. R package version 1.0.7.

Kaur, Jashanjot and P. Kaur Buttar. 2018. "A systematic review on stopword removal algorithms." *Int. J. Futur. Revolut. Comput. Sci. Commun. Eng* 4.

Kelly, Chelsea Rae. 2022. "The situation sounds sketchy." *American Behavioral Scientist*: p. 00027642211066035.

Kennedy, Graeme. 2014. *An Introduction to Corpus Linguistics*. Routledge.

Kennedy, John F. 1962. "Address at Rice University on the nation's space effort."

King, Gary, Jennifer Pan, and Margaret Roberts. 2013. "How censorship in China allows government criticism but silences collective expression." *The American Political Science Review* 107:326–43.

Kjell, Oscar N. E., Salvatore Giorgi, and H. A. Schwartz. 2021. "Text: An R-package for Analyzing and Visualizing Human Language Using Natural Language Processing and Deep Learning." https://www.r-text.org/.

Klebanov, Beata Beigman, Daniel Diermeier, and Eyal Beigman. 2008. "Lexical cohesion analysis of political speech." *Political Analysis* 447–463.

Koehn, Philipp. 2005. "Europarl." In *Proceedings of Machine Translation Summit X*, pp. 79–86.

Konieczny, Piotr. 2009. "Governance, organization, and democracy on the internet." *Sociol. Forum* 24:162–92.

Kozlowski, Austin C., Matt Taddy, and James A. Evans. 2019. "The geometry of culture." *American Sociological Review* 84:905–49.

Krippendorff, Klaus. 2018. *Content Analysis*. SAGE.

Krotov, Vlad, Leigh Johnson, and Leiser Silva. 2020. "Tutorial: Legality and ethics of web scraping." *Communications of the Association for Information Systems* 47:22.

Kučera, Henry and Winthrop Nelson Francis. 1967. *Computational Analysis of Present-Day American English*. Dartmouth Publishing Group.

Kuhn, Max. 2022. *caret*. R package version 6.0-93.

Kuhn, Max and Hadley Wickham. 2020. *Tidymodels*.

Kurtz, Albert K. 1948. "A research test of the Rorschach test." *Pers. Psychol.* 1:41–51.

Kusner, Matt, Yu Sun, Nicholas Kolkin, and Kilian Weinberger. 2015. "From word embeddings to document distances." In *International Conference on Machine Learning*, pp. 957–66. PMLR.

Lakoff, George. 2008. *Women, Fire, and Dangerous Things*. University of Chicago Press.

Larsen, Reif. 2009. *The Selected Works of TS Spivet*. Random House.

Lazarsfeld, Paul F. 1940. *Radio and the Printed Page: An Introduction to the Study of Radio and Its Role in the Communication of Ideas*. Duell, Sloan, & Pearce.

Lee, Daniel and H. Sebastian Seung. 1999. "Learning the parts of objects by non-negative matrix factorization." *Nature* 401:788–91.

Lee, Joo Ho and Jeong Soo Ahn. 1996. "Using n-grams for Korean text retrieval." In *Proceedings of the 19th Annual International ACM SIGIR Conference*, SIGIR '96, pp. 216–24.

Lee, Monica and John Levi Martin. 2014. "Coding, counting and cultural cartography." *American Journal of Cultural Sociology* 3:1–33.

Lee, Monica and John Levi Martin. 2015. "Response to Biernacki, Reed, and Spillman." *American Journal of Cultural Sociology* 3:380–415.

Leech, Geoffrey. 2014. "Preface." In *Learner English on Computer*, edited by Sylviane Granger, pp. xiv–xx. Addison-Wesley-Longman.

Leonawicz, Matthew. 2021. *rtrek*. R package version 0.3.3.

Levy, Omer and Yoav Goldberg. 2014. "Neural word embedding as implicit matrix factorization." In *Advances in Neural Information Processing Systems 27*, edited by Z. Ghahramani, M. Welling, C. Cortes, N. D. Lawrence, and K. Q. Weinberger, pp. 2177–85. Curran Associates.

Li, Zhuofan, Daniel Dohan, and Corey M Abramson. 2021. "Qualitative coding in the computational era." *Socius* 7:23780231211062345.

Liu, Bing, Minqing Hu, and Junsheng Cheng. 2005. "Opinion observer." In *Proceedings of the 14th International Conference on World Wide Web*, pp. 342–51.

Lix, Katharina, Amir Goldberg, Sameer B. Srivastava, and Melissa A. Valentine. 2022. "Aligning Differences: Discursive Diversity and Team Performance." *Management Science* 68:8430–8448.

Llaudet, Elena and Kosuke Imai. 2022. *Data Analysis for Social Science*. Princeton University Press.

Lopez, Christian. 2017. "Unsupervised machine learning: The hclust, pvclust." https://quantdev.ssri.psu.edu/sites/qdev/files/Unsupervised_Machine_Learning_The_mclust_Package_and_others.html.

Lovins, Julie Beth. 1968. "Development of a stemming algorithm." *Mech. Transl. Comput. Linguistics* 11:22–31.

Lucchesi, Lydia R., Petra M. Kuhnert, Jenny L. Davis, and Lexing Xie. 2022. "Smallset Timelines": A Visual Representation of Data Preprocessing Decisions." In Proceedings of the 2022 ACM Conference on Fairness, Accountability, and Transparency, pp. 1136–1153.

Luhn, H. P. 1958. "The automatic creation of literature abstracts." *IBM Journal of Research and Development* 2:159–65.

Lynott, Dermot, Louise Connell, Marc Brysbaert, James Brand, and James Carney. 2020. "The Lancaster Sensorimotor norms." *Behavior Research Methods* 52:1271–91.

Mack, David. 2019. "The "Star Trek: Picard" trailer shows the captain reuniting with seven of nine and data." *BuzzFeed News*. https://www.buzzfeednews.com/article/davidmack/star-trek-picard-trailer-data-seven-nine-patrick-stewart.

Mackenzie, Charles. 1980. *Coded-Character Sets*. Addison-Wesley-Longman.

Malinowski, Bronislaw. 1937. "Infant speech." *Nature* 140:172–3.

Malinowski, Bronislaw. [1947] 2015. *Freedom and Civilization*. Routledge.

Mandelbrot, Benoit. 1953. "An informational theory of the statistical structure of language." *Communication Theory* 84:486–502.

Manning, Christopher, Prabhakar Raghavan, and Hinrich Schütze. 2010. "Introduction to information retrieval." *Natural Language Engineering* 16:100–3.

Manning, Christopher D., Mihai Surdeanu, John Bauer, Jenny Rose Finkel, Steven Bethard, and David McClosky. 2014. "The Stanford CoreNLP natural language processing toolkit." In *Proceedings of 52nd Annual Meeting of the Association for Computational Linguistics*, pp. 55–60.

Martin, Carla D. and Mason A. Porter. 2012. "The extraordinary SVD." *American Mathematical Monthly* 119:838–51.

Martin, John Levi. 2001. "On the limits of sociological theory." *Philosophy of the Social Sciences* 31:187–223.

Martin, John Levi. 2017. *Thinking Through Methods*. University of Chicago Press.

Martin, James R. 1997. "Analysing genre." In *Genre and institutions*, pp. 3–39. Continuum.

Matloff, Norm. 2020. "TidyverseSkeptic." `https://github.com/matloff/TidyverseSkeptic/`.

McClain, Colleen, Regina Widjaya, Gonzalo Rivero, and Aaron Smith. 2021. "Comparing highly active and less active tweeters." Pew Research Center. `https://www.pewresearch.org/internet/2021/11/15/2-comparing-highly-active-and-less-active-tweeters/`.

McDonald, Ryan, et al. 2013. "Universal dependency annotation for multilingual parsing." In *Proceedings of the 51st Annual Meeting of the Association for Computational Linguistics*, pp. 92–7. aclweb.org.

McElreath, Richard. 2020. *Statistical Rethinking*. CRC Press.

McEnery, Tony and Andrew Hardie. 2011. *Corpus Linguistics*. Cambridge University Press.

McKean, Erin. 2002. "L33t-sp34k." *Verbatim, The Language Quarterly* 27:13–4.

McLevey, John. 2021. *Doing Computational Social Science*. SAGE.

McLevey, John V. P., Tyler Crick, Pierson Browne, and Darrin Durant. 2022. "A new method for computational cultural cartography: From neural word embeddings to transformers and Bayesian mixture models." *Canadian Review of Sociology/Revue canadienne de sociologie* 59:228–250.

Merriam-Webster. 2020. "run."

Mihalcea, Rada and Paul Tarau. 2004. "Textrank." In *Proceedings of the 2004 Conference on Empirical Methods in Natural Language Processing*, pp. 404–11. aclweb.org.

Miller, G A. 1957. "Some effects of intermittent silence." *American Journal of Psychology* 70:311–314.

Miller, M. Mark. 1997. "Frame mapping and analysis of news coverage of contentious issues." *Social Science Computer Review* 15:367–78.

Mimno, David. 2013. "mallet." *A wrapper around the Java machine learning tool MALLET*.

Mimno, David, Hanna Wallach, Edmund Talley, Miriam Leenders, and Andrew McCallum. 2011. "Optimizing semantic coherence in topic models." In *Proceedings of the 2011 Conference on Empirical Methods in Natural Language Processing*, pp. 262–72.

Minhas, Shahryar, Peter D. Hoff, and Michael D. Ward. 2019. "Inferential approaches for network analysis." *Political Analysis* 27:208–22.

Mitchell, J. Clyde. 1983. "Case and Situation Analysis." *The Sociological Review* 31:187–211.

Mohr, John. 1994. "Soldiers, mothers, tramps and others." *Poetics* 22:327–57.

Mohr, John. 1998. "Measuring Meaning Structures." *Annual Review of Sociology* 24:345–70.

Mohr, John, Christopher Bail, Margaret Frye, Jennifer Lena, Omar Lizardo, Terence McDonnell, et al. 2020. *Measuring Culture.* Columbia University Press.

Mohr, John and Petko Bogdanov. 2013. "Introduction–Topic models: What they are and why they matter." *Poetics* 41:545–569.

Mohr, John, Robin Wagner-Pacifici, Ronald Breiger, and Petko Bogdanov. 2013. "Graphing the grammar of motives in National Security Strategies." *Poetics* 41:670–700.

Molina, Mario and Filiz Garip. 2019. "Machine learning for sociology." *Annual Review of Sociology* 45: 27–45.

Moore, Matthew. 2008. "The clbuttic mistake." *The Daily Telegraph.*

Mora, G Cristina and Tianna S Paschel. 2020. "Antiblackness as a logic for anti-immigrant resentment." In *Sociological Forum*, volume 35, pp. 918–40. Wiley Online Library.

Mosier, Charles. 1941. "A psychometric study of meaning." *The Journal of Social Psychology* 13:123–40.

Mosteller, Frederick and David Wallace. 1963. "Inference in an authorship problem." *Journal of the American Statistical Association* 58:275–309.

Mouselimis, Lampros. 2022. *fastText.* R package version 1.0.2.

Mu, Jiaqi, Suma Bhat, and Pramod Viswanath. 2017. "All-but-the-top: Simple and effective postprocessing for word representations.". arXiv preprint arXiv:1702.01417

Mullen, Lincoln. 2021. *gender.* R package version 0.6.0.

Mullen, Lincoln. 2023. *genderdata.* R package version 0.6.0.

Mullen, Lincoln, Kenneth Benoit, Os Keyes, Dmitry Selivanov, and Jeffrey Arnold. 2018. "Fast, consistent tokenization of natural language text." *Journal of Open Source Software* 3:655.

Muñoz, John and Cristobal Young. 2018. "We ran 9 billion regressions." *Sociological Methodology* 48:1–33.

Muscio, Alessandro. 2023. "The ambiguous role of science and technology in Marvel superhero comics." *Technol. Forecast. Soc. Change* 186:122149.

Navarro, Danielle. 2022. "Project Structure." https://slides.djnavarro.net/project-structure/#1. Accessed: 2022-6-16.

Neal, Zachary. 2014. "The backbone of bipartite projections." *Social Networks* 39:84–97.

Neal, Zachary. 2017. "Well connected compared to what?" *Environment and Planning* 49:2859–77.

Neal, Zachary. 2022. "backbone." *PLOS One* 17:e0269137.

Nelson, Laura. 2020. "Computational grounded theory: A methodological framework." *Sociological Methods & Research* 49: 3–42.

Nelson, Laura. 2021a. "Cycles of Conflict, a Century of Continuity." *American Journal of Sociology* 127:1–59.

Nelson, Laura. 2021b. "Leveraging the alignment between machine learning and intersectionality." *Poetics* 88:101539.

Nelson, Laura, Derek Burk, Marcell Knudsen, and Leslie McCall. 2021. "The future of coding: A comparison of hand-coding and three types of computer-assisted text analysis methods." *Sociological Methods & Research* 50: 202–237.

Neuendorf, Kimberly. 2017. *The Content Analysis Guidebook*. SAGE.

Newman, Mark. 2001. "Scientific collaboration networks." *Physical Review E* 64:016132.

Newman, Mark E. J. 2003. "Mixing patterns in networks." *Physical Review E* 67:026126.

Nie, Jian-Yun and Fuji Ren. 1999. "Chinese information retrieval." *Information Processing & Management* 4:443–62.

Nissenbaum, Helen. 2009. *Privacy in Context*. Stanford Law Books.

Nouvel, Damien, Maud Ehrmann, and Sophie Rosset. 2016. *Named Entities for Computational Linguistics*. Wiley Online Library.

Odell, Evan. 2019. *guardianapi*. R package version 0.1.1.

Okrent, Arika. 2021. *Highly Irregular*. Oxford University Press.

Olson, David R. 1996. *The World on Paper*. Cambridge University Press.

Ong, Walter. 2013. *Orality and Literacy*. Routledge.

Ooms, Jeroen. 2022a. *hunspell*. R package version 3.0.2.

Ooms, Jeroen. 2022b. *tesseract*. R package version 5.1.0.

Opsahl, Tore, Filip Agneessens, and John Skvoretz. 2010. "Node centrality in weighted networks." *Social Networks* 32:245–51.

Ortuño, M., P. Carpena, P. Bernaola-Galván, E. Muñoz, and A. M. Somoza. 2002. "Keyword detection in natural languages and DNA." *EPL* 57:759.

Osgood, C. E. 1952. "The nature and measurement of meaning." *Psychological Bulletin* 49:197–237.

Padgett, John F. and Christopher K. Ansell. 1993. "Robust Action and the Rise of the Medici, 1400–1434." *American Journal of Sociology* 98:1259–1319.

Paine, Albert. 1912. *Mark Twain: A Biography*. Harper & brothers.

Pardo-Guerra, Juan Pablo and Prithviraj Pahwa. 2022. "The extended computational case method." *Sociol. Methods Res.* 51:1826–67.

Parker, Matt. 2011. "Example waffles charts in R using GGPLOT2." GitHub. https://gist.github.com/mmparker/1358652.

Pechenick, Eitan Adam, Christopher M. Danforth, and Peter Sheridan Dodds. 2015. "Characterizing the Google Books corpus." *PloS One* 10:e0137041.

Pedersen, Thomas Lin. 2022a. *ggraph*. R package version 2.1.0.

Pedersen, Thomas Lin. 2022b. *tidygraph*. R package version 1.2.2.

Pena, José M., Jose Antonio Lozano, and Pedro Larranaga. 1999. "An empirical comparison of four initialization methods for the k-means algorithm." *Pattern Recognition Letters* 20:1027–40.

Pennington, Jeffrey, Richard Socher, and Christopher D. Manning. 2014. "Glove: Global vectors for word representation." In *Proceedings of the 2014 Conference on Empirical Methods in Natural Language Processing (EMNLP)*, pp. 1532–43.

Petrov, Slav, Dipanjan Das, and Ryan McDonald. 2011. "A universal part-of-speech tagset." *arXiv preprint arXiv:1104.2086*.

Pioneer Press. 2007. "'Weird Al's' imitation: funky form of flattery." *St. Paul Pioneer Press*.

Porter, Martin. 2001. "Snowball." http://snowball.tartarus.org/texts/introduction.html.

Porter, Martin, Richard Boulton, and Andrew Macfarlane. 2002. "The english (porter2) stemming algorithm." *Retrieved* 18:2011.

Porter, Martin, et al. 1980. "An algorithm for suffix stripping." *Program* 14:130–7.

Prior, Lindsay. 2003. *Using Documents in Social Research*. SAGE.

Puetz, Kyle, Andrew Davis, and Alexander Kinney. 2021. "Meaning structures in the world polity." *Poetics* 88:101598.

Pury, Cynthia L. S. 2011. "Automation can lead to confounds in text analysis." *Psychological Science* 22:835–6; author reply 837–8.

Quach, Katyanna. 2020. "AI me to the Moon... Carbon footprint for 'training GPT-3' same as driving to our natural satellite and back." https://www.theregister.com/2020/11/04/gpt3_carbon_footprint_estimate/. Accessed: 2022-6-23.

Rakshit, Sandip, Subhadip Basu, and Hisashi Ikeda. 2010. "Recognition of hand-written textual annotations using tesseract open source OCR engine for information Just In Time (iJIT)." arXiv preprint arXiv:1003.5893

Rawson, K. and T. Muñoz. 2016. "Against cleaning." *Curating Menus*. http://curatingmenus.org/articles/against-cleaning/.

Reed, Isaac. 2015. "Counting, interpreting and their potential interrelation in the human sciences." *American Journal of Cultural Sociology* 3:353–64.

Reed, Isaac and Jeffrey Alexander. 2015. *Meaning and Method*. Routledge.

Ribeiro, Filipe N., Matheus Araújo, Pollyanna Gonçalves, Marcos André Gonçalves, and Fabrício Benevenuto. 2016. "SentiBench." *EPJ Data Science* 5:23.

Riffe, Daniel, Stephen Lacy, Brendan R. Watson, and Frederick Fico. 2019. *Analyzing Media Message*. Routledge.

Rinker, Tyler. 2013. *qdapDictionaries*. University at Buffalo/SUNY. version 1.0.7.

Rinker, Tyler. 2015. *entity*. University at Buffalo/SUNY. version 0.1.0.

Rinker, Tyler. 2016. *tagger*. University at Buffalo/SUNY. version 0.0.2.

Rinker, Tyler. 2017. *coreNLPsetup*. University at Buffalo/SUNY. version 0.0.1.

Rinker, Tyler. 2018a. *lexicon*. Buffalo, New York. version 1.2.1. http://github.com/trinker/lexicon.

Rinker, Tyler. 2018b. *termco*. Buffalo, New York. version 0.5.6. http://github.com/trinker/termco.

Rinker, Tyler. 2018c. *textclean: Text Cleaning Tools*. Buffalo, New York. version 0.9.3. https://github.com/trinker/textclean.

Rinker, Tyler. 2018d. *textstem*. Buffalo, New York. version 0.1.4. http://github.com/trinker/textstem.

Rinker, Tyler. 2021. *sentimentr*. Buffalo, New York. version 2.9.0. https://github.com/trinker/sentimentr.

Ripley, B. D. 1996. *Pattern Recognition and Neural Networks*. Cambridge University Press.

Rivera, Lauren A. 2020. "Employer decision making." *Annual Review of Sociology* 46:215–32.

Roberts, Carl. 1989. "Other than counting words." *Social Forces* 68:147–77.

Roberts, Daniel A., Sho Yaida, and Boris Hanin. 2022. *The Principles of Deep Learning Theory*. Cambridge University Press.

Roberts, Margaret, Brandon Stewart, and Edoardo M. Airoldi. 2016. "A model of text for experimentation in the social sciences." *Journal of the American Statistical Association* 111:988–1003.

Roberts, Margaret, Brandon Stewart, and Dustin Tingley. 2019. "stm." *Journal of Statistical Software* 91:1–40.

Roberts, Margaret, Brandon Stewart, Dustin Tingley, Christopher Lucas, Jetson Leder-Luis, Shana Kushner Gadarian, Bethany Albertson, and David G. Rand. 2014. "Structural topic models for open-ended survey responses." *American Journal of Political Science* 58:1064–82.

Robbins, R. H. 1971. "Malinowski, Firth, and 'Context of Situation.'" In *Social Anthropology and Language*, edited by E. Ardener. London: Routledge.

Robinson, David. 2017. "Teach the tidyverse to beginners." http://varianceexplained.org/r/teach-tidyverse/.

Rodriguez, Pedro L. and Arthur Spirling. 2022. "Word embeddings: What works, what doesn't, and how to tell the difference for applied research." *The Journal of Politics* 84:101–115.

Rosa, J. and N. Flores. 2017. "Unsettling race and language." *Language in Society* 46:621–647.

Rose, Dan. 1980. "Malinowski's influence on wittgenstein on the matter of use in language." *Journal of the History of the Behavioral Sciences* 16:145–9.

Roux, Maurice. 2018. "A comparative study of divisive and agglomerative hierarchical clustering algorithms." *Journal of Classification* 35:345–66.

Salganik, Matthew. 2019. *Bit by Bit*. Princeton University Press.

Salganik, Matthew, et al. 2020. "Measuring the predictability of life outcomes with a scientific mass collaboration." *PNAS of the United States of America* 117:8398–403.

Salton, Gerard. 1975. *A Theory of Indexing*. SIAM.

Salton, G. 1981. "The Smart environment for retrieval system evaluation." In *Information Retrieval Experiment*, edited by Karen Sparck Jones, pp. 316–29. Butterworth & Company.

Salton, G., A. Wong, and C. S. Yang. 1975. "A vector space model for automatic indexing." *Communications of the ACM* 18:613–20.

Sanh, Victor, Lysandre Debut, Julien Chaumond, and Thomas Wolf. 2019. "Distil-BERT, a distilled version of BERT: Smaller, faster, cheaper and lighter." arXiv preprint arXiv:1910.01108

Saussure, Ferdinand de. 1986. *Course in General Linguistics*. Bloomsbury Academic.

Schmid, Helmut. 1994. "Probabilistic part-of-speech tagging using decision trees." *Paper presented at the Internaitonal Conference on New Methods in Language Processing*. Manchester, UK. URL: chrome-extension://efaidnbmnnnibpcajpcglclefindmkaj/https://citeseerx.ist.psu.edu/document?repid=rep1&type=pdf&doi=bd0bab6fc8cd43c0ce170ad2f4cb34181b31277d.

Schmidt, Benjamin, Steven T., Piantadosi, and Kyle Mahowald. 2021. "Uncontrolled corpus composition drives an apparent surge in cognitive distortions." *PNAS* 118.

Schofield, Alexandra, Måns Magnusson, and David Mimno. 2017. "Pulling out the stops: Rethinking stopword removal for topic models." In *Proceedings of the 15th Conference of the European Chapter of the Association for Computational Linguistics*, pp. 432–6. aclweb.org.

Schönemann, Peter. 1966. "A generalized solution of the orthogonal procrustes problem." *Psychometrika* 31:1–10.

Schwartz, Tim. 2011. "Culturomics." *Science* 332:36–7.

Schwemmer, Carsten. 2021. *stminsights*. R package version 0.4.1.

Schwendinger, Florian and Emil Hvitfeldt. 2020. *fastTextR*. R package version 2.0.0.

Segev, Elad. 2020. "Textual network analysis: Detecting prevailing themes and biases in international news and social media." *Sociol. Compass* 14.

Selivanov, Dmitriy, Manuel Bickel, and Qing Wang. 2022. *text2vec*. R package version 0.6.3.

Serrano, M. Ángeles, Marián Boguná, and Alessandro Vespignani. 2009. "Extracting the multiscale backbone of complex weighted networks." *PNAS* 106: 6483–8.

Shelley, Mary. 1888. *Frankenstein; or, The Modern Prometheus*. George Routledge and Sons.

Shor, Eran, Arnout van de Rijt, Alex Miltsov, Vivek Kulkarni, and Steven Skiena. 2015. "A Paper ceiling: Explaining the persistent underrepresentation of women in printed news." *American Sociological Review* 80:960–84.

Shor, Eran, Arnout van de Rijt, Charles Ward, Saoussan Askar, and Steven Skiena. 2014. "Is there a political bias?" *Social Science Quarterly* 95:1213–29.

Sievert, Carson and Kenneth Shirley. 2014. "LDAvis." In *Proceedings of the Workshop on Interactive Language Learning, Visualization, and Interfaces*, Baltimore, MD: Association of Computational Linguistics, pp. 63–70.

Silge, Julia and David Robinson. 2016. "tidytext." *JOSS* 1.

Simon, Noah, Jerome Friedman, Trevor Hastie, and Rob Tibshirani. 2011. "Regularization paths for Cox's proportional hazards model via coordinate descent." *Journal of Statistical Software* 39:1–13.

Slowikowski, Kamil. 2022. *ggrepel*. R package version 0.9.2.

Smaha, Rebecca and Christiane Fellbaum. 2015. "How natural are artificial languages?" In *Language Production, Cognition, and the Lexicon*, edited by Núria Gala, Reinhard Rapp, and Gemma Bel-Enguix, pp. 299–312. Springer.

Small, Mario Luis. 2009. "How many cases do I need?." *Ethnography* 10:5–38.

Smith-Lovin, Lynn, et al. 2019. "Mean affective ratings of 968 identities, 853 behaviors, and 660 modifiers by amazon mechanical turk workers in 2015." University of Georgia: Distributed at UGA Affect Control Theory Website. URL: https://act.franklinresearch.uga.edu/.

Speed, John Gilmer. 1893. "Do newspapers now give the news." In *Forum*, volume 15, pp. 705–11.

Spillman, Lyn. 2014. "Mixed methods and the logic of qualitative inference." *Qualitative Sociology* 37:189–205.

Spillman, Lyn. 2015. "Ghosts of straw men." *American Journal of Cultural Sociology* 3:365–79.

Stoltz, Dustin and Marshall Taylor. 2017. "Paying with change." *Poetics* 64:26–39.

Stoltz, Dustin and Marshall Taylor. 2019a. "Concept mover's distance." *Journal of Computational Social Science* 2:293–313.

Stoltz, Dustin and Marshall Taylor. 2019b. "Textual spanning: Finding discursive holes in text networks." *Socius* 5:2378023119827674.

Stoltz, Dustin and Marshall Taylor. 2021. "Cultural cartography with word embeddings." *Poetics* 88:101567.

Stoltz, Dustin and Marshall Taylor. 2022a. *text2map*. R package version 0.1.6.

Stoltz, Dustin and Marshall Taylor. 2022b. *text2map.corpora*. R package version 0.1.4.

Stoltz, Dustin and Marshall Taylor. 2022c. *text2map.pretrained*. R package version 0.1.0.

Stone, Philip, Dexter Dunphy, and Marshall Smith. 1966. *The General Inquirer*, volume 651. M.I.T. Press.

Strang, Gilbert. 2020. *Linear Algebra for Everyone*. Wellesley-Cambridge Press.

Stuhler, Oscar. 2022a. *semgram*. R package version 0.1.0.

Stuhler, Oscar. 2022b. "Who Does What to Whom? Making Text Parsers Work for Sociological Inquiry." *Sociological Methods & Research* 51:1580–1633.

Sumpter, R. S. 2001. "News about news: John G. Speed and the first newspaper content analysis." *Journal of History* 27:64–72.

Sweetser, Eve E. 1988. "Grammaticalization and semantic bleaching." In *Annual Meeting of the Berkeley Linguistics Society*, volume 14, pp. 389–405. journals.linguisticsociety.org.

Sylvester, James Joseph. 1851. *The Collected Mathematical Papers of James Joseph Sylvester: Volume 3, 1870–1883*. Cambridge University Press.

Tausczik, Yla and James Pennebaker. 2010. "The psychological meaning of words." *Journal of Language and Social Psychology* 29:24–54.

Tavares, Hugo. 2018. "Syntax equivalents: base R vs Tidyverse." https:// tavareshugo.github.io/data_carpentry_extras/base-r_tidyverse_ equivalents/base-r_tidyverse_equivalents.html. Accessed: 2022-3-12.

Tavory, Iddo and Stefan Timmermans. 2014. *Abductive Analysis*. University of Chicago Press.

Taylor, Ann, Mitchell Marcus, and Beatrice Santorini. 2003. "The Penn treebank." In *Treebanks*, pp. 5–22. Springer.

Taylor, Marshall. 2020. "Visualization strategies for regression estimates with randomization inference." *The Stata Journal* 20:309–35.

Taylor, Marshall and Dustin Stoltz. 2021. "Integrating semantic directions with concept mover's distance to measure binary concept engagement." *Journal of Computational Social Science* 4:231–42.

Team, RStudio. 2020. *RStudio*. PBC., Boston.

Team, R Core. 2021. *R: A Language and Environment for Statistical Computing*. R Foundation for Statistical Computing.

Tenney, A. A. [1912] 2008. "The scientific analysis of the press." In *The Content Analysis Reader*, edited by Klaus Krippendorf, pp. 16–20.

Thompson, Andrew. 2020. "2.7 million news articles and essays." *Components*. https://components.one/datasets/all-the-news-2-news-articles-dataset/.

Thorndike, Edward L. 1921. *The Teacher's Word Book*. Teacher's College, Columbia University.

Tierney, Graham, Christopher Bail, and Alexander Volfovsky. 2021. "Author clustering and topic estimation for short texts." *arXiv preprint arXiv:2106.09533*.

Tomasello, Michael. 2009. *Constructing a Language*. Harvard University Press.

Traag, Vincent A., Ridho Reinanda, and Gerry van Klinken. 2015. "Elite co-occurrence in the media." *Asian Journal of Social Science* 43:588–612.

Truong, Brandon, Cornelia Caragea, Anna Squicciarini, and Andrea Tapia. 2014. "Identifying valuable information from twitter during natural disasters." *Proceedings of the American Society for Information Science and Technology* 51:1–4.

Tsvetkov, Yulia, Manaal Faruqui, Wang Ling, Guillaume Lample, and Chris Dyer. 2015. "Evaluation of word vector representations by subspace alignment." In *Proceedings of the 2015 Conference on Empirical Methods in Natural Language Processing*, pp. 2049–54. Association for Computational Linguistics.

Tufte, Edward R. 1974. *Data Analysis for Politics and policy*. Prentice-Hall.

Underwood, Ted, Kevin Kiley, Wenyi Shang, and Stephen Vaisey. 2022. "Cohort succession explains most change in literary culture." *Sociological Science* 9:184–205.

Underwood, Ted, Patrick Kimutis, and Jessica Witte. 2020. "NovelTM datasets for English-language fiction, 1700-2009." *Journal of Cultural Analytics* 5:13147.

Unicode. 2022. "The unicode® standard version 15.0 -core specification." Technical report.

US Copyright Office. 2022a. "Copyright in General."

US Copyright Office. 2022b. "More Information on Fair Use."

Ushey, Kevin, J.J. Allaire, and Yuan Tang. 2023. *reticulate*. R package version 1.27.

Uyheng, Joshua and Kathleen Carley. 2020. "Bots and online hate during the COVID-19 pandemic." *Journal of Computational Social Science* 3:445–68.

Vaccaro, Kristen, Karrie Karahalios, Christian Sandvig, Kevin Hamilton, and Cedric Langbort. 2015. "Agree or cancel? Research and terms of service compliance." In *ACM CSCW Ethics Workshop*. URL: chrome-extension://efaidnbmnnnibpcajpcglclefindmkaj/https://s3.amazonaws.com/kvaccaro.com/documents/Agree_Or_Cancel.pdf.

Van de Rijt, Arnout, Eran Shor, Charles Ward, and Steven Skiena. 2013. "Only 15 minutes? The social stratification of fame in printed media." *American Sociological Review* 78:266–89.

van Loon, Austin and Jeremy Freese. 2022. "Word embeddings reveal how fundamental sentiments structure natural language." *The American Behavioral Scientist* p. 00027642211066046.

Van Rijsbergen, C. J. 1979. *Information Retrieval*. Butterworths.

Vapnik, Vlamimir. 1998. *Statistical Learning Theory*. Publishing House of Electronics Industry.

Venables, William, David Smith, and the R Core Team. 2021. "An Introduction to R."

Wagner-Pacifici, Robin, John Mohr, and Ronald Breiger. 2015. "Ontologies, methodologies, and new uses of Big Data in the social and cultural sciences." *Big Data & Society* 2:2053951715613810.

Warnes, Gregory, et al. 2022. *gmodels*. R package version 2.18.1.1.

Warriner, Amy Beth, Victor Kuperman, and Marc Brysbaert. 2013. "Norms of valence, arousal, and dominance for 13,915 English lemmas." *Behavior Research Methods* 45:1191–207.

Weber, Robert Philip. 1984. "Computer-aided content analysis." *Qualitative Sociology* 7:126–47.

Weber, Robert Philip. 1990. *Basic Content Analysis*. SAGE.

Wickham, Hadley. 2007. "Reshaping data with the reshape package." *Journal of Statistical Software* 21:1–20.

Wickham, Hadley. 2010. "A layered grammar of graphics." *Journal of computational and graphical statistics* 19:3–28.

Wickham, Hadley and Garrett Grolemund. 2016. *R for Data Science*. O'Reilly Media, Inc.

Wickham, Hadley, et al. 2019. "Welcome to the tidyverse." *Journal of Open Source Software* 4:1686.

Wijffels, Jan. 2021. *word2vec*. R package version 0.3.4.

Wijffels, Jan. 2023. *udpipe*. R package version 0.8.11.

Wild, Fridolin. 2022. *lsa: Latent Semantic Analysis*. R package version 0.73.3.

Willey, Malcolm M. and William Weinfeld. 1934. "The country weekly and the emergence of 'one-newspaper places'." *Journalism Quarterly* 11:246–57.

Williams, Herve Abdi And. 2010. "Encyclopedia of research design." In *Matrix Algebra*, edited by Neil Salkind, volume 1. SAGE. https://sk.sagepub.com/reference/researchdesign/nv232.xml.

Wilson, Michael. 1988. "MRC psycholinguistic database." *Behavior Research Methods* 20:6–10.

Wimmer, Andreas and Kevin Lewis. 2010. "Beyond and below racial homophily." *American Journal of Sociology* 116:583–642.

Wittgenstein, Ludwig. [1953] 2009. *Philosophical Investigations*. Macmillan.

Yan, Xiaohui, Jiafeng Guo, Yanyan Lan, and Xueqi Cheng. 2013. "A biterm topic model for short texts." In *Proceedings of the 22nd International Conference on World Wide Web*, pp. 1445–56.

Yeomans, Michael. 2021. "A concrete example of construct construction in natural language." *Organizational Behavior and Human Decision Processes* 162:81–94.

Yin, Robert. 2009. *Case Study Research*. SAGE.

Yin, Zi and Yuanyuan Shen. 2018. "On the dimensionality of word embedding." In *Advances in Neural Information Processing Systems 31*, pp. 887–98. Curran Associates, Inc.

Young, Cristobal and Katherine Holsteen. 2017. "Model uncertainty and robustness." *Sociological Methods & Research* 46:3–40.

Young, Michael. 2011. "Malinowski's last word on the anthropological approach to language." *Pragmatics* 21:1–22.

Yu, Shuiyuan, Chunshan Xu, and Haitao Liu. 2018. "Zipf's law in 50 languages": Its structural pattern, linguistic interpretation, and cognitive motivation." https://arxiv.org/abs/1807.01855.

Yung, Vincent. 2021. "A visual approach to interpreting the career of the network metaphor." *Poetics* 88:101566.

Zaeem, Razieh Nokhbeh, Chengjing Li, and K Suzanne Barber. 2020. "On sentiment of online fake news." In *2020 IEEE/ACM International Conference on Advances in Social Networks Analysis and Mining*, pp. 760–67. ieeexplore.ieee.org.

Zeldes, Amir. 2017. "The GUM Corpus." *Language Resources and Evaluation* 51:581–612.

Zhu, Kiros, Zemel, Salakhutdinov, et al. 2015. "Aligning books and movies: Towards story-like visual explanations by watching movies and reading books." *Proceedings of the IEEE International Conference on Computer Vision*, pp. 19–27.

Zipf, George. 1949. *Human Behavior and the Principle of Least Effort*. Addison-Wesley.

Znaniecki, Florian. 1934. *Method of Sociology*. Farrar & Rinehart.

Index